PERSPECTIVES
ON THE STUDY OF FILM

PERSPECTIVES
ON THE STUDY OF FILM

Edited by

John Stuart Katz

The Ontario Institute for Studies in Education, University of Toronto

LITTLE, BROWN AND COMPANY
Boston

Acknowledgments

William Arrowsmith. "Film as Educator" from *The Journal of Aesthetic Education,* 3, no. 3 (July 1969), pp. 75–83. Reprinted by permission of the University of Illinois Press.

Bela Balazs. "In Praise of Theory" and "Der Sichtbare Mensch" from *Theory of the Film,* pp. 17–19 and 39–45. Reprinted by permission of Dobson Books Ltd. and Globus-Buchvertrieb.

George Bluestone. "Time in Film and Fiction" from *Journal of Aesthetics and Art Criticism,* 19, no. 3 (1961), pp. 311–315. Reprinted by permission of The American Society for Aesthetics and the author.

Leo Braudy. "On Two Fronts" adapted from "Newsreel: A Report" from *Film Quarterly,* 22, no. 2, pp. 48–51. © 1969 by The Regents of the University of California. Reprinted by permission of The Regents and the author.

Edmund Carpenter. "The New Languages" from *Explorations in Communications,* edited by Edmund Carpenter and Marshall McLuhan, pp. 162–179. Copyright © 1960 by the Beacon Press. Reprinted by permission of the Beacon Press and Jonathan Cape Ltd.

David Castro and Jerry Stoll. "Profile of Art in Revolution" (1967) reprinted by permission of American Documentary Films.

The Communications Experience. "A New Kind of Writing: Basic Skills Revisited and Revised" from *Media and Methods* (April 1970), pp. 39, 62. Reprinted by permission of the publisher and the authors.

Peter Harcourt. "In Defense of Film History," copyright © 1971 by Peter Harcourt, revised from a paper presented to The American Film Institute–Ontario Institute for Studies in Education Film Seminar, April 1969.

Aldous Huxley. "Education on the Nonverbal Level" from *Daedalus,* the Journal of the American Academy of Arts and Sciences (Spring 1962), pp. 279–293. Reprinted by permission of the publisher.

Pauline Kael. "Circles and Squares: Joys and Sarris" from *i Lost It at the Movies,* by Pauline Kael, pp. 292–319. Copyright © 1963 by Pauline Kael. Reprinted by permission of Little, Brown and Co. and Jonathan Cape Ltd.

John Stuart Katz. "Interaction and Film Study," copyright © 1971 by John Stuart Katz, appeared in an earlier form in *The Journal of Aesthetic Education,* 5, no. 2 (April 1971).

Stanley Kauffmann. "Films and the Future" from *The Humanities in the Schools: A Contemporary Symposium,* edited by A. Taylor, pp. 99–113. Copyright © 1968 by Stanley Kauffmann. Reprinted by permission of the author.

Jonas Mekas. "Movie Journal" from *The Village Voice,* January 8, 1970. Copyrighted by The Village Voice, Inc., 1970. Reprinted by permission of *The Village Voice.*

Marshall McLuhan. "Classroom Without Walls" from *Explorations in Communications,* edited by Edmund Carpenter and Marshall McLuhan, pp. 1–3. Copyright © 1960 by the Beacon Press. Reprinted by permission of the Beacon Press and Jonathan Cape Ltd.

Newsreel. "Newsreel" from *Film Quarterly,* 22, no. 2, pp. 43–48. © 1969 by The Regents of the University of California. Reprinted by permission of The Regents.

Gerald O'Grady. "The Preparation of Teachers of Media" from *The Journal of Aesthetic Education,* 3, no. 3 (July 1969), pp. 113–133. Reprinted by permission of the University of Illinois Press.

Erwin Panofsky. "Style and Medium in the Motion Pictures" from *Critique,* 1, no. 3 (January–February 1947), pp. 5–28. Reprinted by permission of Dr. Gerda Panofsky.

Ted Perry. "The Seventh Art as Sixth Sense" from *Educational Theatre Journal,*

21, no. 1 (1969), pp. 28–35. Reprinted by permission of the American Educational Theatre Association and the author.

Alan C. Purves. "A Model for Curriculum Evaluation in Film," copyright © 1971 by Alan C. Purves, revised from a paper presented to The American Film Institute–Ontario Institute for Studies in Education Film Seminar, April 1969.

Michael Roemer. "The Surfaces of Reality" from *Film Quarterly*, 18, no. 1, pp. 15–22. © 1964 by The Regents of the University of California. Reprinted by permission of The Regents and the author.

Andrew Sarris. "Notes on the *Auteur* Theory in 1962" from *Film Culture*, 27 (Winter 1962–1963), pp. 1–8. Reprinted by permission of the publisher.

Anthony Schillaci. "Film as Environment" from *Saturday Review*, December 28, 1968. Copyright 1968 Saturday Review, Inc. Reprinted by permission of the publisher and the author.

Ralph A. Smith. "Teaching Film as Significant Art," copyright © 1971 by Ralph A. Smith, revised by the author from: "Film as Significant Art," *Screen Education*, 32 (January–February 1966), pp. 3–11, by permission of the publisher; "Film Appreciation as Aesthetic Education," *The Educational Forum*, 30, no. 4 (May 1966), pp. 483–489, by permission of Kappa Delta Pi, an Honor Society in Education; and "Film Study as Aesthetic Education," *Journal of Aesthetic Education*, 3, no. 3 (July 1969), pp. 5–11, by permission of the publisher.

Susan Sontag. "Theatre and Film" from *Styles of Radical Will*, by Susan Sontag, pp. 99–122. Copyright © 1966, 1969 by Susan Sontag. Reprinted by permission of Farrar, Straus & Giroux, Inc., and Martin Secker & Warburg Ltd.

Andres Steinmetz. "Educational Innovation and Evaluation," copyright © 1971 by Andres Steinmetz, revised from a paper presented to The American Film Institute–Ontario Institute for Studies in Education Film Seminar, April 1969.

Stan Vanderbeek. "Re: Vision" from *The American Scholar*, 35, no. 2 (Spring 1966), pp. 335–340. Reprinted by permission of the International Center for the Communication Arts and Sciences, Inc., and the author.

Slavko Vorkapich. "Toward True Cinema" from *Film Culture* (March 1959), pp. 10–17. Reprinted by permission of the publisher.

Sol Worth. "Film as a Non-Art: An Approach to the Study of Film" from *The American Scholar*, 35, no. 2 (Spring 1966), pp. 322–334. Copyright © 1966 by the United Chapters of Phi Beta Kappa. Reprinted by permission of the publisher and the author.

Preface

Film study is increasingly becoming an integral part of both the
formal and informal education of students of all ages. Informally,
that education may consist of seeing and discussing films, reading
reviews, and perhaps making films. Formally, film study may take
place in schools, colleges, universities, and through conferences
and workshops. We hear about not only film study, but also media
studies, screen education, visual literacy, and communications
curricula. Each of these categories tends to suggest a somewhat
different attitude both to film and to the student, but the attitudes do
overlap and are not mutually exclusive.

The study of film does not lend itself to prescriptive dicta, the
apotheosis of "classics," prerequisites, or conventional evaluative
techniques. Film is too flexible and new to education to be saddled
with the academic constraints we associate with more traditional
curricula or subjects. Therefore, a traditional textbook on film or
the study of film seems to be in direct opposition both to the art form
itself and to the potential of film within education.

This book is neither a handbook of questions to ask about
specific films nor a handbook of "facts" to be learned or taught for
successful film study. The issues central to this book are what film is,
how it enhances one's experiences, and how one can better learn
about and understand the medium. The articles in *Perspectives on the
Study of Film* exemplify various approaches toward film and have
been arranged into chapters according to themes and concepts
prevalent in film study.

For encouragement and suggestions in the editing of this book,
the introductions, and my article, I would like to express my gratitude
to the following people: Judith Katz, Kit Laybourne, Gerald
O'Grady, Brenda O'Connor, Terry Massameno, Andrew Effrat, Curt
Oliver, Robert Geller, and Jane Aaron.

Contents

Introduction

Film is an important and an exciting medium. We are told that
students spend as much time watching films and film on television as
they spend in school. Oddly, because of this some people insist that
there is no need to consume school time with film study. If students
see films anyway, why waste time showing and discussing them in
schools? And, a similar argument goes, since film making is
expensive and few students will continue in it professionally, there
is no need for schools to spend time and money on it.

To see, however, is not necessarily to *see*. Without murdering
through dissection, it is possible, as the authors in this volume show,
to increase students' enjoyment and understanding of film. One can
learn to appreciate the medium, realize how it works, and thereby
enhance his understanding of the art form itself and of the world
with which it deals.

Two famous quotations illustrate the artist's desire to make his
readers or viewers better able to perceive and examine themselves
and their relations to the work of art. Joseph Conrad, in the preface to
The Nigger of the Narcissus (1897), said, "My task which I am trying
to achieve is, by the power of the written word to make you hear,
to make you feel — it is, before all, to make you see." In 1903 D. W.
Griffith said, "The task I'm trying to achieve is, above all, to make
you see." A good film can make a viewer *see* in the sense of Conrad
and Griffith. Film study, both formal and informal, can sensitize
the viewer so that he may *better see*, in the sense of understand and
appreciate, both works of art and the world around him.

As educators realize the importance, impact, and viability
of "new media," the study of film increases in schools, colleges, and
universities. It is variously taught as a unique discipline, as part of
the curriculum in art, history, and English, and, in the case of film
making, as a performing or studio art. In one way or another,
educational institutions that have not yet introduced it will

1

eventually incorporate film study. Increasingly, then, the question asked is not just *whether*, but also *how* to study film.

This book brings together articles dealing with the medium of film and with the study of that medium. The authors include film makers, film critics, teachers, educational researchers, and university professors of film, education, and the humanities. It is not just a book "about" film or "about" education. It combines articles on what film is and what it is not with articles on the place of film in education and on the development of approaches, curricula, and evaluation models for film study. The approaches discussed in these pages should interest the casual film viewer as well as teachers, critics, film makers, and students formally studying film. An attempt has been made to include diversified viewpoints and to span levels of formal film study from the elementary school to the university.

The main emphasis of the book is on the study of narrative and documentary feature-length and short films. For the most part, the films discussed are those shown in commercial movie theaters or, in the case of documentaries and shorts, in art houses, in film societies, or on television. Most of the films are available for rental to schools and colleges in 16-millimeter prints.

The articles included here treat film as a medium valuable and viable in and for itself. No attempt has been made to include articles dealing primarily with "audio-visual aids" or instructional films. This book is not a manual of teaching methods, but a collection of perspectives exemplifying various ways of approaching film. The theoretical frameworks into which these articles fit center around the nature of the medium and practical problems in curriculum development and evaluation.

Each of the four chapters in this book consists of articles on a particular aspect of film or film study. Many of the more wide-ranging articles could fit into a number of different chapters and, consequently, the chapters themselves could have been arranged differently. However, chapter divisions were made on the basis of issues and concepts prevalent in film study, and articles were selected and placed into chapters on the basis of their central arguments and hypotheses. Each chapter begins with a short introduction discussing the articles and the relations between articles in that chapter and other chapters in the book.

Chaper 1, "Education and Film Study," centers on the process of education broadly defined and on the place of film within the context of education. Chapter 2, "The Film as Art and Humanities," contains theoretical and critical articles that approach film as an intrinsically valuable art form. The authors in this chapter consider

the medium from the historical, aesthetic, and stylistic points of
view. The authors in Chapter 3, "The Film as Communications,
Environment, and Politics," approach film as a language and as part
of our environment that affects both our life styles and the way
in which we perceive the world around us. Some of the authors in
this section suggest that film has political power to explore and
communicate ideas and concepts not available through other media.
Chapter 4, "Curriculum Design and Evaluation in Film Study,"
is concerned with specific rationales for teaching film and with the
assessment and utilization of film curricula.

1 Film Study and Education

The following articles are addressed, either implicitly or explicitly, to the importance of film study within education. Although they are concerned with various approaches to the study of film, these authors have in common their examination of the experiences film study offers and their belief that the medium merits the attention of educators.

In the first article, "Education on the Nonverbal Level," Aldous Huxley argues for broadening the boundaries of education and thereby sets the stage for others to consider the place of film within education. Huxley says that humans are multiple amphibians, that we each live in and experience many different kinds of worlds. Good education, which helps students make the best of all the worlds in which they are forced to live, would include not only traditional training in the symbol systems of science and the humanities, but also training in what Huxley calls "elementary awareness" and the "nonverbal humanities."

Huxley's analysis of nonverbal education is cosmic and far-reaching, not dealing specifically with film study, but exploring generally the necessity for an affective, spiritual mode of perception. The nonverbal perceptual experiences that he recommends are also the subject of discussion by other authors in this book, especially Marshall McLuhan and Edmund Carpenter. Others, including Bela Balazs in this chapter and Anthony Schillaci in Chapter 3, explicitly discuss ways in which the study of film can deal with these kinds of experiences.

Marshall McLuhan's "Classroom Without Walls" warns that we must incorporate new mass media, including films, into our educational system. If we don't quickly master these new languages they might, because of our lack of understanding, "serve only to weaken or corrupt previously achieved levels of verbal and pictorial culture." Furthermore, McLuhan suggests, students are already

interested in films and can best be taught through that which
they enjoy.

The Communications Experience is a Philadelphia group of
media educators composed of Jon Dunn, Kit Laybourne, and Andres
Steinmetz. In "A New Kind of Writing: Basic Skills Revisited and
Revised," they discuss what have historically been considered basic
skills and develop the idea that new skills in media competency
are now a necessary part of education in a radically changed society.
Their article is adapted from a proposal for the establishment of
media programs designed for use in elementary and high schools.
The major thrusts of the group's work are (1) treating media
competency as a basic skill, and (2) changing the role of the teacher
to that of a facilitator-researcher.

Continuing the argument for film study, but with a different
emphasis, William Arrowsmith in "Film as Educator" foresees the
time when film will prevail as a curriculum in schools and
universities, taking the place and prestige now enjoyed by literature
and the arts. He suggests this possibility because film is a popular art
and students do not feel constrained by it as they frequently do by
literature. Arrowsmith looks at film not only as part of the common
culture, but also as having roots in literature and the classical
tradition. In this respect his approach to film has much in common
with that of Gerald O'Grady in Chapter 4. As a classicist, Arrowsmith
proposes that the teaching of film and literature be juxtaposed. He
further states that the best way to train film makers is by educating
them in the tradition of Homer, Sophocles, Plato, Shakespeare, and
Racine. Finally, Arrowsmith appraises film from the point of view
of its power to educate for social change, to create a humane culture
by having film makers who are both artists and educators.

In the remaining papers in this chapter, two film critics assess
roles and rationales for the study of film. "Films and the Future" is a
paper Stanley Kauffmann delivered at a 1965 meeting chaired by
Harold Taylor to discuss the humanities in the schools. Kauffmann's
approach to film teaching is aimed primarily toward the education of
individuals who will respond in a cultured way to film as a fine art.
As a critic he is not as concerned as a teacher might be that all
students respond to the medium. Rather, he is more concerned with
"touching the few who will respond to the art than with dabbing
every member of the class with a little art veneer." His conclusion
recommends film study not as much for the benefit of the viewer per
se as for the benefit of the art, for he optimistically foresees some
aesthetic change in films resulting from demands by well-educated
audiences.

The two final papers in this chapter are by Bela Balazs, a Hungarian critic. In "In Praise of Theory" he points out the need for teaching people to appreciate films so that they will be more aware and cognizant of this important art and industry. Balazs further argues that film is potentially the greatest instrument for mass influence yet devised and that we must study how it works and what it can do so that we will be able to control it. "In Der Sichtbare Mensch" ("The Faces of Men"), originally published in 1923, Balazs, like Huxley, Carpenter, McLuhan, Vanderbeek, Schillaci, and others represented in this book, explores the value of understanding and utilizing nonverbal language. * Balazs explicitly examines the silent film's ability to do what print cannot do — to show visual man, his movement, gesture, and facial expression. A universal humanity, he argues, can be promoted by film's visual language enabling us to understand each other's emotions.

* These approaches to film as a nonverbal language are somewhat different from approaches to either the grammar or the semiotics of film. See, for example, in the Selected Bibliography (p. 327), Spottiswoode, Lawson, Whitaker, Wollen, Barthes, Metz, Mitry, Sebeok; and, in Chapter 3 of the text, "Film as a Non-Art" by Sol Worth.

Education
on the Nonverbal Level

ALDOUS HUXLEY

Early in the mid-Victorian period the Reverend Thomas Binney, a Congregationalist divine, published a book with the alluring title, *Is It Possible to Make the Best of Both Worlds?* His conclusion was that perhaps it might be possible. In spite of its unorthodox message, or perhaps because of it, the book was a best seller, which only showed, said the more evangelical of Mr. Binney's Nonconformist colleagues and Anglican opponents, how inexpressibly wicked Victorian England really was.

What Mr. Binney's critics had done (and their mistake is repeated by all those who use the old phrase disapprovingly) was to equate "making the best of both worlds" with "serving two masters." It is most certainly very difficult, perhaps quite impossible, to serve Mammon and God simultaneously — to pursue the most sordid interests while aspiring to realize the highest ideals. This is obvious. Only a little less obvious, however, is the fact that it is very hard, perhaps quite impossible, to serve God while failing to make the best of both worlds — of *all* the worlds of which, as human beings, we are the inhabitants.

Man is a multiple amphibian and exists at one and the same time in a number of universes, dissimilar to the point, very nearly, of complete incompatibility. He is at once an animal and a rational intellect; a product of evolution closely related to the apes and a spirit capable of self-transcendence; a sentient being in contact with the brute data of his own nervous system and the physical environment and at the same time the creator of a home-made universe of words and other symbols, in which he lives and moves and has anything from thirty to eighty percent of his being. He is a self-conscious and self-centered ego who is also a member of a moderately gregarious species, an individualist compelled by the population explosion to live at ever closer quarters, and in ever tighter organizations, with millions of other egos as self-centered and as poorly socialized as himself. Neurologically, he is a lately evolved Jekyll-cortex associated with an immensely ancient brain-stem-Hyde. Physiologically, he is a creature whose endocrine system is perfectly adapted to the conditions prevailing in the lower Paleolithic, but living in a metropolis and spending eight hours a day sitting at a desk in an air-conditioned office. Psychologically, he is a highly educated product of twentieth-century civilization, chained, in a state of uneasy and hostile symbiosis, to a disturbingly dynamic unconscious, a wild phantasy and an unpredictable id — and yet capable of falling in love, writing string quartets, and having mystical experiences.

Living amphibiously in all these incommensurable worlds at once, human beings (it is hardly surprising) find themselves painfully confused, uncertain where they stand or who they really are. To provide themselves with a recognizable identity, a niche in the scheme of things that they can call "home," they will give assent to the unlikeliest dogmas, conform to the most absurd and even harmful rules of thought, feeling, and conduct, put on the most extravagant fancy dress and identify themselves with masks that bear almost no resemblance to the faces they cover. "Bovarism" (as Jules de Gaultier calls it) is the urge to pretend that one is something that in fact one is not. It is an urge that manifests itself, sometimes weakly, sometimes with overpowering strength, in all human beings, and one of the conditions of its manifestation is precisely our uncertainty about where we stand or who we are. To explore our multiple amphibiousness with a view to doing something constructive about it is a most laborious process. Our minds are congenitally lazy, and the original sin of the intellect is oversimplification. Dogmatism and bovaristic identification with a stereotype are closely related manifestations of the same kind of intellectual delinquency. "Know thyself." From time immemorial this has been the advice of all the seers and philosophers. The self that they urge us to know is not, of course, the stylized persona with which, bovaristically, we try to become identified; it is the multiple amphibian, the inhabitant of all those incompatible worlds that we must somehow learn to make the best of.

A good education may be defined as one which helps the boys and girls subjected to it to make the best of all the worlds in which, as human beings, they are compelled, willy-nilly, to live. An education that prepares them to make the best of only one of their worlds, or of only a few of them, is inadequate. This is a point on which, in principle, all educators have always agreed. *Mens sana in corpore sano* is an ancient educational ideal and a very good one. Unfortunately, good ideals are never enough. Unless they are accompanied by full instructions regarding the methods by which they may be realized, they are almost useless. Hell is paved with good intentions, and whole periods of history have been made hideous or grotesque by enthusiastic idealists who failed to elaborate the means whereby their lofty aspirations might be effectively, and above all harmlessly, implemented.

Just how good is modern education? How successful is it in helping young people to make the best of all the worlds which, as multiple
amphibians, they have to live in? In a center of advanced scientific
and technical study this question gets asked inevitably in terms of
what may be called the paradox of specialization. In science and
technology specialization is unavoidable and indeed absolutely
necessary. But training for this unavoidable and necessary specialization does nothing to help young amphibians to make the best of their
many worlds. Indeed, it pretty obviously prevents them from doing
anything of the kind. What then is to be done? At the Massachusetts
Institute of Technology and in other schools where similar problems
have arisen, the answer to this question has found expression in a
renewed interest in the humanities. Excessive scientific specialization
is tempered by courses in philosophy, history, literature, and social
studies. All this is excellent so far as it goes. But does it go far
enough? Do courses in the humanities provide a sufficient antidote
for excessive scientific and technical specialization? Do they, in the
terminology we have been using, help young multiple amphibians to
make the best of a substantially greater number of their worlds?

Science is the reduction of the bewildering diversity of unique
events to manageable uniformity within one of a number of symbol
systems, and technology is the art of using these symbol systems so
as to control and organize unique events. Scientific observation is
always a viewing of things through the refracting medium of a
symbol system, and technological praxis is always the handling of
things in ways that some symbol system has dictated. Education in
science and technology is essentially education on the symbolic level.

Turning to the humanities, what do we find? Courses in philosophy, literature, history, and social studies are exclusively verbal.
Observation of and experimentation with nonverbal events have no
place in these fields. Training in the sciences is largely on the symbolic level; training in the liberal arts is wholly and all the time on
that level. When courses in the humanities are used as the only antidote to too much science and technology, excessive specialization in
one kind of symbolic education is being tempered by excessive specialization in another kind of symbolic education. The young amphibians are taught to make the best, not of all their worlds, but only of
two varieties of the same world — the world of symbols. But this
world of symbols is only one of the worlds in which human beings do
their living and their learning. They also inhabit the nonsymbolic
world of unconceptualized or only slightly conceptualized experience. However effective it may be on the conceptual level, an education that fails to help young amphibians to make the best of the inner

and outer universes on the hither side of symbols is an inadequate education. And however much we may delight in Homer or Gibbon, however illuminating in their different ways Pareto and William Law, Hui-neng and Bertrand Russell may strike us as being, the fact remains that the reading of their works will not be of much help to us in our efforts to make the best of our worlds of unconceptualized, nonverbal experience.

And here, before I embark on a discussion of these nonverbal worlds, let me add parenthetically that even on the verbal level, where they are most at home, educators have done a good deal less than they might reasonably have been expected to do in explaining to young people the nature, the limitations, the huge potentialities for evil as well as for good, of that greatest of all human inventions, language. Children should be taught that words are indispensable but also can be fatal — the only begetters of all civilization, all science, all consistency of high purpose, all angelic goodness, and the only begetters at the same time of all superstition, all collective madness and stupidity, all worse-than-bestial diabolism, all the dismal historical succession of crimes in the name of God, King, Nation, Party, Dogma. Never before, thanks to the techniques of mass communication, have so many listeners been so completely at the mercy of so few speakers. Never have misused words — those hideously efficent tools of all the tyrants, war-mongers, persecutors, and heresy-hunters — been so widely and so disastrously influential as they are today. Generals, clergymen, advertisers, and the rulers of totalitarian states — all have good reasons for disliking the idea of universal education in the rational use of language. To the military, clerical, propagandist, and authoritarian mind such training seems (and rightly seems) profoundly subversive. To those who think that liberty is a good thing, and who hope that it may some day become possible for more people to realize more of their desirable potentialities in a society fit for free, fully human individuals to live in, a thorough education in the nature of language, in its uses and abuses, seems indispensable. Whether in fact the mounting pressures of overpopulation and over-organization in a world still enthusiastically dedicated to nationalistic idolatry will permit this kind of subversive linguistic education to be adopted by even the more democratic nations remains to be seen.

And now, after this brief digression, let us return to our main theme, the education of multiple amphibians on levels other than the verbal and the symbolic. "Make the body capable of doing many things," wrote Spinoza. "This will help you to perfect the mind and come to the intellectual love of God." Substitute "psychophysical organism" for "body," and you have here the summary of a program for universal education on the nonsymbolic level, supplemented by a statement of the reasons why such an education is desirable and indeed, if the child is to grow into a fully human being, absolutely necessary. The detailed curriculum for an education in what may be called the nonverbal humanities has still to be worked out. All I can do at this time is to drop a few fragmentary hints.

Two points, to begin with, must be emphatically stressed. First, education in the nonverbal humanities is not just a matter of gymnastics and football, of lessons in singing and folk dancing. All these, of course, are good, but by themselves not good enough. Such traditional methods of training young people in nonverbal skills need to be supplemented, if they are to yield their best results, by other kinds of training, beginning with a thorough training in elementary awareness. And the second point to be remembered is that education in the nonverbal humanities is a process that should be started in the kindergarten and continued through all the years of school and college — and thereafter, as self-education, throughout the rest of life.

At the end of a delightful anthology entited *Zen Flesh, Zen Bones*, its editor, Mr. Paul Reps, has printed an English version of an ancient Tantrik text in which Shiva, in response to Parvati's questions about the nature of enlightened consciousness, gives a list of one hundred and twelve exercises in the art of being aware of inner and outer reality on its nonsymbolic levels. *Gnosce Teipsum*. But how? From the vast majority of our pastors and masters no answer is forthcoming. Here, for a blessed change, is a philosophical treatise that speaks of means as well as of ends, of concrete experience as well as of high abstractions. The intelligent and systematic practice of any half-dozen of these hundred and twelve exercises will take one further towards the realization of the ancient ideal of self-knowledge than all the roaring or pathetic eloquence of generations of philosophers, theologians, and moralists. (Let me add, in passing, that whereas Western philosophy tends to be concerned with the manipulation of abstract symbols for the benefit of the speculative and moralizing intellect, oriental philosophy is almost always essentially operational. "Perform such and such psychophysical operations," the exponents of this philosophy say, "and you will probably find yourself in a state of mind which, like all those who have achieved it in the past, you will regard as self-evidently and supremely valuable. In the context of this state of mind, speculation about man and the universe leads us, as it led earlier thinkers, to the metaphysical doctrine of *Tat tvam asi* [thou art That], and to its ethical corollary — universal compassion. In this philosophy it is the experiential element that is important. Its speculative superstructure is a thing of words, and words, though useful and necessary, should never be taken too seriously.")

Education in elementary awareness will have to include techniques for improving awareness of internal events and techniques for improving awareness of external events as these are revealed by our organs of sense. In his introductions to several of F. M. Alexander's books, John Dewey insisted upon the importance of a properly directed training in the awareness of internal events. It was Dewey's opinion that the training methods developed by Alexander were to education what education is to life in general — an indispensable condition for any kind of improvement. Dewey had himself undergone this training and so knew what he was talking about. And yet in spite of this high praise bestowed by one of the most influential of modern philosophers and educational reformers, Alexander's methods have been ignored, and schoolchildren still receive no training in the kind of internal awareness that can lead to what Alexander described as "creative conscious control."

The educational and therapeutic values of training aimed at heightening awareness of internal events was empirically demonstrated during the first quarter of the present century by the eminently successful Swiss psychiatrist, Dr. Roger Vittoz. And in recent years methods similar to those of Vittoz and to the Tantrik exercises attributed many centuries ago to Shiva have been developed and successfully used both in the treatment of neurotics and for the enrichment of the lives of the normal by the authors of *Gestalt Therapy*, Drs. Frederick F. Perls, Ralph F. Hefferline, and Paul Goodman.

All our mental processes depend upon perception. Inadequate perceiving results in poor thinking, inappropriate feeling, diminished interest in and enjoyment of life. Systematic training of perception should be an essential element in all education.

Our amphibiousness is clearly illustrated in the two modes of our awareness of external events. There is a receptive, more or less unconceptualized, aesthetic and "spiritual" mode of perceiving; and there is also a highly conceptualized, stereotyped, utilitarian, and even scientific mode. In his "Expostulation and Reply" and "The Tables Turned," Wordsworth has perfectly described these two modes of awareness and has assigned to each its special significance and value for the human being who aspires to make the best of both worlds and so, by teaching his psychophysical organism to "do many things," to "perfect the mind and come to the intellectual love of God."

"Why, William, on that old grey stone,
Thus for the length of half a day,
Why, William, sit you thus alone,
And dream your time away?

Where are your books? — that light bequeathed
To beings else forlorn and blind?
Up! Up! and drink the spirit breathed
From dead men to their kind.

You look round on your Mother Earth,
As if she for no purpose bore you;
As if you were her first-born birth,
And none had lived before you."

One morning thus, by Esthwaite lake,
When life was sweet, I knew not why,
To me my good friend Matthew spake,
And thus I made reply.

"The eye it cannot choose but see;
We cannot bid the ear be still;
Our bodies feel, where'er they be,
Against or with our will.

Nor less I deem that there are Powers
Which of themselves our minds impress;
That we can feed this mind of ours
In a wise passiveness.

Think you, 'mid all this mighty sum
Of things for ever speaking,
That nothing of itself will come,
But we must still be seeking?

Then ask not wherefore, here, alone,
Conversing as I may,
I sit upon this old grey stone
And dream my time away."

In "The Tables Turned" it is the poet who takes the offensive against his studious friend. "Up! up! my Friend," he calls, "and quit your books." And then, "Books!" he continues impatiently.

Books! 'tis a dull and endless strife;
Come, hear the woodland linnet;
How sweet his music! on my life,
There's more of wisdom in it.

And hark how blithe the throstle sings!
He too is no mean preacher.
Come forth into the light of things,
Let Nature be your teacher.

One impulse from a vernal wood
May teach you more of man,
Of moral evil and of good
Than all the sages can.

Sweet is the lore which Nature brings;
Our meddling intellect
Mis-shapes the beauteous forms of things —
We murder to dissect.

Enough of Science and of Art;
Close up those barren leaves;
Come forth and bring with you a heart
That watches and receives.

Matthew and William — two aspects of the multiple amphibian that was Wordsworth, that is each one of us. To be fully human, we must learn to make the best of William's world as well as of Matthew's. Matthew's is the world of books, of the social heredity of steadily accumulating knowledge, of science and technics and business, of words and the stock of second-hand notions which we project upon external reality as a frame of reference, in terms of which we may explain, to our own satisfaction, the enigma, moment by moment, of ongoing existence. Over against it stands William's world — the world of sheer mystery, the world as an endless succession of unique events, the world as we perceive it in a state of alert receptiveness with no thought of explaining it, using it, exploiting it for our biological or cultural purposes. As things now stand, we teach young people to make the best only of Matthew's world of familiar words, accepted notions, and useful techniques. We temper a too exclusive concentration on scientific symbols, not with a training in the art of what William calls "wise passiveness," not with lessons in watching and receiving, but with the injunction to concentrate on philosophical and sociological symbols, to read the books that are reputed to contain a high concentration of "the spirit breathed from dead men to their kind." (Alas, dead men do not always breathe a spirit; quite often they merely emit a bad smell.)

It is related in one of the Sutras that on a certain occasion the Buddha preached a wordless sermon to his disciples. Instead of saying anything, he picked a flower and held it up for them to look at. The disciples gaped uncomprehendingly. Only Mahakasyapa understood what the Tathagata was driving at, and all that he did was to smile. Gautama smiled back at him, and when the wordless sermon was over, he made a little speech for the benefit of those who had failed to comprehend his silence. "This treasure of the unquestionable teaching, this Mind of Nirvana, this true form that is without forms, this most subtle Dharma beyond words, this instruction that is to be given and received outside the pale of all doctrines — this I have now handed on to Mahakasyapa." Perceived not as a botanical specimen, not as the analyzed and labeled illustration of a pre-existent symbol system, but as a nameless, unique event, in which all the beauty and the mystery of existence are manifest, a flower can become the means to enlightenment. And what is true of a flower is true, needless to say, of any other event in the inner or outer world — from a toothache to Mount Everest, from a tapeworm to The Well-Tempered Clavichord — to which we choose to pay attention in a state of wise passiveness. And wise passiveness is the condition not only of spiritual insight. ("In prayer," wrote St. Jeanne Chantal, "I always want to *do* something, wherein I do very wrong. . . . By wishing to accomplish something myself, I spoil it all.") In another context, wise passiveness, followed in due course by wise hard work, is the condition of creativity. We do not fabricate our best ideas; they "occur to us," they "come into our heads." Colloquial speech reminds us that, unless we give our subliminal mind a chance, we shall get nowhere. And it is by allowing ourselves at frequent intervals to be wisely passive that we can most effectively help the subliminal mind to do its work. The *cogito* of Descartes should be emended, said Von Baader, to *cogitor*. In order to actualize our potentialities, in order to become fully human and completely ourselves, we must not merely think; we must also permit ourselves to be thought. In Gardner Murphy's words, "Both the historical record of creative thought and the laboratory report of its appearance today, indicate clearly that creative intelligence can spring from the mind that is not strained to its highest pitch, but is utterly at ease." Watching and receiving in a state of perfect ease or wise passiveness is an art which can be cultivated and should be taught on every educational level from the most elementary to the most advanced.

Creativity and spiritual insight — these are the highest rewards of wise passiveness. But those who know how to watch and receive are rewarded in other and hardly less important ways. Receptivity can be a source of innocent and completely harmless happiness. A man or woman who knows how to make the best of both worlds — the world revealed by wise passiveness and the world created by wise activity — tends to find life enjoyable and interesting. Ours is a civilization in which vast numbers of children and adults are so chronically bored that they have to resort during their leisure hours to a regimen of non-stop distractions. Any method which promises to make life seem enjoyable and the commonplaces of everyday experience more interesting should be welcomed as a major contribution to culture and morality.

In *Modern Painters* there is a remarkable chapter on "the Open Sky" — a chapter which even by those who find Ruskin's theology absurd and his aesthetics frequently perverse may still be read with profit and admiring pleasure. "It is a strange thing," Ruskin writes, "how little in general people know about the sky. It is the part of creation in which nature has done more for the sake of pleasing man, more for the sake and evident purpose of talking to him and teaching him, than in any of her works, and it is just the part in which we least attend to her.... There is not a moment in any day of our lives in which nature is not producing (in the sky) scene after scene, picture after picture, glory after glory, and working always upon such exquisite and constant principles of the most perfect beauty, that it is quite certain it is all done for us and intended for our perpetual pleasure." But, in point of fact, does the sky produce in most people the perpetual pleasure which its beauty is so eminently capable of giving? The answer, of course, is No. "We never attend to it, we never make it a subject of thought.... We look upon it ... only as a succession of monotonous and meaningless accidents, too common or too vain to be worthy of a moment of watchfulness or a glance of admiration.... Who, among the chattering crowd, can tell me of the forms and the precipices of the chain of tall white mountains that girded the horizon at noon yesterday? Who saw the narrow sunbeam that came out of the south and smote their summits until they melted and mouldered away in a dust of blue rain? ... All has passed unregretted as unseen; or if the apathy be ever shaken off, if even for an instant, it is only by what is gross or what is extraordinary." A habit of wise passiveness in relation to the everyday drama of the clouds and mist and sunshine can become a source, as Ruskin insists, of endless pleasure. But most of the products of our educational system prefer Westerns and alcohol.

In the art of watching and receiving Ruskin was self-educated. But there seems to be no reason why children should not be taught that wise passiveness which gave this victim of a traumatic childhood so much pleasure and kept him, in spite of everything, reasonably sane for the greater part of a long and productive life. A training in watching and receiving will not turn every child into a great stylist but, within the limits imposed by constitution, temperament, and the circumambient culture, it will make him more sensitive, more intelligent, more capable of innocent enjoyment and, in consequence, more virtuous and more useful to society.

In the United States life, liberty, and the pursuit of happiness are constitutionally guaranteed. But if life hardly seems worth living, if liberty is used for subhuman purposes, if the pursuers of happiness know nothing about the nature of their quarry or the elementary techniques of hunting, these constitutional rights will not be very meaningful. An education in that wise passiveness recommended by

the saints and the poets, by all who have lived fully and worked creatively, might help us to transform the paper promises of a democratic
constitution into concrete contemporary fact.

Let us now consider very briefly two other areas in which an
education in the art of making the best of all our seemingly incommensurable worlds would certainly be helpful and might also turn out
to be practicable within the system now prevailing in our schools and
colleges. It is a matter of observable fact that all of us inhabit a world
of phantasy as well as a world of first-order experience and a world
of words and concepts. In most children and in some adults this
world of phantasy is astonishingly vivid. These people are the visuali-
zers of Galton's classical dichotomy. For them the world presented to
their consciousness by their story-telling, image-making phantasy is
as real as, sometimes more real than, the given world of sense impressions and the projected world of words and explanatory concepts.
Even in nonvisualizers the world of phantasy, though somewhat
shadowy, is still real enough to be retreated into or shrunk from, tormented by or voluptuously enjoyed. The mentally ill are the victims
of their phantasy, and even more or less normal people find themselves tempted into folly, or inhibited from behaving as they know
they ought to behave, by what goes on in the superreal but unrealis-
tic world of their imagination. How can we make the best of this odd,
alien, almost autonomous universe that we carry about with us inside
our skulls?

The question has been partially answered by the apostles of
those numerous religious movements stemming from "New Thought."
Using a vaguely theological language and interpreting the Bible to suit
themselves, they have given a religious form to a number of useful
and practical methods for harnessing imagination and its suggestive
power in the service of individual well-being and social stability. For
about a quarter or perhaps a third of the population their methods
work remarkably well. This is an important fact, of which professional educators should take notice and from whose implications
they should not be ashamed to learn. Unfortunately, men and women
in high academic positions tend to be intellectually snobbish. They
turn up their noses at the nonscientific, distressingly "inspirational"
but still astute and experienced psychologists of the modern heretical
churches. This is deplorable. Truth lives, proverbially, at the bottom
of a well, and wells are often muddy. No genuinely scientific investi-
gator has any right to be squeamish about anything.

And here is another truth-containing well abhorred by academic
scientists of the stricter sort. Excellent techniques for teaching children and adults to make the best of the chaotic world of their phantasy

have been worked out by the Dianeticists and their successors, the Scientologists. Their Imagination Games deserve to be incorporated into every curriculum. Boys and girls, and even grown men and women, find these games amusing and, what is more important, helpful. Made the worst of, our imagination will destroy us; made the best of, it can be used to break up long-established habits of undesirable feeling, to dissipate obsessive fears, to provide symbolic outlets for anger and fictional amends for real frustrations.

In the course of the last three thousand years how many sermons have been preached, how many homilies delivered and commands roared out, how many promises of heaven and threats of hell-fire solemnly pronounced, how many good-conduct prizes awarded and how many childish buttocks lacerated with whips and canes? And what has been the result of all this incalculable sum of moralistic words, and of the rewards and savage punishments by which the verbiage has been accompanied? The result has been history — the successive generations of human beings comporting themselves virtuously and rationally enough for the race to survive, but badly enough and madly enough for it to be unceasingly in trouble. Can we do better in the future than we are doing today, or than our fathers did in the past? Can we develop methods more effective than pious talk and Pavlovian conditioning?

For an answer to these questions — or at least for some hints as to the nature of a possible answer — we must turn to history and anthropology. Like many primitive societies today, many highly civilized societies of the past provided their members with realistically amphibious methods for dealing with negative emotions and the instinctive drives that are incompatible with communal living. In these societies morality and rational behavior were not merely preached and rewarded; they were made easier by the provision of religiously sanctioned safety valves, through which the angry, the frustrated, and the anxiously neurotic could release their aggressive or self-destructive tendencies in a satisfyingly violent and yet harmless and socially acceptable way. In Ancient Greece, for example, the orgies of Dionysus and, at a somewhat later date, the Corybantic dances, sacred to the Great Mother, were safety valves through which rage and resentment found an innocuous outlet, while the paralyzing inhibitions of anxiety were swept away in a wild rush of nervous, muscular, and hormonal activity. In this ethical and therapeutic context Dionysus was known as Lusios, the Liberator. His orgies delivered the participants from the dismal necessity of running amok, or retreating into catatonia, or stoically bottling up their feelings and so giving themselves a psychosomatic illness. Corybantic dancing

was regarded as a form of medical treatment and at the same time as
a religious rite, cathartic to the soul no less than to the adrenalin-
charged body. Which did most for morality and rational behavior — the dialogues of Plato or the orgies of Dionysus, Aristotle's
Ethics or the Corybantic dances? My guess is that, in this competition, Lusios and the Great Mother would be found to have won hands
down.

In a society like ours it would doubtless be impracticable to
revive Maenadism or the congregational antics of the Dionysian
orgies. But the problem of what multiple amphibians should do about
their frustrations and their tendencies to aggression remains acute
and still unsolved. Sixty years ago William James wrote an essay entitled *The Moral Equivalent of War.* It is an excellent essay as far as it
goes; but it does not, unfortunately, go far enough. Moral equivalents
must be found not only for war but also for delinquency, family squab-
bles, bullying, puritanical censoriousness, and all the assorted beast-
liness of daily life. Preaching and conditioning will never of themselves solve these problems. It is obvious that we must take a hint from
the Greeks and provide ourselves with physical safety valves for
reducing the pressure of our negative emotions. No ethical system
which fails to provide such physical safety valves, and which fails to
teach children and their elders how to use them, is likely to be effective. It will be the business of psychologists, physiologists, and sociologists to devise acceptable safety valves, of moralists and clergymen
to provide rationalization in terms of the local value systems and
theologies, and for educators to find a place in the curriculum for
courses in the indispensable art of letting off steam.

And there is another art that merits the educator's closest attention — the art of controlling physical pain. Pain, as recent studies have
made abundantly clear, is not simply a mechanical affair of peripheral receptors and special centers in the brain, and its intensity is
not directly proportional to the extent of the injury which is its cause.
Pain may be aggravated or inhibited by numerous psychological and
even cultural factors. Which means, of course, that to some extent at
least pain is controllable. This fact, needless to say, has been known
from time immemorial, and for the last century and a half (from the
days of Elliotson and Esdaile) has been systematically exploited in
hypnotic anesthesia. Neurological research is now discovering the
organic and functional reasons for these old observations and empirical practices; a somewhat disreputable "wild" phenomenon is in process of being turned into a domesticated scientific fact, consonant
with other well-known facts and safely caged within a familiar sym-
bol-system. Taking advantage of the newfound respectability of hyp-

nosis and suggestion, educators should now include elementary pain control in the curriculum of physical training. Control of pain through suggestion and autosuggestion is an art which, as every good dentist knows, can be learned by most children with the greatest of ease. Along with singing and calisthenics, it should be taught to every little boy and little girl who can learn it.

Training in a closely similar art may prove to be very useful as a part of ethical education. In his book *Auto-Conditioning* Professor Hornell Hart has outlined simple and thoroughly practical methods for changing moods, intensifying motivations, and implementing good intentions. There are no educational panaceas, no techniques that work perfectly in every case. But if autoconditioning produces good results in only twenty or thirty percent of those who have been instructed in the art, it deserves to take its place in every educator's armamentarium.

That we are multiple amphibians is self-evident, and the corollary of this self-evident truth is that we must attack our problems on every front where they arise — on the mental front and on the physiological front, on the front of concepts and symbols and on the front of wordless experience, on the rational front and on the irrational front, the individual front and the social front. But what should be our strategy? How are we to learn and successfully practice the art of attacking on all the fronts simultaneously? Many valuable discoveries were made by the amphibians of earlier times and alien cultures, and many discoveries are being made within our own culture today. These empirical findings of the past and the present should be studied, tested, related to the best scientific knowledge now available, and finally adapted for practical use within our educational systems. Ten million dollars from the coffers of one of the great foundations would pay for the necessary research and large-scale experimentation. Out of such research and experimentation might come, within a few years, a radical improvement in the methods currently used to prepare young people to meet the challenges of their manifold amphibiousness and to make the best of all the strangely assorted worlds in which, as human beings, they are predestined to live.

Classroom Without Walls

MARSHALL MC LUHAN

It's natural today to speak of "audio-visual aids" to teaching, for we still think of the book as norm, of other media as incidental. We also think of the new media (press, radio, TV) as *mass media* and think of the book as an individualistic form — individualistic because it isolated the reader in silence and helped create the Western "I." Yet it was the first product of mass production.

With it everybody could have the same books. It was impossible in medieval times for different students, different institutions, to have copies of the same book. Manuscripts, commentaries, were dictated. Students memorized. Instruction was almost entirely oral, done in groups. Solitary study was reserved for the advanced scholar. The first printed books were "visual aids" to oral instruction.

Before the printing press, the young learned by listening, watching, doing. So, until recently, our own rural children learned the language and skills of their elders. Learning took place outside the classroom. Only those aiming at professional careers went to school at all. Today in our cities, most learning occurs outside the classroom. The sheer quantity of information conveyed by press-magazines-film-TV-radio far exceeds the quantity of information conveyed by school instruction and texts. This challenge has destroyed the monopoly of the book as a teaching aid and cracked the very walls of the classroom so suddenly that we're confused, baffled.

In this violently upsetting social situation, many teachers naturally view the offerings of the new media as entertainment, rather than education. But this carries no conviction to the student. Find a classic that wasn't first regarded as light entertainment. Nearly all vernacular works were so regarded until the 19th century.

Many movies are obviously handled with a degree of insight and maturity at least equal to the level permitted in today's textbooks. Olivier's *Henry V* and *Richard III* assemble a wealth of scholarly and artistic skill, which reveals Shakespeare at a very high level, yet in a way easy for the young to enjoy.

The movie is to dramatic representation what the book was to the manuscript. It makes available to many and at many times and places what otherwise would be restricted to a few at few times and places. The movie, like the book, is a ditto device. TV shows to 50,-

22

000,000 simultaneously. Some feel that the value of experiencing a book is diminished by being extended to many minds. This notion is always implicit in the phrases "mass media," "mass entertainment" — useless phrases obscuring the fact that English itself is a mass medium.

Today we're beginning to realize that the new media aren't just mechanical gimmicks for creating worlds of illusion, but new languages with new and unique powers of expression. Historically, the resources of English have been shaped and expressed in constantly new and changing ways. The printing press changed not only the quantity of writing but also the character of language and the relations between author and public. Radio, film, TV pushed written English toward the spontaneous shifts and freedom of the spoken idiom. They aided us in the recovery of intense awareness of facial language and bodily gesture. If these "mass media" should serve only to weaken or corrupt previously achieved levels of verbal and pictorial culture, it won't be because there's anything inherently wrong with them. It will be because we've failed to master them as new languages in time to assimilate them to our total cultural heritage.

These new developments, under quiet analytic survey, point to a basic strategy of culture for the classroom. When the printed book first appeared, it threatened the oral procedures of teaching and created the classroom as we now know it. Instead of making his own text, his own dictionary, his own grammar, the student started out with these tools. He could study not one but several languages. Today these new media threaten, instead of merely reinforce, the procedures of this traditional classroom. It's customary to answer this threat with denunciations of the unfortunate character and effect of movies and TV, just as the comic book was feared and scorned and rejected from the classroom. Its good and bad features in form and content, when carefully set beside other kinds of art and narrative, could have become a major asset to the teacher.

Where student interest is already focused is the natural point at which to be in the elucidation of other problems and interests. The educational task is not only to provide basic tools of perception but also to develop judgment and discrimination with ordinary social experience.

Few students ever acquire skill in analysis of newspapers. Fewer have any ability to discuss a movie intelligently. To be articulate and discriminating about ordinary affairs and information is the mark of an educated man. It's misleading to suppose there's any basic difference between education and entertainment. This distinction merely relieves people of the responsibility of looking into the matter. It's like setting up a distinction between didactic and lyric poetry on the ground that one teaches, the other pleases. However, it's always been true that whatever pleases teaches more effectively.

A New Kind of Writing: Basic Skills Revisited and Revised

THE COMMUNICATIONS EXPERIENCE

There is a story, often repeated in Tanzania, about the Christian missionaries who took over the schooling in a Wachagga village and taught with great dedication the basic skills of readin', 'ritin', 'rithmetic, and reverence for the Lord. The missionaries did a fine job, sanctified by their own zeal, and when they left, all the young Wachaggans in the village had mastered the basics and could read, 'rite, 'rithmetize, and revere. By *all the young Wachaggans*, that is, we mean the sole two youngsters who accidentally survived the lions, sharks, drought, heat, European clothing, etc. This experience gave rise to the old Tanzanian proverb, "Caveat discipulus," which translates roughly "Beware of pedagogues peddling basic skills."

The Wachagga in their savage innocence recognized too late a truth about basic skills which is overlooked by an equally overwhelming number of Americans and American educators in their civilized ignorance. That the basic survival skills in any society are determined by the actual nature of that society itself and not by misperceptions or well-intentioned wishes about the nature of that society or culture. This civilized ignorance is evidenced in the increased public and professional outcry for a return to "good ole basic education" whose 3R basic skills were based on a view of a "good ole culture" which is, empirically speaking, long gone. Like the

Wachaggans, we are in danger of losing an entire generation unless we examine the nature of our culture as it exists and the nature of the forces which set its tone and emphases before we decide a priori upon the skills needed in that culture.

In preparing our proposal we considered basic skills as those competencies necessary for one to realize a meaningful and autonomous life in the mainstream of his culture. From the Wachagga we learned that those basic competencies are determined by the nature of the culture. We also realized that as the forces which set a culture's tone and emphases change, it is reasonable to expect that the role of those competencies which have served as basic skills in the past also changes.

As both society and the classrooms within it are examined in this context, the massive intrusion of mass communications during the past two decades becomes an obviously ever more important force in shaping that culture. That the impact of media and technology upon our society and especially upon the young in our society is formidable is rarely disputed. The data show that people are spending more time with the media, gathering more information from the media, and basing more decisions on media inputs; kids are spending more time with television than with teachers, seeing more films than reading books. Yet, while this revolution has radically changed our society, the basic skills being taught in the schools have not changed correspondingly. Further while the role of the teacher in this media and information enriched society is also altered, basic teaching skills have not kept pace. These realizations led to the two major thrusts of our work: (1) treating media competency as a basic skill and (2) changing the role of the teacher in an as yet ill-defined science of education to that of facilitator-researcher.

In all facets of contemporary life, powerful, far reaching ideas and related technologies are developing. Crucial to harnessing these world shaping forces is achieving a responsible and knowing relationship among men and between man and his environment. Man's technology can be considered as attempts at getting into an ever more communicative and, hence, more meaningful relationship with his environment, and we consider the common communications media in exactly those terms. Hence we have defined the concept of Communications Skills as including human relations skills and "media competency" in addition to the usual literacy and computational skills. Media competency is the basic skill which has to do with the ability to both recognize the impact upon the individual of the content and the form of communications media and to learn to use these in order to respond with feeling, individuality, and constructive concern to basic problems and issues in society. It has to do, therefore, with attempts at isolating and becoming conscious of the ways media shape the environment and man, and the ways in which man shapes his life through the use of media. The term "media" is used broadly here, including print and non-print communication channels as well as those buildings, organizations, and rituals which man creates in order to organize himself for purposeful life experiences.

In developing the concept of media competency as a basic skill, we began by considering the classroom as a mini-society not immune to the conflicts which rage in the society at large, and focus on the elements of communication within that mini-society. For example, explicitly teaching language from the viewpoint of another communications mode necessarily points out such things as the relationships information creates and the arbitrariness of language conventions. It also leaves open the possibility for considering body language, non-verbal communications, and visual information systems as equally important communications channels. It is useful to note that a critical disposition towards print, and awareness of its limitations and the print based standards imposed on learning and expression — all nagging problems — may themselves be placed in perspective when other communications forms become more prominent in education.

An interesting requirement emerges in making *the concept of communication* central — the dynamics of people working in groups must be dealt with because interpersonal behavior becomes the medium of the message. In this area of *Human Relations Skills,* personal growth and development become recognized for the reason that as the individual begins to understand and construct his own language he begins to understand and know himself. In the context of the group, this personality development is encouraged and socialized, and as groups work together they create, adapt, and change society. When such community, personal growth, and human relations centered aims become prime, it means that the usual subject matter will have to be approached from a broader conceptual basis.

A first step in working these ideas out in practice involves achieving a working understanding of various media forms *per se.* Since, for the sake of consistency, these learnings must be carried out in a way sensitive to the communication needs of the individuals involved, they must be self-directed. *This places certain demands on tactics of educational research* and leads to the following two interests.

The first is having students learn about the media forms available to them so that throughout their adult lives they may use these forms as learning mediums themselves. Our work has as an implicit first objective the establishment of opportunities for people to learn filmmaking, photography, television, etc. and to study how others have used and are using the modes of communications. A long range additional outcome of our work would concentrate on self-directed human relations training experiences. That is, individuals (teachers as well as learners) would use multi-media resources in order to reflect upon their own individual and group behavior and modes of communication and to invent techniques and activities designed to help personal growth according to personal diagnosis. In a sense, such activities from the very beginning will often provide a context for learning about the technical aspects of electro-chemical mass communications media.

The second interest and second concern of our work is an attempt at laying a foundation for a way of thinking about instruction which will provide a more fluent and organic way of conceptualizing inquiry into and about the educational process. However, we see clearly that such work must be grounded in practice and must emerge almost of itself from practice, so that what is being proposed is in a sense "action research." This means that traditional expectations about research and evaluation design must be amended. That is not to say that there is little interest in rigorous work and objecive assessment. Quite to the contrary, work can only sensibly proceed if careful attempts are made to describe and observe, conceptualize, criticize assumptions and values, and isolate important variables and their mode of interaction so that it is possible to study the delicate interplay between what seems cause and what seems effect. Still even if there existed a compelling "science" of education under prevailing conditions those who actually teach our children will remain but funnels unless they take part in formulating questions and in studying the student relationships in which they are engaged. If such a fundamental change in the teacher's role can be effected, we believe that there is great hope that the practice of education, complete with context and participants, will become the actual ground for building a *new science of education.* Those who actually participate in education will become — and for the first time, in a real sense — the investigators of education. The point that we are concerned with here is, quite simply, that humanistic education must build its own science of education.

In this view, teachers themselves will take more of an active role in studying themselves, their teaching, and their classrooms. The concept of teacher as research-evaluator, or better, teacher as facilitator, can emphasize the role of teacher as a receptive person who helps the student obtain suitable feedback on his own actions. In keeping with our basic concept of communication, the primary role of the teacher in the classroom can be described in terms of his function as a facilitator — one who helps modify the environment and helps provide the kind of structure that the unique individual needs in order to act, express himself, experiment, and learn from his mistakes and successes. If teaching requires freedom from certain constraints and freedom to be exploratory on the part of teachers and students, and if, to remain flexible and responsive, teaching must adapt and adjust to the teacher's qualitative judgments, then the help that the teacher will find most useful has to do with ways in which the teacher can make his judgements as precise, valid, and reliable as possible. This view of evaluation — evaluation primarily aimed at guiding the instructional process as it unfolds — is a neglected one but a necessary one if education is to fare better on the fields of basic skills than did the Wachagga youngsters.

There is another proverb, also oft repeated in Tanzania, about the zealous missionaries' success in foisting the same inappropriate skills on hipper youngsters in the next village down the road. It goes "De mortuis nil nisi bonum" which translates roughly "A poached pedagogue in every pot." The morals of these tales are patent. If we ignore skills which are required by the nature of society and its technologies, our students will not lead meaningful and autonomous lives, and if education fails to teach these required skills in appropriate manners, it too will be heading inevitably toward the pot. The name of the experience, as always, is communications.

Film as Educator

WILLIAM ARROWSMITH

In humanistic education the future lies with film. Of this I am firmly convinced. I do not mean by this either "audio-visualism" or educational filmstrips. I mean that film will be not only the future medium of instruction, but that film also will challenge and eventually claim the place and prestige accorded to literature and the arts in the traditional curriculum. In short, film not merely as medium but as curriculum, too. This conviction rests upon a faith that human society cannot do without the humanities, cannot forsake its faith in the project of making men more fully human, helping men to "become the thing they are." If real education — and not merely the transmission of knowledge — is to take place, a curriculum is required which corroborates and exemplifies moral discovery, the making of a fate, the hunger for identity. Literature and the arts have always been at the heart of the humanities because they provided just such corroboration; our most enduring use for art has been precisely in education — and it is an end worthy of art, this "expansion of love beyond ourselves," which Nietzsche called education.

But I recognize, with distress and sadness, that this literature which is for me so crucial a curriculum that I cannot imagine my life without it, is for others, especially many young people, no longer at the center of things. It has come to seem to them artificial, even faintly anachronistic; its conventions suddenly seem conventional, labored, and unreal. Its crucial illusion crippled, participation becomes constrained or even impossible. This constraint comes not only from the comparative spaciousness and realism of the new media, the superior complexity and power of their conventions, but also from the way in which literature is too often taught; that is, as technical or professional virtuosity or as a decorative cultural "accomplishment." We have become very adept, as Edgar Friedenberg points out, "at driving cadmium rods into the seething mass of our cultural heritage and rendering it inactive."[1] The schools do it by castrating art, by disguising its true subversiveness, or by forcing it to yield a crop of acceptable clichés. The universities do it by treating literature as though it were written not for our enjoyment and instruction, but as part of a curriculum, for analysis and instruction.

The constraint students feel with literature has noticeably increased as scholarly attitudes have moved from the graduate schools to the undergraduate and even the secondary curricula. Constraint now becomes the rule; the student begins to suspect, resent, and reject a literary culture and education that flourish apparently for their own sakes or for their professors', without pertinence to his life. And so the conventions that support the art of the spoken word — the artificialities that used not to trouble us, that we took in our stride once — begin to seem dubious and then to dissolve. One no longer feels the necessity of the style, or its necessities are no longer

---

[1] The Humanities in the School, ed. Harold Taylor (New York: Citation Press, 1968), p. 145.

ours. Constraint is not easly unlearned; and poetry and drama seem
now no longer second nature, but come to us increasingly touched by
the self-consciousness of all high culture that has been educationally
formalized. I have heard Jesuits say that they could not teach in clerical garb, because the authority of their robes tainted the subjects
they taught, troubling education with the problems of resented or
refused authority. It is the same with the spoken arts in education;
what is bad and merely authoritative or professional in education has
corrupted them and weakened their enabling conventions. They no
longer speak to us naturally, and our responses are becoming fatally
self-conscious. Or so it seems to me.

Film itself may be highly self-conscious, but it is surely unique in
possessing audiences who take it naturally, who attend to it without
fuss or pretense or shame; who for the most part trust its makers and
feel unmistakably at ease with its conventions. People go to movies
as they go to take a bath or a stroll. You cannot assume that one
student in ten has read a given book; chances are high that half the
students will have seen — and seen well, or at least intensely — any
film you care to mention. What is more, students see films with a
natural confidence, a confidence unembarrassed by the grosser kinds
of self-consciousness. By comparison, audiences for poetry, drama,
or music are notoriously unsure, inclined either to dogmatic arro-
gance or deferential ignorance. The fear of the expert — the academic
expert above all — hovers over them. But in film the climate is freer,
more tolerant. The experts have not yet invaded the film and claimed
it "No Trespassing — For Experts Only. Everybody Else Get Out!" as
scholars have done with the Renaissance and musicologists with
baroque music; or in literature where one sees the sad spectacle of
writers and periods that were once of enormous seminal significance
to the general reader and that, thanks to the claims of scholars, and
the reluctance of the non-expert to take on the expert, have been rendered almost wholly useless and inaccessible.

In this openness and exemption from the self-consciousness of
"high" culture lies the enormous promise of film. Its technical possibilities are, of course, staggering, but they would have almost no significance unless the audience could accept them easily and naturally
within the context of conventions that audiences feel at home with.
Indeed, one of my fears in the wave of technical experiment in film
now is that the experiments may succeed in making the audience as
killingly conscious of the camera and mere technical artifice as they
are now mostly unconscious of it, content to accept a tale or a visual
sequence as though it possessed its own internal necessity and could
no more be questioned than wind on water. In saying this, I run the

risk of offending those who are eager to see film accorded an equal place — i.e., a *technical* place — alongside the other arts. But the unique situation of film is surely that it comes to us, not as a part of our educationally acquired "high" culture, but as part of the common culture itself.

It may be that films are still a part of common culture because film began not as an art but as an industry, and for a long time refused to be taken, or to take itself, seriously. But whatever the reason, the film-maker enjoys in this respect a precious advantage over all his peers in the other arts. Only he has a real hope of creating on this basis an art which is not only great but also popular. What the novel was to the nineteenth century, the film might be to the twentieth: *the* genre, the only genre wholly congenial to the majority of a culture. In ancient Greece tragedy was just such a genre — popular, democratic, of enormous appeal to all classes; anything but the tiresome Mandarin nonsense it has become in modern production. Even in Italy as late as thirty years ago Italian opera was an unmistakably popular art form; you heard it as a matter of course on bar radios and in piazzas, interspersed with vivid comment. Now the same music brings dismay and anger and cries of *Abbassa la radio!* This currency, this conventional acceptability and viability belong, as I say, uniquely to film. And they suggest just how enormous an influence film might come to exert throughout the culture.

I said earlier that film would come to prevail in the educational curriculum of schools and universities, and that it would do so not only as a medium but also as a curriculum. It will be able to do this, I suggest, precisely because it is itself still a part of common culture and therefore can be meaningfully utilized in programs of general education. At present, general education is in disrepair and disesteem throughout the learned world. But general education was not defeated by its own inadequacy but by the professionalization of universities. Specialists cannot, for obvious reasons, confer a general education any more than plumbers can design a landscape. And general education in this country withered because specialists could not be persuaded to educate themselves or their students except as specialists. Yet our need for a valid form of general education is urgent, and grows more urgent all the time. We have learned recently how terrible is the cost to culture of its rejection by those who, because they have no stake in it, cannot use it. How, for instance, can you meaningfully teach Greek tragedy — with its conviction of each man's freedom to find his own fate and his responsibility for it — to those who have never experienced such freedom, who lack precisely the power to alter their fates or even to find them? You cannot. And what the ghetto child violently refuses, the middle-class child accepts because it is sugared with the promise of later material success. What we desperately need is a general education, a general curriculum, which could focus the realities of our present existence, present them as fact or hypothesis in a telling way — which could deal with our obsessions and tell the truth about our lives. Such a curriculum clearly must be designed and taught in such a way that it does not elicit irrelevant refusal or suspicion — that is, a curriculum whose style and conventions would seem, because shared by both teacher and student, to carry their own necessities, to require neither apology nor defense. That curriculum is film, a medium which is instantly acceptable, which provides, as reading does not, an immediate and shared experience of unparalleled intensity, which is still largely unencumbered by a scholarly literature, and whose vitality and future seem undeniable.

But it is not merely a matter of intensity and community. Here, after all, we have an art that is wholly available to the whole world, a truly ecumenical art. Given only subtitles, it is accessible to anyone, anywhere. And precisely because it *can* go anywhere, it tends to have, at least among the great directors, precisely the kind of ecumenical ambitions — the hope of reaching all mankind — that great writers, to some degree always imprisoned in the parish of their language, have hungered for. Even if the culture is formidably remote — — Korean, say, or even Indian — the director can quickly and vividly familiarize it as no writer conceivably can. Yet the only purpose of familiarizing it must be to transcend what he has familiarized — to speak to *any man* in *any* place. Ecumenical ambitions may produce pretentious failures — but at least they will not produce a precious art. If there is little comfort in living in an age of violent change, of feeling only transitional, always uncertain of where one is or might be going, it is in such conditions, especially when they are universal, that we can hope for something like a Homeric vision, for a generous image of humanity. And the hope is measurably augmented when artists of great talent — I think of Kurosawa and Antonioni — apply themselves to portraying the human psyche — its powers and weaknesses — as it strives to adapt to nearly unbearable change, to the destruction of the very ecology by which it was once — and may still be — fatally defined. This is, admittedly, a theme particularly suited to film, which can show with compelling beauty and detail the relation betweeen psyche and ecology, which can re-create the old poetry of earth and the nightmarish new world in stunning proximity. But it is also one of the great universal themes — perhaps *the* great theme of the age — and it is, *I* think, no accident that it should be film — that ecumenical art — that is now attempting to treat it.

I know of no art with such potential for stating our problems, complexities, anxieties, and powers more naturally or comprehensively than film. And this is why film seems to me a *natural* curriculum — a curriculum-in-process, a creative project — with which to replace much of what we now do in literature and philosophy and humanities. At least film is where we might most intelligently begin, taking advantage of an existing motivation, of a living art form — in order to deepen and widen common culture. There is always the chance — doubtless high — that we shall stultify film in the process, but I cannot see how serious educators can fail to make use of the most powerful art-form that has ever existed, above all when that art has an unmistakable popular life. One would have to be *mad* not to use it. There is no way of guaranteeing that we shall not abuse it too. But, unlike the other arts, film is intrinsically *interdisciplinary;* it *fuses* all the existing arts in a new mode whose marvellous complexity will defeat all but the ablest academic critics. It is a medium congenial to ideas, and to *present* ideas above all, and its hunger for an ecumenical audience should, at least for now, keep it relatively honest. Ideally, I think such a film curriculum should be complemented by literature — literature which criticizes the film, or which is criticized or amplified by the film. For I assume that the past still matters enormously and still has things to teach us, and also that the past can be bettered by present achievement — and that this rivalry between dead and living, this effort by the present to outdo the *past — imitare superando* — is supremely educational. In a time when the old are despised by the young, and the young feared by the old, it stands to reason that the past will seem irrelevant to the present. But surely it is not; certainly all education in the humanities is based on the premise of the relevance of the past to the present — that present which is, as Whitehead said, "holy ground."

The present is, like our culture, an *oecumene.* We are all ecumenical men and good Europeans these days. But the human *oecumene* runs backward too; it includes the dead, no less than Australian bushmen and the Hairy Ainu. And the dead are the vast majority. "Now that you're in Hell, Timon," the poet asks the famous misanthrope, "which do you prefer, the darkness or the light?" "The light, man. There are more of you here in Hell." The living are not diminished by honor done the dead. These, I suppose, are the pieties one expects of classicists, but I enter them as a protest against the jaunty McLuhanite modernity and the perky technical *hybris* of too many cineasts. Any valid general education should strive to keep past and present in constant creative and critical connection. Resnais's *Hiroshima mon Amour*, for instance, should be set against the poem it unknowingly, I suspect, imitates — the *Iliad.* And the point of the contrast should not be to batter the modern work with the ancient masterpiece, but to show why, in this case, in strategy and taste and power, the ancient work does so much more compellingly what the modern tries to do. Here, I would want to say, is a case of crucial cultural rivalry. Resnais attempted an honorable task; he attempted — probably unknowingly — the greatest theme of the greatest poet; a theme we badly need for our own time, and whose power and viability can be glimpsed in the passionate enthusiasm this rather poor film aroused among the young.

Or one might perhaps show how Antonioni, allusively and powerfully, attempts to create for film a visual vocabulary capable of taking what is still alive in the art of the past and renewing it in a fresh context. Thus in *Blow-Up*, when the photographer returns to find the corpse in the park, we see him look at the bare grass, the body gone, while the leaves scatter in a fresh dawn wind around him; and he turns suddenly and looks upward, and the camera holds momentarily on the leafy branch overhead; nothing but the leaves and the wind-sound. And then at the close of the film, as the camera holds on the photographer, his eyes fill with tears as he turns, in the grip of a starker reality now, unable to participate any longer in the illusion of the mummers' tennis — turns and looks at the green grass. And then he too is gone, and there is only the grass left, under and behind the closing legend. Ephemerality, anonymity, the vision of man's days like the grass and the leaves, and the great Homeric figure: "As is the generation of leaves, so is that of men. One generation is born, and another dies. . . . " All these are in the aura of Antonioni's work. An aura of visual association, utterly without educated snobbery or pretense, a re-creation in cinematic terms of the oldest metaphors of human anonymity and impermanence in a world of change. In *La Notte* the same theme: the millionaire Milanese Trimalchio who seeks to leave a permanent monument; in the grass a battered marble Roman head, all permanence, gazed at by a fascinated cat, all animal transcience. In *L'Eclisse*, as Ricardo leaves Vittoria's apartment, one sees above the gate, perfectly squared in iron, an Umbrian landscape of the fourteenth century — the old poetry of earth framed by the imprisoning enclosures of the new megalopolis. In *The Red Desert*, the Sardinian beach fantasy, the girl, a brown and gawky adolescent, runs to hide, peering out from the green shrubbery; and she brings irresistibly to mind one of Gauguin's Tahitian girls — the cultural suggestion supporting the psychological purpose of the fantasy — the wonder and fear that accompany the arrival of "the other"; the waking out of oneself. None of these echoes, I stress, function for cultural show; they are rather Antonioni's way of using the past, transmuting it, and making it newly available, for contrast or for direct statement. In this respect, this attempt to affiliate himself in a cinematic — but not a literary — way to a great literary and artistic tradition, Antonioni is unique.

This, of course, is merely a suggestion of the sort of connection that can legitimately be found when past and present, literature and film, are meaningfully juxtaposed. The result of such juxtapositions would be, it seems to me, to demonstrate one of the ideal relations of past and present and to show unmistakably the pertinence of the past, whether achievement or challenge. A legitimate form of general education could be created on the basis of the available film resources, and the effect of such education would be both to rescue literature and to enrich film. Let me say bluntly that I think the education of film-makers could be remarkably improved if they could be brought into a reasonably respectful and lively relation to past literature and the arts. I have the distinct impression that film-makers are all too often lamentably ignorant or even contemptuous of the literary tradition whose rightful inheritors they are. If they were not, they would not make many of the films they now make, and many of their dreadful adaptations of literary material would show either more respect for the orginal or more imaginative and radical adaptation than one now sees. And they would be bolder in appropriating material which is conducive to their ends. We need, in short, educated film-makers if we are to entrust the curriculum of education to them. I personally fail to see how one can legitimately expect to improve the training of film-makers except by educating them well in the great tradition of Homer, Sophocles, Plato, Shakespeare, and Racine. The achievements of film are already impressive, but they are not so impressive that we can lightly condone mere technical virtuosity combined with a radical illiteracy. The film-maker is as much the heir of literature as the American is the heir of Europe. But he lacks the humility to seize his inheritance, perhaps because, like most Americans, he cannot rid himself of his obsession with money and his populist assumption that literature and the past are either boring or bunk.

Let me close by saying that I think the mission of the film-maker goes far beyond mere artistic prowess or achievement. The film-maker alone has the opportunity, in conjunction with the other mass media, to reshape and reinvigorate the culture. The novelist has lost his chance; the poets and dramatists no longer have one. The educators have for the most part renounced education. And that means that the great task of education in our times — the creation of a humane culture in its apparent absence or defeat — rests with the maker of

films. Art is not enough. Or rather we need an art that can perform
the task of education — the task that literature and the other arts
once performed until they somehow lost the consent on which their
power was based. The legacy of literature, however, is immense.
What is required is the kind of sensibility that can seize it and trans-
mute it to another medium, with equal power and simplicity and complexity, much as Montaigne and Shakespeare seized and transmuted
the classical world they found in Plutarch, or as the Greek dramatists
deliberately democratized the aristocratic ethos of *arete* they found
in Homer and the poets. It is an art of translation that I am speaking
of here — translation so accurate that it controls the matter and
power of the original, and so radical that it utterly reshapes, transmog-
rifies, the values it discovers. You can transform great talent into
genius only by energizing it in a task that requires exceptional
powers, that makes talent transcend itself. Neither entertainment nor
what we conventionally call art are likely to do it; we need a
vision — and Vergilian powers in both artist and educator — that will
transcend both art and entertainment. I suggest education, by which I
mean both art and entertainment, be subsumed in a higher effort.

Films and the Future

STANLEY KAUFFMANN

I begin with comments on an occasion that I think is directly related
to the subject of this meeting — the opening of the new Lincoln
Center Repertory Theatre in 1965 with a production of *Danton's
Death*. Those of you who are interested in these matters may have
read that the company in fact started in 1963 in a temporary building
and was generally coolly received, that its then management, of successful Broadway types, was roundly disapproved by most serious
critics, that the appointment of a new management — Blau and Irving
of the San Francisco Actors' Workshop — was generally hailed. I was
among the hailers because, although I had never seen a Workshop

production, I knew the plays they had been doing, the atmosphere they had created, and that Blau and Irving had gained their reputations by turning their backs on what the commercial theatre signifies. Then came the first Blau-Irving production in New York. One cannot, of course, reach final decisions about them or about the future growth of the company on the basis of one production, but this time, as against the first management's productions, there was a feeling not of rage but of hopelessness. *Danton's Death* was poorly produced in every regard, and I felt that I was facing, not Broadway slicked-up superficial art, but an exponent of American bankruptcy in the performing arts, that the poverty on the stage was *our* poverty, that that stage was a combination mirror and magnifying glass.

Or to take another instance that leads back to the subject of this meeting, Federico Fellini, the Italian film director, was in New York recently, and in conversation he said: "I have been in New York five or six times, and each time it seems to me made up of pieces of dreams I had when I was a boy. Why have I never seen New York rightly used in an American film? And where are the good new American films altogether?"

I replied, not entirely evasively, that the answer would entail a concise restatement of American history — and not just its cultural history. So instead, I asked him to have another drink.

These two instances are not meant as glib evidence that this country is bankrupt of artistic talent, because it most certainly is not. But I'm here specifically as a commentator on the theatre and on films, and these two arts are at present in especially poor estate in contrast to several other American arts; and since these two arts are most clearly related to large audiences, their condition seems to me to reflect mercilessly the condition of the American public; this, by easy progress, this relates to the education, expectancies, appetites of that public.

I'd like now to state my conclusion to make clear what I'm progressing toward. It is simply this — art of any kind is a circular process. It is obviously not made without artists; less obviously, but equally pertinently, it is not made, for long or well, without a responsive audience. Talent is a relative constant in the human race; it flowers when there is the right public soil. We all know of individual exceptions to this, artists who worked all their lives, unaccepted and unknown; but they are exceptions. The great eras in any art — painting, music, poetry, architecture, drama — were sustained by appetites in a society. The elements that produce that appetite are many and are tightly interwoven — political, economic, religious, the home, the school. None of them can, rationally, be entirely isolated from the others. But, recognizing the irrationality, we can discuss what teachers can do with young people to improve appetites for art in this country's future.

In this matter it is important to start with a clear, unsentimentalized view, free of democratic fallacies. A very small proportion of any country's population has at any time had a strong interest in art. I think it is a dangerous mistake to assume, as a dynamics in the teaching of humanities, that that proportion must be increased. If it happened to be increased, that would be lovely. What is much more important is, first, that it be maintained, and second, that it be continually refined.

The aims of the teacher and the hopes of the critic are not necessarily identical. The teacher presumably wants to send out every pupil more of a whole-souled being than he was when he came in. Theoretically, at least, he has equal responsibility to every pupil, to enlighten the pupil to the best of both their abilities in the subject he teaches, in the time and at the stage that their meeting takes place. As a citizen, I applaud; as a critic, I don't much care. That is, I am much more concerned with touching the few who will respond to the art than with dabbing every member of the class with a little art veneer. Of course one cannot reliably know in advance who the responsive few will be, and therefore the approach must be to the whole class. What I am concerned with is the *intent* of the approach, so that when those few are reached, they are given help instead of — as often happens — hindrance that may take years to overcome. It is culturally more important that those few get some glimmer of the mysteries and uncertainties of art than that the majority be given a few facile certainties to make them feel they have a grip on the subject. When I was in grammar school and high school, music appreciation exams consisted of the teacher playing brief snatches on the phonograph and asking us to write down the name of the composer and the title of the piece. It bred a good number of graduates who felt that the ability to name the composer and title was the mark of the musical connoisseur.

I am not going to discuss here the subject of awakening latent creative artistic ability in students. That can happen and does happen, but it is necessarily much rarer than this matter of cultivating a demanding audience. Anyway, it follows, both socially and educatively, if that audience is properly cultivated.

Thus my view of the teaching of the arts is that it ought never to be construed as in any way a parallel to the teaching of arithmetic or reading or geography, of which everyone must know something. It is not necessary — to the individual or to society — that every individual feels some link or responsibility to fine art; that concept is delusory, fallacious, and corrosive. It *is* important that every student be given a chance to find out whether he responds to fine art. I should judge that the only way to grade this approach is in terms of the student's age, what his experience of life and his possible imaginative reach may be. Within that framework, nothing but the best should be given him — in materials or in guidance. The former is relatively easy to give him, the latter less so.

This decade is one of insistent cultural explosion. The explosion has so far been largely in terms of the measurable, producible, and controllable: the building of theatres and galleries, the endowing of artists, individually and in groups, and assisting performing artists to tour. In other words, it has largely been in terms of masonry and money. We have yet to learn whether this activity has any effect on the creation of art, good or null. It will most likely have a favorable effect on interpretive art — the performance of music, of dance, of plays. As for the rest, we do not yet know, and the subject is clouded by imponderables that prohibit prophecy. If statistics are taken as chief guide, as they are in such a vulgar and distorted book as *The Culture Consumers* by Alvin Toffler, then the cultural explosion could turn out to be one of the worst disasters in the artistic life of this country: an approach that equates the clicking of museum turn-stiles with the growth of taste. Just think of the millions who filed past Michelangelo's "Pietá" at the New York World's Fair. If they had been truly affected by it, they would have come out and burned down the rest of the Fair.

The chief safeguard against what we may call numerism is progressive, unpetrified elitism. Fine art is not for everybody, Tolstoy and his disciples notwithstanding. Democracy is a political theory, not an aesthetic one. Any teacher who is not an advocate of elitism, who does not approach the subject of art as the abbot of a religious order approaches novices to find out which ones truly have the voca-tion, instead of trying to recruit them all — such a teacher is in my view a menace.

A word must be said about the manifestations of art that pre-ponderate. We are all well aware these days that in the world of art, fine art does not exist alone. It coexists with popular art, which in the last two hundred years or so has grown in proportionate amount and in influence. This growth has zoomed since the Second World War, for reasons that are familiar. Mass culture is now so large, so perva-sive, that it cannot be omitted from any discussion of art. In the audi-ence arts — films, the theatre, television — mass culture is so impor-tant and employs so many skilled people that it is rightfully in the province of serious criticism. No serious literary critic would concern himself with the latest best-selling historical romance simply because it was decently constructed and bearably written. But a serious film critic might well have to concern himself with the film made from that book because of the executant artists concerned, who may for various reasons have to operate within commercial films only and whose work needs comment, and because the power — in dream and fantasy — of the film version of the novel is so enormously intensified that it becomes both more influential and more interesting. Besides, fine art of our day often uses some of the modes and manners of the mass art. For example, in the theatre, *Guys and Dolls* raised musical comedy to a new dimension; in films *Dr. Strangelove* grew out of science fiction and popular topical fiction.

Two points can be concluded from this, I believe: (1) no firm line can be drawn between fine art and popular art; (2) equally, they are not mistakable one for the other. The moviegoer who doesn't like a good Western is malnourished and contemporaneously malformed; the polemicist of the popular who tells us that Westerns, or similar pictures, are what films are *for* is also malformed. There can no longer be any doubt that fine art derives some vitality, some ideas of method, some tonalities, from popular art, and by no means always in terms of parody or patronization or — if I may use an already tedious word — camp. Similarly, for the cultivated person, there is little doubt — in the vast majority of instances — as to what is fine art, even when it uses popular elements. One rough definition might be that fine art aims to be more than it seems, aims to have resonances larger than its materials. The popular has no such aim. It often does have such resonances, but they are incidental and accidental. Fine art is the use of experience as illumination; popular art is experience as entertainment. Popular art can take care of itself; the very essence of its being is that it thrives without subsidy, support, or study or else it dies. It is or is not. Fine art needs all those elements that popular art can scorn, plus some cultivation — some training — of its audience.

The surge and power of popular art, its constant and rightful appearance as a subject of serious discussion, have further muddled a clear view of artistic standards. The necessity to understand the relevance of popular art is sometimes misconstrued as an argument for alteration of standards. I think it is simply an argument for greater catholicity. It would be a failure in the teaching of art to ignore the existence and value of the popular. It would be a further facet of democratic sentimentality to equate it, in any degree, with serious art. And this is not to say that the standards of art are fixed. They are like the rules of grammar: if there are not rules, there is no grammar; but they must respond to life, usage, pertinence.

Let me now move on to the specific art in which that confusion is most likely to occur — the film — not to define further the differences between the popular and the fine, but to comment on some benefits of the latter. I scant the drama because, as far as the secondary school is concerned, the drama is treated much like literature, with the exception that it can be read aloud in class — assigning roles to different students — a device which, if it is not necessarily enlightening, is at least an antidote to possible boredom.

Film is quite a different matter. It has a number of assets, which I'll come to, and one fundamental advantage it shares with only one other art. It comes to the student exactly in the form in which it was made by the artist. This is true of only one other art — literature of the English language. Recorded music is wonderful, but it is not in the form intended by the composer. Reproductions of painting, photographs, models of architecture, and translations of foreign literature, all these are often excellent; none is the original work of art. Only literature in English and the film are available in a classroom exactly as they came from the maker's hand. They are thus the two arts that are safest from intrusions of middlemen en route, including teachers, and since film has some unique powers and attractions, it is, in that sense, the safer of the two.

I must be clear that I'm speaking about films that have been made as art, not educational films, such as the Encyclopaedia Britannica films in the humanities or factual films meant to instruct. These are educational tools, which may or may not be good; they stand in relation to the films I'm discussing as textbooks and syllabus guides stand to literature. The films I mean are the ones available in the many catalogs of film rental firms, the ones that have been made and shown all over the world as works of some degree of art. They are available in 16-millimeter prints, and all you need in order to bring American or Swedish or Japanese or Indian artists making art into a classroom in Ashtabula or Tucson is a 16-millimeter projector and a modest budget.

I'll skip any exegesis of the general values of artistic experience for those capable of it and concentrate on some specific values of film:[1]

1. In an age imbued with technological interests, this is the one art that flowers out of technology. Excepting architecture, film is the one art that can capitalize directly on the twentieth-century luxuriance of applied science. Some composers and some sculptors are trying to bridge the gap between art and science with the use of electric and

---

[1] Some of the following material is adapted from the essay, "The Film Generation," in my book *A World on Film* (New York: Harper and Row, 1966).

electronic components. The film-maker has no choice; he *must* use electronic equipment. This contributes to a sense of junction with his society, with membership in the present. The technological interest and the interest in applied science of American youth are notable, not to say notorious. I think they and the audiences of all ages share the film-maker's feeling of union with the present, perhaps unconsciously; I think that the scientific skills involved are in themselves a link between them and the artist. Lately we have heard much of Marshall McLuhan's thesis that "the medium is the message." Insofar as McLuhan is not a salesman of McLuhan, there is some insight to be found in his work, and insofar as these insights have relevance to future society, they certify that this technological ambience of films is of prime socio-cultural importance.

2. Through the film, the world of surfaces and physical detail has again become material for art. Young people, if they are anything more than clods, are professional discoverers, and in no way are they more alert than to their physical environment. The film has taken over from the novel the primary function of creating material reality. It has exalted this function, for instead of merely making a mosaic of details into which life also fits, the film manages to create poetry out of doorknobs, breakfasts, and furniture. Trivial details, of which everyone's universe is made, can once again be transmuted into metaphor, contributing to imaginative act.

A complementary, powerful fact is that this principle operates whether the film-maker is concerned with it or not. In any film except those with fantastic settings, whether the director's aim is naturalistic or romantic or symbolic or anything else, the physical world, through the mysteries of photography, never stops insisting on its presence and relevance.

This phenomenon gives some verity even to many mediocre films and gives great vitality to a film by a good artist. Indeed, out of this phenomenon, it can be argued that the film discovered pop art half a century ago, digested this minor achievement, then continued on its way.

3. The film form as such seems particularly apt for the treatment of many of the pressing questions of our day. I don't think this an inappropriate point in relation to high school students who, I am told, read Hemingway, Faulkner, and Pasternak. Nor do I mean by "pressing questions" such limited adolescent questions as juvenile delinquency. Such a film, for example, as *The Sound of Trumpets* by the young Italian, Ermanno Olmi, is one that any responsive high school student could appreciate and should see — a film about a youth's first job in an immense corporation in Milan.

The film form's particular strength in this area is its ability to externalize certain psychical matters that, for example, the theatre cannot easily deal with; it can relate them to physical environment in a manner that the theatre cannot contain nor the novel quite duplicate. The film can dramatize post-Freudian man, his habitat, and the relation between the two.

4. Film is, as I have noted, the one art that is available to the whole world at once, exactly as it was first made. With subtitles, it is the only art involving language that can be enjoyed in a language of which one is ignorant. (I except opera, where the language rarely needs to be understood precisely.)

The point is not the spreading of information or amity, as in USIA or UNESCO films; the point is emotional relationship and debt. If one has been moved by, say Japanese actors in Japanese settings, in actions of Japanese life that have resonated against one's own experience, there is a connection with Japan that is deeper than the benefits of propaganda or travelogue.

Obviously similar experience — emotional and spiritual — is available through other arts but rarely with the imperial ease of the film. As against foreign literature, foreign films have an advantage besides accessibilty in the original language. The Japanese novelist invites us to re-create the scene in imagination. The Japanese film-maker provides the scene for us with a vividness that our minds cannot equal in a foreign setting. Thus our responses can begin at a more advanced point and can more easily, although not more strongly, be stimulated and heightened. This universality and this relative simultaneity of response have made us all members of a much larger empathetic community than has been immediately possible before in history.

5. Film has one great benefit by accident — its youth — which I believe makes it especially attractive to the young. The motion-picture camera is only about seventy-five years old, and that's a generous estimate. It is this freshness, relative to the other arts, that gives young people not only the excitement of the potentials of the form but a strong proprietary feeling about it. The film belongs to them.

These are five of the reasons why, I believe, films can be of special interest and effect with young people — why I believe they are important in any curriculum concerned with culture. I repeat an earlier reason — the film is the art form probably best insured against the teaching of culture, against the rough usage it must get at the hands of most teachers and the possible blunting to which it is liable even in the hands of good teachers in the routines of the classroom and the processes of explication.

But this statement needs counterbalance. Despite the statistics of the cultural explosion, we seem to be living in the end of an age of belief in the death of art. Ever since Flaubert, we have been hearing about the death of the novel; composers are telling us that both tonality and atonality are finished; painters are telling us that art as planned mimesis — even mimesis of the imagination or fantasy — is finished. Whether the term "finished" is accurate or not, certainly all the arts are going through profound metamorphoses. It is so clear that old forms within each art are dying, that belief in that truth is no longer a useful progressive tenet. We may find out before the end of this century whether a new culture is possible or whether all cultural life is going to divide into two phases — museum-keeping and mere activity — or whether there will be a third phase. Museum-keeping I define as the obvious with painting and sculpture but also as the maintenance of repertories of Shakespeare and Ibsen, of Beethoven and Bach, of libraries of Dickens and Yeats. Mere activity I define as, for example, most chance music, action or pop or op painting, underground cinema, Park Avenue architecture.

The third function — about which we cannot yet tell — is the possible evolution of a new pertinent culture, relevant to the new societies that are going to keep evolving one after another, possibly with increasing rapidity, a culture with a relationship analogous to that of previous cultures with previous societies, in terms of affirmation of community, a source of inspiration and consolation. There is no guarantee that art is not dying — all art; that it will not be completely supplanted by arty activity — for a while — until even that dies out. But neither is there a guarantee that art will die. A relevant and vital future culture may be possible if, in the process of metamorphosis, we adapt but do not jettison the standards that thousands of years of art have given us.

Among the strongest facts militating toward the survival of art — toward a new socially pertinent art that is sensibly derivative of the past — is the fact of the film. And this is where the schools come in: the creation of an audience that *demands* film that is true — that is socially and culturally apposite yet reflective of human history — is, as I said at the outset, one way to insure that we will *get* the film that we would like to have. One way to create that audience is for those young people who might constitute that audience to get early exposure to good films — maximum exposure with maximally helpful discourse.

In short, to put it in reverse order, the high school teachers of this country can expose their classes to good films; and the susceptible members of those classes may become the audience that can do much to evoke good films in the future. Those future good films may help to bridge the passage from a disintegrating cultural age to the integration of another without losing our rich heritage. It is a large statement and a large order; but then, why shouldn't it be?

In Praise of Theory

BELA BALAZS

DANGERS OF IGNORANCE

We all know and admit that film art has a greater influence on the minds of the general public than any other art. The official guardians of culture note the fact with a certain amount of regret and uneasiness. But too few of us are sufficiently alive to the dangers that are an inevitable consequence of this fact. Nor do we realize clearly enough that we must be better connoisseurs of the film if we are not to be as much at the mercy of perhaps the greatest intellectual and spiritual influence of our age as to some blind and irresistible elemental force. And unless we study its laws and possibilities very carefully, we shall not be able to control and direct this potentially greatest instrument of mass influence ever devised in the whole course of human cultural history. One might think that the theory of this art would naturally be regarded as the most important field for present-day art theory. No one would deny to-day that the art of the motion picture is *the* popular art of our century — unfortunately not in the sense that it is the product of the popular spirit but the other way round, in the sense that the mentality of the people, and particularly of the urban population, is to a great extent the product of this art, an art that is at the same time a vast industry. Thus the question of educating the public to a better, more critical appreciation of the films is a question of the mental health of the nations. Nevertheless, too few of us have yet realized how dangerously and irresponsibly we have failed to promote such a better understanding of film art.

WHY ARE PEOPLE NOT TAUGHT
TO APPRECIATE FILMS?

Nowadays social considerations are taken into account in the cultural sphere no less than in others. Nevertheless, the aesthetics of the film are nowhere included in the official teaching of art appreciation. Our academies have sections for literature and every established art, but none for the new art of our day — the film. It was not until 1947 that the first film-maker was elected to the French *Académie*. At our universities there are chairs for literature and all arts except that of the film. The first Art Academy which included the theory of film art in its curriculum was opened in Prague in 1947. The text-books used in our secondary schools discuss the other arts but say nothing of the film. Millions hear about the aesthetics of literature and painting who will never make use of such knowledge because they read no books and look at no pictures. But the millions who frequent the movies are left without guidance — no one teaches them to appreciate film art.

NEED FOR GENERAL CULTURE

There are numerous film schools in the world and no one denies that there may be need of a theory of the film — for specialists. In Paris, in London, and elsewhere, film institutes and scientific film societies have been formed to study the "science" of the film. But what is needed is not specialized knowledge: it is a general level of culture. No one who had not the faintest conception of literature or music would be considered well educated. A man who had never heard of Beethoven or Michelangelo would be out of place among people of culture. But if he has not the faintest idea of the rudiments of film art and had never heard of Asta Nielsen or David Wark Griffith, he might still pass for a well-educated, cultured person, even on the highest level. The most important art of our time is that about which one need know nothing whatever. And yet it is an urgent need that we should cultivate enough discrimination to influence the art which shapes the popular taste in the highest degree. Until there is a chapter on film art in every text-book on the history of art and on aesthetics; until the art of the film has a chair in our universities and a place in the curriculum of our secondary schools, we shall not have firmly established in the consciousness of our generation this most important artistic development of our century.

Der Sichtbare Mensch

BELA BALAZS

This chapter which deals with the visual culture developed through the silent film is taken from my book *Der Sichtbare Mensch*. In it I hailed the silent film as a turning-point in our cultural history, not suspecting that the sound film would soon come to oust it. The truth which stated a then existing reality has remained true, but the reality it dealt with has bolted like a runaway horse and has made new observations and interpretations necessary. Nevertheless, this chapter may be of interest not merely as a chapter in the history of film theory. Nor does it perhaps retain its interest only because the picture still remains the essence of the film and its visual content. Lines of development are never rigidly set. They often proceed in a round-about way, throwing the light of old knowledge on to new paths through dialectical interaction. Because I believe that we have now come to such a doubling back in the development of the film, when the already once accomplished and then again lost achievements of the silent film are about to be revalued and restored, I want to quote here what I wrote in 1923 about the silent film:

The discovery of printing gradually rendered illegible the faces of men. So much could be read from paper that the method of conveying meaning by facial expression fell into desuetude.

Victor Hugo wrote once that the printed book took over the part played by the cathedral in the Middle Ages and became the carrier of the spirit of the people. But the thousands of books tore the one spirit, embodied in the cathedral, into thousands of opinions. The word broke the stone into a thousand fragments, tore the church into a thousand books.

The visual spirit was thus turned into a legible spirit and visual culture into a culture of concepts. This of course had its social and economic causes, which changed the general face of life. But we paid little attention to the fact that, in conformity with this, the face of individual men, their foreheads, their eyes, their mouths, had also of necessity and quite concretely to suffer a change.

At present a new discovery, a new machine is at work to turn the attention of men back to a visual culture and give them new faces. This machine is the cinematographic camera. Like the printing press, it is a technical device for the multiplication and distribution of products of the human spirit; its effect on human culture will not be less than that of the printing press.

For not to speak does not mean that one has nothing to say. Those who do not speak may be brimming over with emotions which can be expressed only in forms and pictures, in gesture and play of feature. The man of visual culture uses these not as substitutes for words, as a deaf-mute uses his fingers. He does not think in words, the syllables of which he sketches in the air like the dots and dashes of the Morse code. The gestures of visual man are not intended to convey concepts which can be expressed in words, but such inner experiences, such non-rational emotions which would still remain unexpressed when everything that can be told has been told. Such emotions lie in the deepest levels of the soul and cannot be approached by words that are mere reflexions of concepts; just as our musical experiences cannot be expressed in rationalized con-cepts. What appears on the face and in facial expression is a spiritual experience which is rendered immediately visible without the inter-mediary of words.

In the golden age of the old visual arts, the painter and sculptor did not merely fill empty space with abstract shapes and forms, and man was not merely a formal problem for the artist. Painters could paint the spirit and the soul without becoming "literary," for the soul and the spirit had not yet been confined in concepts capable of expression only by means of words; they could be incarnated without residue. That was the happy time when paintings could still have a "theme" and an "idea," for the idea had not yet been tied to the con-cept and to the word that named the concept. The artist could present in its primary form of manifestation the soul's bodily incarnation in gesture or feature. But since then the printing press has grown to be the main bridge over which the more remote interhuman spiritual exchanges take place and the soul has been concentrated and crystal-lized chiefly in the word. There was no longer any need for the sub-tler means of expression provided by the body. For this reason our bodies grew soulless and empty — what is not in use, deteriorates.

The expressive surface of our body was thus reduced to the face alone and this not merely because the rest of the body was hidden by clothes. For the poor remnants of bodily expression that remained to us the little surface of the face sufficed, sticking up like a clumsy sem-aphore of the soul and signalling as best it could. Sometimes a gesture of the hand was added, recalling the melancholy of a mutilated torso. In the epoch of word culture the soul learnt to speak but had grown almost invisible. Such was the effect of the printing press.

Now the film is about to inaugurate a new direction in our culture. Many million people sit in the picture houses every evening and purely through vision, experience happenings, characters, emotions, moods, even thoughts, without the need for many words. For words do not touch the spiritual content of the pictures and are merely passing instruments of as yet undeveloped forms of art. Humanity is already learning the rich and colourful language of gesture, movement and facial expression. This is not a language of signs as a substitute for words, like the sign-language of the deaf-and-dumb — it is the visual means of communication, without intermediary of souls clothed in flesh. Man has again become visible.

Linguistic research has found that the origins of language lie in expressive movement, that is, that man when he began to speak moved his tongue and lips to no greater extent than the other muscles of his face and body — just as an infant does to-day. Originally the purpose was not the making of sounds. The movement of tongue and lips was at first the same spontaneous gesturing as every other expressive movement of the body. That the former produced sounds was a secondary, adventitious phenomenon, which was only later used for practical purposes. The immediately visible message was thus turned into an immediately audible message. In the course of this process, as in every translation, a great deal was lost. It is the expressive movement, the gesture, that is the aboriginal mother-tongue of the human race.

Now we are beginning to remember and re-learn this tongue. It is still clumsy and primitive and very far removed as yet from the refinements of word art. But already it is beginning to be able sometimes to express things which escape the artists of the word. How much of human thought would remain unexpressed if we had no music! The now developing art of facial expression and gesture will bring just as many submerged contents to the surface. Although these human experiences are not rational, conceptual contents, they are nevertheless neither vague nor blurred, but as clear and unequivocal as is music. Thus the inner man, too, will become visible.

But the old visible man no longer exists to-day and the new visible man is not yet in existence. As I have said before, it is the law of nature that unused organs degenerate and disappear, leaving only rudiments behind. The animals that do not chew lose their teeth. In the epoch of word culture we made little use of the expressive powers of our body and have therefore partly lost that power. The gesturing of primitive peoples is frequently more varied and expressive than that of the educated European whose vocabulary is infinitely richer. A few more years of film art and our scholars will discover that cinematography enables them to compile encyclopedias of facial expression, movement and gesture, such as have long existed for words in the shape of dictionaries. The public, however, need not wait for the gesture encyclopedia and grammars of future academies: it can go to the pictures and learn it there.

We had, however, when we neglected the body as a means of expression, lost more than mere corporal power of expression. That which was to have been expressed was also narrowed down by this neglect. For it is not the same spirit, not the same soul that is expressed once in words and once in gestures. Music does not express the same thing as poetry in a different way — it expresses something quite different. When we dip the bucket of words in the depths, we bring up other things than when we do the same with gestures. But let no one think that I want to bring back the culture of movement and gesture in place of the culture of words, for neither can be a substitute for the other. Without a rational, conceptual culture and the scientific development that goes with it there can be no social and hence no human progress. The connecting tissue of modern society is the word spoken and written, without which all organization and planning would be impossible. On the other hand fascism has shown us where the tendency to reduce human culture to subconscious emotions in place of clear concepts would lead humanity.

What I am talking about is only art and even here there is no question of displacing the more rational art of the word. There is no reason why we should renounce one sort of human achievement in favour of another. Even the most highly developed musical culture need not crowd out some more rational aspect of culture.

But to return to the simile of the bucket: we know that the wells that dry up are the wells from which no water is dipped. Psychology and philology have shown that our thoughts and feelings are determined *a priori* by the possibility of expressing them. Philology is also aware that it is not only concepts and feelings that create words, but that it is also the other way round: words give rise to concepts and feelings. This is a form of economy practised by our mental constitution which desires to produce unusable things just as little as does our physical organism. Psychological and logical analysis has shown that words are not merely images expressing our thoughts and feelings but in most cases their *a priori* limiting forms. This is at the root of the danger of stereotyped banality which so often threatens the educated. Here again the evolution of the human spirit is a dialectical process. Its development increases its means of expression and the increase of means of expression in its turn facilitates and accelerates its development. Thus if then the film increases the possibilities of expression, it will also widen the spirit it can express.

Will this newly developing language of facial expression and expressive gesture bring human beings closer to each other or the contrary? Despite the tower of Babel there were concepts common to all behind the different words and one could also learn the languages of others. Concepts on the other hands, have, in civilized communities, a content determined by convention. A universally valid grammar was an even more potent unifying principle holding together the individuals who in bourgeois society were prone to become estranged and isolated from each other. Even the literature of extreme subjectivism used the common vocabulary and was thus preserved from the loneliness of final misunderstanding.

But the language of the gestures is far more individual and personal than the language of words, although facial expression, too, has its habitual forms and conventionally accepted interpretations, to such an extent that one might — and should — write a comparative "gesturology" on the model of comparative linguistics. Nevertheless this language of facial expression and gesture, although it has a certain generally accepted tradition, lacks the severe rules that govern grammar and by the grace of our academies are compulsory for us all. No school prescribes that you must express your cheerfulness by this sort of smile and your bad humour with that sort of wrinkled brow. There are no punishable errors in this or that facial expression, although children doubtless do observe and imitate such conventional grimaces and gestures. On the other hand, these are more immediately induced by inner impulses than are words. Yet it will probably be the art of the film after all which may bring together the peoples and nations, make them accustomed to each other, and lead them to mutual understanding. The silent film is free of the isolating walls of language differences. If we look at and understand each other's faces and gestures, we not only understand, we also learn to feel each other's emotions. The gesture is not only the outward projection of emotion, it is also its initiator.

The universality of the film is primarily due to economic causes — which are always the most compelling causes. The making of a film is so expensive that only very few nations have a home market sufficient to make film production pay. But one of the preconditions of the international popularity of any film is the universal comprehensibility of facial expression and gesture. Specific national characteristics will in time be permissible only as exotic curiosities and a certain levelling of "gesturology" will be inevitable. The laws of the film market permit only universally comprehensible facial expressions and gestures, every nuance of which is understood by princess and working girl alike from San Francisco to Smyrna. We now already have a situation in which the film speaks the only uni-

versal, common world language understood by all. Ethnic peculiari-
ties, national specialities sometimes can lend style and colour to a
film, but can never become factors in causing the story to move on,
because the gestures which convey the meaning and decide the
course of the action must be uniformly comprehensible to every audience everywhere, otherwise the producer will lose money on the film.

The silent film helped people to become physically accustomed
to each other and was about to create an international human type.
When once a common cause will have united men within the limits of
their own race and nation, then the film which makes visible man
equally visible to everyone, will greatly aid in levelling physical
differences between the various races and nations and will thus be
one of the most useful pioneers in the development towards an international universal humanity.

2 The Film as Art and Humanities

The following articles specifically treat film as an art form, as an aesthetic entity. The authors are professional film critics, film makers, and aestheticians. Their primary concern is not with the formal study of film, but more broadly with the exploration of the essence, history, and technique of the medium. However, the ways in which these authors perceive film and their analyses of how the medium works are of great importance to film study.

"Style and Medium in the Motion Pictures," by the late Erwin Panofsky, is one of the few classics in film literature. It was first published in 1934 by the Department of Art and Archaeology of Princeton University. Panofsky revised and brought the piece up to date in 1947, but he did not change his basic constructs. Later, when asked if he wished to revise again, he stated that he wanted the piece to remain as it appeared in 1947. Although much of the article is dated and one can find exceptions in contemporary film to some of Panofsky's ideas, he succinctly traces the art of the film from its primitive beginnings, analyzing film's relationship to other arts, its conventions, and its technical developments. Panofsky raises issues that still appear in film theory and criticism, particularly the issues of filmic time and space, film as a visual medium, and film's manipulation of physical reality.

Susan Sontag, in "Theatre and Film," concentrates on the comparison between these two arts, making particular reference to Panofsky's essay. She argues against the popular view that what is genuinely "theatrical" is different from what is genuinely "cinematic," documenting her thesis with a close analysis of theater and film and of some of Panofsky's basic theories. She questions two widely held irreconcilable positions in the arts today: (1) that barriers between media should be broken down and the media synthesized into one eclectic art; and (2) that art forms should purify themselves and incorporate only those qualities distinctive to that art. Sontag

challenges several of the assumptions of film historians, critics, and
aestheticians and firmly states her conviction that even the most
obvious differences between the two arts, such as their use of time
and space, should be reexamined.

The comparison between film and other arts continues with
"Time in Film and Fiction" by George Bluestone. His consideration of
the relation between film and the novel, a relation that has been
stressed by critics almost as much as that between film and theater,
centers on the way in which each of the forms treats the concepts of
time and space. Bluestone contends that although both the novel and
film are time arts, the formative principle in the novel is time and the
formative principle in film is space. Furthermore, he argues, the novel
has three tenses and film has only one, the present. Bluestone, too,
refers to issues raised by Panofsky, particularly film's "dynamization
of space" and "spacialization of time" and the principle of
"coexpressibility." Bluestone interprets the latter as the phenomenon
"according to which a moving picture — even when it has learned to
talk — remains a picture that moves, and does not convert itself into a
piece of writing that is enacted." Panofsky and Bluestone, along with
Balazs, Roemer, Mekas, and others in this book, assert the primacy of
the visual image in film, thus relegating talk, narration, sound, and
music to supporting but important roles.

The relation between physical reality and what is seen on the
screen has long been a subject of controversy among film critics and
theorists. Michael Roemer, in "The Surfaces of Reality," examines
the nature of film in an attempt to understand its effectiveness as an
art form. He states that film succeeds best when it is concrete, when
it renders meaning in physical terms by using the language of the
commonplace. The appearance of reality is preserved in a good film,
Roemer says, but the art of the film maker comes about by his
carefully controlling and arranging photographed and recorded
images of life into a structured whole. Following in the tradition of
film theorist Siegfried Kracauer, Roemer approaches film as the
"redemption of physical reality," the surface verisimilitude
concerned with the details of everyday life.

Ted Perry, in "The Seventh Art as Sixth Sense," views the art
of film and its relation to reality from a different perspective. In
discussing experience mediated by the cinematic process, Perry
argues that the cinema experience is unique because film produces
a model of the environment that is different from other images of the
environment. Within the context of Brunerian psychology, he notes
that what we call "reality" is simply our perception constructed from

the information collected by our nervous system. Film, therefore, is able to create new realities, not just "redeem" them. Perry is interested in film's ability to produce unique yet realistic images of the environment and, therefore, alter man's perceptions and insights. He discusses how *Last Year at Marienbad* dispenses with conventions of time and space and presents its own reality, demonstrating that the cinema "does not have to duplicate supposed mental processes but can function in a way that the mind cannot, thereby extending and amplifying the mind."

In "Toward True Cinema" Slavko Vorkapich discusses two aspects of the motion picture — recording and creative — and argues that only the latter is true art. He claims that most films are not examples of the creative use of motion picture devices and techniques, but are instead examples only of the use of recording instruments and processes. Vorkapich's emphasis is on the development of film's visual language independent of the traditions of literature and the theater. Cinematography, he suggests, is the "getting of visual-dynamic-meaningful elements, which creative cutting combines into living entities." In the second part of the article, Vorkapich suggests a method for increasing the visual awareness of film students.

If, as these authors suggest, film is considered an art, then the question of who performs the role of artist remains. Panofsky compares the making of a film to the building of a medieval cathedral. Unlike a painting or a novel, it is not the work of one man but requires the combined efforts of many persons, each with different skills. One theory of film, the *auteur,* proposes in its simplest form that certain directors — *auteurs* — have pervasive personalities which mold and make distinguishable, and frequently distinguished, the films they direct. One of the classic statements on the theory is Andrew Sarris's "Notes on the *Auteur* Theory in 1962." After a discussion of Andre Bazin's critique of *la politique des auteurs,* Sarris elaborates three main premises of the *auteur* theory, which he visualizes as concentric circles: technique, personal style, and interior meaning. Sarris ends by discussing his own pantheon of *auteurs* and citing examples of how the *auteur* theory can work in the specific practice of film criticism.

In direct response to the Sarris article, critic Pauline Kael's "Circles and Squares: Joys and Sarris" closely examines the premises of Sarris's three-circle model, the *auteur* theory itself, and film criticism in general. Kael argues against the theory, stating that criticism should be an eclectic art and that critics who follow a narrow approach will fail to perceive and to help others perceive originality and importance in new works. * Her warning against a simple answer or formula as the only way of looking at a film should be of particular relevance to those interested in the study of film. At the end of her article, she discusses the relationship between Sarris, Jonas Mekas, the *auteur* theory, and experimental film makers.

The final article in this chapter, by Jonas Mekas, film critic and authority on experimental film, deals with the non-narrative film and the nature of the artist and the film critic. In "Movie Journal," Mekas discusses how criticism of these films, which he calls lyrics, poems, or "avant-garde films," differs from that of the narrative, commercial films with which most of the authors in this chapter are concerned.

* Sarris has published two rejoinders: "The *Auteur* Theory and the Perils of Pauline," *Film Quarterly,* 16, no. 4 (1963), 26–33; and "Notes on the *Auteur* Theory in 1970," *Film Comment,* 6, no. 3 (Fall 1970), 7–9. Neither has been reprinted here because they do not significantly further either the argument with Kael or Sarris's original concept of the *auteur* theory.

Style and Medium
in the Motion Pictures

ERWIN PANOFSKY

Film art is the only art the development of which men now living have witnessed from the very beginnings; and this development is all the more interesting as it took place under conditions contrary to precedent. It was not an artistic urge that gave rise to the discovery and gradual perfection of a new technique; it was a technical invention that gave rise to the discovery and gradual perfection of a new art.

From this we understand two fundamental facts. First, that the primordial basis of the enjoyment of moving pictures was not an objective interest in a specific subject matter, much less an aesthetic interest in the formal presentation of subject matter, but the sheer delight in the fact that things seemed to move, no matter what things they were. Second, that films — first exhibited in "kinetoscopes," viz., cinematographic peep shows, but projectable to a screen since as early as 1894 — are, originally, a product of genuine folk art (whereas, as a rule, folk art derives from what is known as "higher art"). At the very beginning of things we find the simple recording of movements: galloping horses, railroad trains, fire engines, sporting events, street scenes. And when it had come to the making of narrative films these were produced by photographers who were anything but "producers" or "directors," performed by people who were anything but actors, and enjoyed by people who would have been much offended had anyone called them "art lovers."

The casts of these archaic films were usually collected in a "café" where unemployed supers or ordinary citizens possessed of a suitable exterior were wont to assemble at a given hour. An enterprising photographer would walk in, hire four or five convenient characters and make the picture while carefully instructing them what to do: "Now, you pretend to hit this lady over the head"; and (to the lady): "And you pretend to fall down in a heap." Productions like these were shown, together with those purely factual recordings of "movement for movement's sake," in a few small and dingy cinemas mostly frequented by the "lower classes" and a sprinkling of youngsters in quest of adventure (about 1905, I happen to remember, there was only one obscure and faintly disreputable *kino* in the whole city of Berlin, bearing, for some unfathomable reason, the English name of

"The Meeting Room"). Small wonder that the "better classes," when they slowly began to venture into these early picture theaters, did so, not by way of seeking normal and possibly serious entertainment, but with that characteristic sensation of self-conscious condescension with which we may plunge, in gay company, into the folkloristic depths of Coney Island or a European kermis; even a few years ago it was the regulation attitude of the socially or intellectually prominent that one could confess to enjoying such austerely educational films as *The Sex Life of the Starfish* or films with "beautiful scenery," but never to a serious liking for narratives.

Today there is no denying that narrative films are not only "art" — not often good art, to be sure, but this applies to other media as well — but also, besides architecture, cartooning and "commercial design," the only visual art entirely alive. The "movies" have re-established that dynamic contact between art production and art consumption which, for reasons too complex to be considered here, is sorely attenuated, if not entirely interrupted, in many other fields of artistic endeavor. Whether we like it or not, it is the movies that mold, more than any other single force, the opinions, the taste, the language, the dress, the behavior, and even the physical appearance of a public comprising more than 60 per cent of the population of the earth. If all the serious lyrical poets, composers, painters and sculptors were forced by law to stop their activities, a rather small fraction of the general public would become aware of the fact and a still smaller fraction would seriously regret it. If the same thing were to happen with the movies the social consequences would be catastrophic.

In the beginning, then, there were the straight recordings of movement no matter what moved, viz., the prehistoric ancestors of our "documentaries"; and, soon after, the early narratives, viz., the prehistoric ancestors of our "feature films." The craving for a narrative element could be satisfied only by borrowing from older arts, and one should expect that the natural thing would have been to borrow from the theater, a theater play being apparently the *genus proximum* to a narrative film in that it consists of a narrative enacted by persons that move. But in reality the imitation of stage performances was a comparatively late and thoroughly frustrated development. What happened at the start was a very different thing. Instead of imitating a theatrical performance already endowed with a certain amount of motion, the earliest films added movement to works of art originally stationary, so that the dazzling technical invention might achieve a triumph of its own without intruding upon the sphere of higher culture. The living language, which is always right, has endorsed this sensible choice when it still speaks of a "moving picture" or, simply, a "picture," instead of accepting the pretentious and fundamentally erroneous "screen play."

The stationary works enlivened in the earliest movies were indeed pictures: bad nineteenth-century paintings and postcards (or waxworks à la Madame Tussaud's), supplemented by the comic strips — a most important root of cinematic art — and the subject matter of popular songs, pulp magazines and dime novels; and the films descending from this ancestry appealed directly and very intensely to a folk art mentality. They gratified — often simultaneously — first, a primitive sense of justice and decorum when virtue and industry were rewarded while vice and laziness were punished; second, plain sentimentality when "the thin trickle of a fictive love interest" took its course "through somewhat serpentine channels," or when Father, dear Father returned from the saloon to find his child dying of diphtheria; third, a primordial instinct for bloodshed and cruelty when Andreas Hofer faced the firing squad, or when (in a film of 1893–94) the head of Mary Queen of Scots actually came off; fourth, a taste for mild pornography (I remember with great pleasure a French film of *ca.* 1900 wherein a seemingly but not really well-rounded lady as well as a seemingly but not really slender one were shown changing to bathing suits — an honest, straightforward *porcheria* much less objectionable than the now extinct Betty Boop films and, I am sorry to say, some of the more recent Walt Disney productions); and, finally, that crude sense of humor, graphically described as "slapstick," which feeds upon the sadistic and the pornographic instinct, either singly or in combination.

Not until as late as *ca.* 1905 was a film adaptation of *Faust* ventured upon (cast still "unknown," characteristically enough), and not until 1911 did Sarah Bernhardt lend her prestige to an unbelievably funny film tragedy, *Queen Elizabeth of England.* These films represent the first conscious attempt at transplanting the movies from the folk art level to that of "real art"; but they also bear witness to the fact that this commendable goal could not be reached in so simple a manner. It was soon realized that the imitation of a theater performance with a set stage, fixed entries and exits, and distinctly literary ambitions is the one thing the film must avoid.

The legitimate paths of evolution were opened, not by running away from the folk art character of the primitive film but by developing it within the limits of its own possibilities. Those primordial archetypes of film productions on the folk art level — success or retribution, sentiment, sensation, pornography, and crude humor — could blossom forth into genuine history, tragedy and romance, crime and adventure, and comedy, as soon as it was realized that they could be transfigured — not by an artificial injection of literary values but by the exploitation of the unique and specific possibilities of the new medium. Significantly, the beginnings of this legitimate development antedate the attempts at endowing the film with higher values of a foreign order (the crucial period being the years from 1902 to *ca.* 1905), and the decisive steps were taken by people who were laymen or outsiders from the viewpoint of the serious stage.

These unique and specific possibilities can be defined as *dynamization of space* and, accordingly, *spatialization of time.* This statement is self-evident to the point of triviality but it belongs to that kind of truths which, just because of their triviality, are easily forgotten or neglected.

In a theater, space is static, that is, the space represented on the stage, as well as the spatial relation of the beholder to the spectacle, is unalterably fixed. The spectator cannot leave his seat, and the setting of the stage cannot change, during one act (except for such incidentals as rising moons or gathering clouds and such illegitimate reborrowings from the film as turning wings or gliding backdrops). But, in return for this restriction, the theater has the advantage that time, the medium of emotion and thought conveyable by speech, is free and independent of anything that may happen in visible space. Hamlet may deliver his famous monologue lying on a couch in the middle distance, doing nothing and only dimly discernible to the spectator and listener, and yet by his mere words enthrall him with a feeling of intensest emotional action.

With the movies the situation is reversed. Here, too, the spectator occupies a fixed seat, but only physically, not as the subject of an aesthetic experience. Aesthetically, he is in permanent motion as his eye identifies itself with the lens of the camera, which permanently shifts in distance and direction. And as movable as the spectator is, as movable is, for the same reason, the space presented to him. Not only bodies move in space, but space itself does, approaching, receding, turning, dissolving and recrystallizing as it appears through the controlled locomotion and focusing of the camera and through the cutting and editing of the various shots — not to mention such special effects as visions, transformations, disappearances, slow-motion and fast-motion shots, reversals and trick film. This opens up a world of possibilities of which the stage can never dream. Quite apart from such photographic tricks as the participation of disembodied spirits in the action of the *Topper* series, or the more effective wonders wrought by Roland Young in *The Man Who Could Work Miracles,* there is, on the purely factual level, an untold wealth of themes as inaccessible to the "legitimate" stage as a fog or a snowstorm is to the sculptor; all sorts of violent elemental phenomena and, conversely, events too microscopic to be visible under normal conditions (such as the life-saving injection with the serum flown in at the very last moment, or the fatal bite of the yellow-fever mosquito); full-scale battle scenes; all kinds of operations, not only in the surgical sense but also in the sense of any actual construction, destruction, or experimentation, as in *Louis Pasteur* or *Madame Curie;* a really grand party, moving through many rooms of a mansion or a palace. Features like these, even the mere shifting of the scene from one place to another by means of a car perilously negotiating heavy traffic or a motorboat steered through a nocturnal harbor, will not only always retain their primitive cinematic appeal but also remain enormously effective as a means of stirring the emotions and creating suspense. In addition, the movies have the power, entirely denied to the theater, to convey psychological experiences by directly projecting their content to the screen, substituting, as it were, the eye of the beholder for the consciousness of the character (as when the imaginings and hallucinations of the drunkard in the otherwise overrated *Lost Weekend* appear as stark realities instead of being described by mere words). But any attempt to convey thought and feelings exclusively, or even primarily, by speech leaves us with a feeling of embarrassment, boredom, or both.

What I mean by thoughts and feelings "conveyed exclusively, or even primarily, by speech" is simply this: Contrary to naïve expectation, the invention of the sound track in 1928 has been unable to change the basic fact that a moving picture, even when it has learned to talk, remains a picture that moves and does not convert itself into a piece of writing that is enacted. Its substance remains a series of visual sequences held together by an uninterrupted flow of movement in space (except, of course, for such checks and pauses as have the same compositional value as a rest in music), and not a sustained study in human character and destiny transmitted by effective, let alone "beautiful," diction. I cannot remember a more misleading statement about the movies than Mr. Eric Russell Bentley's in the spring number of the *Kenyon Review*, 1945: "The potentialities of the talking screen differ from those of the silent screen in adding the dimension of dialogue — which could be poetry." I would suggest: "The potentialities of the talking screen differ from those of the silent screen in integrating visible movement with dialogue which, therefore, had better not be poetry."

All of us, if we are old enough to remember the period prior to 1928, recall the old-time pianist who, with his eyes glued on the screen, would accompany the events with music adapted to their mood and rhythm; and we also recall the weird and spectral feeling overtaking us when this pianist left his post for a few minutes and the film was allowed to run by itself, the darkness haunted by the monotonous rattle of the machinery. Even the silent film, then, was never mute. The visible spectacle always required, and received, an audible accompaniment which, from the very beginning, distinguished the film from simple pantomime and rather classed it — *mutatis mutandis* — with the ballet. The advent of the talkie meant not so much an "addition" as a transformation: the transformation of musical sound into articulate speech and, therefore, of quasi pantomime into an entirely new species of spectacle which differs from the ballet, and agrees with the stage play, in that its acoustic component consists of intelligible words, but differs from the stage play and agrees with the ballet in that this acoustic component is not detachable from the visual. In a film, that which we hear remains, for good or worse, inextricably fused with that which we see; the sound, articulate or not, cannot express any more than is expressed, at the same time, by visible movement; and in a good film it does not even attempt to do so. To put it briefly, the play — or, as it is very properly called, the "script" — of a moving picture is subject to what might be termed the *principle of coexpressibility*.

Empirical proof of this principle is furnished by the fact that, wherever the dialogical or monological element gains temporary prominence, there appears, with the inevitability of a natural law, the "close-up." What does the close-up achieve? In showing us, in magnification, either the face of the speaker or the face of the listeners or both in alternation, the camera transforms the human physiognomy into a huge field of action where — given the qualification of the performers — every subtle movement of the features, almost imperceptible from a natural distance, becomes an expressive event in visible space and thereby completely integrates itself with the expressive content of the spoken word; whereas, on the stage, the spoken word makes a stronger rather than a weaker impression if we are not permitted to count the hairs in Romeo's mustache.

This does not mean that the scenario is a negligible factor in the making of a moving picture. It only means that its artistic intention differs in kind from that of a stage play, and much more from that of a novel or a piece of poetry. As the success of a Gothic jamb figure depends not only upon its quality as a piece of sculpture but also, or even more so, upon its integrability with the architecture of the portal, so does the success of a movie script — not unlike that of an opera libretto — depend, not only upon its quality as a piece of literature but also, or even more so, upon its integrability with the events on the screen.

As a result — another empirical proof of the coexpressibility principle — good movie scripts are unlikely to make good reading and have seldom been published in book form; whereas, conversely, good stage plays have to be severely altered, cut, and, on the other hand, enriched by interpolations to make good movie scripts. In Shaw's *Pygmalion*, for instance, the actual process of Eliza's phonetic education and, still more important, her final triumph at the grand party, are wisely omitted; we see — or, rather, hear — some samples of her gradual linguistic improvement and finally encounter her, upon her return from the reception, victorious and splendidly arrayed but deeply hurt for want of recognition and sympathy. In the film adaptation, precisely these two scenes are not only supplied but also strongly emphasized; we witness the fascinating activities in the laboratory with its array of spinning disks and mirrors, organ pipes and dancing flames, and we participate in the ambassadorial party, with many moments of impending catastrophe and a little counterintrigue thrown in for suspense. Unquestionably these two scenes, entirely absent from the play, and indeed unachievable upon the stage, were the highlights of the film; whereas the Shavian dialogue, however severely cut, turned out to fall a little flat in certain moments. And wherever, as in so many other films, a poetic emotion, a musical outburst, or a literary conceit (even, I am grieved to say, some of the wisecracks of Groucho Marx) entirely lose contact with visible movement, they strike the sensitive spectator as, literally, out of place. It is certainly terrible when a soft-boiled he-man, after the suicide of his mistress, casts a twelve-foot glance upon her photograph and says something less-than-coexpressible to the effect that he will never forget her. But when he recites, instead, a piece of poetry as sublimely more-than-coexpressible as Romeo's monologue at the bier of Juliet, it is still worse. Reinhardt's *Midsummer Night's Dream* is probably the most unfortunate major film ever produced; and Olivier's *Henry V* owes its comparative success, apart from the all but providential adaptability of this particular play, to so many *tours de force* that it will, God willing, remain an exception rather than set a pattern. It combines "judicious pruning" with the interpolation of pageantry, nonverbal comedy and melodrama; it uses a device perhaps best designated as "oblique close-up" (Mr. Olivier's beautiful face inwardly listening to but not pronouncing the great soliloquy); and, most notably, it shifts between three levels of archaeological reality: a reconstruction of Elizabethan London, a reconstruction of the events of 1415 as laid down in Shakespeare's play, and the reconstruction of a performance of this play on Shakespeare's own stage. All this is perfectly legitimate; but, even so, the highest praise of the film will always come from those who, like the critic of the *New Yorker*, are not quite in sympathy with either the movies *au naturel* or Shakespeare *au naturel*.

As the writings of Conan Doyle potentially contain all modern mystery stories (except for the tough specimens of the Dashiell Hammett school), so do the films produced between 1900 and 1910 preestablish the subject matter and methods of the moving picture as we know it. This period produced the incunabula of the Western and the crime film (Edwin S. Porter's amazing *Great Train Robbery* of 1903) from which developed the modern gangster, adventure, and mystery pictures (the latter, if well done, is still one of the most honest and genuine forms of film entertainment, space being doubly charged with time as the beholder asks himself not only "What is going to happen?" but also "What has happened before?"). The same period saw the emergence of the fantastically imaginative film (*Méliès*) which was to lead to the expressionist and surrealist experiments (*The Cabinet of Dr. Caligari, Sang d'un Poète*, etc.), on the one hand, and to the more superficial and spectacular fairy tales à la Arabian Nights, on the other. Comedy, later to triumph in Charlie Chaplin, the still insufficiently appreciated Buster Keaton, the Marx Brothers and the pre-Hollywood creations of René Clair, reached a respectable level in Max Linder and others. In historical and melodramatic films the foundations were laid for movie iconography and movie symbolism, and in the early work of D. W. Griffith we find, not only remarkable attempts at psychological analysis (*Edgar Allan Poe*) and social criticism (*A Corner in Wheat*) but also such basic technical innovations as the long shot, the flashback and the close-up. And modest trick films and cartoons paved the way to Felix the Cat, Popeye the Sailor, and Felix's prodigious offspring, Mickey Mouse.

Within their self-imposed limitations the earlier Disney films, and certain sequences in the later ones,[1] represent, as it were, a

---

[1] I make this distinction because it was, in my opinion, a fall from grace when *Snow White* introduced the human figure and when *Fantasia* attempted to picturalize The World's Great Music. The very virtue of the animated cartoon is to animate, that is to say endow lifeless things with life, or living things with a different kind of life. It effects a metamorphosis, and such a metamorphosis is wonderfully present in Disney's animals, plants, thunderclouds and railroad trains. Whereas his dwarfs, glamourized princesses, hillbillies, baseball players, rouged centaurs and *amigos* from South America are not transformations but caricatures at best, and fakes or vulgarities at worst. Concerning music, however, it should be born in mind that its cinematic use is no less predicated upon the principle of coexpressibility than is the cinematic use of the spoken word.

chemically pure distillation of cinematic possibilities. They retain the most important folkloristic elements — sadism, pornography, the humor engendered by both, and moral justice — almost without dilution and often fuse these elements into a variation on the primitive and inexhaustible David-and-Goliath motif, the triumph of the seemingly weak over the seemingly strong; and their fantastic independence of the natural laws gives them the power to integrate space with time to such perfection that the spatial and temporal experiences of sight and hearing come to be almost interconvertible. A series of soap bubbles, successively punctured, emits a series of sounds exactly corresponding in pitch and volume to the size of the bubbles; the three uvulae of Willie the Whale — small, large and medium — vibrate in consonance with tenor, bass and baritone notes; and the very concept of stationary existence is completely abolished. No object in creation, whether it be a house, a piano, a tree or an alarm clock, lacks the faculties of organic, in fact anthropomorphic, movement, facial expression and phonetic articulation. Incidentally, even in normal, "realistic" films the inanimate object, provided that it is dynamizable, can play the role of a leading character as do the ancient railroad engines in Buster Keaton's *General* and *Niagara Falls*. How the earlier Russian films exploited the possibility of heroizing all sorts of machinery lives in everybody's memory; and it is perhaps more than an accident that the two films which will go down in history as the great comical and the great serious masterpiece of the silent period bear the names and immortalize the personalities of two big ships: Keaton's *Navigator* (1924) and Eisenstein's *Potemkin* (1925).

The evolution from the jerky beginnings to this grand climax

There is music permitting or even requiring the accompaniment of visible action (such as dances, ballet music and any kind of operatic compositions) and music of which the opposite is true; and this is, again, not a question of quality (most of us rightly prefer a waltz by Johann Strauss to a symphony by Sibelius) but one of intention. In *Fantasia* the hippopotamus ballet was wonderful, and the Pastoral Symphony and "Ave Maria" sequences were deplorable, not because the cartooning in the first case was infinitely better than in the two others (cf. above), and certainly not because Beethoven and Schubert are too sacred for picturalization, but simply because Ponchielli's "Dance of the Hours" is coexpressible while the Pastoral Symphony and the "Ave Maria" are not. In cases like these even the best imaginable music and the best imaginable cartoon will impair rather than enhance each other's effectiveness.

Experimental proof of all this was furnished by Disney's recent *Make Mine Music* where The World's Great Music was fortunately restricted to Prokofieff. Even among the other sequences the most successful ones were those in which the human element was either absent or reduced to a minimum; Willie the Whale, the Ballad of Johnny Fedora and Alice Blue-Bonnet, and, above all, the truly magnificent Goodman Quartet.

offers the fascinating spectacle of a new artistic medium gradually becoming conscious of its legitimate, that is, exclusive, possibilities and limitations — a spectacle not unlike the development of the mosaic, which started out with transposing illusionistic genre pictures into a more durable material and culminated in the hieratic supernaturalism of Ravenna; or the development of line engraving, which started out as a cheap and handy substitute for book illumination and culminated in the purely "graphic" style of Dürer.

Just so the silent movies developed a definite style of their own, adapted to the specific conditions of the medium. A hitherto unknown language was forced upon a public not yet capable of reading it, and the more proficient the public became the more refinement could develop in the language. For a Saxon peasant of around 800 it was not easy to understand the meaning of a picture showing a man as he pours water over the head of another man, and even later many people found it difficult to grasp the significance of two ladies standing behind the throne of an emperor. For the public of around 1910 it was no less difficult to understand the meaning of the speechless action in a moving picture, and the producers employed means of clarification similar to those we find in medieval art. One of these were printed titles or letters, striking equivalents of the medieval *tituli* and scrolls (at a still earlier date there even used to be explainers who would say, *viva voce*, "Now he thinks his wife is dead but she isn't" or "I don't wish to offend the ladies in the audience but I doubt that any of them would have done that much for her child"). Another, less obtrusive method of explanation was the introduction of a fixed iconography which from the outset informed the spectator about the basic facts and characters, much as the two ladies behind the emperor, when carrying a sword and a cross respectively, were uniquely determined as Fortitude and Faith. There arose, identifiable by standardized appearance, behavior and attributes, the well-remembered types of the Vamp and the Straight Girl (perhaps the most convincing modern equivalents of the medieval personifications of the Vices and Virtues), the Family Man, and the Villain, the latter marked by a black mustache and walking stick. Nocturnal scenes were printed on blue or green film. A checkered tablecloth meant, once for all, a "poor but honest" milieu; a happy marriage, soon to be endangered by the shadows from the past, was symbolized by the young wife's pouring the breakfast coffee for her husband; the first kiss was invariably announced by the lady's gently playing with her partner's necktie and was invariably accompanied by her kicking out with her left foot. The conduct of the characters was predetermined accordingly. The poor but honest laborer who, after leaving his little house with the checkered tablecloth, came upon an abandoned baby could not but take it to his home and bring it up as best he could; the Family Man could not but yield, however temporarily, to the temptations of the Vamp. As a result these early melodramas had a highly gratifying and soothing quality in that events took shape, without the complications of individual psychology, according to a pure Aristotelian logic so badly missed in real life.

Devices like these became gradually less necessary as the public grew accustomed to interpret the action by itself and were virtually abolished by the invention of the talking film. But even now there survive — quite legitimately, I think — the remnants of a "fixed attitude and attribute" principle and, more basic, a primitive or folkloristic concept of plot construction. Even today we take it for granted that the diphtheria of a baby tends to occur when the parents are out and, having occurred, solves all their matrimonial problems. Even today we demand of a decent mystery film that the butler, though he may be anything from an agent of the British Secret Service to the real father of the daughter of the house, must not turn out to be the murderer. Even today we love to see Pasteur, Zola or Ehrlich win out against stupidity and wickedness, with their respective wives trusting and trusting all the time. Even today we much prefer a happy finale to a gloomy one and insist, at the very least, on the observance of the Aristotelian rule that the story have a beginning, a middle and an ending — a rule the abrogation of which has done so much to estrange the general public from the more elevated spheres of modern writing. Primitive symbolism, too, survives in such amusing details as the last sequence of Casablanca where the delightfully crooked and right-minded préfet de police casts an empty bottle of Vichy water into the wastepaper basket; and in such telling symbols of the supernatural as Sir Cedric Hardwicke's Death in the guise of a "gentleman in a dust-coat trying" (On Borrowed Time) or Claude Rains's Hermes Psychopompos in the striped trousers of an airline manager (Here Comes Mister Jordan).

The most conspicuous advances were made in directing, lighting, camera work, cutting and acting proper. But while in most of these fields the evolution proceeded continuously — though, of course, not without detours, breakdowns and archaic relapses — the development of acting suffered a sudden interruption by the invention of the talking film; so that the style of acting in the silents can already be evaluated in retrospect, as a lost art not unlike the painting technique of Jan van Eyck or, to take up our previous simile, the burin technique of Dürer. It was soon realized that acting in a silent film neither meant a pantomimic exaggeration of stage acting (as was generally and erroneously assumed by professional stage actors who more and more frequently condescended to perform in the movies), nor could dispense with stylization altogether; a man photographed while walking down a gangway in ordinary, everyday-life fashion looked like anything but a man walking down a gangway when the result appeared on the screen. If the picture was to look both natural and meaningful the acting had to be done in a manner equally different from the style of the stage and the reality of ordinary life; speech had to be made dispensable by establishing an organic relation between the acting and the technical procedure of cinephotography — much as in Dürer's prints color had been made dispensable by establishing an organic relation between the design and the technical procedure of line engraving.

This was precisely what the great actors of the silent period accomplished, and it is a significant fact that the best of them did not come from the stage, whose crystallized tradition prevented Duse's only film, Cenere, from being more than a priceless record of Duse. They came instead from the circus or the variety, as was the case of Chaplin, Keaton and Will Rogers; from nothing in particular, as was the case of Theda Bara, of her greater European parallel, the Danish actress Asta Nielsen, and of Garbo; or from everything under the sun, as was the case of Douglas Fairbanks. The style of these "old masters" was indeed comparable to the style of line engraving in that it was, and had to be, exaggerated in comparison with stage acting (just as the sharply incised and vigorously curved tailles of the burin are exaggerated in comparison with pencil strokes or brushwork), but richer, subtler and infinitely more precise. The advent of the talkies, reducing if not abolishing this difference between screen acting and stage acting, thus confronted the actors and actresses of the silent screen with a serious problem. Buster Keaton yielded to temptation and fell. Chaplin first tried to stand his ground and to remain an exquisite archaist but finally gave in, with only moderate success (The Great Dictator). Only the glorious Harpo has thus far successfully refused to utter a single articulate sound; and only Greta Garbo succeeded, in a measure, in transforming her style in principle. But even in her case one cannot help feeling that her first talking picture, Anna Christie, where she could ensconce herself, most of the time, in mute or monosyllabic sullenness, was better than her later performances; and in the second, talking version of Anna Karenina, the weakest moment is certainly when she delivers a big Ibsenian speech to her husband, and the strongest when she silently moves along the platform of the railroad station while her despair takes shape in the consonance of her movement (and expression) with the movement of the nocturnal space around her, filled with the real noises of the trains and the imaginary sound of the "little men with the iron hammers" that drives her, relentlessly and almost without her realizing it, under the wheels.

Small wonder that there is sometimes felt a kind of nostalgia for the silent period and that devices have been worked out to combine the virtues of sound and speech with those of silent acting, such as the "oblique close-up" already mentioned in connection with *Henry V*; the dance behind glass doors in *Sous les Toits de Paris*; or, in the *Histoire d'un Tricheur*, Sacha Guitry's recital of the events of his youth while the events themselves are "silently" enacted on the screen. However, this nostalgic feeling is no argument against the talkies as such. Their evolution has shown that, in art, every gain entails a certain loss on the other side of the ledger; but that the gain remains a gain, provided that the basic nature of the medium is realized and respected. One can imagine that, when the cavemen of Altamira began to paint their buffaloes in natural colors instead of merely incising the contours, the more conservative cavemen foretold the end of paleolithic art. But paleolithic art went on, and so will the movies. New technical inventions always tend to dwarf the values already attained, especially in a medium that owes its very existence to technical experimentation. The earliest talkies were infinitely inferior to the then mature silents, and most of the present technicolor films are still inferior to the now mature talkies in black and white. But even if Aldous Huxley's nightmare should come true and the experiences of taste, smell and touch should be added to those of sight and hearing, even then we may say with the Apostle, as we have said when first confronted with the sound track and the technicolor film, "We are troubled on every side, yet not distressed; we are perplexed, but not in despair."

From the law of time-charged space and space-bound time, there follows the fact that the screenplay, in contrast to the theater play, *has no aesthetic existence independent of its performance, and that its characters have no aesthetic existence outside the actors.*

The playwright writes in the fond hope that his work will be an imperishable jewel in the treasure house of civilization and will be presented in hundreds of performances that are but transient variations on a "work" that is constant. The script-writer, on the other hand, writes for one producer, one director and one cast. Their work achieves the same degree of permanence as does his; and should the same or a similar scenario ever be filmed by a different director and a different cast there will result an altogether different "play."

Othello or Nora are definite, substantial figures created by the

playwright. They can be played well or badly, and they can be "interpreted" in one way or another; but they most definitely exist, no
matter who plays them or even whether they are played at all. The
character in a film, however, lives and dies with the actor. It is not
the entity "Othello" interpreted by Robeson or the entity "Nora"
interpreted by Duse; it is the entity "Greta Garbo" incarnate in a
figure called Anna Christie or the entity "Robert Montgomery" incarnate in a murderer who, for all we know or care to know, may forever remain anonymous but will never cease to haunt our memories.
Even when the names of the characters happen to be Henry VIII or
Anna Karenina, the king who ruled England from 1509 to 1547 and
the woman created by Tolstoy, they do not exist outside the being of
Garbo and Laughton. They are but empty and incorporeal outlines
like the shadows in Homer's Hades, assuming the character of reality
only when filled with the lifeblood of an actor. Conversely, if a movie
role is badly played there remains literally nothing of it, no matter
how interesting the character's psychology or how elaborate the
words.

What applies to the actor applies, *mutatis mutandis*, to most of
the other artists, or artisans, who contribute to the making of a film:
the director, the sound man, the enormously important cameraman,
even the make-up man. A stage production is rehearsed until everything is ready, and then it is repeatedly performed in three consecutive
hours. At each performance everybody has to be on hand and does
his work; and afterward he goes home and to bed. The work of the
stage actor may thus be likened to that of a musician, and that of the
stage director to that of a conductor. Like these, they have a certain
repertoire which they have studied and present in a number of complete but transitory performances, be it *Hamlet* today and *Ghosts*
tomorrow, or *Life with Father per saecula saeculorum*. The activities
of the film actor and the film director, however, are comparable, respectively, to those of the plastic artist and the architect, rather than
to those of the musician and the conductor. Stage work is continuous
but transitory; film work is discontinuous but permanent. Individual
sequences are done piecemeal and out of order according to the most
efficient use of sets and personnel. Each bit is done over and over
again until it stands; and when the whole has been cut and composed
everyone is through with it forever. Needless to say that this very
procedure cannot but emphasize the curious consubstantiality that
exists between the person of the movie actor and his role. Coming
into existence piece by piece, regardless of the natural sequence of
events, the "character" can grow into a unified whole only if the
actor manages to be, not merely to play, Henry VIII or Anna Karenina
throughout the entire wearisome period of shooting. I have it on the

best of authorities that Laughton was really difficult to live with in
the particular six or eight weeks during which he was doing — or
rather being — Captain Bligh.

It might be said that a film, called into being by a co-operative
effort in which all contributions have the same degree of permanence,
is the nearest modern equivalent of a medieval cathedral; the role of
the producer corresponding, more or less, to that of the bishop or
archbishop; that of the director to that of the architect in chief; that
of the scenario writers to that of the scholastic advisers establishing
the iconographical program; and that of the actors, cameramen, cut-
ters, sound men, make-up men and the divers technicians to that of
those whose work provided the physical entity of the finished product, from the sculptors, glass painters, bronze casters, carpenters and
skilled masons down to the quarry men and woodsmen. And if you
speak to any one of these collaborators he will tell you, with perfect
bona fides, that his is really the most important job — which is quite
true to the extent that it is indispensable.

This comparison may seem sacrilegious, not only because there
are, proportionally, fewer good films than there are good cathedrals,
but also because the movies are commercial. However, if commercial
art be defined as all art not primarily produced in order to gratify the
creative urge of its maker but primarily intended to meet the requirements of a patron or a buying public, it must be said that noncommercial art is the exception rather than the rule, and a fairly recent and
not always felicitous exception at that. While it is true that commercial art is always in danger of ending up as a prostitute, it is equally
true that noncommercial art is always in danger of ending up as an
old maid. Noncommercial art has given us Seurat's "Grande Jatte"
and Shakespeare's sonnets, but also much that is esoteric to the point
of incommunicability. Conversely, commercial art has given us much
that is vulgar or snobbish (two aspects of the same thing) to the point
of loathsomeness, but also Dürer's prints and Shakespeare's plays.
For, we must not forget that Dürer's prints were partly made on com-
mission and partly intended to be sold in the open market; and that
Shakespeare's plays — in contrast to the earlier masques and inter-
mezzi which were produced at court by aristocratic amateurs and
could afford to be so incomprehensible that even those who
described them in printed monographs occasionally failed to grasp
their intended significance — were meant to appeal, and did appeal,
not only to the select few but also to everyone who was prepared to
pay a shilling for admission.

It is this requirement of communicability that makes commercial
art more vital than noncommercial, and therefore potentially much
more effective for better or for worse. The commercial producer can

both educate and pervert the general public, and can allow the general public — or rather his idea of the general public — both to educate and to pervert himself. As is demonstrated by a number of excellent films that proved to be great box office successes, the public does not refuse to accept good products if it gets them. That it does not get them very often is caused not so much by commercialism as such as by too little discernment and, paradoxical though it may seem, too much timidity in its application. Hollywood believes that it must produce "what the public wants" while the public would take whatever Hollywood produces. If Hollywood were to decide for itself what it wants it would get away with it — even if it should decide to "depart from evil and do good." For, to revert to whence we started, in modern life the movies are what most other forms of art have ceased to be, not an adornment but a necessity.

That this should be so is understandable, not only from a sociological but also from an art-historical point of view. The processes of all the earlier representational arts conform, in a higher or lesser degree, to an idealistic conception of the world. These arts operate from top to bottom, so to speak, and not from bottom to top; they start with an idea to be projected into shapeless matter and not with the objects that constitute the physical world. The painter works on a blank wall or canvas which he organizes into a likeness of things and persons according to his idea (however much this idea may have been nourished by reality); he does not work with the things and persons themselves even if he works "from the model." The same is true of the sculptor with his shapeless mass of clay or his untooled block of stone or wood; of the writer with his sheet of paper or his dictaphone; and even of the stage designer with his empty and sorely limited section of space. It is the movies, and only the movies, that do justice to that materialistic interpretation of the universe which, whether we like it or not, pervades contemporary civilization. Excepting the very special case of the animated cartoon, the movies organize material things and persons, not a neutral medium, into a composition that receives its style, and may even become fantastic or pretervoluntarily symbolic,[2] not so much by an interpretation in the

---

[2] I cannot help feeling that the final sequence of the new Marx Brothers film *Night in Casablanca* — where Harpo unaccountably usurps the pilot's seat of a big airplane, causes incalculable havoc by flicking one tiny little control after another, and waxes the more insane with joy the greater the disproportion between the smallness of his effort and the magnitude of the disaster — is a magnificent and terrifying symbol of man's behavior in the atomic age. No doubt the Marx Brothers would vigorously reject this interpretation; but so would Dürer have done had anyone told him that his "Apocalypse" foreshadowed the cataclysm of the Reformation.

artist's mind as by the actual manipulation of physical objects and
recording machinery. The medium of the movies is physical reality as
such: the physical reality of eighteenth-century Versailles — no
matter whether it be the original or a Hollywood facsimile indistinguishable therefrom for all aesthetic intents and purposes — or of a
suburban home in Westchester; the physical reality of the Rue de
Lappe in Paris or of the Gobi Desert, of Paul Ehrlich's apartment in
Frankfurt or of the streets of New York in the rain; the physical reality of engines and animals, of Edward G. Robinson and Jimmy
Cagney. All these objects and persons must be organized into a work
of art. They can be arranged in all sorts of ways ("arrangement" comprising, of course, such things as make-up, lighting and camera
work); but there is no running away from them. From this point of
view it becomes evident that an attempt at subjecting the world to
artistic prestylization, as in the expressionist settings of *The Cabinet
of Dr. Caligari* (1919), could be no more than an exciting experiment
that could exert but little influence upon the general course of events.
To prestylize reality prior to tackling it amounts to dodging the problem. The problem is to manipulate and shoot unstylized reality in
such a way that the result has style. This is a proposition no less
legitimate and no less difficult than any proposition in the older arts.

Theatre and Film

SUSAN SONTAG

Does there exist an unbridgeable gap, even opposition, between the
two arts? Is there something genuinely "theatrical," different in kind
from what is genuinely "cinematic"?

Virtually all opinion holds that there is. A commonplace of discussion has it that film and theatre are distinct and even antithetical
arts, each giving rise to its own standards of judgment and canons of
form. Thus Erwin Panofsky argues in his celebrated essay "Style and
Medium in the Motion Pictures" (1934, rewritten in 1956) that one of
the criteria for evaluating a movie is its freedom from the impurities

of theatricality, and that, to talk about film, one must first define "the basic nature of the medium." Those who think prescriptively about the nature of live drama, less confident in the future of that art than the cinéphiles in theirs, rarely take a comparably exclusivist line.

The history of cinema is often treated as the history of its emancipation from theatrical models. First of all from theatrical "frontality" (the unmoving camera reproducing the situation of the spectator of a play fixed in his seat), then from theatrical acting (gestures needlessly stylized, exaggerated — needlessly, because now the actor could be seen "close up"), then from theatrical furnishings (unnecessary distancing of the audience's emotions, disregarding the opportunity to immerse the audience in reality). Movies are regarded as advancing from theatrical stasis to cinematic fluidity, from theatrical artificiality to cinematic naturalness and immediateness. But this view is far too simple.

Such oversimplification testifies to the ambiguous scope of the camera eye. Because the camera can be used to project a relatively passive, unselective kind of vision — as well as the highly selective ("edited") vision generally associated with movies — cinema is a medium as well as an art, in the sense that it can encapsulate any of the performing arts and render it in a film transcription. (This "medium" or non-art aspect of film attained its routine incarnation with the advent of television. There, movies themselves became another performing art to be transcribed, miniaturized on film.) One can film a play or ballet or opera or sporting event in such a way that film becomes, relatively speaking, a transparency, and it seems correct to say that one is seeing the event filmed. But theatre is never a "medium." Thus, because one can make a movie of a play but not a play of a movie, cinema had an early but fortuitous connection with the stage. Some of the earliest films were filmed plays. Duse and Bernhardt are on film — marooned in time, absurd, touching; there is a 1913 British film of Forbes-Robertson playing Hamlet, a 1923 German film of Othello starring Emil Jannings. More recently, the camera has preserved Helene Weigel's performance of Mother Courage with the Berliner Ensemble, the Living Theatre production of The Brig (filmed by the Mekas brothers), and Peter Brook's staging of Weiss' Marat/Sade.

But from the beginning, even within the confines of the notion of film as a "medium" and the camera as a "recording" instrument, other events than those occurring in theatres were taken down. As with still photography, some of the events captured on moving photographs were staged but others were valued precisely because they

were *not* staged — the camera being the witness, the invisible spectator, the invulnerable voyeuristic eye. (Perhaps public happenings,
"news," constitute an intermediate case between staged and unstaged
events; but film as "newsreel" generally amounts to using film as a
"medium.") To create on film a *document* of a transient reality is a
conception quite unrelated to the purposes of theatre. It only appears
related when the "real event" being recorded happens to be a theatrical performance. In fact, the first use of the motion-picture camera
was to make a documentary record of unstaged, casual reality;
Lumière's films from the 1890's of crowd scenes in Paris and New
York antedate any filming of plays.

The other paradigmatic non-theatrical use of film, which dates
from the earliest period of movie-making with the celebrated work of
Méliès, is the creation of illusion, the construction of fantasy. To be
sure, Méliès, (like many directors after him) conceived of the rectan-
gle of the screen on analogy with the proscenium stage. And not only
were the events staged; they were the very stuff of invention: impossible journeys, imaginary objects, physical metamorphoses. But this,
even adding the fact that Méliès situated his camera in front of the
action and hardly moved it, does not make his films theatrical in an
invidious sense. In their treatment of persons as things (physical
objects) and in their disjunctive presentation of time and space,
Méliès' films are quintessentially "cinematic" — so far as there is
such a thing.

If the contrast between theatre and films doesn't lie in the materials represented or depicted in a simple sense, this contrast survives
in more generalized forms.

According to some influential accounts, the boundary is virtually
an ontological one. Theatre deploys artifice while cinema is committed to reality, indeed to an ultimately physical reality which is
"redeemed," to use Siegfried Kracauer's striking word, by the
camera. The aesthetic judgment that follows from this venture in
intellectual map-making is that films shot in real-life settings are
better (i.e., more cinematic) than those shot in a studio. Taking Flaherty and Italian neo-realism and the *cinéma-vérité* of Rouch and
Marker and Ruspoli as preferred models, one would judge rather
harshly the era of wholly studio-made films inaugurated around 1920
by *The Cabinet of Dr. Caligari*, films with ostentatiously artificial
décor and landscapes, and applaud the direction taken at the same
period in Sweden, where many films with strenuous natural settings
were being shot on location. Thus, Panofsky attacks *Dr. Caligari* for
"pre-stylizing reality," and urges upon cinema "the problem of

manipulating and shooting unstylized reality in such a way that the
result has style."

But there is no reason to insist on a single model for film. And it
is helpful to notice how the apotheosis of realism in cinema, which
gives the greatest prestige to "unstylized reality," covertly advances a
definite political-moral position. Films have been rather too often
acclaimed as the democratic art, the preeminent art of mass society.
Once one takes this description seriously, one tends (like Panofsky
and Kracauer) to wish that movies continue to reflect their origins in
a vulgar level of the arts, to remain loyal to their vast unsophisticated
audience. Thus, a vaguely Marxist orientation collaborates with a
fundamental tenet of romanticism. Cinema, at once high art and
popular art, is cast as the art of the authentic. Theatre, by contrast,
means dressing up, pretense, lies. It smacks of aristocratic taste and
the class society. Behind the objection of critics to the stagy sets of
Dr. Caligari, the improbable costumes and florid acting of Renoir's
Nana, the talkiness of Dreyer's *Gertrud* as "theatrical" lay the judgment that such films were false, that they exhibited a sensibility both
pretentious and reactionary which was out of step with the democratic and more mundane sensibility of modern life.

Anyway, whether aesthetic defect or no in the particular case,
the synthetic "look" in films is not necessarily a misplaced theatrical-
ism. From the beginning of film history, there were painters and
sculptors who claimed that cinema's true future resided in artifice,
construction. Not figurative narration or storytelling of any kind
(either in a relatively realistic or in a "surrealistic" vein) but abstraction was film's true destiny. Thus, Theo van Doesburg in his essay of
1929, "Film as Pure Form," envisages film as the vehicle of "optical
poetry," "dynamic light architecture," "the creation of a moving
ornament." Films will realize "Bach's dream of finding an optical
equivalent for the temporal structure of a musical composition."
Though only a few film-makers — for example, Robert Breer —
continue to pursue this conception of film, who can deny its claim to
be cinematic?

Could anything be more alien to the nature of theatre than such a
degree of abstraction? Let's not answer that question too quickly.

Panofsky derives the difference between theatre and film as a
difference between the *formal* conditions of seeing a play and those
of seeing a movie. In the theatre, "space is static, that is, the space
represented on the stage, as well as the spatial relation of the
beholder to the spectacle, is unalterably fixed," while in the cinema,

"the spectator occupies a fixed seat, but only physically, not as the subject of an aesthetic experience." In the theatre, the spectator cannot change his angle of vision. In the cinema, the spectator is "aesthetically . . . in permanent motion as his eye identifies with the lens of the camera, which permanently shifts in distance and direction."

True enough. But the observation does not warrant a radical dissociation of theatre and film. Like many critics, Panofsky has a "literary" conception of the theatre. In contrast to theatre, conceived of as basically dramatized literature (texts, words), stands cinema, which he assumes to be primarily "a visual experience." This means defining cinema by those means perfected in the period of silent films. But many of the most interesting movies today could hardly be described adequately as images with sound added. And the most lively work in the theatre is being done by people who envisage theatre as more than, or different from, "plays" from Aeschylus to Tennessee Williams.

Given his view, Panofsky is as eager to hold the line against the infiltration of theatre by cinema as the other way around. In the theatre, unlike movies, "the setting of the stage cannot change during one act (except for such incidentals as rising moons or gathering clouds and such illegitimate reborrowings from film as turning wings or gliding backdrops)." Not only does Panofsky assume that theatre means plays, but by the aesthetic standard he tacitly proposes, the model play would approach the condition of No Exit, and the ideal set would be either a realistic living room or a blank stage. No less arbitrary is his complementary view of what is illegitimate in film: all elements not demonstrably subordinate to the image, more precisely, the moving image. Thus Panofsky asserts: "Wherever a poetic emotion, a musical outburst, or a literary conceit (even, I am grieved to say, some of the wisecracks of Groucho Marx) entirely loses contact with visible movement, they strike the sensitive spectator as, literally, out of place." What then of the films of Bresson and Godard, with their allusive, thoughtful texts and their characteristic refusal to be primarily a visual experience? How could one explain the extraordinary rightness of Ozu's relatively immobilized camera?

Part of Panofsky's dogmatism in decrying the theatrical taint in movies can be explained by recalling that the first version of his essay appeared in 1934 and undoubtedly reflects the recent experience of seeing a great many bad movies. Compared with the level that film reached in the late 1920's it is undeniable that the average quality of films declined sharply in the early sound period. Although a number of fine, audacious films were made during the very first years of sound,

the general decline had become clear by 1933 or 1934. The sheer dull-
ness of most films of this period can't be explained simply as a regres-
sion to theatre. Still, it's a fact that film-makers in the 1930's did turn
much more frequently to plays than they had in the preceding decade
—filming stage successes such as *Outward Bound, Rain, Dinner at
Eight, Blithe Spirit, Faisons un Rêve, Twentieth Century, Boudu
Sauvé des Eaux*, the Pagnol trilogy, *She Done Him Wrong, Der Dreigro-
schen Oper, Anna Christie, Holiday, Animal Crackers, The Petrified
Forest*, and many, many more. Most of these films are negligible as art;
a few are first-rate. (The same can be said of the plays, though there is
scant correlation between the merits of the movies and of the stage
"originals.") However, their virtues and faults cannot be sorted out
into a cinematic versus a theatrical element. Usually, the success of
movie versions of plays is measured by the extent to which the script
rearranges and displaces the action and deals less than respectfully
with the spoken text — as do certain English films of plays by Wilde
and Shaw, the Olivier Shakespeare films (at least *Henry V*), and Sjö-
berg's *Miss Julie*. But the basic disapproval of films which betray their
origins in plays remains. (A recent example: the outrage and hostility
which greeted Dreyer's masterly *Gertud*, because of its blatant fidelity to the 1904 Danish play on which it is based, with characters conversing at length and quite formally, with little camera movement and
most scenes filmed in medium shot.)

My own view is that films with complex or formal dialogue, films
in which the camera is static or in which the action stays indoors, are
not necessarily theatrical — whether derived from plays or not. *Per
contra*, it is no more part of the putative "essence" of movies that the
camera must rove over a large physical area than it is that the sound
element in a film must always be subordinate to the visual. Though
most of the action of Kurosawa's *The Lower Depths*, a fairly faithful
transcription of Gorky's play, is confined to one large room, this film
is just as cinematic as the same director's *Throne of Blood*, a very
free and laconic adaption of *Macbeth*. The claustrophobic intensity
of Melville's *Les Enfants Terribles* is as peculiar to the movies as the
kinetic élan of Ford's *The Searchers* or the opening train journey in
Renoir's *La Bête Humaine*.

A film does become theatrical in an invidious sense when the
narration is coyly self-conscious. Compare Autant-Lara's *Occupe-toi
d'Amélie*, a brilliant cinematic use of the conventions and materials
of boulevard theatre, with Ophuls' clumsy use of similar conventions
and materials in *La Ronde*.

In his book *Film and Theatre* (1936), Allardyce Nicoll argues that the difference between the two arts, both forms of dramaturgy, is that they use different kinds of characters. "Practically all effectively drawn stage characters are types [while] in the cinema we demand individualization . . . and impute greater power of independent life to the figures on the screen." (Panofsky, by the way, makes exactly the same contrast but in reverse: that the nature of films, unlike that of plays, requires flat or stock characters.)

Nicoll's thesis is not as arbitrary as it may at first appear. A little-remarked fact about movies is that the moments that are plastically and emotionally most successful, and the most effective elements of characterization, often consist precisely of "irrelevant" or unfunctional details. (One random example: the ping-pong ball the schoolmaster toys with in Ivory's *Shakespeare Wallah*.) Movies thrive on the narrative equivalent of a technique familiar from painting and photography: off-centering. Hence, the pleasing disunity or fragmentariness of the characters of many of the greatest films, which is probably what Nicoll means by "individualization." In contrast, linear coherence of detail (the gun on the wall in the first act that must go off by the end of the third) is the rule in Occidental narrative theatre, and gives rise to the impression of the unity of the characters (a unity that may be equivalent to the construction of a "type").

But, even with these adjustments, Nicoll's thesis doesn't work so far as it rests on the idea that "when we go to the theatre, we expect theatre and nothing else." For what is this theatre-and-nothing-else if not the old notion of artifice? (As if art were ever anything else, some arts being artificial but others not.) According to Nicoll, when we sit in a theatre "in every way the 'falsity' of a theatrical production is borne in upon us, so that we are prepared to demand nothing save a theatrical truth." Quite a different situation obtains in the cinema, Nicoll holds. Every member of the movie audience, no matter how sophisticated, is on essentially the same level; we all believe that the camera cannot lie. As the film actor and his role are identical, the image cannot be dissociated from what is imaged. We experience what cinema gives us as the truth of life.

But couldn't theatre dissolve the distinction between the truth of artifice and the truth of life? Isn't that just what theatre as ritual seeks to do? Isn't that the aim of theatre conceived as an *exchange* with an audience? — something that films can never be.

Panofsky may be obtuse when he decries the theatrical taint in movies, but he is sound when he points out that, historically, theatre is only one of the arts feeding into cinema. As he remarks, it is apt that films came to be known popularly as moving pictures rather than as "photoplays" or "screen plays." Cinema derives less from the theatre, from a performance art, an art that already moves, than it does from forms of art which were stationary. Nineteenth-century historical paintings, sentimental postcards, the museum of wax figures à la Madame Tussaud, and comic strips are the sources Panofsky cites. Another model, which he surprisingly fails to mention, is the early narrative uses of still photography — like the family photo album. The stylistics of description and scene-building developed by certain nineteenth-century novelists, as Eisenstein pointed out in his brilliant essay on Dickens, supplied still another prototype for cinema.

Movies are images (usually photographs) that move, to be sure. But the distinctive cinematic unit is not the image but the principle of connection between the images: the relation of a "shot" to the one that preceded it and the one that comes after. There is no peculiarly "cinematic" as opposed to "theatrical" mode of linking images.

If an irreducible distinction between theatre and cinema does exist, it may be this. Theatre is confined to a logical or *continuous* use of space. Cinema (through editing, that is, through the change of shot — which is the basic unit of film construction) has access to an alogical or *discontinuous* use of space.

In the theatre, actors are either in the stage space or "off." When "on," they are always visible or visualizable in contiguity with each other. In the cinema, no such relation is necessarily visible or even visualizable. (Example: the last shot of Paradjanov's *Shadows of Our Forgotten Ancestors*.) Some of the films considered objectionably theatrical are those which seem to emphasize spatial continuities, like Hitchcock's virtuoso *Rope* or the daringly anachronistic *Gertrud*. But closer analysis of both these films would show how complex their treatment of space is. The long takes increasingly favored in sound films are, in themselves, neither more nor less cinematic than the short takes characteristic of silents.

Thus, cinematic virtue does not reside in the fluidity of the movement of the camera or in the mere frequency of the change of shot. It consists in the arrangement of screen images and (now) of sounds. Méliès, for example, though he didn't go beyond the static positioning of his camera, had a very striking conception of how to *link* screen images. He grasped that editing offered an equivalent to the magician's sleight of hand — thereby establishing that one of the distinctive aspects of film (unlike theatre) is that anything can happen, that there is nothing that cannot be represented convincingly. Through editing, Méliès presents discontinuities of physical substance and behavior. In his films, the discontinuities are, so to speak, practical, functional; they accomplish a transformation of ordinary reality. But the continuous reinvention of space (as well as the option of temporal indeterminacy) peculiar to film narration does not pertain only to the cinema's ability to fabricate "visions," to show the viewer a radically altered world. The most "realistic" use of the motion-picture camera also involves a discontinuous account of space, insofar as all film narration has a "syntax," composed of the rhythm of associations and disjunctions. (As Cocteau has written, "My primary concern in a film is to prevent the images from flowing, to oppose them to each other, to anchor them and join them without destroying their relief." But such a conception of film syntax need hardly entail, as Cocteau thinks, rejecting movies as "mere entertainment instead of a vehicle for thought.")

In marking the boundary between theatre and film, the issue of the continuity of space seems to me more fundamental than the obvious contrast between theatre as an organization of movement in three-dimensional space (like dance) and cinema as an organization of plane space (like painting). The theatre's capacities for manipulating space and time are simply much cruder and more labored than those of film. Theatre cannot equal the cinema's facilities for the strictly controlled repetition of images, for the duplication or matching of word and image, and for the juxtaposition and overlapping of images. (With advanced lighting techniques and an adept use of scrim, one can now "dissolve in" or "dissolve out" on the stage. But no technique could provide an equivalent on the stage of the "lap dissolve.")

Sometimes the division between theatre and film is located as the difference between the play and the film script. Theatre has been described as a mediated art, presumably because it usually consists of a preexistent play mediated by a particular performance which offers one of many possible interpretations of the play. Film, in contrast, is regarded as unmediated — because of its larger-than-life scale and more unrefusable impact on the eye, and because (in Panofsky's words) "the medium of the movies is physical reality as such" and the characters in a movie "have no aesthetic existence outside the actors." But there is an equally valid sense which shows movies to be the mediated art and theatre the unmediated one. We see what happens on the stage with our own eyes. We see on the screen what the camera sees.

In the cinema, narration proceeds by ellipsis (the "cut" or change of shot); the camera eye is a unified point of view that continually displaces itself. But the change of shot can provoke questions, the simplest of which is: from *whose* point of view is the shot seen? And the ambiguity of point of view latent in all cinematic narration has no equivalent in the theatre. Indeed, one should not underestimate the aesthetically positive role of *disorientation* in the cinema. Examples: Busby Berkeley dollying back from an ordinary-looking stage already established as some thirty feet deep to disclose a stage area three hundred feet square; Resnais panning from character X's point of view a full 360 degrees to come to rest upon X's face.

Much also may be made of the fact that, in its concrete existence, cinema is an *object* (a product, even) while theatre results in a *performance*. Is this so important? In a way, no. Art in all its forms, whether objects (like films or painting) or performances (like music or theatre), is first a mental act, a fact of consciousness. The object aspect of film and the performance aspect of theatre are only means — means to the experience which is not only "of" but "through" the film and the theatre event. Each subject of an aesthetic experience shapes it to his own measure. With respect to any *single* experience, it hardly matters that a film is identical from one projection of it to another while theatre performances are highly mutable.

The difference between object art and performance art underlies Panofsky's observation that "the screenplay, in contrast to the theatre play, has no aesthetic existence independent of its performance," so that characters in movies *are* the stars who enact them. It is because each film is an object, a totality that is set, that movie roles are identical with the actors' performances; while in the theatre (in the Occident, an artistic totality that is generally additive rather than organic) only the written play is "fixed," an object (literature) and therefore existing apart from any staging of it.

But these qualities of theatre and film are not, as Panofsky apparently thought, unalterable. Just as movies needn't necessarily be designed to be shown at all in theatre situations (they can be intended for more continuous and casual viewing: in the living room, in the bedroom, or on public surfaces like the façades of buildings), so a movie *may* be altered from one projection to the next. Harry Smith, when he runs off his films, makes each projection an unrepeatable performance. And, again, theatre is not just about preexisting plays which get produced over and over, well or badly. In Happenings, street or guerilla theatre, and certain other recent theatre events, the "plays" are identical with their productions in precisely the same sense as the screenplay is identical with the unique film made from it.

Despite these developments, however, a large difference still remains. Because films are objects, they are totally manipulable, totally calculable. Films resemble books, another portable art-object; making a film, like writing a book, means constructing an inanimate thing, every element of which is determinate. Indeed, this determinacy has or can have a quasi-mathematical form in films, as it does in music. (A shot lasts a certain number of seconds, "matching" two shots requires a change of angle of so many degrees.) Given the total determinacy of the result on celluloid (whatever the extent of the director's conscious intervention), it was inevitable that some film directors would want to devise schemas to make their intentions more exact. Thus, it was neither perverse nor primitive of Busby Berkeley to have used only one camera to shoot the whole of each of his mammoth dance numbers. Every "set-up" was designed to be shot from only one, exactly calculated angle. Working on a far more self-conscious level of artistry than Busby Berkeley, Bresson has declared that, for him, the director's task consists in finding the single way of doing each shot that is correct. No image is justified in itself, according to Bresson, but rather in the exactly specifiable relation it bears to the chronologically adjacent images — which relation constitutes its "meaning."

But theatre allows only the loosest approximation to this sort of formal concern and to this degree of aesthetic responsibility on the part of the director, which is why French critics justly speak of the director of a film as its "author." Because they are performances, events that are always "live," what takes place on a theatre stage is not subject to an equivalent degree of control and cannot admit a comparably exact integration of effects.

It would be foolish to conclude that superior films are those resulting from the greatest amount of conscious planning on the part of the director or those which objectify a complex plan (though the director may not have been aware of it, and proceeded in what seemed to him an intuitive or instinctive way). Plans may be faulty or ill-conceived or sterile. More important, the cinema admits of a number of quite different kinds of sensibility. One gives rise to the kind of formalized art to which cinema (unlike theatre) is naturally adapted. Another has produced an impressive body of "improvised" cinema. (This should be distinguished from the work of some film-makers, notably Godard, who have become fascinated with the "look" of improvised, documentary cinema, used for formalistic ends.)

Nevertheless, it seems indisputable that cinema, not only potentially but by its nature, is a more rigorous art than theatre. This capacity for formal rigor, combined with the accessibility of mass audiences, has given cinema an unquestioned prestige and attractiveness as an art form. Despite the extreme emotional resources of "pure theatre" demonstrated by Julian Beck and Judith Malina's Living Theatre and Jerzy Grotowski's Theatre Laboratory, theatre as an art form gives the general impression of having a problematic future.

More than a failure of nerve must account for the fact that thea- tre, this seasoned art, occupied since antiquity with all sorts of local offices — enacting sacred rites, reinforcing communal loyalty, guiding morals, provoking the therapeutic discharge of violent emotions, con- ferring social status, giving practical instruction, affording entertain- ment, dignifying celebrations, subverting established authority — is now on the defensive before movies, this brash art with its huge, amorphous, passive audience. But the fact is undeniable. Meanwhile, movies continue to maintain their astonishing pace of formal articula- tion. (Take the commercial cinema of Europe, Japan, and the United States since 1960, and consider what the audiences of these films in less than a decade have become habituated to in the way of increas- ingly elliptical storytelling and visualization.)

But note: this youngest of the arts is also the most heavily bur- dened with memory. Cinema is a time machine. Movies preserve the past, while theatres — no matter how devoted to the classics, to old plays — can only "modernize." Movies resurrect the beautiful dead; present, intact, vanished or ruined environments; embody without irony styles and fashions that seem funny today; solemnly ponder irrelevant or naïve problems. The historical particularity of the real- ity registered on celluloid is so vivid that practically all films older than four or five years are saturated with pathos. (The pathos I am describing is not simply that of old photographs, for it overtakes ani- mated cartoons and drawn, abstract films as well as ordinary movies.) Films age (being objects) as no theatre event does (being always new). There is no pathos of mortality in theatre's "reality" as such, nothing in our response to a good performance of a Mayakovsky play comparable to the aesthetic role of the emotion of nostalgia when we see in 1966 a film by Pudovkin.

Also worth noting: compared with the theatre, innovations in cinema seem to be assimilated more efficiently, seem altogether more sharable — among other reasons, because new films are quickly and widely circulated. And, partly because virtually the entire body of accomplishment in film can be consulted in the present (in film li- braries, of which the most celebrated is the Cinemathèque Française), most film-makers are more knowledgeable about the entire history of their art than most theatre directors are about even the very recent past of theirs.

The key word in most discussions of cinema is "possibility." There is a merely classifying use of the word, as in Panofsky's engaging judgment that "within their self-imposed limitations the early Disney films . . . represent, as it were, a chemically pure distillation of cinematic possibilities." But behind this relatively neutral usage lurks a more polemical sense of cinema's possibilities, in which what is regularly intimated is the obsolescence of theatre and its supersession by films.

Thus, Panofsky describes the mediation of the camera eye as opening "up a world of possibility of which the stage can never dream." Already in 1924, Artaud declared that motion pictures had made the theatre obsolete. Movies "possess a sort of virtual power which probes into the mind and uncovers undreamt-of possibilities. . . . When this art's exhiliration has been blended in the right proportions with the psychic ingredient it commands, it will leave the theatre far behind and we will relegate the latter to the attic of our memories." (When sound came in, though, Artaud became disenchanted with films and returned to theatre.)

Meyerhold, facing the challenge head on, thought the only hope for theatre lay in a wholesale emulation of the cinema. "Let us 'cinematify' the theatre," he urged, meaning that the staging of plays should be "industrialized," theatres must accommodate audiences in the tens of thousands rather than in the hundreds. Meyerhold also seemed to find some relief in the idea that the coming of sound signaled the downfall of movies. Believing that the international appeal of films depended entirely on the fact that screen actors (unlike theatre actors) didn't have to speak any particular language, he was unable to imagine in 1930 that technology (dubbing, subtitling) could solve the problem.

Is cinema the successor, the rival, or the revivifyer of the theatre?

Sociologically, it is certainly the rival — one of many. Whether it is theatre's successor depends partly on how people understand and use the decline of theatre as an art form. One can't be sure that theatre is not in a state of irreversible decline, spurts of local vitality notwithstanding. And art forms *have* been abandoned (though not necessarily because they become "obsolete").

But why should theatre be rendered obsolete by movies? Predictions of obsolescence amount to declaring that a something has one particular task (which another something may do as well or better). But has theatre one particular task or aptitude? One which cinema is better able to perform?

Those who predict the demise of the theatre, assuming that cinema has engulfed its function, tend to impute a relation between films and theatre reminiscent of what was once said about photography and painting. If the painter's job really had been no more than fabricating likenesses, then the invention of the camera might indeed have made painting obsolete. But painting is hardly just "pictures," any more than cinema is just theatre democratized and made available to the masses (because it can be reproduced and distributed in portable standardized units).

In the naïve tale of photography and painting, painting was reprieved when it claimed a new task: abstraction. As the superior realism of photography was supposed to have liberated painting, allowing it to go abstract, cinema's superior power to represent (not merely to stimulate) the imagination may appear to have similarly emboldened the theatre, inviting the gradual obliteration of the conventional "plot."

This was how it was supposed to be, but not how it in fact turned out. Actually, painting and photography evidence parallel development rather than a rivalry or a supersession. And, at an uneven rate, so do theatre and film. The possibilities for theatre that lie in going beyond psychological realism, thereby achieving greater abstractness, are equally germane to the future of narrative films. Conversely, the idea of movies as witness to real life, testimony rather than invention or artifice, the treatment of collective historical situations rather than the depiction of imaginary personal "dramas," seems equally relevant to theatre. Alongside documentary films and their sophisticated heir, cinéma-vérité, one can place the new documentary theatre, the so-called "theatre of fact," exemplified in plays by Hochhuth, in Weiss' The Investigation, in Peter Brook's recent projects for a production called US with the Royal Shakespeare company in London.

Despite Panofsky's strictures, there seems no reason for theatre and film not to exchange with each other, as they have been doing right along.

The influence of the theatre upon films in the early years of cinema history is well known. According to Kracauer, the distinctive lighting of Dr. Caligari (and of many German films of the early 1920's) can be traced to an experiment with lighting that Max Reinhardt made shortly before on the stage in his production of Sorge's The Beggar. Even in this period, however, the impact was reciprocal. The accomplishments of the "expressionist film" were immediately absorbed by the expressionist theatre. Stimulated by the cinematic technique of the "iris-in," stage lighting took to singling out a lone player or some segment of the scene, masking out the rest of the stage. Rotating sets tried to approximate the instantaneous displacement of the camera eye. (More recently, reports have come of ingenious lighting techniques used by the Gorky Theatre in Leningrad, directed since 1956 by Georgy Tovstonogov, which allow for incredibly rapid scene changes taking place behind a horizontal curtain of light.)

Today traffic seems, with few exceptions, entirely one way: film to theatre. Particularly in France and in Central and Eastern Europe, the staging of many plays is inspired by the movies. The aim of adapting neo-cinematic devices for the stage (I exclude the outright use of films within the theatre production) seems mainly to tighten up the theatrical experience, to approximate the cinema's absolute control of the flow and location of the audience's attention. But the conception can be even more directly cinematic. An example is Josef Svoboda's production of *The Insect Play* by the Čapek brothers at the Czech National Theatre in Prague (recently seen in London), which frankly attempted to install a mediated vision upon the stage, equivalent to the discontinuous intensifications of the camera eye. According to a London critic's account, "the set consisted of two huge, faceted mirrors slung at an angle to the stage, so that they reflect whatever happens there defracted as if through a decanter stopper or the colossally magnified eye of a fly. Any figure placed at the base of their angle becomes multiplied from floor to proscenium; further out, and you find yourself viewing it not only face to face but from overhead, the vantage point of a camera slung to a bird or a helicopter."

Marinetti was perhaps the first to propose the use of films as one element in a theatre experience. Writing between 1910 and 1914, he envisaged the theatre as a final synthesis of all the arts; and as such it had to draw in the newest art form, movies. No doubt the cinema also recommended itself for inclusion because of the priority Marinetti gave to existing forms of popular entertainment, such as the variety theatre and the *café chantant*. (He called his projected total art form "the Futurist Variety Theatre.") And at that time scarcely anyone considered cinema anything but a vulgar art.

After World War I, similar ideas appear frequently. In the total-theatre projects of the Bauhaus group in the 1920's (Gropius, Piscator, etc.) film had an important place. Meyerhold insisted on its use in the theatre, describing his program as fulfilling Wagner's once "wholly utopian" proposals to "use all means available from the other arts." Alban Berg specified that a silent film of the developing story was to be projected in the middle of Act 2 of his opera *Lulu*. By now, the employment of film in theatre has a fairly long history which includes the "living newspaper" of the 1930's, "epic theatre," and Happenings. This year marked the introduction of a film sequence into Broadway-level theatre. In two successful musicals, London's *Come Spy with Me* and New York's *Superman*, both parodic in tone, the action is interrupted to lower a screen and run off a movie showing the pop-art hero's exploits.

But thus far the use of film within live theatre events has tended to be stereotyped. Film is often employed as *document*, supportive of or redundant to the live stage events (as in Brecht's productions in East Berlin). Its other principal use is as *hallucinant*; recent examples are Bob Whitman's Happenings, and a new kind of nightclub situation, the mixed-media discothèque (Andy Warhol's The Plastic Inevitable, Murray the K's World). From the point of view of theatre, the interpolation of film into the theatre experience may be enlarging. But in terms of what cinema is capable of, it seems a reductive, monotonous use of film.

What Panofsky perhaps could not have realized when he wrote his essay is that much more than the "nature" of a specific art "medium" is at stake. The relation between film and theatre involves not simply a static definition of the two arts, but sensitivity to the possible course of their radicalization.

Every interesting aesthetic tendency now is a species of radicalism. The question each artist must ask is: What is *my* radicalism, the one dictated by *my* gifts and temperament? This doesn't mean all contemporary artists believe that art progresses. A radical position isn't necessarily a forward-looking position.

Consider the two principal radical positions in the arts today. One recommends the breaking down of distinctions between genres; the arts would eventuate in one art, consisting of many different kinds of behavior going on at the same time, a vast behavioral magma or synesthesia. The other position recommends the maintaining and clarifying of barriers between the arts, by the intensification of what each art distinctively is; painting must use only those means which pertain to painting, music only those which are musical, novels those which pertain to the novel and to no other literary form, etc. The two positions are, in a sense, irreconcilable — except that both are invoked to support the perennial modern quest for the definitive art form.

An art may be proposed as definitive because it is considered the most rigorous or most fundamental. For these reasons, Schopenhauer suggested and Pater asserted that all art aspires to the condition of music. More recently, the thesis that all the arts are leading toward one art has been advanced by enthusiasts of the cinema. The candidacy of film is founded on its being both so exact and, potentially, so complex a combination of music, literature, and the image.

Or, an art may be proposed as definitive because it is held to be most inclusive. This is the basis of the destiny for theatre held out by Wagner, Marinetti, Artaud, Cage — all of whom envisage theatre as a total art, potentially conscripting all the arts into its service. And as the ideas of synesthesia continue to proliferate among painters, sculptors, architects, and composers, theatre remains the favored candidate for the role of summative art. In this conception, theatre's role must disparage the claims of cinema. Partisans of theatre would argue that while music, painting, dance, cinema, and utterance can all converge on a "stage," the film object can only become bigger (multiple screens, 360 degree projection, etc.) or longer in duration or internally more articulated and complex. Theatre can be anything, everything; in the end, films can only be more of what they specifically (that is to say, cinematically) are.

Underlying the more grandiose apocalyptic expectations for both arts is a common animus. In 1923 Béla Bálacz, anticipating in great detail the thesis of Marshall McLuhan, described movies as the herald of a new "visual culture" which will give us back our bodies, and particularly our faces, which have been rendered illegible, soulless, unexpressive by the centuries-old ascendancy of "print." An animus against literature, against the printing press and its "culture of concepts," also informs most interesting thinking about the theatre in our time.

No definition or characterization of theatre and cinema can be taken for granted — not even the apparently self-evident observation that both cinema and theatre are temporal arts. In theatre and cinema, like music (and unlike painting), everything is not present all at once. But there are significant developments today pointing up the atemporal aspect of these forms. The allure of mixed-media forms in theatre suggests not only a more elongated and more complex "drama" (like Wagnerian opera) but also a more compact theatre experience which approaches the condition of painting. This prospect of compactness is broached by Marinetti; he calls it simultaneity, a leading notion of Futurist aesthetics. As the final synthesis of all the arts, theatre "would use the new twentieth century devices of electricity and the cinema; this would enable plays to be extremely short, since all these technical means would enable the theatrical synthesis to be achieved in the shortest possible space of time, as all the elements could be presented simultaneously."

The source of the idea of art as an act of violence pervading cinema and theatre is the aesthetics of Futurism and of Surrealism; its principal texts are, for theatre, the writings of Artaud and, for cinema, two films of Luis Buñuel, *L'Age d'Or* and *Un Chien Andalou*. (More recent examples: the early plays of Ionesco, at least as conceived; the "cinema of cruelty" of Hitchcock, Clouzot, Franju, Robert Aldrich, Polanski; work by the Living Theatre; some of the neo-cinematic light shows in experimental theatres and discothèques; the sound of late Cage and LaMonte Young.) The relation of art to an audience understood to be passive, inert, surfeited, can only be assault. Art becomes identical with aggression.

However understandable and valuable this theory of art as an assault on the audience is today (like the complementary notion of art as ritual), one must continue to question it, particularly in the theatre. For it can become as much a convention as anything else and end, like all theatrical conventions, by reinforcing rather than challenging the deadness of the audience. (As Wagner's ideology of a total theatre played its role in confirming the philistinism of German culture.)

Moreover, the depth of the assault must be assessed honestly. In the theatre, this means not "diluting" Artaud. Artaud's writings express the demand for a totally open (therefore flayed, self-cruel) consciousness of which theatre would be one adjunct or instrument. No work in the theatre has yet amounted to this. Thus, Peter Brook has astutely and forthrightly disclaimed that his company's work in the "Theatre of Cruelty," which culminated in his celebrated production of *Marat/Sade*, is genuinely Artaudian. It is Artaudian, he says, in a trivial sense only. (Trivial from Artaud's point of view, not from ours.)

For some time, all useful ideas in art have been extremely sophisticated. Take, for example, the idea that everything is what it is and not another thing: a painting is a painting; sculpture is sculpture; a poem is a poem, not prose. Or the complementary idea: a painting can be "literary" or sculptural, a poem can be prose, theatre can emulate and incorporate cinema, cinema can be theatrical.

We need a new idea. It will probably be a very simple one. Will we be able to recognize it?

Time in Film and Fiction

GEORGE BLUESTONE

In their illuminating discussion of literature and the other arts, René Wellek and Austin Warren compare literature to the fine arts and music, but they follow modern criticism in neglecting motion pictures. I do not claim of course that the cinema has any priority on our attention. The cinema is no more nor less useful than painting or music or sculpture in declaring its autonomy as an art form, or in sharpening by vivid contrasts the contours of literature. I do suggest that the film, having principles of its own, offers still another fruitful comparison which helps define both forms. The treatment of time in fiction and film shows us once again that at a high conceptual level there appear certain common patterns in the manner of Walzel's *Wechselseitige Erhellung der Künste,* and, at the material level, certain crucial differences in the manner of Lessing's *Laocoön.* In the few comparative studies already available, we can easily find parallel approaches. Claude-Edmond Magny (in her *L'Age du roman Américain*) finding a cinematic "exaltation of the instant" in Hemingway, follows the way of Walzel. Albert Laffay ("Le Récit, le Monde, et le Cinema," *Les Temps Modernes* [May–June 1947]), discovering that the cinema differs not only in materials but in the way it structures both story and reality, follows the way of Lessing. In comparing the two media, we must blend the two approaches, but it is Lessing, I think, who has the final say.

To begin with, the novel has three tenses; the film only one. From this follows almost everything one can say about time in both media. By now, we are familiar with Bergson's distinction between two kinds of time: chronological time measured in more or less discrete units, as in clocks and metronomes; and psychological time which distends or compresses in consciousness and appears in continuous flux. What are the comparative abilities of fiction and film to render these types of time?

A. A. Mendilow, in *Time and the Novel,* describes language as "A medium consisting of consecutive units constituting a forward-moving linear form of expression that is subject to the three characteristics of time — transience, sequence and irreversibility." But we must remember that Mendilow is here referring to chronological time only. And chronological time in the novel exists on three levels: the duration of the reading; the narrator's time; and the span of the narrative

91

events. That the three chronologies may harmonize is due entirely to
the willingness of the reader to suspend disbelief and to accept the
authority of convention. As long as the novelist is not troubled by the
bargain into which he enters with his reader, the three levels do not
come into serious conflict.

As early as the eighteenth century, Laurence Sterne saw the
essential paradox of this convention. If the novelist chooses to chronicle a series of events up to the present moment, he discovers that by
the time he commits a single event to paper, the present moment has
already slipped away. And if the novelist discovers that it takes a
chronological year to record a fictional day, as Sterne did, how is one
ever to overcome the durational lag between art and life? If the present moment is constantly renewed, how can prose, which is fixed,
ever hope to capture it? Whenever a novelist chooses for his province
a sequence of events which cannot be completed until the present
moment, the three levels come into open conflict. In Sterne and Gide,
that conflict becomes more central than conflicts between the characters.

The film is spared at least some of this uneasiness because one of
the levels is omitted. Since the camera is always the narrator, we
need concern ourselves only with the duration of the viewing and the
time-span of the narrative events. Even when a narrator appears in
the film, the essential fact is unaltered. When Francis begins telling
the story of Dr. Caligari, the camera shows his face; then the camera
shifts to the scene of the story and there takes over the telling. What
has happened is not so much that Francis has turned over the role of
narrator to the omniscient camera as that the omniscient camera has,
from the beginning, included Francis as part of the narrative.

The range of chronological time for reader and viewer are rather
fluid, yet more or less fixed by convention. Where a novel can be
read in anywhere from two to fifty hours, a film generally runs one or
two. *Intolerance* runs over two hours; the uncut version of *Les
Enfants du Paradis* over three; and *Gone with the Wind* and *War and
Peace* slightly less than four. Since the fictional events in both novel
and film may range from the fleeting duration of a dream, as in *Scar-
let Street* and *Finnegans Wake*, to long but finite stretches of human
history, as in *Intolerance* and *Orlando*, the sense of passing time is
infinitely more crucial than the time required for reading or viewing.

We may note, of course, that a fifty-hour novel has the advantage of achieving a certain density, that "solidity of specification"
which James admired, simply because the reader has lived with it
longer. Because its mode of beholding allows stops and starts, thumb-
ing back, skipping, flipping ahead, and so lets the reader set his own
pace, a novel can afford diffuseness where the film must economize.

Where a novel allows the reader to control his rate, the film viewer is bound by the relentness rate of a projector which he cannot control. The results, as may be expected, are felt in the contrast between the loose, more variegated conventions of the novel, and the tight, more compact conventions of the film.

In the last analysis, however, it is the qualitative rather than the quantitative difference that militates against blurring the distinctions between fiction and film. For the moment we shift from chronological to psychological time, certain unique problems arise.

Here I speak of psychological time in roughly two ways. The first suggests that the human mind is capable of accelerating and collapsing the "feel" of time to the point where each individual may be said to possess his own time-system. The second suggests, beyond this variability in rate, the kind of flux which, being fluid and interpenetrable, and lacking in sharp boundaries, can scarcely be measured at all.

As long as the kind of time we are talking about implies discrete units in a series, language seems roughly adequate to the task. For example, the observation that chronological time crowded with activity, the sense of time passing quickly, seems "long" in retrospect, whereas chronological time taken up with dull and undifferentiated activity (the sense of time passing slowly) seems "short" in retrospect still has built into it a concept of measurement. It assumes the clock as a standard, for this kind of psychological time seems "long" or "short" in terms of certain normative expectancies. It assumes a normative "feel" for chronological time which may be distended or compressed by the stress of the moment, or by memory.

Here language is still appropriate to its task. Mendilow points out, for example, that in *Tom Jones* each book draws on a progressively greater length of the reader's clock time to cover a progressively shorter period of fictional time. So that where Book Three covers five years, Books Nine and Ten cover twelve hours each. Both for Tom Jones and the reader, the events of the five weeks which occupy the last two thirds of the novel will seem "longer" than the events of the twenty years which occupy the first third.

Compression and distension of time have their exact equivalents in the film's use of speed-up and slow-motion. The cinema has developed a new kind of presentational reality, what V. I. Pudovkin calls filmic space and filmic time; what Erwin Panofsky calls the Dynamization of Space and the Spatialization of Time. The theatrical producer, says Pudovkin,

> ... works with real actuality which though he may always remould, yet forces him to remain bound by the laws of real space

and real time. The film director, on the other hand, has as his
material the finished recorded celluloid. . . . The elements of reality
are fixed on those pieces; by combining them in his selected
sequence according to his desire, the director builds up his own
"filmic" time and "filmic" space.

The director creates a new reality, the most important characteristic of which is that laws of space and time which are ordinarily
invariable or inescapable become "tractable and obedient." Hollywood's silent comedians made superb use of this freedom. James
Agee has noted how Mack Sennett, realizing "the tremendous drum-
like power of mere motion to exhilarate," gave inanimate objects a
mischievous life of their own, "broke every law of nature the tricked
camera could serve him for and made the screen dance like a witches'
Sabbath." No previous narrative art has been able to achieve such
graphic effects.

Not only is space liberated but *because* it is liberated, time is,
too. Anyone who has seen the remarkable slow-motion sequence in
Zéro de Conduite can attest to the dramatic power of distended time.
By interfering and only by interfering with clock time was Jean Vigo
able to render the dream-like essence of the pillow fight.

Similarly, it is easy to find innumerable examples of accelerated
motion in Hollywood where the emphasis has always been on the
murderous pace of the comic chase. Chaplin outraces the Keystone
cops. W. C. Fields weaves in and out of traffic at eighty miles an
hour. Time is distorted in the opposite direction, but the principle
remains the same. Spatial mobility makes time more flexible.

As for the kind of rhythmic progression one finds in music, the
film has an exact parallel in the principles of montage. Not only does
each shot take its meaning both from preceding shots and from future
expectations, but the use of sound in music and dialogue provides a
complex system of counterpoint.

As soon as we enter the realm of the time-flux, however, we not
only broach all but insoluble problems for the novel; we also find a
sharp divergence between prose and cinema. The transient, sequential, and irreversible character of language is no longer adequate. In
this kind of experimental time, past and present lose their identity as
discrete sections of time. The present becomes "specious" because
on second glance it is seen as fused with the past, obliterating the line
between them.

By drawing from Sturt's *Psychology of Time* Mendilow lends
support to the idea that the whole of experience is implicit in every
moment of the present. "One of the reasons for the feeling of pastness," according to Sturt,

is that we are familiar with the things or events that we recognize as past. But it remains true that this feeling of familiarity is a *present* experience, and therefore logically should not arouse a concept of the past. On the other hand, a present impression (or memory) of something which is past is different from a present impression of something which is present but familiar from the past.

How this operates in practice may be seen when we attempt to determine precisely which of two past events is prior, and in what manner the distinction between the memory of a past thing and the impression of a present thing is to be made. At first glance, we seem perfectly able to deduce which of two remembered events is prior.

On second thought, however, it seems as if, apart from deduction, the memory of a past event comes to me with its pastness built in as it were. The image I have of my friend *includes* the information that this is the way he looked the year *before* he died. We are caught in a perpetual present permeated in this fashion by a remembered past. This obliteration between past and present is precisely the problem which confronts the novelist who wishes to catch the flux in language. If he is faced with the presentness of consciousness on the one hand, and the obliteration of a discrete past and present on the other, how is he to express these phenomena in a language which relies on tenses?

Whether we use William James' "stream of consciousness," Ford Madox Ford's "chronological looping," or Henri Bergson's "*durée,*" we find the same problem: language, consisting as it does of bounded, discrete units cannot satisfactorily represent the unbounded and continuous. We have a sign to cover a thing's "becoming"; and one to cover a thing's "having become"; but "becoming" is a present participle, "become" a past participle, and our language has thus far offered no way of showing the continuity between them. So elusive has been the *durée* that the novelist has submitted to the steady temptation of trying to escape time entirely. His failure to do so dramatizes the medium's limitation. Speaking of Gertrude Stein's attempt to emancipate fiction from the tyranny of time, E. M. Forster notes the impasse: "She fails, because as soon as fiction is completely delivered from time it cannot express anything at all."

To be sure, there seem to be intuitive moments of illumination in Proust during which a forgotten incident floats up from oblivion in its pristine form and seems, for the moment, to become free of time. Proust's involuntary memory fuses the experience of his mother's madeleine cake with the earlier experience of Aunt Leonie's, and the intervening time seems obliterated. But it is precisely the point of

Proust's agonizing effort that — despite our ability, through involuntary memory, to experience simultaneously events "with countless intervening days between" — there is always a sense in which these events remain "widely separated from one another in Time." The recognition of this conflict helps us understand why every formulation which attempts to define a "timeless" quality in a novel seems unsatisfactory, why Mendilow's attempt to find an "ideal time" in Kafka seems to say little more than that Kafka was not plagued by the problem. In the end, the phrase "timeless moment" poses an insuperable contradiction in terms.

The film-maker, in his own and perhaps more acute way, also faces the problem of how to render the flux of time. Pictures have no tenses. Unfolding in a perpetual present, like visual perception itself, they cannot express either a past or a future. One may argue that dialogue and music provide doors through which past and future may enter. Dialogue, after all, is language, and language does have referential tenses. A character whose face appears before us may talk about his past and thereby permeate his visual present with a kind of psychic past.

At best, however, sound is a secondary advantage which does not seriously threaten the primacy of the spatial image. When Ellen, the housekeeper in the film of *Wuthering Heights,* her withered face illumined by the fire, begins telling her story to Lockwood, we do sense a certain tension between story-teller and story. But in the film we can never shake our attention loose from the physical presence of the teller. The image of her face has priority over the sound of her voice. This phenomenon is essentially what Panofsky calls the "principle of coexpressibility," according to which a moving picture — even when it has learned to talk — remains a picture that moves, and does not convert itself into a piece of writing that is enacted. That is why Shakespearean films which fail to adapt the fixed space of the stage to cinematic space so often seem static and talky.

In the novel, the line of dialogue stands naked and alone; in the film, the spoken word is subsumed in the spatial image. In a film, according to Panofsky, "That which we hear remains, for good or worse, inextricably fused with that which we see." Our seeing — and therefore our sense of the present — remains primary.

If dialogue and music are inadequate to the task of capturing the flux, the film's constant motion is another matter. At first the film seems bound by discrete sections, much as the novel is bound by discrete words. At the film's outer limit stands the frame; and within the frame appear the distinct outlines of projected objects, each cut as by a razor's edge. But the effect of running off the frames is startingly different from running off the sentence. For whether the words in a novel come to me as non-verbal images or as verbal meanings, I can still detect a distinct subject and predicate. If I say, "The top spins on the table," my mind assembles the top, then the spinning, then the table (unless of course I am capable of absorbing the sentence all at once, in which case the process extends to a paragraph composed of discrete sentences). But on the screen I simply perceive a shot of a top spinning on a table, a shot in which subject and predicate appear fused. Not only is the top indistinguishable from its spinning, but at every moment the motion of the top seems to contain the history of its past motion. It is true that the image of the top stimulated by the sentence resembles the image of the top stimulated by the film in the sense that both contain the illusion of continuous motion. Yet this resemblance does not appear in the *process* of cognition. It appears only after the fact, as it were, only after the component parts have been assembled. Although the mental, residual images do meet in rendering the top's continuity of motion, it is in the mode of *apprehending* them that we find the qualitative difference.

It is the motion of the film's *present* which is unique. Montage depends for its effects on instantaneous successions of different spatial entities which are constantly exploding against each other. But a succession of such variables would quickly become incomprehensible without a constant to stabilize them. In the film, that constant is motion. No matter how diverse the moving spaces which explode against each other, movement itself pours over from shot to shot, binding as it blurs.

So powerful is this continuity, regardless of the *direction* of the motion, that at times we tend to forget the boundaries of both frame and projected object. We attend to the motion only. In those moments when motion alone floods our attention and spatial attributes seem forgotten, we suddenly come as close as the film is able to fulfilling the essential requirement of the time-flux — the boundaries are no longer perceptible. The transience of the photographic shot falls away before the sweeping permanence of the motion. Past and present seem fused, and we have magically accomplished before us a spatial analogue for the temporal flux.

If the film is incapable of maintaining the illusion for very long, if its spatial attributes, being primary, presently assert themselves, if the film's spatial appeal to eye overwhelms its temporal appeal to mind, it is nevertheless true that the film, above all other non-verbal arts, comes closest to rendering the time-flux. The film's linear progression, and what Panofsky calls the "Dynamization of Space" permits us to intuit the durée insofar as it can, in spatial art, be intuited at all.

My analysis, then, permits a usable distinction between the two media. Both novel and film are time arts, but whereas the formative principle in the novel is time, the formative principle in the film is space. Whereas the novel takes its space for granted and forms its narrative in a complex of time values, the film takes its time for granted and forms its narrative in configurations of space. Both film and novel create the illusion of psychologically distorted time and space, but neither destroys time or space. The novel renders the illusion of space by going from point to point in time; the film renders time by going from point to point in space. The novel abides by, yet explores, the possibilities of psychological law; the film abides by, yet explores, the possibilities of optical law.

Where the twentieth-century novel has achieved the shock of novelty by explosions of words, the twentieth-century film has achieved a comparable shock by explosions of visual images. It is a phenomenon which invites detailed investigation that the rise of the film, which preempted the picturing of bodies in nature, coincides exactly with the rise of the modern novel which preempted human consciousness.

The Surfaces of Reality

MICHAEL ROEMER

As Siegfried Kracauer effectively demonstrates, the camera photographs the skin; it cannot function like an X-ray machine and show us what is underneath. This does not mean, however, that the filmmaker has no control over the surfaces rendered by his camera. On the contrary, he chooses his surfaces for their content, and through their careful selection and juxtaposition builds a structure of feeling and meaning that are the core of his work.

There are times in the history of the medium when story, treatment and performance drift so far into a studio never-never land that
we cannot help but make a virtue of "pure" reality, as free from
interference on the part of the film-maker as possible — even at the
risk of creating something shapeless. This should not, however,
obscure the fact that a film, like a poem or painting, is basically an
artifact.

The assertion that film is nothing more than a documentary
recording of reality undoubtedly stems from the fact that the medium
must render all meaning in physical terms. This affinity for real surfaces, combined with great freedom of movement both in time and
space, brings film closer than any other medium to our own random
experience of life. Even the realistic playwright, who — until the
advent of the camera — came closest to rendering the appearance of
reality, is often forced in his structure to violate the very sense of life
he is trying to create. But the film-maker can use the flexible
resources at his command to approximate the actual fabric of reality.
Moreover, he need not heighten his effects in order to communicate,
for he can call on the same sensibilities in his audience that we use in
life itself.

All of us bring to every situation, whether it be a business meeting or a love affair, a social and psychological awareness which helps
us understand complex motivations and relationships. This kind of
perception, much of it nonverbal and based on apparently insignificant clues, is not limited to the educated or gifted. We all depend on
it for our understanding of other people and have become extremely
proficient in the interpretation of subtle signs — a shading in the
voice, an averted glance. This nuanced awareness, however, is not
easily called upon by the arts, for it is predicated upon a far more
immediate and total experience than can be provided by literature
and the theater, with their dependence on the word, or by the visual
arts — with their dependence on the image. Only film renders experience with enough immediacy and totality to call into play the perceptual processes we employ in life itself.

The fact that film exercises this sort of perceptual capacity is, I
believe, one of its chief appeals to us. It gives us practice in the delicate and always somewhat uncertain skill of finding out what is going
on. As an extreme example, take these lines from *Marty*. They are
spoken in a dance hall during the first encounter between a lonely
man and a lonely girl. She says: "I'm twenty-nine years old. How old
are you?" And he answers: "Thirty-six."

On the stage or the printed page these lines would fall ludicrously flat. But on the screen, when spoken by performers who can

make every detail yield a wealth of meaning, they instantly convey — as they would in life itself — a complex web of feeling: the
girl's fear that she might be too old for the man, her need to come
right to the point, her relief when he turns out to be older, and finally
a mutual delight that their relationship has crossed its first hurdle.

Film thrives on this kind of intimate detail, for the camera
reports it so closely that nothing essential is lost to the eye or ear.
The camera makes it possible to use the stuff of life itself, without
amplification or overstatement and without any loss in dramatic
value. What is achieved in a large action or an explicit moment on the
stage can be rendered just as dramatically on the screen in small and
implicit terms, for it is not the magnitude of a gesture that makes it
dramatic but its meaning and intention.

This is *not* to say that the medium is most aptly used on the kind
of everyday story told in *Marty*, or that low-key dialogue without
conflict or strong feeling is always effective on the screen. I quote the
scene merely as an example of the medium's capacity for finding
meaning in the detail of everyday life and would like to suggest that
out of such detail, out of the ordinary surfaces of life, the film-maker
can structure *any* kind of situation and story — lyrical or dramatic,
historical or contemporary.

Like so many films that deal with the past, Dreyer's *Passion de
Jeanne D'Arc* might well have been filled with violent action and
theatrical confrontations. Instead the story is told in terms of mundane detail. Thus Jeanne is betrayed at a critical moment by a priest
who averts his eyes when she turns to him for help. There is no call
for anything more explicit. The betrayal is what matters, and the
camera renders it far more credibly and forcefully in a mundane
detail than it would be in a highly dramatized gesture.

In *Rashomon* and *The Seven Samurai* Kurosawa deals with
events of the thirteenth and sixteenth centuries in the most everyday
terms. He knows that our basic daily experience of reality has not
changed much over the centuries: a war between bandits and samurai
in a feudal Japanese village was as full of mud and rain, as gritty and
as grotesque as a twentieth-century skirmish. Film at its best uses the
language of ordinary experience — but uses it subtly and artfully.

In a contemporary setting, Bresson's *A Man Escaped* chronicles
the efforts of a French resistance fighter to break out of a German
prison. Much of the film takes place within the confines of a cell and
the camera records how he painstakingly prepares his escape by
fashioning tools out of spoons and rope out of blankets. It is all very
ordinary and physical, but out of the grimy detail emerges a devout
and heroic assertion of life and human freedom and of the need to

preserve them in the face of all odds. In the hands of a sensitive film-maker the ordinary moment becomes a channel for deep feeling and a sequence of apparently insignificant scenes is structured into a world of great complexity.

This use of ordinary surfaces requires great skill and discipline since the audience can sense every false move and movement, every false note in the dialogue, every unsubstantiated relationship. The very thing that works *for* the film-maker if he can master it — reality — can quickly turn against him, so that the most ordinary moment becomes utterly unreal. Not surprisingly most directors avoid the challenge and set their stories in unfamiliar parts, among unusual people and in unusual circumstances.

Because most good films use the language of the commonplace, they tend to have an unassuming appearance, whereas films that make a large claim — that speak nobly and poetically about life, love and death — almost invariably prove to be hollow. A good film is concrete: it creates a sequence of objective situations, actual relationships between people, between people and their circumstances. Thus each moment becomes an objective correlative; that is, feeling (or meaning) rendered in actual, physical terms: objectified.

By contrast, most movies are a series of conventional communicative gestures, dialogues, and actions. Most movie-makers *play* on the feelings of their audience by setting up a sequence of incidents that have a proven effect. The events are not rendered; they are merely *cited*. The films do not use the vocabulary of actuality but rather a second-hand language that has proven effective in other films — a language that is changed only when the audience no longer responds.

This language of conventions gives most pictures the appearance of ludicrous unreality fifteen or twenty years after they have been acclaimed as masterpieces. The dramatic conventions of the 1940's are recognized as a system of hollow clichés by the sixties. When *The Best Years of Our Lives* was first shown, references to the war were enough to make an audience feel strongly about a situation or character without any substantiation whatever; there were feelings abroad which, when touched, produced the desired effect. By 1964 this is no longer true and the tissue of the film disintegrates.

Audiences can be "played" by a skillful movie-maker with a fair amount of predictability, so that even discriminating audiences are easily taken in. At the beginning of Bergman's *Wild Strawberries* Professor Borg dreams that he is on a deserted street with all its doors and windows shuttered tight. He looks up at a clock that has no hands and pulls out his own watch only to find that its hands are missing also. A man appears on the corner with his head averted; when he turns, he has no face and his body dissolves into a pool on the sidewalk. A glass hearse comes down the street and spills a coffin that opens. Borg approaches and discovers his own body in the coffin. The corpse comes to life and tries to pull him in.

The nightmare quality in this sequence is derivative. The deserted, shuttered street, the clock and watch without hands, the glass hearse, the faceless man are all conventions familiar to surrealist painting and literature. Bergman uses them skillfully and with conviction to produce an effect in the audience, but they are not true film images, derived from life and rendered in concrete, physical terms.

There is a similar nightmare in Dreyer's *Vampire*. A young man dreams that he has entered a room with an open coffin in it. He approaches and discovers that he himself is the corpse. The camera now assumes the point-of-view of the dead man: we look up at the ceiling. Voices approach and two carpenters appear in our field of vision. They close the coffin with a lid but we continue to look out through a small glass window. Talking indistinctly, they nail down the lid and plane the edges of the wood. The shavings fall onto the window. One of them has put a candle down on the glass and wax drips onto it. Then the coffin is lifted up and we pass close under the ceiling, through the doorway, beneath the sunlit roofs and the church steeple of a small town — out into the open sky.

Here the detail is concrete: an experience is rendered, not cited; the situation is objective and out of it emerges, very powerfully, the feeling that Dreyer is after: a farewell to life, a last confined look at the earth before the coffin is lowered into the grave. Once again we note that the unassuming detail can render a complex feeling (or meaning) which eludes the more obviously ambitious but abstract statement.

Good film dialogue, too, has this concrete quality. Like the speech of everyday life, it does not tell you *directly* what is felt or meant. One might call it symptomatic dialogue: symptomatic because it is a surface manifestation of what is going on inside the person. The dialogue in most films is, of course, the opposite: a direct statement of feeling or meaning: "I love you"; "I am so happy"; "You are this"; "I am that." But just as the action should be a physical or surface correlative that permits the audience to discover for itself the implicit meaning, so the dialogue should be a *surface* that renders its content by implication — not directly. The two lines quoted from *Marty* are good film dialogue. In contrast, here is an incident from Bergman's *The Seventh Seal*.

Shortly before his death the knight Antonius Block shares a meal with a young couple in front of their covered wagon. "I shall always remember this moment," he says. "The silence, the twilight, the bowls of strawberries and milk, your faces in the evening light. Mikhael sleeping, Jof with his lyre. I'll try to remember what we have talked about. I'll carry this moment between my hands as carefully as if it were a bowl filled to the brim with fresh milk. And it will be an adequate sign — it will be enough for me."

Without this lengthy and explicit verbalization, one would have little insight into the feelings of Antonius Block. The situation itself does not communicate them and Bergman uses dialogue as a way of getting us to understand and feel something the film itself does not render. In Kurosawa's *Ikiru*, a petty official who is dying of cancer and trying desperately to give meaning to his life by pushing a playground project through the sterile bureaucracy, stops on his way home from work to look at the evening sky. "It's beautiful," he says to his companion, "but I have no time." Here the dialogue is part of the objective situation. No direct statement is needed since the man and his feelings are clear.

What is true for dialogue is equally true for performance. A good film performance is a carefully integrated sequence of concrete actions and reactions that render the feelings and thoughts of a character. It is not a system of hollow gestures that, like bad dialogue, *tell* the audience what is going on. Most film performances are drawn from the vast repertory of acting conventions. Conversely, the good film actor — whether trained in the Method or not — tries to render feelings through the use of surface correlatives. He is not concerned with the demonstration of feeling but with the symptom of feeling.

Chaplin's best work is continuously physical and concrete. If his performance in *The Gold Rush* had been generalized (or conventionalized) the scene in which he boils and eats his shoe would have become preposterous. He executes it, however, in the most careful physical detail. While the shoe is cooking, he pours water over it as if he were basting a bird. He carves and serves it with meticulous care, separating the uppers from the sole as though boning a fish. Then he winds the limp laces around his fork like spaghetti and sucks each nail as if it were a delicate chicken bone. Thus a totally incongruous moment is given an absolute, detailed physicality; the extraordinary is made ordinary, credible — and therefore funny.

It must be noted again that while the screen exceeds all other media in verisimilitude, its reality is nevertheless a *mode*. We appear to be looking at reality but are actually looking at a representation of it that may be as carefully structured as a still-life by Cézanne. The film-maker uses the surfaces of life itself — literal photographic images and accurately reproduced sounds. But the arrangement of these images and sounds is totally controlled. Each moment, each detail is carefully coordinated into the structure of the whole — just like the details in a painting or poem. By artfully controlling his images, the film-maker presents an unbroken realistic surface; he preserves the appearance of reality.

This means that he should at no time interpose himself between audience and action. He must be absent from the scene. An example of this is the use of the camera. In the standard film the camera is often editorial; the director uses it to *point out* to the audience what he wants them to see. Imagine a scene between husband and wife: we see them in a medium-shot, talking; then we cut to a close-up of the woman's hand and discover that she is slipping her wedding ring off and on. The director has made his point: we now know that she is unhappily married. But by artificially lifting the detail out of context and bringing it to our attention, the autonomous reality of the scene is violated and the audience becomes aware of the film-maker. Of course a good director may also be said to use the camera editorially — to point out what he wants us to see. But he never seems to be doing so; he preserves the appearance of an autonomous reality on the screen. The moment with the ring would have been incidental to the scene — for the camera must follow the action, not lead it.

Since the process of editing is an obvious and continued intrusion by the film-maker on the material, an editor tries to make most of his cuts in such a way that the cut itself will be obscured. In order to cut from a medium-shot to a close-up of a man, he will probably use a moment when the man rises from a chair or turns rapidly. At such a time the audience is watching the action and is unaware of the jump; once again, the effort is to preserve an apparently autonomous reality.

At the end of *Notti di Cabiria* the girl and the man she has just married are sitting in a restaurant. We see her from the back, talking. Then Fellini cuts to a shot from the front and we see that she has taken out a large wad of bank notes — her savings. We immediately realize, with something of a shock, that the man is after her money. If Fellini had actually *shown* us Cabiria taking the money out of her pocketbook, the moment would have become self-conscious and overloaded with meaning; we would have had too much time to get the point. By jumping the moment and confronting us suddenly with the money, Fellini renders the meaning *and* preserves the apparent autonomy of the situation.

Spontaneity, the sense that what is happening on the screen is

happening for the first time and without plan or direction, is an essential factor in establishing a reality. It is also extremely difficult to
achieve since a huge industry has sprung up around the medium, putting enormous financial and technical pressure on the moment before
the camera. Years of routine and a high degree of established skill in
every department of film-making all conspire against it. From writing
and casting to the angles of the camera a monstrous if unintended
predictability crushes all life. Even a strong director is often helpless
against the machinery; and even location shooting, which should be a
liberating force, turns into a dead-end when a huge crew descends on
the place, seals it off hermetically and effectively turns it into a
studio. The channels have been set up too long and too well; all
vision is trapped into standardized imagery and the living moment
cannot survive.

For this reason an almost improvised film — like *Shadows* or
Breathless, made without great skill or art by relatively inexperienced
people — can carry far greater conviction than the standard theatrical
product. In spite of obvious flaws there is a spontaneity to the action
that endows it with life. Of course the experienced director, working
in freedom and under good conditions, can achieve spontaneity without relying on improvisation. Kurosawa shot parts of *The Seven
Samurai* with several cameras; this made it unnecessary for the
actors to repeat, and so deaden, the action with every shift in camera
position. Chaplin, on the other hand, used to rehearse and shoot end-
lessly to achieve a perfect but seemingly effortless result. Both men
were after the same thing: spontaneity — and with it, reality.

Our sense of reality is so delicately attuned that certain moments
are better left off the screen or the situation is destroyed. This is
especially true for violence and death. When someone's head is cut
off in a fiction film we know perfectly well that a trick is employed
and unless a scene of this kind is handled with great care, it ends up
being incredible or even funny. Similarly, when someone dies on the
screen and remains in full view, many of us cannot resist watching
for the slightest sign of life in the supposed corpse. We are pitting our
own sense of reality against the movie-maker's; needless to say, *we*
come out on top and the scene is destroyed.

In Dreyer's unproduced script on the life of Christ he describes
the crucifixion by showing us the back of the cross, with the points of
the nails splintering through the wood. On the screen these would be
undeniably real nails going through real wood, and the authenticity of
the moment would not be challenged. If, however, Dreyer had chosen
to show us the cross from the front we would know absolutely that
the nails going through the *flesh* are a deception — and the suffering
figure would turn into a performer.

The nail splintering through the wood forces us to use our imagination — forces us to visualize what is happening on the other side of
the cross. This involves us in a far deeper participation than could be
achieved by the spurious horror of a nail going through the flesh of
an actor.

There is something to be learned here about the entire process of
perception in film. If we are explicitly told something, as we are in
most pictures we remain passive and essentially outsiders. If, however, we have to draw our *own* conclusions on the basis of evidence
presented, as we do in life itself, we cannot help but participate. We
become actively involved. When we are told something explicitly, we
are in a sense deprived of the experience. It has been digested for us
and we are merely informed of the results, or the meaning. But it is
experience we are after, even if it remains vicarious experience.

This brings us to another characteristic of the medium — one that
is profoundly related to our previous discussion. Although the experience of the motion picture audience remains essentially vicarious,
film comes closer than any other medium to giving us the illusion of a
primary experience. This has been studied by psychologists who have
found that the dark theater, the bright hypnotic screen, the continuous
flow of images and sounds, and the large anonymous audience in
which we are submerged all contribute to a suspension of self-awareness and a total immersion in the events on the screen.

Beyond this, however, the medium itself encourages the illusion
of a primary participation. The camera can induce an almost physical
response — so that when Chaplin sits on a hypodermic needle in the
lair of a dope fiend, or when Dreyer's Jeanne d'Arc has her head
shaved and some of the hair falls onto her lip, the sensation produced
in us is almost physical. Moreover, this physical participation is not
limited to sharp sensory detail; it extends to the realm of movement.

Most directors think of the screen as of a *picture frame* within
which each shot is carefully composed. They emphasize the *pictorial*
quality of film. But while the medium is visual, it is not pictorial in
the conventional sense. A sequence of beautifully composed shots
tends to leave the audience outside the frame — spectators who are
continually aware of the director's fine eye for composition. A good
director tries to eliminate this distance between audience and action,
to destroy the screen as a picture frame, and to drag the audience
through it into the reality of the scene. That is the function of the
running shots in *Rashomon* and of the extraordinarily emphatic
camerawork of Fellini, who leans subtly into every movement and
propels us into the action kinesthetically. By contrast, we have the

autonomous camera motion and stiff pictorial composition of most films.

Images of movement rather than beautifully composed shots are at the heart of the medium, and significantly some of the most haunting moments in film derive their effect from motion. In Vigo's *L' Atalante*, a bride on her wedding night, still dressed in her white gown, walks along the deck of a moving barge. The barge moves forward, she is walking toward the stern, and the camera is set on the edge of the canal, so that there is a dark stationary line in the foreground. The combination of the silent forward gliding of the barge with the backward motion of the girl, whose gown and veil are streaming in the wind, has a profound emotional impact; it renders perfectly both her feelings and our own.

At the end of *Ikiru* the dying bureaucrat has succeeded in building the playground. It is a winter night; the camera moves slowly past a jungle-gym; beyond it we see the old man, swaying to and fro on a child's swing and singing to himself under the falling snow. The various components of this scene are hard to separate: the hoarse, cracked voice of the dying man; his happiness; the song itself. But the motion of the camera, the falling snow, and the slow movement of the swing certainly contribute to the extraordinary sense of peace and reconciliation that is communicated by the image.

A last example: in Dreyer's *Day of Wrath*, a witch is burned in a seventeenth-century town. We see her bound to the top rungs of a tall ladder. Then Dreyer cuts to a long-shot and side view: on the left a huge pile of faggots is burning; to the right soldiers are raising the ladder toward the fire by means of long poles. When it stands perpendicular, they topple it forward so that the woman falls screaming across the entire frame toward the flames. The falling arc described by the victim is rendered in coldly objective terms, from far away — but it transmits her terror completely and draws us relentlessly into the action.

Kurosawa has developed a way of staging that makes it hard for an audience to remain detached. On the theory that no one should be seen entirely from the back, many directors stage their scenes in a three-quarter view. As a result, no one is seen full-face: we look at the actors, but they look away. In *Rashomon* and *The Seven Samurai*, however, the actors either have their backs to camera or face us frontally. When they face us, they are all but looking at us — with only their eyes turned slightly left or right of lens to indicate that they are addressing each other and not us. Of course a face seen frontally is much more exposed than a three-quarter view, and far less likely to leave us detached.

Film can further strengthen the illusion of a primary experience by using a subjective point-of-view. In the ancient and Elizabethan theaters, while we remain in objective possession of the entire stage, the poetry and particularly the soliloquy can focus our attention on one person and shift it to his point-of-view. At any given moment the world can be seen through his eyes, subjectively. In the realistic theater, with its fidelity to the surfaces of everyday life, this has become difficult if not impossible. We *know* how Ibsen's Nora sees the world but except for rare moments do not *experience* it from her point-of-view. She cannot, as it were, reach out and envelop us in her vision — as Hamlet and Lear can.

On the screen it again becomes possible to shift from an objective vision of a person to a vision of what *he* sees. This is done continually, often with little understanding or control. We see a girl enter a room in an objective shot. Then the camera renders what *she* sees: there is a party and her husband is talking to another woman. The next moment might be objective again, or it might be seen from the husband's point-of-view. Montage makes it possible to shift from objective to subjective, or from one subjective point-of-view to another. Film can render a place, a person, or a situation not just as they are but in the context of the protagonist's experience — *as* his experience. A point-of-view can be so carefully articulated that we comprehend every object, every passing figure, every gesture and mood in terms of the protagonist. The medium thus extends the meaning of realistic surfaces beyond their objective value; it renders them in their subjective context as well.

This brings us to an apparent paradox, for we have insisted throughout that film is at its best when rendering an objective situation. It is true, of course, that a moment can be rendered subjectively on the screen and still retain its objective reality. When the girl sees her husband talking to another woman, we see them through her eyes and so become privy to a subjective state. But the husband and the other women are *in themselves* rendered objectively: they look no different; they are not affected by the point-of-view. The basic language of the medium, the realistic surface, has not been violated. The same may be said of most flash-backs: a subjective recollection is rendered — but in objective, undistorted terms.

There are, however, moments on the screen in which the realistic surface is in fact destroyed and a purely subjective state is created. The processional at the end of Vigo's *Zéro de Conduite* is shot in slow-motion, with the boys in their white gowns gliding through a snow of pillow feathers to the accompaniment of a totally distorted but oddly ecstatic song. In such scenes, and it must be noted that while they are often attempted they do not often succeed, the reality of the feeling is so compelling that an audience accepts and assimilates a totally subjective image. The participation is so intensive that instead of rejecting an image we know to be "unreal," we enter into it eagerly.

When successful, scenes of this kind are deeply moving for they are predicated on a rare and free flow of feeling between audience and material. But they are moments of grace and cannot be counted on — like those rare moments in a performance when pure feeling breaks out of the actor and is communicated directly, without the mediation of a physical correlative.

By and large the language of the medium remains the surface of reality, and there seem to be few experiences that cannot be rendered in this language. Moreover, there is a great challenge in making the commonplaces of life, that have so long eluded art, yield up their meaning and take their rightful place in the larger patterns of existence. Film is indeed, as Kraeauer put it, the redemption of physical reality. For we are finally able to use the much-despised and ephemeral detail of everyday life, the common physical dross, and work it into the gold of art.

The Seventh Art
as Sixth Sense

TED PERRY

One of the problems which has occupied film theorists is the ontological relationship between the objects in front of the camera and the image subsequently seen on the screen. The problem arises because film is thought of as the most realistic of the media; that is, it seems to be capable of producing an image which shares the ontological status of its model. The image seems to be a re-presentation of what was in front of the camera. This representational quality has bothered film theorists for it seems to imply that the image is only a copy of what is in front of the camera. If the image is only a copy, it has no aesthetic stature of its own. The Russians suggested in response to this problem that the formative elements were contained in montage, in the way in which the units of meaning were juxtaposed. The German expressionists suggested that such things as decor and camera work were the formative forces. Other theorists, such as Arnheim, have presented very comprehensive cases for the way in which the medium is not at all realistic but a highly conventionalized abstraction of the world in front of the camera. The most recent discussion of this problem is found in the works of André Bazin and Jean Mitry, with Bazin maintaining that the film image reveals reality itself and Mitry countering with the view that the image is a unique perception, co-ordinate with the world in front of the camera but uniquely different from that world. Much of this discussion, of course, is plagued with a lack of definition and a confusion over the use of such terms as reality. Moreover, except for the arguments advanced by Bazin and Mitry, the discussion has centered around specifying what are the formative elements of the cinema. What has not been done with any precision, I think, is to specify the ontological status of the cinema. In other words, given the formative elements of the cinema, what is the relationship between the film poem and nature, between the experience mediated by the cinematic process and the experience available without the cinematic process? While this particular issue is the generative force behind the paper which follows, I would like to believe that the position argued herein is applicable not only to film but to most of what is called art.

Simply stated, the argument I wish to make is that the cinema experience is totally unique and in no sense an experience available prior to, or apart from, the cinema. There is no such thing as the camera which acts as a recording device, reproducing some world which exists in front of the camera. The world on the screen is a world constituted by the cinematic process, regardless of the degree to which it seems faithful to a world supposed to exist in front of the camera.

This opinion of the cinema has its basis in certain views of cognitive growth and in the nature of the mind.[1] These theories suggest that one of the most important ways man has of dealing with his environment is by constructing an image or representation of the environment within his nervous system. In other words, by processing and coding the information available to him, man

---

[1] The terms mind and nervous system are both used in this paper to refer to the self which perceives, remembers, imagines, feels, conceives, reasons, wills, etc.

produces a representation or an image of the environment. Bruner
suggests that there are several types of representations, namely
enactive, iconic, and symbolic.[2] Once a person has learned to ride a
bicycle, for instance, his nervous system contains the enactive
representation of bicycle riding, and it would take only a moment for
him to implement that representation when he used a bicycle. The
nervous system also contains numerous iconic representations, that
is, images which stand for perceptual events. Symbolic representation,
on the other hand, functions primarily through language. Words, and
combinations of words, stand for phenomena. Through these three
modes of representation, and perhaps others, man constructs images
of his environment which enable him to cope with, and relate himself
to, the environment.

One might conclude very readily that human cognitive growth is
essentially the development of the internal capacities necessary to
process and code information into more and more complex and
useful representations. The anthropological evidence seems to
indicate, however, that cognitive growth has occurred, not through
the development of the nervous system, that is, from the inside out,
but rather from the outside in. Man's cognitive growth seems to
follow from his use of tools and other extensions of his nervous
system. In other words, man's growth seems to follow from his ability
to construct more and more complex and meaningful images or
representations, and the growth in his ability to create these
representations comes about through the creation and use of implementation systems which unlock and amplify certain human powers.
Some implementation systems serve to amplify motor acts, as with
the wheel and the lever; other implementation systems serve to amplify perceptions, as with the telephone and radar; and other implementation systems amplify ratiocinative activities, as with language.
Cognitive growth occurs through the use of these implementation sys-
ems, or amplifiers of human powers, because, as Bruner says:

> Any implement system, to be effective, must produce an appropri-
> ate internal counterpart, an appropriate skill necessary for organiz-
> ing sensorimotor acts, for organizing percepts, and for organizing
> our thoughts in a way that matches them to the requirements of
> implement systems.[3]

To summarize, then, cognitive growth seems to occur as man
builds new images or representations of his environment; he builds
new images by making use of implementation systems which amplify

[2] Jerome S. Bruner, "The Course of Cognitive Growth," *American Psychologist,* XIX, No. 1 (1964), 2.
    [3] *Ibid.,* p. 1.

his powers. Human growth, therefore, occurs as innovative implementation systems are developed. These innovations are transmitted to us,
Bruner notes, by agents of the culture; that is, by prototypic "ways of
responding, ways of looking and imaging, and most important, ways
of translating what one has encountered into language."[4]

There are some important aspects of this argument about the
course of cognitive growth. In the first place, it is important to note
that what man calls reality is merely a conglomerate of the various
images or representations produced by his nervous system. When
amplified by various implementation systems, the nervous system
may be capable of producing multiple images of the environment, but
they are still images and not the environment itself. For instance, the
perceptual system, without amplification, is not sensitive to the infrared portion of the electromagnetic spectrum. Thus the infrared is
not included in the usual image of reality or the environment. If
man's perceptual system were sensitive to the infrared, any image of
the environment would have to include that information. In short,
images of the environment are limited by the sensitivity of the
perceptual system. A person's image of reality is not a copy of what
is "out there," for he is only sensitive to part of the information. In
other words, what man calls reality is merely an image, or better yet,
a conglomerate of various images, and this reality is constructed from
the information collected by the nervous system. The data given to
man's perceptual system are by no means all of the data "out there."
What man calls reality, then, is nothing more than the representation
constructed out of the kaleidoscopic chaos of information given to
the sensory apparatus. The amazing thing, of course, is that to man
this symbolic world, these images in the nervous system, seems to be
the world, *the* non-ego. The images of the environment seem to be the
environment.

There is another very important aspect of this argument about
the nature of cognitive growth. In the use of such terms as image and
representation, there is an implication that the symbolic processes
produce a copy of the environment. It seems to me, however, that
there is a good deal of evidence, both theoretical and experimental, to
suggest that the mind or nervous system is constitutive in knowing;
that is, the mind in some sense adds to what it is given. The
constitutive power of the mind is derived not only from the
operations of the mind itself but also from the implementation
systems used by the mind to amplify its powers. All means of
knowing alter and shape what is known. Language, for instance, is
not only a symbol system which produces a representation of the en-

4 *Ibid.*, p. 13.

vironment, it is also a lattice work which determines how man perceives the environment. By manipulating language, for instance, it is possible to produce a new reality from the same information. The transformational rules of grammar provide a syntactic means of re-working the "realities" one has encountered. Not only, for instance, did the man play the piano, but the piano was played by the man. As Bruner points out, for instance:

> Once the child has succeeded in internalizing language as a cognitive instrument, it becomes possible for him to represent and systematically transform the regularities of experience with far greater flexibility and power than ever before.[5]

Some implementation systems are capable of producing several images of reality, all based on the same data and all providing us with the opportunity for new insights, new thoughts, and new actions. The transformation which is true within one implementation system, such as language, is also true across implementation systems; that is, each implementation system produces a different image of the en-vironment, a different reality, one based upon the sensitivity of the system and the principles of processing and coding information. Certain images of the environment are useful in one situation and not in others. The iconic representation of a bicycle is not very helpful in learning to ride a bicycle; an enactive representation of bicycle riding cannot be sent through the mail. Every image of the environment serves a different function. The more images man has of his environment, the more realities, the more he unlocks his internal skills or capacities and the more able he is to cope with his en-vironment. He produces additional images of the environment by creating and using multiple implementation systems because each im-plementation system produces a different image of the environment, a different reality. I do not mean to imply that the various im-plementation systems produce images which are merely different facets of the environment. Each system constitutes the image it produces; that is, it adds to and restructures the information given to it. To say that the various implementation systems are constitutive is to say that they are capable of producing new insights.

Given these views of cognitive processes, I think it is possible to make several statements about the cinema experience, with particular reference to the relationship between man's experience of the environment without the camera intervening and the experience me-diated by the camera and the film-maker.

In the first place, I should think the cinema may be seen as an

[5] *Ibid.*, p. 4.

innovative implementation system which is capable of amplifying human powers to the point of achieving new images or re-presentations of the environment. In this sense, the cinema is an extension of man's nervous system, an extension which informs man about the environment. It informs man, not so much by producing new information but rather by changing man, by altering his patterns of perception so that he receives new insights. As an extension of the nervous system or the mind, the cinema has the power of translating experience into new forms, more useful and understandable. Film creates new realities. It is a way of letting go of the environment in order to grasp it in a new way. As an extension of the nervous system, the cinema is a means of amplifying man's rational and perceptual powers.

This image of the environment produced by the cinema is not a copy of the environment because the medium, the cinema, is constitutive. No matter how objective the cinema might seem to be, nevertheless, as a medium of knowing it does shape and add to the information it processes and codes. The cinema therefore produces a new model or representation of the environment, absolutely separate from the environment and uniquely different from other images of the environment. This view by no means is meant to imply that what the cinema does is imitate some aspect of the world presently hidden from man or that it selects and abstracts from the environment, as Arnheim seems to imply at times. Rather, like the mind, or any other medium of knowing, the cinema is constitutive. Just as the mind adds to what is known in order to produce a unique perception, so also does the cinema. The formative processes of the mind and those of the cinema enable each to constitute a unique image of the environment, a new reality. The things the cinema shows do not and cannot exist prior to the cinema; they are constituted by the cinema. Just as there is no world wholly external to human beings, so also is there no world wholly external to the camera which the camera might record and reproduce.

An emphasis upon the constitutive power of the mind or the camera should not overlook, however, that both the mind and the camera are imitative and creative. They are imitative to the extent that they depend upon the external stimuli, and they are creative to the extent that they provide new insights through the constitutive power of the implementation system. The cinematic image may be very realistic, i.e., it may look like images produced by many other implementation systems and the unamplified nervous system, or the cinematic image may be so highly particularized and uniquely constituted by the medium that the viewer sees only moving shapes and colors. In any case, the point is that the cinema enables the mind to produce an image of the world which the mind could not produce through its unamplified system, and this image of the environment is a new insight constituted by the implementation system. Film creates new realities.

There are some immediate implications of the position I am trying to argue. In the first place, the argument serves as a means of understanding many people's boredom with certain newer forms of theater and film. I suspect that the reason these films bore many people is not because the films or plays are uninteresting or bad, but rather because these films and plays present new images of the environment. These new images of the environment cannot be absorbed into the construct man calls reality without making some adjustments in the construct. It is much easier to believe that the construct is a complete, authoritative, accurate picture of reality, if not reality itself. A few images of the environment are therefore taken as sufficient for all the environment, and no new insights are possible. When the universe is a closed system, the film and the theater are expected to reflect a closed notion of what constitutes reality. If this purpose is violated, the resulting films and plays seem dull, boring, and sometimes even infuriating, depending upon how closely integrated are the viewer's notions of reality and his own ego.

Man's images of the environment are *the* world for him; the images are reality. Once these images are accepted as the last word about the environment, however, and become the total picture of reality, then all implementation systems are expected to provide images which are mere replications of this closed world. The experimental evidence indicates that prejudiced persons, for instance, tend to conform the facts of experience into mutations appropriate to their prejudices. Once any man's images of the environment are accepted as the final word about reality, then there is no longer any possibility for forms such as the film or theater to present a new perception, a new image; films and plays are not allowed to constitute a reality but merely to replicate what man takes to be reality.

The film *Last Year at Marienbad* is a good example of what I am discussing. The film's uniqueness, in part, lies in the way it makes use of the motion picture medium to construct a world which cannot be transposed into normal experience. Most films and plays, for instance, specify very precisely what is present reality, what is imagined, what is dreamed, and precisely when the transitions occur from one kind of reality to another. *Last Year at Marienbad* dispenses with these conventions, presenting several realities simultaneously and never specifying what is dreamed, what is remembered, or what is present fact. The film was severely criticized because its events could not be transposed into a narrative which would conform to the usual experience of man caught by the laws of space and time. The defense of the film rests with the argument presented in this paper. The film presents a reality all its own, one constituted by the camera, one which is not meant to reflect some other image of the environment; that is, the film makes no attempt to duplicate the reality construct produced by another implementation system or by the unamplified nervous system. Robbe-Grillet, the author of the scenario, states just this position:

> The universe in which the entire film occurs is, characteristically, that of a perpetual present which makes all resources to memory impossible. This is a world without a past, a world which is self-sufficient at every moment and which obliterates itself as it proceeds. This man, this woman begin existing only when they appear on the screen the first time; before that they are nothing; and, once the projection is over, they are again nothing. Their existence lasts only as long as the film lasts. There can be no reality outside the images we see, the worlds we hear.[6]

Most people find the film boring. I suggest that they find the film boring, and even infuriating, because it offers a new reality, a new perception, a fresh image of the environment. Most people are unwilling to admit this new reality into the construct they think to be reality. If they like experimental films at all, these people prefer that such films adhere to a discontinuity of form which approximates what is thought to be the way in which the inner processes of the mind work. Last Year at Marienbad demonstrates that the cinema does not have to duplicate supposed mental processes but can function in a way that the mind cannot, thereby extending and amplifying the mind.

There are several other implications to be derived from the view that the cinema is a constitutive extension of the nervous system. If cognitive growth occurs by the creation and use of implementation systems which amplify human powers in order to produce new images of the environment, it is also possible that cognitive growth ceases when man accepts his present images or representations of the environment as the final word about the environment. For example, once man accepts his present ways of seeing as the only ways of seeing, then in this area cognitive growth ceases. Consequently, it

---

[6] Alain Robbe-Grillet, For a New Novel, trans. by Richard Howard (New York, 1965), p. 152.

seems to me that one could logically argue for certain newer forms of artistic expression as means of breaking down habitual patterns of seeing. The light show, for instance, seems to be uniquely capable of bombarding the nervous system to the point of overloading. The theory is that this overloading may result in habitual perceptual patterns being bypassed and altered. I do not mean to imply that such artistic forms allow man to reach some sort of noumenal world, but rather that these forms aid in bypassing and correcting the sensory transformations and habitual patterns of seeing in order to produce a clearer, more truthful phenomenal picture of the environment. The same argument would hold true, I think, for the artistic forms produced by non-human means, such as computers, for those forms produced by random methods of organization and construction, and also for those artistic forms in which the spectator is asked to participate in the creation of the art object, perhaps by rearranging its parts. All of these forms, I suggest, are ways of bypassing habitual patterns of perception, of correcting some of those sensory transformations which produce inadequate phenomenal pictures of the world. In short, these new artistic forms are ways of helping man to expand and adjust the construct he calls reality, his world.

If the cinema is truly an implementation system which amplifies human powers and is capable of producing new realities, new images of the environment, then it seems to me there are grounds for suggesting that the impact of the cinema is derived in part from the fact that it presents an image which is both real and unreal; that is, an image which has the illusion of the familiar but which is actually a new perception. No one can doubt the realistic illusion of the motion picture image. It has "thereness," as Robbe-Grillet says. The illusion is so complete that people such as John Wayne and Humphrey Bogart seem to have the same status as a next door neighbor, despite the fact that for most people John Wayne was never anything more than a flickering pattern of shadow and light on a screen. The images man takes to be so real, however, are not just very faithful reproductions but something constituted by the cinematic process. The John Wayne that the viewer knows is a person who only exists on the screen, i.e., in the cinema experience; no doubt that is why it is such a shock and surprise to meet the flesh and blood counterpart of the screen personality. To a great extent, then, the film draws its power, not from being such a good copy of the environment, or what man takes to be reality, but from being a new perception and a new image of the environment which is also realistic, i.e., which has the illusion of being like so many other images man already has. The cinematic process produces something new with the character of being something familiar. Indeed, Robbe-Grillet says that what most attracts the artist to the cinema is the "possibility of presenting with all the appearance of incontestable objectivity what is, also, only dream or memory — in a word, what is only imagination."[7]

An argument that the cinema is a constitutive extension of the nervous system may also support the view, once stated by Oscar Wilde, that life imitates art. In other words, by using a number of implementation systems to produce multiple images of the world, man is better able to know, and to come to grips with, the environment. It is partly through the images of the world produced by the cinema that man comes to know life. This view does not mean that life is something out there which the cinema leads man to discover, for all man ever knows are the images, the shadows dancing on the wall of the Platonic cave. Life is itself composed of, and constituted by, the images man has of his environment. The images are his reality.

In summary, the view I have tried to present is merely that the cinema offers man a way of producing new, unique images of the environment. As such, the cinema is an extension of man's nervous system which is capable of altering his patterns of perception, of introducing new insights. Such a cinema produces experiences uniquely different from the experiences produced without the cinematic process, and therefore its ontological status is different from that of a mere reproduction or from that of a mere discoverer of things hidden in the environment. The ontological status of the cinema is more akin to that of the images produced by man's perceptual organization; that is, the images produced by the cinematic process are related to the environment in much the same way as the images produced by man's perceptual organization. Each image, whether produced by man's perceptual organization or by the cinema, is constituted by different systems, one by the mind or the nervous system and one by the mind with the cinema plugged into it. Man mistakenly tends to label as reality only the image which his perceptual organization produces. Reality is the product of many images, those produced by the perceptual organization, those produced by the cinema, and those produced by many other implementation systems. Finally, then, film is not just a new way of seeing things, it is also a way of seeing new things, things which did not and could not have existed prior to or apart from the cinema. The cinema therefore is not just a way of reaching out to get new information, but a way of processing the existing information so as to produce a new image of the environment, much as transformational

[7] *Ibid.,* p. 149.

grammar allows man to transpose units of meaning in order to produce new images, new realities. Given the same information, the implementation system can produce an image of the man playing the piano or one of the piano being played by the man. Each image is a different reality, a unique insight. The cinema is a tool which allows man to produce new, unique images of the environment. The more images man has, the more he unlocks his internal capacities necessary to organize these new images, and therefore the more complete and full are the lives that man creates for himself.

Toward True Cinema

SLAVKO VORKAPICH

PART ONE: TWO ASPECTS OF THE MOTION PICTURE: RECORDING AND CREATIVE

The name *motion picture* may stand merely for the technical process which consists in a rapid succession of pictures projected on a screen, or for any kind of popular entertainment produced and presented in such a way, or, among other things, for a truly creative use of a rapid succession of pictures projected on a screen. The name is a general one and a general name is expected to cover a variety of things. But a special meaning of a general name like *painting* becomes immediately apparent when it is placed in a simple context, for example, in "Teaching Painting at a University." Obviously here the sense of creative use of the tools of painting is intended, and not house — or furniture — painting and other similar uses of brush and paint. It may be worth noting that in the case of *painting* the general name is reserved for the creative use of the medium, while other uses have to be qualified.

Now, with the word *creative*, especially in connection with motion pictures, one can get into real semantic and philosophic difficulties if one tries to prove as true one's assumptions about it.

One of my claims is that most of the films made so far are

examples not of creative use of motion picture devices and techniques, but examples of their use as recording instruments and processes only. There are extremely few motion pictures that may be cited as instances of creative use of the medium, and from these only fragments and short passages may be compared to the best achievements in other arts.

Often, when a specific example, like the lunch hour sequence in the documentary *The City*, is mentioned, a number of listeners would come up with some such question: "You mean a series of quick cuts?" — "Do you think it is possible to make a whole picture like that?" — If I mention McLaren's *Fiddle-Dee-Dee*: "Oh, you mean abstract shapes dancing to music?" — If I describe passages from Cocteau's *Beauty and the Beast*, some jump at the conclusion that I mean fantasy and symbolism, and if, with some hesitation, I mention some of my own work I can almost hear a few of them thinking: "Now we know! You mean camera tricks! You mean montage: the Hollywood kind, not the Eisenstein kind! You mean flip-flops and wipes and zooms and the camera on the flying trapeze!"

Perhaps the right answer would be: Yes, all of these things and much more. But first let me try to explain what may *not* be considered as the creative use of the medium, what may be called the *recording* use only, or an *extension* of some other medium of communication or expression.

The technical nature of the film medium is such that it may very easily and profitably be utilized as such an extension. In this sense it may be compared to various uses of printing of words; to various uses of still photography: reporting, keeping records of events, people, things, etc.; to uses of drawing and painting for scientific exposition such as diagrams, charts, and illustrations in books on biology, botany, medicine, etc.; or it may be compared to various uses of the sound recording devices for preserving speeches, lectures, memorable performances of music or for making transcriptions of radio shows. In fact, the film medium *is* used mostly as an extension of each of the various media mentioned. And it is natural that the chief value in such films should lie in that which is recorded: the event, the performance, the person, or the object photographed and the verbal and sound accompaniment that usually goes with it. Rarely is it required that the value consist in a unique filmic structure about the subject.

The fact that some of these recordings have been so effective and at times emotionally very moving may have led many people into believing that this efficient power came from the medium itself. Now, no one would call a *phonograph record* of a master conductor's in-

terpretation of a great composer's composition — no one would call
that record a musical masterpiece, no matter how technically perfect
it was. But, quite often, technically polished *visual* and sound
recordings of great performances in various fields have been hailed as
great films. This applies, equally, to most dramatic or story films. Let
me illustrate this with a hypothetical example.

Suppose, we take a piece of creative writing, e.g., the famous
soliloquy from Hamlet, and, suppose, we photograph with a motion
picture camera that passage just as it is printed on the page in a book.
Or, for this particular shot, we may have had the monologue printed
on parchment in some fancy type designed by a creative typographer,
and we may, for extra embellishment, use some real "mood" lighting,
like throwing a faint shadow of "a bare bodkin" upon the page. Now
would this, in a "rapid succession of pictures projected on a screen",
give us a motion picture? Technically, yes. But what creative
contribution was achieved by the use of the motion picture camera,
apart from giving us another *record of Shakespeare's* creative work?
Obviously, none.

Suppose we elaborate a little more on our shooting of the
monologue and we get a creative actor and we dress him in a costume
designed by a creative designer and put him in a setting designed by a
creative art director and we light him with lights full of mood and
photograph him with a motion picture camera and register on film all
his expressive actions and gestures and movements of his lips and
tongue and cheeks and record his voice on the best sound system
available. What do we get this time? A performance really worth
preserving and showing all over the world. *But what have we as*
makers of the picture created except making an embellished record
of an actor's acting of a writer's writing? Again the answer is: obviously nothing. No matter how "amazingly lifelike" the picture may
seem, strictly speaking, this is what was actually achieved: from a
living creative performance a shadow was abstracted by mechanical
means. This applies also to complete photoplays. *Photo plays,* how
precisely descriptive that name is!

At this point the thought of the close-up as a real filmic
contribution usually comes up. The close view is not something
specifically filmic, if it is taken in the sense of something brought
closer or magnified for closer scrutiny only. Long before the advent
of the film, the close-up was to be found in all except stage arts and
music. Portraits and still lives in painting, sculpture, and still
photography; descriptive detail in literature.

There is a controversy about who "invented" the close-up.
Probably the inventor got the idea from observing someone in the

audience of a theater — a *legitimate* theater, of course — who was using a pair of binoculars to see an actor's or an actress' face at close range. And it is mainly in this telescopic sense that the close-up is still used. No doubt that it adds dramatic emphasis to a photoplay and thus makes up for some of the loss of the performers' living presence. Still we are talking in terms of the theater, and still we are using the medium to record bits of that other art, the actor's creative acting. Let me at this point make clear that I am not opposed to the use of the film medium as an extension of the theater, I only object to calling such extension creative use of the unique characteristics inherent in cinematography.

Considered filmically or creatively, the close-up has two main functions: visual-dynamic and associative. Close-up here means close view of anything relatively small. We react bodily, kinesthetically to any visual change. As a rule the bigger the change the stronger the reaction. For example, in a sudden cut from a long view of an object to a very close view of it there is, always, an inevitable optical and kinesthetic impact, an explosive magnification, a sudden leap forward. If the object is in motion, the close-up intensifies this motion; as a rule, the greater the area of the screen is in motion the greater the intensity. This seems obvious. And thinking in these terms, one should, obviously, be led into thinking of *degrees* of change, impact, and intensity, and how important — if one hopes to use film creatively — the relative organization of these factors must be. To use a visual medium artistically is to make the visual parts "go well together." Problems of duration, harmony, contrast, proportion, and rhythm, are involved in this sort of visual-dynamic organization, i.e., cutting, which is quite different from editing a sequence of long shots, medium shots, and close-ups according to literary-dramatic requirements only. And a little more thinking in this direction leads one to deeper fundamental differences, through proper shooting for that sort of cutting, down to the original conception, to the problem of how to express a theme filmically. And that is a long way from the stage.

In a close-up an object appears somehow dissociated from its context. It is thus more or less liberated and made available for new combinations, both in respect of its visual values and meaning connotations. The latter are called "association-fields" by Gyorgy Kepes in his remarkable book *Language of Vision*. (Although primarily a study of visual principles operative in static graphic arts, this book is full of fruitful suggestions applicable to motion pictures.) In certain combinations with other fields an object acquires a quality that may be compared to that of a poetic image, but this similarity should not be taken too literally. Each different aspect of the same object has a unique quality and thus it differs from a word, which is more readily variable in a different context. The possibilities of creative organization of filmic imagery are so little known and explored (to some extent by Cocteau) that it seems like an insolence to compare our crude gropings with masterpieces of other arts.

It is clear that the emphasis here is on visual values. But this means more than striking photography, unusual camera angles, and ingenious dolly and boom shots. It is not a question of artistically composed tableaux. It is a problem of composing visually, but in time. Individual shots may be incomplete, as individual musical tones are incomplete in themselves, but they must be "just right and go well together" with other shots, as tones must with other tones, to make complete and esthetically satisfying units. Beautiful photography is only surface embellishment, while *cinematography* is the gathering of visual-dynamic-meaningful elements, which creative cutting combines into living entities.

The emphasis, then, is on the development of a visual dynamic language, independent of literature and theatrical traditions. The emphasis on the visual aspect does not exclude creative use of sound. It is, however, somewhat amusing to read a chapter on "counterpoint between sound and image" when no one can claim to have mastered the fundamental organization of the factors spoken of in connection with the close-up.

No doubt, the film medium is related, in some ways, to other arts. But relation does not imply imitation. It may learn from other media, but, if it is to be dignified with the name of art, it must not merely copy. In art "speaking likeness" is not a criterion of value.

PART TWO: A METHOD OF TEACHING
THE CREATIVE USE OF THE MEDIUM

In essential ways the motion picture medium is unique. And to the study of the possibilities inherent in the medium a method has to be worked out. I can give here only a rough idea of certain aspects of such a method, based on my own experiences teaching film at the Department of Cinema at the University of Southern California.

The teaching should be based on a literal interpretation of the name of the medium: *motion pictures. Pictures* should be taken in the sense of *images*. The goal is integration of motion, image, meaning, and sound, but at the beginning the emphasis should be laid on the first part of the name: *motion.*

An effort should be made to dissociate the meaning of the word from certain undesirable connotations. It does not stand merely for stage action, nor a certain type of agitation now so popular with film directors. This may be exemplified by the "movements" of a star, who, during the span of a brief dialogue moves from the couch to the fireplace and to the window, where with a toss she turns her back to her lover and comes to rest, staring out of the window. Nor does it stand merely for a perpetual agitation of the camera, also very popular with the movie directors, who treat the camera like an infant who is not satisfied until it is perambulated or dollied about. The students are asked to make a fresh mental start, if they can, by forgetting, for a while, the daily film fare they have seen. It is then explained that a whole new world is open to them for exploration: the world of motion.

The invention of the cinematic tools has not only given us the means to make "amazingly lifelike" recordings, it has also extended, immensely, the possibility of a heightened perceptual grasp of reality.

In static visual arts students are trained in a sensitive perception of the shape of things, while here they are directed toward a keener perception of the *shapes of the motions* that things generate. At first they are required to observe simple motions. An example of a simple motion would be a segment of space as it is cut out by a door opening or closing, a complex motion would be one traced by a newspaper dancing high in the wind. The emphasis is on object motion, because of the geometric simplicity of such motions. The students are requested to observe, analyze, compare, classify, and describe these motions.

The human perceptive mechanism is such that it may interpret as motion certain phenomena where no actual motion occurs. This was thoroughly investigated by Gestalt psychologists and is called phi-phenomenon or apparent movement. "Under appropriate conditions successive presentation of two lights at two points not too distant from each other results in an experience of movement from the first to the second" (Koehler). Our experiments show that there is a sensation of displacement or a visual leap in a cut between any two sufficiently different shots. This may be demonstrated very vividly if short strips of the shots, approximately ten frames each, are rapidly alternated. In certain cases a clear transformation of one shape into another may be experienced. By making their own selections of shots or designs and intercutting them in various ways students become aware of a new purely filmic force: more or less intense visual impact that occurs at each cut.

The project following these exercises consists in a thorough observation of a complete simple activity or occupation where a limited variety of motions is involved. Again the emphasis is on the motions of objects, for example in the wrapping of a package, preparing food, loading of a truck, etc. The complete action is broken down into as many simple motions as possible and each is shot from a great variety of angles. This kind of analysis, or over-analysis, is different from recording previously discussed. Here the motion picture camera is in its natural element. This process is really a filmic liberation of bits of dynamic visual energies, extracted from a simple event in reality. Each angle is selected to take hold of a single clear visual note. None is intended for an individual display as a "best shot" in the picture, not any more than a note is intended to be the best in a melody. In the re-creation of the event in cutting, each filmic facet acquires value only by its place in the total filmic structure. And the student's sense for structure grows out of these exercises in analysis.

Sometimes, in cutting, the movements are slightly overlapped, i.e. each new fragment begins a little back of the point already reached by the preceding fragment; in other words, in each new strip a small fraction of the preceding movement is repeated. Often surprisingly beautiful effects result. A sort of rhythmical time-stretching occurs. There are several striking instances of this effect in Eisenstein's earlier films.

Most students soon will become aware that very simple everyday actions may be made exciting by means of filmic analysis, and that there is a new kind of visual beauty to be found in the ordinary world around them. One can say that where there is physical action there is visual poetry.

The next stage in the student's work should consist in exploring the associative possibilities between images. Students should be asked to make simple statements entirely by visual means. Some may become capable of expressing truly poetic moods; those with vivid imaginations may bring in surprisingly effective free combinations of images, while others may succeed in making simple documentaries interesting and visually exciting.

The work done this way may be compared to the creation of simple melodies. Once the student has mastered this elementary process, he should be prepared to orchestrate several movements within a shot and to achieve a more complex organization of images for themes of greater complexity, so that perhaps, some day, he may learn how to make, not *photoplays*, but dramatic *motion pictures*.

Notes on the Auteur Theory in 1962

ANDREW SARRIS

> I call these sketches Shadowgraphs, partly by the designation to remind you at once that they derive from the darker side of life, partly because like other shadowgraphs they are not directly visible. When I take a shadowgraph in my hand, it makes no impression on me, and gives me no clear conception of it. Only when I hold it up opposite the wall, and now look not directly at it, but at that which appears on the wall, am I able to see it. So also with the picture which I wish to show here, an inward picture which does not become perceptible until I see it through the external. This external is perhaps quite unobtrusive but not until I look through it, do I discover that inner picture which I desire to show you an inner picture too delicately drawn to be outwardly visible, woven as it is of the tenderest moods of the soul.
>
> — Soren Kierkegaard, *Either/Or*

An exhibitor once asked me if an old film I had recommended was *really* good or good only according to the *auteur* theory. I appreciate the distinction. Like the alchemists of old, *auteur* critics are notorious for rationalizing leaden clinkers into golden nuggets. Their judgments are seldom vindicated because few spectators are conditioned to perceive in individual works the organic unity of a director's career. On a given evening, a film by John Ford must take its chances as if it were a film by Henry King. Am I implying that the weakest Ford is superior to the strongest King? Yes! This kind of unqualified affirmation seems to reduce the *auteur* theory to a game of aesthetic solitaire with all the cards turned face up. By *auteur* rules, the Fords will come up aces as invariably as the Kings will come up deuces. Presumably we can all go home as soon as the directorial signature is flashed on the screen. To those who linger, *The Gunfighter* (King 1950) may appear worthier than *Flesh* (Ford 1932). (And how deeply one must burrow to undermine Ford!) No matter. The *auteur* theory is unyielding. If, by definition, Ford is invariably superior to King, any evidence to the contrary is merely an optical illusion. Now what could be sillier than this inflexible attitude? Let us abandon the absurdities of the *auteur* theory so that we may return to the chaos of common sense.

My labored performance as devil's advocate notwithstanding, I intend to praise the *auteur* theory, not to bury it. At the very least, I would like to grant the condemned system a hearing before its execution. The trial has dragged on for years, I know, and everyone is now bored by the abstract reasoning involved. I have little in the way of new evidence or new arguments, but I would like to change some of my previous testimony. What follows is consequently less a manifesto than a credo, a somewhat disorganized credo, to be sure, expressed in formless notes rather than in formal brief.

I. AIMEZ-VOUS BRAHMS?

> Goethe? Shakespeare? Everything signed with their names is considered good, and one wracks one's brains to find beauty in their stupidities and failures, thus distorting the general taste. All these great talents, the Goethes, the Shakespeares, the Beethovens, the Michelangelos, created, side by side with their masterpieces, works not merely mediocre, but quite simply frightful.
>
> — Tolstoy, *Journal*, 1895–1899

The preceding quotation prefaces the late Andre Bazin's famous critique of *la politique des auteurs* which appeared in the *Cahiers du Cinema* of April 1957. Because no comparably lucid statement opposing the *politique* has appeared since that time, I would like to discuss some of Bazin's arguments with reference to the current situation. (I except, of course, Richard Roud's penetrating article, *The French Line*, which dealt mainly with the post-*nouvelle vague* situation when the *politique* had degenerated into McMahonism.)

As Tolstoy's observation indicates, *la politique des auteurs* antedates the cinema. For centuries, the Elizabethan *politique* has decreed the reading of every Shakespearean play before any encounter with the Jonsonian repertory. At some point between *Timon of Athens* and *Volpone*, this procedure is patently unfair to Jonson's reputation. But not really. On the most superficial level of artistic reputations, the *auteur* theory is merely a figure of speech. If the man in the street could not invoke Shakespeare's name as an identifiable cultural reference, he would probably have less contact with all things artistic. The Shakespearean scholar, by contrast, will always be driven to explore the surrounding terrain with the result that all the Elizabethan dramatists gain more rather than less recognition through the pre-eminence of one of their number. Therefore on balance, the *politique* as a figure of speech does more good than harm.

Occasionally, some iconoclast will attempt to demonstrate the fallacy of this figure of speech. We will be solemnly informed that *The Gambler* was a potboiler for Dostoevski in the most literal sense of the word. In Jacques Rivette's *Paris nous appartient*, Jean-Claude Brialy asks Betty Schneider if she would still admire *Pericles* if it were not signed by Shakespeare. Zealous musicologists have played *Wellington's Victory* so often as an example of inferior Beethoven that I have grown fond of the piece, atrocious as it is. The trouble with such iconoclasm is that it presupposes an encyclopedic awareness of the *auteur* in question. If one is familiar with every Beethoven composition, *Wellington's Victory*, in itself, will hardly tip the scale toward Mozart, Bach or Schubert. Yet, that is the issue raised by the *auteur* theory. If not Beethoven, who? And why? Let us say that the *politique* for composers went Mozart, Beethoven, Bach and Schubert. Each composer would represent a task force of compositions, arrayed by type and quality with the mighty battleships and aircraft carriers flanked by flotillas of cruisers, destroyers and minesweepers. When the Mozart task force collides with the Beethoven task force, symphonies roar against symphonies, quartets maneuver against quartets, and it is simply no contest with the operas. As a single force, Beethoven's nine symphonies outgun any nine of Mozart's forty-one symphonies, both sets of quartets are almost on a par with Schubert's, but *The Magic Flute*, *The Marriage of Figaro* and *Don Giovanni* will blow poor *Fidelio* out of the water. Then, of course, there is Bach with an entirely different deployment of composition and instrumentation. The Haydn and Handel cultists are moored in their inlets ready to join the fray, and the moderns with their nuclear noises are still mobilizing their forces.

It can be argued that any exact ranking of artists is arbitrary and pointless. Arbitrary up to a point, perhaps, but pointless, no. Even Bazin concedes the polemical value of the *politique*. Many film critics would rather not commit themselves to specific rankings ostensibly because every film should be judged on its own merits. In many instances, this reticence masks the critic's condescension to the medium. Since it has not been firmly established that the cinema is an art at all, it requires cultural audacity to establish a pantheon for film directors. Without such audacity, I see little point in being a film critic. Anyway, is it possible to honor a work of art without honoring the artist involved? I think not. Of course, any idiot can erect a pantheon out of hearsay and gossip. Without specifying any work, the Saganesque seducer will ask quite cynically, "Aimez-vous Brahms?" The fact that Brahms is included in the pantheon of highbrow pick-ups does not invalidate the industrious criticism which justifies the composer as a figure of speech.

Unfortunately, some critics have embraced the *auteur* theory as a short-cut to film scholarship. With a "you-see-it-or-you-don't" attitude toward the reader, the particularly lazy *auteur* critic can save himself the drudgery of communication and explanation. Indeed, at their worst, *auteur* critiques are less meaningful than the straightforward plot reviews which pass for criticism in America. Without the necessary research and analysis, the *auteur* theory can degenerate into the kind of snobbish racket which is associated with the merchandising of paintings.

It was largely against the inadequate theoretical formulation of *la politique des auteurs* that Bazin was reacting in his friendly critique. (Henceforth, I will abbreviate *la politique des auteurs* as the *auteur* theory to avoid confusion.) Bazin introduces his arguments within the context of a family quarrel over the editorial policies of *Cahiers*. He fears that by assigning reviews to admirers of given directors, notably Alfred Hitchcock, Jean Renoir, Roberto Rossellini, Fritz Lang, Howard Hawks and Nicholas Ray, every work, major and minor, of these exalted figures is made to radiate the same beauties of style and meaning. Specifically, Bazin notes a distortion when the kindly indulgence accorded the imperfect work of a Minnelli is coldly withheld from the imperfect work of Huston. The inherent bias of the *auteur* theory magnifies the gap between the two films.

I would make two points here. First, Bazin's greatness as a critic, (and I believe strongly that he was the greatest film critic who ever lived,) rested in his disinterested conception of the cinema as a universal entity. It follows that he would react against a theory which cultivated what he felt were inaccurate judgments for the sake of dramatic paradoxes. He was, if anything, generous to a fault, seeking in every film some vestige of the cinematic art. That he would seek justice for Huston vis-à-vis Minnelli on even the secondary levels of creation indicates the scrupulousness of his critical personality.

However, my second point would seem to contradict my first. Bazin was wrong in this instance insofar as any critic can be said to be wrong in retrospect. We are dealing here with Minnelli in his *Lust for Life* period and Huston in his *Moby Dick* period. Both films can be considered failures on almost any level. The miscasting alone is disastrous. The snarling force of Kirk Douglas as the tormented Van Gogh, the brutish insensibility of Anthony Quinn as Gauguin, and the nervously scraping tension between these two absurdly limited actors, deface Minnelli's meticulously objective decor, itself inappropriate for the mood of its subject. The director's presentation of the paintings themselves is singularly unperceptive in the repeated failure to maintain the proper optical distance from canvases which arouse the spectator less by their detailed draughtsmanship than by the shock of a *gestalt* wholeness. As for *Moby Dick*, Gregory Peck's Ahab deliberates long enough to let all the demons flee the *Pequod*, taking Melville's Lear-like fantasies with them. Huston's epic technique with its casually shifting camera viewpoint then drifts on an intellectually becalmed sea toward a fitting rendezvous with a rubber whale. These two films are neither the best nor the worst of their time. The question is which deserves the harder review. And there's the rub. At the time, Huston's stock in America was higher than Minnelli's. Most critics expected Huston to do "big" things, and, if they thought about it all, expected Minnelli to stick to "small" things like musicals. Although neither film was a critical failure, audiences stayed away in large enough numbers to make the cultural respectability of the projects suspect. On the whole, *Lust for Life* was more successful with the audiences it did reach than was *Moby Dick*.

In retrospect, *Moby Dick* represents the turning downward of Huston as a director to be taken seriously. By contrast, *Lust for Life* is simply an isolated episode in the erratic career of an interesting stylist. The exact size of Minnelli's talent may inspire controversy, but he does represent something in the cinema today. Huston is virtually a forgotten man with a few actors' classics behind him surviving as the ruins of a once-promising career. Both Eric Rohmer, who denigrated Huston in 1957, and Jean Domarchi, who was kind to Minnelli that same year, somehow saw the future more clearly on an *auteur* level than did Bazin. As Santayana has remarked: "It is a great advantage for a system of philosophy to be substantially true." If the *auteur* critics of the Fifties had not scored so many coups of clairvoyance, the *auteur* theory would not be worth discussing in the Sixties. I must add that, at the time, I would have agreed with Bazin on this and every other objection to the *auteur* theory, but subsequent history, that history about which Bazin was always so mystical, has substantially confirmed most of the principles of the *auteur* theory. Ironically, most of the original supporters of the *auteur* theory have now abandoned it. Some have discovered more useful *politiques* as directors and would-be directors. Others have succumbed to a European-oriented pragmatism where intention is now more nearly equal to talent in critical relevance. Luc Moullet's belated discovery that Samuel Fuller was, in fact, fifty years old, signaled a reorientation of *Cahiers* away from the American cinema. (The handwriting was already on the wall when Truffaut remarked recently that where he and his colleagues had "discovered" *auteurs*, his successors have "invented" them.)

Bazin then explores the implications of Giraudoux' epigram:

"There are no works; there are only authors." Truffaut has seized upon this paradox as the battle-cry of *la politique des auteurs*. Bazin casually demonstrates how the contrary can be argued with equal probability of truth or error. He subsequently dredges up the equivalents of *Wellington's Victory* for Voltaire, Beaumarchais, Flaubert and Gide to document his point. Bazin then yields some ground to Rohmer's argument that the history of art does not confirm the decline with age of authentic geniuses like Titian, Rembrandt, Beethoven, or nearer to us, Bonnard, Matisse and Stravinsky. Bazin agrees with Rohmer that it is inconsistent to attribute senility only to aging film directors while at the same time honoring the gnarled austerity of Rembrandt's later style. This is one of the crucial propositions of the *auteur* theory because it refutes the popular theory of decline for aging giants like Renoir and Chaplin, and asserts instead that as a director becomes older, he is likely to become more profoundly personal than most audiences and critics can appreciate. However, Bazin immediately retrieves his lost ground by arguing that whereas the senility of directors is no longer at issue, the evolution of an art-form is. Where directors fail and fall is in the realm not of psychology but of history. If a director fails to keep pace with the development of his medium, his work will become obsolescent. What seems like senility is in reality a disharmony between the subjective inspiration of the director and the objective evolution of the medium. By making this distinction between the subjective capability of an *auteur* and the objective value of a work in film history, Bazin reinforces the popular impression that the Griffith of *Birth of a Nation* is superior to the Griffith of *Abraham Lincoln* in the perspective of timing which similarly distinguishes the Eisenstein of *Potemkin* from the Eisenstein of *Ivan the Terrible*, the Renoir of *La Grande Illusion* from the Renoir of *Picnic in the Grass* and the Welles of *Citizen Kane* from the Welles of *Arkadin*.

I have embroidered Bazin's actual examples for the sake of greater contact with the American scene. In fact, Bazin implicitly denies a decline in the later works of Chaplin and Renoir, and never mentions Griffith. He suggests circuitously that Hawks' *Scarface* is clearly superior to Hawks' *Gentlemen Prefer Blondes* although the *auteur* critics would argue the contrary. Bazin is particularly critical of Rivette's circular reasoning on *Monkey Business* as the proof of Hawks' genius. "One sees the danger," Bazin warns, "which is an aesthetic cult of personality."

Bazin's taste, it should be noted, was far more discriminating than that of American film historians. Films Bazin cites as un-questionable classics are still quite debatable here in America.

After all, *Citizen Kane* was originally panned by James Agee, Richard Griffith and Bosley Crowther, and *Scarface* has never been regarded as one of the landmarks of the American cinema by native critics. I would say that the American public has been ahead of its critics on both *Kane* and *Scarface*. Thus to argue against the *auteur* theory in America is to assume that we have anyone of Bazin's sensibility and dedication to provide an alternative, and we simply don't.

Bazin finally concentrates on the American cinema which invariably serves as the decisive battleground of the *auteur* theory whether over *Monkey Business* or *Party Girl*. Unlike most "serious" American critics, Bazin likes Hollywood films, but not solely because of the talent of this or that director. For Bazin, the distinctively American comedy, western and gangster genres have their own mystiques apart from the personalities of the directors concerned. How can one review an Anthony Mann western, Bazin asks, as if it were not an expression of the genre's conventions. Not that Bazin dislikes Anthony Mann's westerns. He is more concerned with otherwise admirable westerns which the *auteur* theory rejects because their directors happen to be unfashionable. Again, Bazin's critical generosity comes to the fore against the negative aspects of the *auteur* theory.

Some of Bazin's arguments tend to overlap each other as if to counter rebuttals from any direction. He argues in turn that the cinema is less individualistic an art than painting or literature, that Hollywood is less individualistic than other cinemas, and that even so, the *auteur* theory never really applies anywhere. In upholding historical determinism, Bazin goes so far as to speculate that if Racine had lived in Voltaire's century, it is unlikely that Racine's tragedies would have been any more inspired than Voltaire's. Presumably the Age of Reason would have stifled Racine's Neo-classical impulses. Perhaps. Perhaps not. Bazin's hypothesis can hardly be argued to a verifiable conclusion, but I suspect somewhat greater reciprocity between an artist and his *Zeitgeist* than Bazin would allow. He mentions more than once, and in other contexts, capitalism's influence on the cinema. Without denying this influence, I still find it impossible to attribute X directors and Y films to any particular system or culture. Why should the Italian cinema be superior to the German cinema after one war when the reverse was true after the previous one? As for artists conforming to the spirit of their age, that spirit is often expressed in contradictions whether of Stravinsky and Sibelius, Fielding and Richardson, Picasso and Matisse, Chateaubriand and Stendhal. Even if the artist does not spring from the idealized head of Zeus, free of the embryonic stains of history, history itself is profoundly affected by his arrival. If we cannot imagine Griffith's *October* or Eisenstein's *Birth of a Nation* because we find it difficult to transpose one artist's unifying conceptions of Lee and Lincoln to the other's dialectical conceptions of Lenin and Kerensky, we are nevertheless compelled to recognize other differences in the personalities of these two pioneers beyond their respective cultural complexes. It is with these latter differences that the *auteur* theory is most deeply concerned. If directors and other artists cannot be wrenched from their historical environments, aesthetics is reduced to a subordinate branch of ethnography.

I have not done full justice to the subtlety of Bazin's reasoning and to the civilized skepticism with which he propounds his own arguments as slight probabilities rather than absolute certainties. Contemporary opponents of the *auteur* theory may feel that Bazin himself is suspect as a member of the *Cahiers* family. After all, Bazin does express qualified approval of the *auteur* theory as a relatively objective method of evaluating films apart from the subjective perils of impressionistic and ideological criticism. Better to analyze the director's personality than the critic's nerve centers or politics. Nevertheless, Bazin makes his stand clear by concluding: "This is not to deny the role of the author, but to restore to him the preposition without which the noun is only a limp concept. 'Author,' undoubtedly, but *of* what?"

Bazin's syntactical flourish raises an interesting problem in English usage. The French preposition "de" serves many functions, but among others, those of possession and authorship. In English, the preposition "by" once created a scandal in the American film industry when Otto Preminger had the temerity to advertise *The Man With the Golden Arm* as a film "by Otto Preminger." Novelist Nelson Algren and the Screenwriter's Guild raised such an outcry that the offending preposition was deleted. Even the noun "author" (which I cunningly mask as "*auteur*") has a literary connotation in English. In general conversation, an "author" is invariably taken to be a writer. Since "by" is a preposition of authorship and not of ownership like the ambiguous "de," the fact that Preminger both produced and directed *The Man With the Golden Arm* did not entitle him in America to the preposition "by." No one would have objected to the possessive form: "Otto Preminger's *The Man With the Golden Arm*." But even in this case, a novelist of sufficient reputation is usually honored with the possessive designation. Now this is hardly the case in France where *The Red and the Black* is advertised as "un film de Claude Autant-Lara." In America, "directed by" is all the director can claim when he is not also a well-known producer like Alfred Hitchcock or Cecil B. De Mille.

Since most American film critics are oriented toward literature or journalism rather than toward future film-making, most American film criticism is directed toward the script instead of toward the screen. The writer-hero in *Sunset Boulevard* complains that people don't realize that someone "writes a picture; they think the actors make it up as they go along." It would never occur to this writer or to most of his colleagues that people are even less aware of the director's function.

Of course, the much-abused man in the street has a good excuse not to be aware of the *auteur* theory even as a figure of speech. Even on the so-called classic level, he is not encouraged to ask aimez-vous Griffith or aimez-vous Eisenstein? Instead, it is which Griffith and which Eisenstein? As for less acclaimed directors, he is lucky to find their names in the fourth paragraph of the typical review. I doubt that most American film critics really believe that an indifferently directed film is comparable to an indifferently written book. However, there is little point in wailing at the Philistines on this issue, particularly when some progress is being made in telling one director from another, at least when the film comes from abroad. The Fellini, Bergman, Kurosawa and Antonioni promotions have helped push more directors up to the first paragraph of a review even ahead of the plot synopsis. So we mustn't complain.

Where I wish to redirect the argument is toward the relative position of the American cinema as opposed to the Foreign cinema. Some critics have advised me that the *auteur* theory only applies to a small number of artists who make personal films, not to the run-of-the-mill Hollywood director who takes whatever assignment is available. Like most Americans who take films seriously, I have always felt a cultural inferiority complex about Hollywood. Just a few years ago, I would have thought it unthinkable to speak in the same breath of a "commercial" director like Hitchcock and a "pure" director like Bresson. Even today, *Sight and Sound* uses different type-sizes for Bresson and Hitchcock films. After years of tortured revaluation, I am now prepared to stake my critical reputation, such as it is, on the proposition that Alfred Hitchcock is artistically superior to Robert Bresson by every criterion of excellence, and further, that, film for film, director for director, the American cinema has been consistently superior to that of the rest of the world from 1915 through 1962. Consequently, I now regard the *auteur* theory primarily as a critical device for recording the history of the American cinema, the only cinema in the world worth exploring in depth beneath the frosting of a few great directors at the top.

These propositions remain to be proven and, I hope, debated. The proof will be difficult because direction in the cinema is a nebulous force in literary terms. In addition to its own jargon, the director's craft often pulls in the related jargons of music, painting, sculpture, dance, literature, theatre, architecture, all in a generally futile attempt to describe the indescribable. What is it the old jazz man says of his art? If you gotta ask what it is, it ain't? Well, the cinema is like that. Criticism can only attempt an approximation, a reasonable preponderance of accuracy over inaccuracy. I know the exceptions to the *auteur* theory as well as anyone. I can feel the human attraction of an audience going one way when I am going the other. The temptations of cynicism, common sense and facile culture-mongering are always very strong, but somehow I feel that the *auteur* theory is the only hope for extending the appreciation of personal qualities in the cinema. By grouping and evaluating films according to directors, the critic can rescue individual achievements from an unjustifiable anonymity. If medieval architects and African sculptors are anonymous today, it is not because they deserved to be. When Ingmar Bergman bemoans the alienation of the modern artist from the collective spirit which rebuilt the Cathedral at Chartres, he is only dramatizing his own individuality for an age which has rewarded him handsomely for the travail of his alienation. There is no justification for penalizing Hollywood directors for the sake of collective mythology. So invective aside, aimez-vous Cukor?

II. WHAT IS THE AUTEUR THEORY?

As far as I know, there is no definition of the *auteur* theory in the English language, that is, by any American or British critic. Truffaut has recently gone to great pains to emphasize that the *auteur* theory was merely a polemical weapon for a given time and a given place, and I am willing to take him at his word. But lest I be accused of misappropriating a theory no one wants anymore, I give the *Cahiers* critics full credit for the original formulation of an idea which reshaped my thinking on the cinema. First of all, how does the *auteur* theory differ from a straightforward theory of directors. Ian Cameron's article, "Films, Directors and Critics" in *Movie* of September 1962, makes an interesting comment on this issue: "The assumption which underlies all the writing in *Movie* is that the director is the author of a film, the person who gives it any distinctive quality. There are quite large exceptions, with which I shall deal later." So far, so good, at least for the *auteur* theory which even allows for exceptions. However, Cameron continues: "On the whole we accept the cinema of directors, although without going to the farthest-out extremes of the *la politique des auteurs* which makes it difficult to think of a bad director making a good film and almost impossible to think of a good director making a bad one." We are back to Bazin again although Cameron naturally uses different examples. That three otherwise divergent critics like Bazin, Roud and Cameron make essentially the same point about the *auteur* theory suggests a common fear of its abuses. I believe there is a misunderstanding here about what the *auteur* theory actually claims, particularly since the theory itself is so vague at the present time.

First of all, the *auteur* theory, at least as I understand it and now intend to express it, claims neither the gift of prophecy nor the option of extracinematic perception. Directors, even *auteurs*, do not always run true to form, and the critic can never assume that a bad director will always make a bad film. No, not always, but almost always, and that is the point. What is a bad director, but a director who has made many bad films? What is the problem then? Simply this: the badness of a director is not necessarily considered the badness of a film. If Joseph Pevney directed Garbo, Cherkassov, Olivier, Belmondo, and Harriet Andersson in *The Cherry Orchard*, the resulting spectacle might not be entirely devoid of merit with so many subsidiary *auteurs* to cover up for Joe. In fact, with this cast and this literary property, a Lumet might be safer than a Welles. The realities of casting apply to directors as well as actors, but the *auteur* theory would demand the gamble with Welles, if he were willing.

Marlon Brando has shown us that a film can be made without a director. Indeed, *One-Eyed Jacks* is more entertaining than many films with directors. A director-conscious critic would find it difficult to say anything good or bad about direction which is non-existent. One can talk here about photography, editing, acting, but not direction. The film even has personality, but like *The Longest Day* and *Mutiny on the Bounty*, it is a cipher directorially. Obviously, the *auteur* theory cannot possibly cover every vagrant charm of the cinema. Nevertheless, the first premise of the *auteur* theory is the technical competence of a director as a criterion of value. A badly directed or undirected film has no importance in a critical scale of values, but one can make interesting conversation about the subject, the script, the acting, the color, the photography, the editing, the music, the costumes, the décor etc. That is the nature of the medium. You always get more for your money than mere art. Now by the *auteur* theory, if a director has no technical competence, no elementary flair for the cinema, he is automatically cast out from the pantheon of directors. A great director has to be at least a good director. This is true in any art. What constitutes directorial talent is more difficult to define abstractly. There is less disagreement, however, on this first level of the *auteur* theory than there will be later.

The second premise of the *auteur* theory is the distinguishable personality of the director as a criterion of value. Over a group of films, a director must exhibit certain recurring characteristics of style which serve as his signature. The way a film looks and moves should have some relationship to the way a director thinks and feels. This is an area where American directors are generally superior to foreign directors. Because so much of the American cinema is commissioned, a director is forced to express his personality through the visual treatment of material rather than through the literary content of the material. A Cukor who works with all sorts of projects has a more developed abstract style than a Bergman who is free to develop his own scripts. Not that Bergman lacks personality, but his work has declined with the depletion of his ideas largely because his technique never equaled his sensibility. Joseph L. Mankiewicz and Billy Wilder are other examples of writer-directors without adequate technical mastery. By contrast, Douglas Sirk and Otto Preminger have moved up the scale because their miscellaneous projects reveal a stylistic consistency.

The third and ultimate premise of the *auteur* theory is concerned with interior meaning, the ultimate glory of the cinema as an art. Interior meaning is extrapolated from the tension between a director's personality and his material. This conception of interior meaning comes close to what Astruc defines as *mise-en-scène,* but not quite. It is not quite the vision of the world a director projects, nor quite his attitude toward life. It is ambiguous in any literary sense because part of it is imbedded in the stuff of the cinema and cannot be rendered in non-cinematic terms. Truffaut has called it the temperature of the director on the set, and that is a close approximation of its professional aspect. Dare I come out and say what I think it to be is an élan of the soul?

Lest I seem unduly mystical, let me hasten to add that all I mean by soul is that intangible difference between one personality and another, all other things being equal. Sometimes, this difference is expressed by no more than a beat's hesitation in the rhythm of a film. In one sequence of *La Règle du jeu,* Renoir gallops up the stairs, turns to his right with a lurching movement, stops in hop-like uncertainty when his name is called by a coquettish maid, and then, with marvelous post-reflex continuity, resumes his bearishly shambling journey to the heroine's boudoir. If I could describe the musical grace note of that momentary suspension, and I can't, I might be able to provide a more precise definition of the *auteur* theory. As it is, all I can do is point at the specific beauties of interior meaning on the screen, and later catalogue the moments of recognition.

The three premises of the *auteur* theory may be visualized as three concentric circles, the outer circle as technique, the middle circle personal style, and the inner circle interior meaning. The corresponding roles of the director may be designated as those of a technician, a stylist and an *auteur*. There is no prescribed course by which a director passes through the three circles. Godard once remarked that Visconti had evolved from a *metteur-en-scène* to an *auteur* while Rossellini had evolved from an *auteur* to a *metteur-en-scène*. From opposite directions, they emerged with comparable status. Minnelli began and remained in the second circle as a stylist; Bunuel was an *auteur* even before he had assembled the technique of the first circle. Technique is simply the ability to put a film together with some clarity and coherence. Nowadays it is possible to become a director without knowing too much about the technical side, even the crucial functions of photography and editing. An expert production crew could probably cover up for a chimpanzee in the director's chair. How do you tell the genuine director from the quasi-chimpanzee? After a given number of films, a pattern is established.

In fact, the *auteur* theory itself is a pattern theory in constant flux. I would never endorse a Ptolemaic constellation of directors in a fixed orbit. At the moment, my list of *auteurs* runs something like this through the first twenty: Ophuls, Renoir, Mizoguchi, Hitchcock, Chaplin, Ford, Welles, Dreyer, Rossellini, Murnau, Griffith, Sternberg, Eisenstein, Stroheim, Bunuel, Bresson, Hawks, Lang, Flaherty, Vigo. This list is somewhat weighted toward seniority and established reputations. In time, some of these *auteurs* will rise, some will fall, and some will be displaced by either new directors or rediscovered ancients. Again, the exact order is less important than the specific definitions of these and as many as two hundred other potential *auteurs*. I would hardly expect any other critic in the world to fully endorse this list, especially on faith. Only after thousands of films have been revaluated, will any personal pantheon have a reasonably objective validity. The task of validating the *auteur* theory is an enormous one, and the end will never be in sight. Meanwhile, the *auteur* habit of collecting random films in directorial bundles will serve posterity with at least a tentative classification.

Although the *auteur* theory emphasizes the body of a director's work rather than isolated masterpieces, it is expected of great directors that they make great films every so often. The only possible exception to this rule I can think of is Abel Gance, whose greatness is largely a function of his aspiration. Even with Gance, *La Roue* is as close to being a great film as any single work of Flaherty's. Not that single works matter that much. As Renoir has observed, a director spends his life on variations of the same film.

Two recent omnibus films — *Boccaccio 70* and *The Seven Capital Sins* — unwittingly reinforced the *auteur* theory by confirming the relative standing of the many directors involved. If I had not seen either film, I would have anticipated that the order of merit in *Boccaccio 70* would be Visconti, Fellini and De Sica, and in *The Seven Capital Sins*, Godard, Chabrol, Demy, Vadim, De Broca, Molinaro. (Dhomme, Ionesco's stage director and an unknown quantity in advance, turned out to be the worst of the lot.) There might be some argument about the relative badness of De Broca and Molinaro, but otherwise, the directors ran true to form by almost any objective criterion of value. However, the main point here is that even in these frothy, ultra-commercial servings of entertainment, the contribution of each director had less in common stylistically with the work of other directors on the project than with his own previous work.

Sometimes a great deal of corn must be husked to yield a few kernels of internal meaning. I recently saw *Every Night at Eight*, one of the many maddeningly routine films Raoul Walsh has directed in his long career. This 1935 effort featured George Raft, Alice Faye, Frances Langford and Patsy Kelly in one of those familiar plots about radio shows of the period. The film keeps moving along in the pleasantly unpretentious manner one would expect of Walsh until one incongruously intense scene with George Raft thrashing about in his sleep, revealing his inner fears in mumbling dream talk. The girl he loves comes into the room in the midst of his unconscious avowals of feeling, and listens sympathetically. This unusual scene was later amplified in *High Sierra* with Humphrey Bogart and Ida Lupino. The point is that one of the screen's most virile directors employed an essentially feminine narrative device to dramatize the emotional vulnerability of his heroes. If I had not been aware of Walsh in *Every Night at Eight*, the crucial link to *High Sierra* would have passed unnoticed. Such are the joys of the *auteur* theory.

Circles and Squares:
Joys and Sarris

PAULINE KAEL

> ... the first premise of the *auteur* theory is the technical competence of a director as a criterion of value. ... The second premise of the *auteur* theory is the distinguishable personality of the director as a criterion of value. ... The third and ultimate premise of the *auteur* theory is concerned with interior meaning, the ultimate glory of the cinema as an art. Interior meaning is extrapolated from the tension between a director's personality and his material. ...
>
> Sometimes a great deal of corn must be husked to yield a few kernels of internal meaning. I recently saw *Every Night at Eight*, one of the many maddeningly routine films Raoul Walsh has directed in his long career. This 1935 effort featured George Raft, Alice Faye, Frances Langford and Patsy Kelly in one of those familiar plots about radio shows of the period. The film keeps moving along in the pleasantly unpretentious manner one would expect of Walsh until one incongruously intense scene with George Raft thrashing about in his sleep, revealing his inner fears in mumbling dream talk. The girl he loves comes into the room in the midst of his unconscious avowals of feeling, and listens sympathetically. This unusual scene was later amplified in *High Sierra* with Humphrey Bogart and Ida Lupino. The point is that one of the screen's most virile directors employed an essentially feminine narrative device to dramatize the emotional vulnerability of his heroes. If I had not been aware of Walsh in *Every Night at Eight*, the crucial link to *High Sierra* would have passed unnoticed. Such are the joys of the *auteur* theory.
>
> — Andrew Sarris, "Notes on the *Auteur* Theory in 1962,"
> *Film Culture*, Winter 1962–1963.

Perhaps a little more corn should be husked; perhaps, for example, we can husk away the word "internal" (is "internal meaning" any different from "meaning"?). We might ask why the link is "crucial"? Is it because the device was "incongruously intense" in *Every Night at Eight* and so demonstrated a try for something *deeper* on Walsh's part? But if his merit is his "pleasantly unpretentious manner" (which is to say, I suppose, that, recognizing the limitations of the script, he wasn't trying to do much) then the incongruous device was probably a misconceived attempt that disturbed the manner — like a bad playwright interrupting a comedy scene because he cannot resist the opportunity to tug at your heartstrings. We might also ask why this narrative device is "essentially feminine": is it more feminine than masculine to be asleep, or to talk in one's sleep, or to reveal feelings? Or, possibly, does Sarris regard the device as feminine because the listening woman becomes a sympathetic figure and emotional understanding is, in this "virile" context, assumed to be essentially feminine? Perhaps only if one accepts the narrow notions of virility so common in our action films can this sequence be seen as "essentially feminine," and it is amusing that a critic can both support these clichés of the male world and be so happy when they are violated.

This is how we might quibble with a different *kind* of critic but we would never get anywhere with Sarris if we tried to examine what he is saying sentence by sentence.

So let us ask, what is the meaning of the passage? Sarris has noticed that in *High Sierra* (not a very good movie) Raoul Walsh repeated an uninteresting and obvious device that he had earlier used in a worse movie. And for some inexplicable reason, Sarris concludes that he would not have had this joy of discovery without the *auteur* theory.

But in every art form, critics traditionally notice and point out the way the artists borrow from themselves (as well as from others) and how the same devices, techniques, and themes reappear in their work. This is obvious in listening to music, seeing plays, reading novels, watching actors; we take it for granted that this is how we perceive the development or the decline of an artist (and it may be necessary to point out to *auteur* critics that repetition without development is decline). When you see Hitchcock's *Saboteur* there is no doubt that he drew heavily and clumsily from *The 39 Steps*, and when you see *North by Northwest* you can see that he is once again toying with the ingredients of *The 39 Steps* — and apparently having a good time with them. Would Sarris not notice the repetition in the Walsh films without the *auteur* theory? Or shall we take the more cynical view that without some commitment to Walsh as an *auteur*, he probably wouldn't be spending his time looking at these movies?

If we may be permitted a literary analogy, we can visualize Sarris researching in the archives of the *Saturday Evening Post*, tracing the development of Clarence Budington Kelland, who, by the application of something like the *auteur* theory, would emerge as a much more important writer than Dostoyevsky; for in Kelland's case Sarris's three circles, the three premises of the *auteur* theory, have

been consistently congruent. Kelland is technically competent (even
"pleasantly unpretentious"), no writer has a more "distinguishable
personality," and if "interior meaning" is what can be extrapolated
from, say *Hatari!* or *Advise and Consent* or *What Ever Happened to
Baby Jane?* then surely Kelland's stories with their attempts to force a
bit of character and humor into the familiar plot outlines are loaded
with it. Poor misguided Dostoyevsky, too full of what he has to say to
bother with "technical competence," tackling important themes in
each work (surely the worst crime in the *auteur* book) and with his
almost incredible unity of personality and material leaving you
nothing to extrapolate from, he'll never make it. If the editors of
Movie ranked authors the way they do directors, Dostoyevsky would
probably be in that almost untouchable category of the "ambitious."

It should be pointed out that Sarris's defense of the *auteur*
theory is based not only on aesthetics but on a rather odd pragmatic
statement: "Thus to argue against the *auteur* theory in America is to
assume that we have anyone of Bazin's sensibility and dedication to
provide an alternative, and we simply don't." Which I take to mean
that the *auteur* theory is necessary in the absence of a critic who
wouldn't need it. This is a new approach to aesthetics, and I hope
Sarris's humility does not camouflage his double-edged argument. If
his aesthetics is based on expediency, then it may be expedient to
point out that it takes extraordinary intelligence and discrimination
and taste to *use* any theory in the arts, and that without those
qualities, a theory becomes a rigid formula (which is indeed what is
happening among *auteur* critics). The greatness of critics like Bazin in
France and Agee in America may have something to do with their
using their full range of intelligence and intuition, rather than relying
on formulas. Criticism is an art, not a science, and a critic who
follows rules will fail in one of his most important functions:
perceiving what is original and important in *new* work and helping
others to see.

THE OUTER CIRCLE

> ... the first premise of the *auteur* theory is the technical compe-
> tence of a director as a criterion of value.

This seems less the premise of a theory than a commonplace of
judgment, as Sarris himself indicates when he paraphrases it as, "A
great director has to be at least a good director." But this commonplace, though it *sounds* reasonable and basic, is a shaky premise: sometimes the greatest artists in a medium bypass or violate

the simple technical competence that is so necessary for hacks. For example, it is doubtful if Antonioni could handle a routine directorial assignment of the type at which John Sturges is so proficient (*Escape from Fort Bravo* or *Bad Day at Black Rock*), but surely Antonioni's *L'Avventura* is the work of a great director. And the greatness of a director like Cocteau has nothing to do with mere technical competence: his greatness is in being able to achieve his own personal expression and style. And just as there were writers like Melville or Dreiser who triumphed over various kinds of technical incompetence, and who were, as artists, incomparably greater than the facile technicians of their day, a new great film director may appear whose very greatness is in his struggling toward grandeur or in massive accumulation of detail. An artist who is not a good technician can indeed create new standards, because standards of technical competence are based on comparisons with work already done.

Just as new work in other arts is often attacked because it violates the accepted standards and thus seems crude and ugly and incoherent, great new directors are very likely to be condemned precisely on the grounds that they're not even good directors, that they don't know their "business." Which, in some cases, is true, but does it matter when that "business" has little to do with what they want to express in films? It may even be a hindrance, leading them to banal slickness, instead of discovery of their own methods. For some, at least, Cocteau may be right: "The only technique worth having is the technique you invent for yourself." The director must be judged on the basis of what he produces — his films — and if he can make great films without knowing the standard methods, without the usual craftsmanship of the "good director," then that is the way he works. I would amend Sarris's premise to, "In works of a lesser rank, technical competence can help to redeem the weaknesses of the material." In fact it seems to be precisely this category that the *auteur* critics are most interested in — the routine material that a good craftsman can make into a fast and enjoyable movie. What, however, makes the *auteur* critics so incomprehensible, is not their *preference* for works of this category (in this they merely follow the lead of children who also prefer simple action films and westerns and horror films to works that make demands on their understanding) but their truly astonishing inability to exercise taste and judgment *within* their area of preference. Moviegoing kids are, I think, much more reliable guides to this kind of movie than the *auteur* critics: every kid I've talked to knows that Henry Hathaway's *North to Alaska* was a surprisingly funny, entertaining movie and *Hatari!* (classified as a "masterpiece" by half the *Cahiers Conseil des Dix,* Peter Bogdanovich, and others) was a terrible bore.

THE MIDDLE CIRCLE

> ... the second premise of the *auteur* theory is the distinguishable personality of the director as a criterion of value.

Up to this point there has really been no theory, and now, when Sarris begins to work on his foundation, the entire edifice of civilized standards of taste collapses while he's tacking down his floorboards. Traditionally, in any art, the personalities of all those involved in a production have been a factor in judgment, but that the *distinguishability* of personality should in itself be a criterion of value completely confuses *normal* judgment. The smell of a skunk is more distinguishable than the perfume of a rose; does that make it better? Hitchcock's personality is certainly more distinguishable in *Dial M for Murder, Rear Window, Vertigo,* than Carol Reed's in *The Stars Look Down, Odd Man Out, The Fallen Idol, The Third Man, An Outcast of the Islands,* if for no other reason than because Hitchcock repeats while Reed tackles new subject matter. But how does this distinguishable personality function as a criterion for judging the works? We recognize the hands of Carné and Prévert in *Le Jour se Lève,* but that is not what makes it a beautiful film; we can just as easily recognize their hands in *Quai des Brumes* — which is not such a good film. We can recognize that *Le Plaisir* and *The Earrings of Madame de ...* are both the work of Ophuls, but *Le Plaisir* is not a great film, and *Madame de ...* is.

Often the works in which we are most aware of the personality of the director are his worst films — when he falls back on the devices he has already done to death. When a famous director makes a good movie, we look at the movie, we don't think about the director's personality; when he makes a stinker we notice his familiar touches because there's not much else to watch. When Preminger makes an expert, entertaining whodunit like *Laura,* we don't look for his personality (it has become part of the texture of the film); when he makes an atrocity like *Whirlpool,* there's plenty of time to look for his "personality" — if that's your idea of a good time.

It could even be argued, I think, that Hitchcock's uniformity, his mastery of tricks, and his cleverness at getting audiences to respond according to his calculations — the feedback he wants and gets from them — reveal not so much a personal style as a personal theory of audience psychology, that his methods and approach are not those of an artist but a prestidigitator. The *auteur* critics respond just as Hitchcock expects the gullible to respond. This is not so surprising — often the works *auteur* critics call masterpieces are ones that seem to reveal the contempt of the director for the audience.

It's hard to believe that Sarris seriously attempts to apply "the distinguishable personality of the director as a criterion of value" because when this premise becomes troublesome, he just tries to brazen his way out of difficulties. For example, now that John Huston's work has gone flat[1] Sarris casually dismisses him with: "Huston is virtually a forgotten man with a few actors' classics behind him. . . ." If *The Maltese Falcon*, perhaps the most high-style thriller ever made in America, a film Huston both wrote and directed, is not a director's film, what is? And if the distinguishable personality of the director is a criterion of value, then how can Sarris dismiss the Huston who comes through so unmistakably in *The Treasure of Sierra Madre*, *The African Queen*, or *Beat the Devil*, or even in a muddled Huston film like *Key Largo*? If these are actors' movies, then what on earth is a director's movie?

Isn't the *auteur* theory a hindrance to clear judgment of Huston's movies and of his career? Disregarding the theory, we see some fine film achievements and we perceive a remarkably distinctive directorial talent; we also see intervals of weak, half-hearted assignments like *Across the Pacific* and *In This Our Life*. Then, after *Moulin Rouge*, except for the blessing of *Beat the Devil*, we see a career that splutters out in ambitious failures like *Moby Dick* and confused projects like *The Roots of Heaven* and *The Misfits*, and strictly commercial projects like *Heaven Knows, Mr. Allison*. And this kind of career seems more characteristic of film history, especially in the United States, than the ripening development and final mastery envisaged by the *auteur* theory — a theory that makes it almost de rigeur to regard Hitchcock's American films as superior to his early English films. Is Huston's career so different, say, from Fritz Lang's? How is it that Huston's early good — almost great — work, must be rejected along with his mediocre recent work, but Fritz Lang, being sanctified as an *auteur*, has his bad recent work praised along with his good? Employing more usual norms, if you respect the Fritz Lang who made *M* and *You Only Live Once*, if you enjoy the excesses

---

[1] And, by the way, the turning point came, I think, not with *Moby Dick*, as Sarris indicates, but much earlier, with *Moulin Rouge*. This may not be so apparent to *auteur* critics concerned primarily with style and individual touches, because what was shocking about *Moulin Rouge* was that the content was sentimental mush. But critics who accept even the worst of Minnelli probably wouldn't have been bothered by the fact that *Moulin Rouge* was soft in the center, it had so many fancy touches at the edges.

of style and the magnificent absurdities of a film like *Metropolis*, then
it is only good sense to reject the ugly stupidity of *Journey to the Lost
City*. It is an insult to an artist to praise his bad work along with his
good; it indicates that you are incapable of judging either.

A few years ago, a friend who reviewed Jean Renoir's University
of California production of his play *Carola*, hailed it as "a work of
genius." When I asked my friend how he could so describe this very
unfortunate play, he said, "Why, of course, it's a work of genius. Renoir's a genius, so anything he does is a work of genius." This could
almost be a capsule version of the *auteur* theory (just substitute
Hatari! for *Carola*) and in this reductio ad absurdum, viewing a work
is superfluous, as the judgment is a priori. It's like buying clothes by
the label: this is Dior, so it's good. (This is not so far from the way the
auteur critics work, either.)

Sarris doesn't even play his own game with any decent attention
to the rules: it is as absurd to praise Lang's recent bad work as to
dismiss Huston's early good work; surely it would be more consistent
if he also tried to make a case for Huston's bad pictures? That would
be more consistent than devising a category called "actors' classics"
to explain his good pictures away. If *The Maltese Falcon* and *The
Treasure of Sierra Madre* are actors' classics, then what makes
Hawks's *To Have and Have Not* and *The Big Sleep* (which were obviously tailored to the personalities of Bogart and Bacall) the work of
an *auteur*?

Sarris believes that what makes an *auteur* is "an élan of the
soul." (This critical language is barbarous. Where else should élan
come from? It's like saying "a digestion of the stomach." A film critic
need not be a theoretician, but it is necessary that he know how to
use words. This might, indeed, be a first premise for a theory.) Those
who have this élan presumably have it forever and their films reveal
the "organic unity" of the directors' careers; and those who don't
have it — well, they can only make "actors' classics." It's ironic that a
critic trying to establish simple "objective" rules as a guide for
critics who he thinks aren't gifted enough to use taste and
intelligence, ends up — where, actually, he began — with a theory
based on mystical insight. This might really make demands on the
auteur critics if they did not simply take the easy way out by
arbitrary decisions of who's got "it" and who hasn't. Their decisions
are not merely not based on their theory; their decisions are *beyond*
criticism. It's like a woman's telling us that she feels a certain dress
does something for her: her feeling has about as much to do with
critical judgment as the *auteur* critics' feeling that Minnelli *has* "it,"
but Huston never had "it."

Even if a girl had plenty of "it," she wasn't expected to keep it forever. But this "élan" is not supposed to be affected by the vicissitudes of fortune, the industrial conditions of moviemaking, the turmoil of a country, or the health of a director. Indeed, Sarris says, "If directors and other artists cannot be wrenched from their historical environments, aesthetics is reduced to a subordinate branch of ethnography." May I suggest that if, in order to judge movies, the *auteur* critics must wrench the directors from their historical environments (which is, to put it mildly, impossible) so that they can concentrate on the detection of that "élan," they are reducing aesthetics to a form of idiocy. Élan as the permanent attribute Sarris posits can only be explained in terms of a cult of personality. May I suggest that a more meaningful description of élan is what a man feels when he is working at the height of his powers — and what we respond to in works of art with the excited cry of "This time, he's really done it" or "This shows what he could do when he got the chance" or "He's found his style" or "I never realized he had it in him to do anything so good," a response to his joy in creativity.

Sarris experiences "joy" when he recognizes a pathetic little link between two Raoul Walsh pictures (he never does explain whether the discovery makes him think the pictures are any better) but he wants to see artists in a pristine state — their essences, perhaps? — separated from all the life that has formed them and to which they try to give expression.

THE INNER CIRCLE

> The third and ultimate premise of the *auteur* theory is concerned with interior meaning, the ultimate glory of the cinema as an art. Interior meaning is extrapolated from the tension between a director's personality and his material.

This is a remarkable formulation: it is the opposite of what we have always taken for granted in the arts, that the artist expresses himself in the unity of form and content. What Sarris believes to be "the ultimate glory of the cinema as an art" is what has generally been considered the frustrations of a man working against the given material. Fantastic as this formulation is, it does something that the first two premises didn't do: it clarifies the interests of the *auteur* critics. If we have been puzzled because the *auteur* critics seemed so deeply involved, even dedicated, in becoming connoisseurs of trash, now we can see by this theoretical formulation that trash is indeed their chosen province of film.

Their ideal *auteur* is the man who signs a long-term contract, directs any script that's handed to him, and expresses himself by shoving bits of style up the crevasses of the plots. If his "style" is in conflict with the story line or subject matter, so much the better — more chance for tension. Now we can see why there has been so much use of the term "personality" in this aesthetics (the term which seems so inadequate when discussing the art of Griffith or Renoir or Murnau or Dreyer) — a routine, commercial movie can sure use a little "personality."

Now that we have reached the inner circle (the bull's eye turns out to be an empty socket) we can see why the shoddiest films are often praised the most. Subject matter is irrelevant (so long as it isn't treated sensitively — which is bad) and will quickly be disposed of by *auteur* citics who know that the smart director isn't responsible for that anyway; they'll get on to the important subject — his *mise-en-scène*. The director who fights to do something he cares about is a square. Now we can at least begin to understand why there was such contempt toward Huston for what was, in its way, a rather extraordinary effort — the *Moby Dick* that failed; why *Movie* considers Roger Corman a better director than Fred Zinnemann and ranks Joseph Losey next to God, why Bogdanovich, Mekas, and Sarris give their highest critical ratings to *What Ever Happened to Baby Jane?* (mighty big crevasses there). If Carol Reed had made only movies like *The Man Between* — in which he obviously worked to try to make something out of a ragbag of worn-out bits of material — he might be considered "brilliant" too. (But this is doubtful: although even the worst Reed is superior to Aldrich's *Baby Jane*, Reed would probably be detected, and rejected, as a man interested in substance rather than sensationalism.)

I am angry, but am I unjust? Here's Sarris:

> A Cukor who works with all sorts of projects has a more developed abstract style than a Bergman who is free to develop his own scripts. Not that Bergman lacks personality, but his work has declined with the depletion of his ideas largely because his technique never equaled his sensibility. Joseph L. Mankiewicz and Billy Wilder are other examples of writer-directors without adequate technical mastery. By contrast, Douglas Sirk and Otto Preminger have moved up the scale because their miscellaneous projects reveal a stylistic consistency.

How neat it all is — Bergman's "work has declined with the depletion of his ideas largely because his technique never equaled his sensibility." But what on earth does that mean? How did Sarris perceive Bergman's sensibility except through his technique? Is Sarris saying what he seems to be saying, that if Bergman had developed more "technique," his work wouldn't be dependent on his ideas? I'm afraid this *is* what he means, and that when he refers to Cukor's "more developed abstract style" he means by "abstract" something unrelated to ideas, a technique not dependent on the content of the films. This is curiously reminiscent of a view common enough in the business world, that it's better not to get too involved, too personally interested in business problems, or they take over your life; and besides, you don't function as well when you've lost your objectivity. But this is the *opposite* of how an artist works. His technique, his *style*, is determined by his range of involvements, and his preference for certain themes. Cukor's style is no more *abstract*(!) than Bergman's: Cukor has a range of subject matter that he can handle and when he gets a good script within his range (like *The Philadelphia Story* or *Pat and Mike*) he does a good job; but he is at an immense *artistic* disadvantage, compared with Bergman, because he is dependent on the ideas of so many (and often bad) scriptwriters and on material which is often alien to his talents. It's amusing (and/or depressing) to see the way *auteur* critics tend to downgrade writer-directors — who are in the best position to use the film medium for personal expression.

Sarris does some pretty fast shuffling with Huston and Bergman; why doesn't he just come out and admit that writer-directors are disqualified by his third premise? They can't arrive at that "interior meaning, the ultimate glory of the cinema" because a writer-director has no tension between his personality and his material, so there's nothing for the *auteur* critic to extrapolate from.

What is all this nonsense about extrapolating "interior" meaning from the tension between a director's personality and his material? A competent commercial director generally does the best he can with what he's got to work with. Where is the "tension"? And if you can locate some, what kind of meaning could you draw out of it except that the director's having a bad time with lousy material or material he doesn't like? Or maybe he's trying to speed up the damned production so he can do something else that he has some *hopes* for? Are these critics honestly (and futilely) looking for "interior meanings" or is this just some form of intellectual diddling that helps to sustain their pride while they're viewing silly movies? Where is the tension in Howard Hawks's films? When he has good material, he's capable of better than good direction, as he demonstrates in films like *Twentieth Century, Bringing Up Baby, His Girl Friday*; and in *To Have and Have Not* and *The Big Sleep* he demonstrates that with help from the actors, he can jazz up ridiculous scripts. But what "interior meaning" can be extrapolated from an enjoyable, harmless, piece of kitsch like *Only Angels Have Wings*; what can the *auteur* critics see in it beyond the sex and glamor and fantasies of the high-school boys' universe — exactly what the mass audience liked it for? And when Hawks's material and/or cast is dull and when his heart isn't in the production — when by the *auteur* theory he should show his "personality," the result is something soggy like *The Big Sky*.

George Cukor's modest statement, "Give me a good script and I'll be a hundred times better as a director"[2] provides some notion of how a director may experience the problem of the given material. What can Cukor do with a script like *The Chapman Report* but try to kid it, to dress it up a bit, to show off the talents of Jane Fonda and Claire Bloom and Glynis Johns, and to give the total production a little flair and craftsmanship. At best, he can make an entertaining bad movie. A director with something like magical gifts *can* make a silk purse out of a sow's ear. But if he has it in him to do more in life than make silk purses, the triumph is minor — even if the purse is lined with gold. Only by the use of the *auteur* theory does this little victory become "ultimate glory." For some unexplained reason those traveling in *auteur* circles believe that making that purse out of a sow's ear is an infinitely greater accomplishment than making a solid carrying case out of a good piece of leather (as, for example, a Zinnemann does with *From Here to Eternity* or *The Nun's Story*).

I suppose we should be happy for Sirk and Preminger, elevated up the glory "scale," but I suspect that the "stylistic consistency" of, say, Preminger, could be a matter of his *limitations*, and that the only way you could tell he made some of his movies was that he used the same players so often (Linda Darnell, Jeanne Crain, Gene Tierney, Dana Andrews, et al., gave his movies the Preminger look). But the argument is ludicrous anyway, because if Preminger shows stylistic consistency with subject matter as varied as *Carmen Jones, Anatomy of a Murder*, and *Advise and Consent*, then by any rational standards he should be attacked rather than elevated. I don't think these films are stylistically consistent, nor do I think Preminger is a great director — for the very simple reason that his films are consistently superficial and facile. (*Advise and Consent*, an *auteur* "master-

---

[2] In another sense, it is perhaps immodest. I would say, give Cukor a clever script with light, witty dialogue, and he will know what to do with it. But I wouldn't expect more than glossy entertainment. (It seems almost too obvious to mention it, but can Sarris really discern the "distinguishable personality" of George Cukor and his "abstract" style in films like *Bhowani Junction, Les Girls, The Actress, A Life of Her Own, The Model and the Marriage Broker, Edward, My Son, A Woman's Face, Romeo and Juliet, A Double Life*? I wish I could put him to the test. I can only *suspect* that many *auteur* critics would have a hard time seeing those telltale traces of the beloved in their works.)

piece" — Ian Cameron, Paul Mayersberg, and Mark Shivas of *Movie* and Jean Douchet of *Cahiers du Cinéma* rate it first on their ten best lists of 1962 and Sarris gives it his top rating — seems not so much Preminger-directed as other-directed. That is to say, it seems calculated to provide what as many different groups as possible want to see: there's something for the liberals, something for the conservatives, something for the homosexuals, something for the family.) An editorial in *Movie* states: "In order to enjoy Preminger's films the spectator must apply an unprejudiced intelligence; he is constantly required to examine the quality not only of the characters' decisions but also of his own reactions," and "He presupposes an intelligence active enough to allow the spectator to make connections, comparisons and judgments." May I suggest that this spectator would have better things to do than the editors of *Movie* who put out Preminger issues? They may have, of course, the joys of discovering links between *Centennial Summer, Forever Amber, That Lady in Ermine,* and *The Thirteenth Letter,* but I refuse to believe in these ever-so-intellectual protestations. The *auteur* critics aren't a very *convincing* group.

I assume that Sarris's theory is not based on his premises (the necessary causal relationships are absent), but rather that the premises were devised in a clumsy attempt to prop up the "theory." (It's a good thing he stopped at three: a few more circles and we'd really be in hell, which might turn out to be the last refinement of film tastes — Abbott and Costello comedies, perhaps?) These critics work embarrassingly hard trying to give some semblance of intellectual respectability to a preoccupation with mindless, repetitious commercial products — the kind of action movies that the restless, rootless men who wander on Forty-second Street and in the Tenderloin of all our big cities have always preferred just because they could respond to them without thought. These movies soak up your time. I would suggest that they don't serve a very different function for Sarris or Bogdanovich or the young men of *Movie* — even though they devise elaborate theories to justify soaking up their time. An educated man must have to work pretty hard to set his intellectual horizons at the level of *I Was a Male War Bride* (which, incidentally, wasn't even a good *commercial* movie).

"Interior meaning" seems to be what those in the know know. It's a mystique — and a mistake. The *auteur* critics never tell us by what divining rods they have discovered the élan of a Minnelli or a Nicholas Ray or a Leo McCarey. They're not critics; they're inside dopesters. There must be another circle that Sarris forgot to get to — the one where the secrets are kept.

OUTSIDE THE CIRCLES,
OR WHAT IS A FILM CRITIC?

I suspect that there's some primitive form of Platonism in the underbrush of Sarris's aesthetics.[3] He says, for example, that "Bazin's greatness as a critic . . . rested in his disinterested conception of the cinema as a universal entity." I don't know what a "universal entity" is, but I rather imagine Bazin's stature as a critic has less to do with "universals" than with intelligence, knowledge, experience, sensitivity, perceptions, fervor, imagination, dedication, lucidity — the traditional qualities associated with great critics. The role of the critic is to help people see what is in the work, what is in it that shouldn't be, what is not in it that could be. He is a good critic if he helps people understand more about the work than they could see for themselves; he is a great critic, if by his understanding and feeling for the work, by his passion, he can excite people so that they want to experience more of the art that is there, waiting to be seized. He is not necessarily a bad critic if he makes errors in judgment. (Infallible taste is inconceivable; what could it be measured against?) He is a bad critic if he does not awaken the curiosity, enlarge the interests and understanding of his audience. The art of the critic is to transmit his knowledge of and enthusiasm for art to others.

I do not understand what goes on in the mind of a critic who thinks a *theory* is what his confrères need because they are not "great" critics. Any honest man can perform the critical function to the limits of his tastes and powers. I daresay that Bogdanovich and V. F. Perkins and Rudi Franchi and Mark Shivas and all the rest of the new breed of specialists know more about movies than some people and could serve at least a modest critical function if they could remember that art is an expression of human experience. If they are men of feeling and intelligence, isn't it time for them to be a little ashamed of their "detailed criticism" of movies like *River of No Return?*

I believe that we respond most and best to work in any art form (and to other experience as well) if we are pluralistic, flexible, relative in our judgments, if we are eclectic. But this does not mean a scrambling and confusion of systems. Eclecticism is not the same as lack of scruple; eclecticism is the selection of the best standards and

---

[3] This might help to explain such quaint statements as: Bazin "was, if anything, generous to a fault, seeking in every film some vestige of the cinematic art" — as if cinema were not simply the movies that have been made and are being made, but some preëxistent entity. If Bazin thought in these terms, does Sarris go along with him?

principles from various systems of ideas. It requires more care, more orderliness to be a pluralist than to apply a single theory. Sarris, who thinks he is applying a single theory, is too undisciplined to recognize the conflicting implications of his arguments. If he means to take a Platonic position, then is it not necessary for him to tell us what his ideals of movies are and how various examples of film live up to or fail to meet his ideals? And if there is an ideal to be achieved, an objective standard, then what does élan have to do with it? (The ideal could be achieved by plodding hard work or by inspiration or any other way; the method of achieving the ideal would be as irrelevant as the "personality" of the creator.) As Sarris uses them, vitalism and Platonism and pragmatism do not support his *auteur* theory; they undermine it.

Those, like Sarris, who ask for objective standards seem to want a theory of criticism which makes the critic unnecessary. And he *is* expendable if categories replace experience; a critic with a single theory is like a gardener who uses a lawn mower on everything that grows. Their desire for a theory that will solve all the riddles of creativity is in itself perhaps an indication of their narrowness and confusion; they're like those puzzled, lost people who inevitably approach one after a lecture and ask, "But what is your basis for judging a movie?" When one answers that new films are judged in terms of how they extend our experience and give us pleasure, and that our ways of judging how they do this are drawn not only from older films but from other works of art, and theories of art, that new films are generally related to what is going on in the other arts, that as wide a background as possible in literature, painting, music, philosophy, political thought, etc., helps, that it is the wealth and variety of what he has to bring to new works that makes the critic's reaction to them valuable, the questioners are always unsatisfied. They wanted a simple answer, a formula; if they approached a chef they would probably ask for the one magic recipe that could be followed in all cooking.

And it is very difficult to explain to such people that criticism is exciting just because there is no formula to apply, just because you must use everything you are and everything you know that is relevant, and that film criticism is particularly exciting just because of the multiplicity of elements in film art.

This range of experience, and dependence on experience, is pitifully absent from the work of the *auteur* critics; they seem to view movies, not merely in isolation from the other arts, but in isolation even from their own experience. Those who become film specialists early in life are often fixated on the period of film during which they first began going to movies, so it's not too surprising that the *Movie* group — just out of college and some still in — are so devoted to the films of the forties and fifties. But if they don't widen their interests to include earlier work, how can they evaluate films in anything like their historical continuity, how can they perceive what is distinctive in films of the forties? And if they don't have interests outside films, how can they evaluate what goes on in films? Film aesthetics as a distinct, specialized field is a bad joke: the *Movie* group is like an intellectual club for the intellectually handicapped. And when is Sarris going to discover that aesthetics is indeed a branch of ethnography; what does he think it is — a sphere of its own, separate from the study of man in his environment?

SOME SPECULATIONS ON THE APPEAL
OF THE AUTEUR THEORY

If relatively sound, reasonably reliable judgments were all that we wanted from film criticism, then *Sight and Sound* might be considered a great magazine. It isn't, it's something far less — a good, dull, informative, well-written, safe magazine, the best film magazine in English, but it doesn't satisfy desires for an excitement of the senses. Its critics don't often outrage us, neither do they open much up for us; its intellectual range is too narrow, its approach too professional. (If we recall an article or review, it's almost impossible to remember which Peter or which Derek wrote it.) Standards of quality are not enough, and *Sight and Sound* tends to dampen enthusiasm. *Movie*, by contrast, seems spirited: one feels that these writers do, at least, love movies, that they're not condescending. But they too, perhaps even more so, are indistinguishable read-alikes, united by fanaticism in a ludicrous cause; and for a group that discounts content and story, that believes the director is the *auteur* of what gives the film value, they show an inexplicable fondness — almost an obsession — for detailing plot and quoting dialogue. With all the zeal of youth serving an ideal, they carefully reduce movies to trivia.

It is not merely that the *auteur* theory distorts experience (all theory does that, and helps us to see more sharply for having done so) but that it is an aesthetics which is fundamentally anti-art. And this, I think, is the most serious charge that can possibly be brought against an aesthetics. The *auteur* theory, which probably helped to liberate the energies of the French critics, plays a very different role in England and with the *Film Culture* and New York *Film Bulletin* *auteur* critics in the United States — an anti-intellectual, anti-art role.

The French *auteur* critics, rejecting the socially conscious, problem pictures so dear to the older generation of American critics, became connoisseurs of values in American pictures that Americans took for granted, and if they were educated Americans, often held in contempt. The French adored the American gangsters, and the vitality, the strength, of our action pictures — all those films in which a couple of tough men slug it out for a girl, after going through hell together in oil fields, or building a railroad, or blazing a trail. In one sense, the French were perfectly right — these were often much more skillfully made and far more interesting visually than the movies with a message which Americans were so proud of, considered so *adult*. Vulgar melodrama with a fast pace can be much more exciting — and more honest, too — than feeble, pretentious attempts at drama — which usually meant just putting "ideas" into melodrama, anyway. Where the French went off was in finding elaborate intellectual and psychological meanings in these simple action films. (No doubt we make some comparable mistakes in interpreting French films.)

Like most swings of the critical pendulum, the theory was a *corrective*, and it helped to remind us of the energies and crude strength and good humor that Europeans enjoyed in our movies. The French saw something in our movies that their own movies lacked; they admired it, and to some degree, they have taken it over and used it in their own way (triumphantly in *Breathless* and *Shoot the Piano Player*, not very successfully in their semi-American thrillers). Our movies were a product of American industry, and in a sense, it was America itself that they loved in our movies — our last frontiers, our robber-barons, our naiveté, our violence, our efficiency and speed and technology, our bizarre combination of sentimentality and inhuman mechanization.

But for us, the situation is different. It is good for us to be reminded that our mass culture is not altogether poisonous in its effect on other countries, but what is appealingly exotic — "American" — for them is often intolerable for us. The freeways of cities like Los Angeles may seem mad and marvelous to a foreign visitor; to us they are the nightmares we spend our days in. The industrial products of Hollywood that we grew up on are not enough to satisfy our interests as adults. We want a great deal more from our movies than we get from the gangster carnage and the John Ford westerns that Europeans adore. I enjoy some movies by George Cukor and Howard Hawks but I wouldn't be much interested in the medium if that were all that movies could be. We see many elements in foreign films that our movies lack. We also see that our films have lost the beauty and innocence and individuality of the silent period, and the sparkle and wit of the thirties. There was no special reason for the French critics, preoccupied with *their* needs, to become sensitive to *ours*. And it was not surprising that, in France, where film directors work in circumstances more comparable to those of a dramatist or a composer, critics would become fixated on American directors, not understanding how confused and inextricable are the roles of the front office, the producers, writers, editors, and all the rest of them — even the marketing research consultants who may pretest the drawing powers of the story and stars — in Hollywood. For the French, the name of a director *was* a guide on what American films to see; if a director was associated with a certain type of film that they liked, or if a director's work showed the speed and efficiency that they enjoyed. I assume that anyone interested in movies uses the director's name as some sort of guide, both positive and negative, even though we recognize that at times he is little more than a stage manager. For example, in the forties, my friends and I would keep an eye out for the Robert Siodmak films and avoid Irving Rapper films (except when they starred Bette Davis whom we wanted to see even in bad movies); I avoid Mervyn LeRoy films (though I went to see *Home Before Dark* for Jean Simmons's performance); I wish I could avoid Peter Glenville's pictures but he uses actors I want to see. It's obvious that a director like Don Siegel or Phil Karlson does a better job with what he's got to work with than Peter Glenville, but that doesn't mean there's any pressing need to go see every tawdry little gangster picture Siegel or Karlson directs; and perhaps if they tackled more difficult subjects they wouldn't do a better job than Glenville. There is no rule or theory involved in any of this, just simple discrimination; we judge the man from his films and learn to predict a little about his next films, we don't judge the films from the man.

But what has happened to the judgment of the English and New York critics who have taken over the *auteur* theory and used it to erect a film aesthetics based on those commercial movies that answered a need for the French, but which are not merely ludicrously inadequate to our needs, but are the results of a system of production that places a hammerlock on American directors? And how can they, with straight faces, probe for deep meanings in these products? Even the kids they're made for know enough not to take them seriously. How can these critics, sensible enough to deflate our overblown message movies, reject the total content of a work as unimportant and concentrate on signs of a director's "personality" and "interior meaning"? It's understandable that they're trying to find movie art in the loopholes of commercial production — it's a harmless hobby and we all play it now and then. What's incomprehensible is that they *prefer* their loopholes to unified film expression. If they weren't so determined to exalt products over works that attempt to express human experience, wouldn't they have figured out that the *mise-en-scène* which they seek out in these products, the director's personal style which comes through despite the material, is only a mere suggestion, a hint of what an artist can do when he's in control of the material, when the whole film becomes expressive? Isn't it obvious that *mise-en-scène* and subject material — form and content — can be judged separately only in bad movies or trivial ones? It must be black comedy for directors to read this new criticism and discover that films in which they felt trapped and disgusted are now said to be their masterpieces. It's an aesthetics for 1984: failure is success.

I am too far from the English scene to guess at motives, and far away also from New York, but perhaps close enough to guess that the Americans (consciously or unconsciously) are making a kind of social comment: like the pop artists, the New Realists with their comic strips and Campbell's soup can paintings, they are saying, "See what America is, this junk is the fact of our lives. Art and avant-gardism are phony; what isn't any good, is good. Only squares believe in art. The artifacts of industrial civilization are the supreme truth, the supreme joke." This is a period when men who consider themselves creative scoff at art and tradition. It is perhaps no accident that in the same issue of *Film Culture* with Sarris's *auteur* theory there is a lavishly illustrated spread on "The Perfect Filmic Appositeness of Maria Montez" — a fairly close movie equivalent for that out-sized can of Campbell's soup. The editor, Jonas Mekas, has his kind of social comment. This is his approach to editing a film magazine: "As long as the 'lucidly minded' critics will stay out, with all their 'form,' 'content,' 'art,' 'structure,' 'clarity,' 'importance' — everything will be all right, just keep them out. For the new soul is still a bud, still going through its most dangerous, most sensitive stage." Doesn't exactly make one feel welcome, does it? I'm sure I don't know what the problem is: are there so many "lucidly minded" critics in this country (like Andrew Sarris?) that they must be fought off? And aren't these little "buds" that have to be protected from critical judgments the same little film makers who are so convinced of their importance that they can scarcely conceive of a five-minute film which doesn't end with what they, no doubt, regard as the ultimate social comment: the mushroom cloud rising. Those "buds" often behave more like tough nuts.

Sarris with his love of commercial trash and Mekas who writes of the "cul-de-sac of Western culture" which is "stifling the spiritual life of man" seem to have irreconcilable points of view. Sarris with his joys in Raoul Walsh seems a long way from Mekas, the spokesman for the "independent film makers" (who couldn't worm their way into Sarris's outer circle). Mekas makes statements like "The new artist, by directing his ear inward, is beginning to catch bits of man's true vision." (Dear Lon Chaney Mekas, please get your ear out of your eye. Mekas has at least one thing in common with good directors: he likes to dramatize.) But to love trash and to feel that you are stifled by it are perhaps very close positions. Does the man who paints the can of Campbell's soup love it or hate it? I think the answer is both: that he is obsessed by it as a fact of our lives and a symbol of America. When Mekas announces, "I don't want any part of the Big Art Game" he comes even closer to Sarris. And doesn't the *auteur* theory fit nicely into the pages of an "independent film makers" journal when you consider that the work of those film makers might compare very unfavorably with good films, but can look fairly interesting when compared with commercial products. It can even look original to those who don't know much film history. The "independent film makers," Lord knows, are already convinced about their importance as the creative figures — the *auteurs*; a theory which suggested the importance of writing to film art might seriously damage their egos. They go even farther than the *auteur* critics' notion that the script is merely something to transcend: they often act as if anyone who's concerned with scripts is a square who doesn't dig film. (It's obvious, of course, that this aesthetic based on images and a contempt for words is a function of economics and technology, and that as soon as a cheap, lightweight 16mm camera with good synchronous sound gets on the market, the independent film makers will develop a different aesthetic.)

The *auteur* theory, silly as it is, can nevertheless be a dangerous theory — not only because it constricts the experience of the critics who employ it, but because it offers nothing but commercial goals to the young artists who may be trying to do something in film. *Movie* with its celebration of Samuel Fuller's "brutality" and the Mackie Mekas who "knows that everything he has learned from his society about life and death is false" give readers more of a charge than they get from the limp pages of *Sight and Sound* and this journal. This is not intended to be a snide remark about *Sight and Sound* and *Film Quarterly*: if they are not more sensational, it is because they are attempting to be responsible, to hoard the treasures of our usable past. But they will be wiped off the cinema landscape, if they can't meet the blasts of anti-art with some fire of their own.

The union of Mekas and Sarris may be merely a marriage of con-

venience; but if it is strong enough to withstand Sarris's "Hello and
Goodby to the New American Cinema" (in the *Village Voice,* September 20, 1962), perhaps the explanation lies in the many shared
attitudes of the Mekas group and the *auteur* critics. Neither group, for
example, is interested in a balanced view of a film; Mekas says he
doesn't believe in "negative criticism" and the *auteur* critics (just like
our grammar-school teachers) conceive of a review as "an appreciation." The directors they reject are so far beyond the pale that their
films are not even considered worth discussion. (Sarris who distributes zero ratings impartially to films as varied as *Yojimbo, The Man-
churian Candidate,* and *Billy Budd* could hardly be expected to take
time off from his devotional exercises with Raoul Walsh to explain
why these films are worthless.) Sarris, too, can resort to the language
of the hipster — "What is it the old jazz man says of his art? If you
gotta ask what it is, it ain't? Well, the cinema is like that." This is
right at home in *Film Culture,* although Sarris (to his everlasting
credit) doesn't employ the accusatory, paranoid style of Mekas: "You
criticize our work from a purist, formalistic and classicist point of
view. But we say to you: What's the use of cinema if man's soul goes
rotten?" The "you" is, I suppose, the same you who figures in so
much (bad) contemporary prophetic, righteous poetry and prose, the
"you" who is responsible for the Bomb and who, by some fantastically self-indulgent thought processes, is turned into the enemy, the
critic. Mekas, the childlike, innocent, pure Mekas, is not about to be
caught by "the tightening web of lies"; he refuses "to continue the
Big Lie of Culture." I'm sure that, in this scheme, any attempt at clear
thinking immediately places us in the enemy camp, turns us into the
bomb-guilty "you," and I am forced to conclude that Mekas is not
altogether wrong — that if we believe in the necessity (not to mention
the beauty) of clear thinking, we are indeed his enemy. I don't know
how it's possible for anyone to criticize his work from a "purist, formalistic and classicist point of view" — the method would be too far
from the object; but can't we ask Mekas: is man's soul going to be in
better shape because your work is protected from criticism? How
much nonsense dare these men permit themselves? When Sarris tells
us, "If the *auteur* critics of the Fifties had not scored so many coups
of clairvoyance, the *auteur* theory would not be worth discussing in
the Sixties," does he mean any more than that he has taken over the
fiats of the *auteur* critics in the fifties and goes on applying them in
the sixties? Does he seriously regard his own Minnelli-worship as
some sort of objective verification of the critics who praised Minnelli
in the fifties? If that's his concept of critical method, he might just
as well join forces with other writers in *Film Culture.* In addition to

Mekas ("Poets are surrounding America, flanking it from all sides,")
there is, for example, Ron Rice: "And the beautiful part about it all
is that you can, my dear critics, scream protest to the skies, you're too
late. The Musicians, Painters, Writers, Poets and Film-Makers all fly
in the same sky, and know Exactly where It's 'AT.' " Rice knows
where he's at about as much as Stan Brakhage who says, "So the
money vendors have begun it again. To the catacombs then. . . ." In
the pages of *Film Culture* they escape from the money changers in
Jerusalem by going to the catacombs in Rome. "Forget ideology,"
Brakhage tells us, "for film unborn as it is has no language and
speaks like an aborigine." We're all familiar with Brakhage's passion
for obstetrics, but does being a primitive man mean being a foetus?
I don't understand that unborn aborigine talk, but I'm prepared to
believe that grunt by grunt, or squeal by squeal, it will be as meaningful as most of *Film Culture*. I am also prepared to believe that for
Jonas Mekas, culture is a "Big Lie." And Sarris, looking for another
culture under those seats coated with chewing gum, coming up now
and then to announce a "discovery" like Joanne Dru, has he found
his spiritual home down there?

Isn't the anti-art attitude of the *auteur* critics, both in England
and here, implicit also in their peculiar emphasis on virility? (Walsh
is, for Sarris, "one of the screen's most virile directors." In *Movie* we
discover: "When one talks about the heroes of *Red River*, or *Rio
Bravo*, or *Hatari!* one is talking about Hawks himself. . . . Finally everything that can be said in presenting Hawks boils down to one simple
statement: here is a man.") I don't think critics would use terms like
"virile" or "masculine" to describe artists like Dreyer or Renoir; there
is something too *limited* about describing them this way (just as when
we describe a woman as sensitive and feminine, we are indicating her
special nature). We might describe Kipling as a virile writer but who
would think of calling Shakespeare a virile writer? But for the *auteur*
critics calling a director virile is the highest praise because, I suggest,
it is some kind of assurance that he is not trying to express himself in
an art form, but treats moviemaking as a professional job. (*Movie*:
Hawks "makes the very best adventure films because he is at one
with his heroes. . . . Only Raoul Walsh is as deeply an adventurer as
Hawks. . . . Hawks' heroes are all professionals doing jobs —
scientists, sheriffs, cattlemen, big game hunters: real professionals
who know their capabilities. . . . They know exactly what they can do
with the available resources, expecting of others only what they
know can be given.") The *auteur* critics are so enthralled with their
narcissistic male fantasies (*Movie*: "Because Hawks' films and their
heroes are so genuinely mature, they don't need to announce the fact

for all to hear") that they seem unable to relinquish their schoolboy notions of human experience. (If there are any female practitioners of *auteur* criticism, I have not yet discovered them.) Can we conclude that, in England and the United States, the *auteur* theory is an attempt by adult males to justify staying inside the small range of experience of their boyhood and adolescence — that period when masculinity looked so great and important but art was something talked about by poseurs and phonies and sensitive-feminine types? And is it perhaps also their way of making a comment on our civilization by the suggestion that trash is the true film art? I ask; I do not know.

Movie Journal

JONAS MEKAS

There are moments in my life when I think that Andrew Sarris was born under a much luckier star than I was. He chose (or was given) as his field of interest and enjoyment the narrative film. He goes to see Hitchcock's "Topaz" and he writes a column about it. He tells the plot of the film (it takes about one third of his column), he talks about the actors (it takes another big chunk of his column), then he discusses the social, the political ideas or references or implications of the film, etc. etc. — and there goes his column. There is plenty to write about. But I have seen the films of Bob Branaman 10 times by now and I still don't know what or how to write about him. As an aesthetic accomplishment, in the domain of film lyricism, Bob Branaman's work is superior to the latest by Hitchcock. But how to talk about Bob Branaman? Or the films of Piero Heliczer, also perfect lyrical expressions? How to discuss them intelligently and fruitfully? Have you noticed that I have practically never reviewed a film by Brakhage, the greatest film-maker making films today?

But there must be a way of talking about them. I intend, in my future columns — this is my challenge for the year 1970 — to try to deal with this problem. Last week, for the fourth or fifth time, I saw the films of Gerald Malanga. I used to dismiss his films. Oh, I used to say, here is another poet who wants to make films. Why don't they stick to their literature! But after the most recent viewing — and I am talking specifically about "In Search of the Miraculous" and "The Preraphaelite Dream" — I have managed to escape my own prejudices and now I have no doubt that Malanga's work has its place in film repertory.

Immediately after seeing Malanga's work, I summed it up for myself: Gerald is a lyrical romanticist. Why did I say so? How did I come to such a conclusion? My method must be similar to that of an art critic. There is a tendency, in movie criticism, to avoid any comparisons or methods that are either borrowed from other arts or resemble those of the other arts. I think such fears are unnecessary. The fact is, that when you watch a film, you are absorbing various visual impressions. I watched the films of Malanga, and the various details, the moods of the details, the people, the faces, and the pace of the camera, the textures, the choices of landscapes — all these impressions set me in a romantic mood. The pace was that of a memory, languorous. The people, the glimpses of people as they were walking in the gardens, and parks, and streets; the "ruins" of the civilizations, the cities; the young people (the romantic die young) standing, gazing; Malanga himself carrying a huge bouquet of red roses, standing on a bridge, looking into the river (in Rome); everything contributes toward a certain melancholy lyricism which pervades the film.

In Bob Branaman there is nothing of that sort. No pace, no detail, no structure that would set me in a romantic disposition. The images run in a fast pace, a lyrical staccato of frames, of images, disconnected from each other, but connected by a certain quality of feeling that has a minimum of emotion. It's more a feeling of form and materials than that of a specific emotion. Images: nature, people, cities — only brief fragments — definitely a notebook, a lyrical sketch book, lyrical memories; but with no great attachment, with no dwelling for too long on any one detail or place (which we have in the case of Malanga — all romantics seem to be attracted again and again to the same moods, places, and "ruins"; but not so a lyricist). There is a certain carelessness of attitude, or let me say lightness of attitude, present in Branaman. A pure lyricist has a light foot and sets you in a light mood. The pace, the structuring is bent toward that purpose — while Malanga's structures are heavier, and always with emotional undertones. There is an undertone in Branaman (or, say, in Brakhage's "Songs") too. But the undertone is not so much an emotion but some kind of mental quality. Form always has to do with mental qualities, with structures of thought and matter. It's nonsense that lyric is about "nothing." That's how art pulls us into the essence of things, through the form — and the form is thought. And that's where the true beauty of a pure lyricist like Branaman or Brakhage of the "Songs" lies. And that's where the curse of the romantics is: their sentimental attachments never really leave them, never really permit them to reach the core of things, that is a pure form. But this is not to put the work of Malanga down: there is enough, there are enough beauties and enough gold in the surface areas of our experience to keep us busy for a long time.

Because of the difficulties of discussing the non-narrative cinema, this cinema enjoys only a very small circle of followers. And nobody practically writes about it. I have seen film-makers cornering the newspaper movie reviewers: why don't you write about our films? What could they write! A reviewer of a new book of poetry, be it the *New York Review of Books* or the *New York Times* Sunday book supplement, or *Caterpillar* — he can at least quote a line or two. But what can a movie reviewer do? He can't quote movies. And since there is no plot to tell, no characters to talk about, and no timely political ideas to refer to — he says nothing. I wish I had a television program to discuss and "review" the avant-garde film. As for magazines and newspapers, it will be up to the new generation of film critics to work out the proper language, terminology, and method of discussing the non-narrative film.

THE CABINET OF DR. CALIGARI (1919)

Directed by Robert Wiene

The Museum of Modern Art/Film Stills Archive

... An attempt at subjecting the world to artistic prestylization, as in the expressionist settings of *The Cabinet of Dr. Caligari* (1919), could be no more than an exciting experiment that could exert but little influence upon the general course of events. To prestylize reality prior to tackling it amounts to dodging the problem.

— *Erwin Panofsky*

Behind the objection of critics to the stagy sets of *Dr. Caligari* ... lay the judgment that such films were false, that they exhibited a sensibility both pretentious and reactionary which was out of step with the democratic and more mundane sensibility of modern life.

— *Susan Sontag*

BATTLESHIP POTEMKIN
(1925)

Directed by Sergei Eisenstein

By making this distinction between the subjective capability of an *auteur* and the objective value of a work in film history, Bazin reinforces the popular impression that the Griffith of *Birth of a Nation* is superior to the Griffith of *Abraham Lincoln* in the perspective of timing which similarly distinguishes the Eisenstein of *Potemkin* from the Eisenstein of *Ivan the Terrible*....

— *Andrew Sarris*

How the earlier Russian films exploited the possibility of heroizing all sorts of machinery lives in everybody's memory; and it is perhaps more than accident that the two films which will go down in history as the great comical and the great serious masterpiece of the silent period bear the names and immortalize the personalities of two big ships: Keaton's *Navigator* (1924) and Eisenstein's *Potemkin* (1925).

— *Erwin Panofsky*

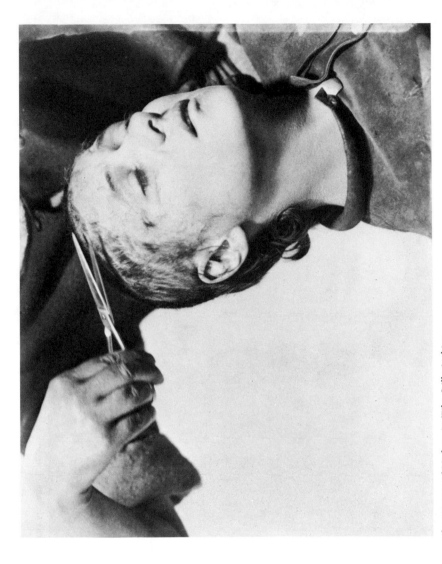

PASSION DE JEANNE D'ARC
(1928)

Directed by Carl Dreyer

The camera can induce an almost physical response — so that when . . . Dreyer's Jeanne d'Arc has her head shaved and some of the hair falls onto her lip, the sensation produced in us is almost physical.

— *Michael Roemer*

UN CHIEN ANDALOU (1928)

Directed by Luis Bunuel

The source of the idea of art as an act of violence pervading cinema and theatre is the aesthetics of Futurism and of Surrealism; its principal texts are, . . . for cinema, two films of Luis Bunuel, *L'Age d'Or* and *Un Chien Andalou.*

— *Susan Sontag*

THE GREAT DICTATOR (1940)

Directed by Charles Chaplin

The advent of the talkies, reducing if not abolishing this difference between screen acting and stage acting, thus confronted the actors and actresses of the silent screen with a serious problem. . . . Chaplin first tried to stand his ground and to remain an exquisite archaist but finally gave in, with only moderate success (*The Great Dictator*).

— *Erwin Panofsky*

The Museum of Modern Art/Film Stills Archive
Courtesy: Janus Films, Inc.

RASHOMON (1950)

Directed by Akira Kurosawa

In *Rashomon* and *The Seven Samarai* Kurosawa deals with events of the thirteenth and sixteenth centuries. . . . Film at its best uses the language of ordinary experience — but uses it subtly and artfully.

— *Michael Roemer*

The Seventh Seal is significant art because it is interesting to perception and says something important in a unique way. The same sorts of things can be said about . . . *Rashomon*.

— *Ralph A. Smith*

BREATHLESS (1960)

Directed by Jean-Luc Godard

Spontaneity, the sense that what is happening on the screen is happening for the first time and without plan or direction, is an essential factor in establishing a reality.... An almost improvised film — like *Shadows* or *Breathless*, made without great skill or art by relatively inexperienced people — can carry far greater conviction than the standard theatrical product.

— *Michael Roemer*

The French saw something in our movies that their own movies lacked; they admired it, and to some degree, they have taken it over and used it in their own way (triumphantly in *Breathless* . . .).

— *Pauline Kael*

LAST YEAR AT MARIENBAD
(1961)

Directed by Alain Resnais

Last Year at Marienbad demonstrates that the cinema does not have to duplicate supposed mental processes but can function in a way that the mind cannot, thereby extending and amplifying the mind.

— *Ted Perry*

Last Year at Marienbad made the clock as limply shapeless as one of Salvador Dali's watches. . . .

— *Anthony Schillaci*

BONNIE AND CLYDE (1967)

Directed by Arthur Penn

. . . Clyde's anger toward Captain Frank Haymer of the fabulous Texas Rangers is first provoked by his realization that Haymer is bounty hunting in Missouri for the Barrow gang instead of back home "protectin' the ranchin' poor folks."

— *Peter Harcourt*

The performance of youthful audiences in discussion of contemporary film indicates their freedom from the judgmental screen which blurs so many films for other generations. In speaking of *Bonnie and Clyde*, late high school kids and young adults do not dwell upon the career of crime or the irregularity of the sexual relationship, but upon other things. The development of their love fascinates young people. . . .

— *Anthony Schillaci*

2001: A SPACE ODYSSEY
(1968)

Directed by Stanley Kubrick

Many films succeed by virtue of what they leave out. *2001: A Space Odyssey* is such a film, its muted understatement creating gaps in the action that invite our inquiry. Only a square viewer wants to know where the black monolith came from and where it is going. For most of the young viewers to whom I have spoken, it is just there.

— *Anthony Schillaci*

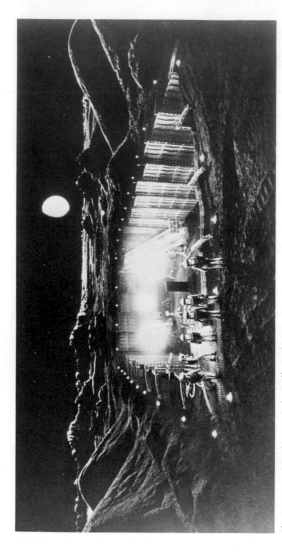

Courtesy: American Documentary Films

IN THE YEAR OF THE PIG   (1969)

Directed by Emile de Antonio

The Film as Politics

The challenge to "controlled" public information . . . must come
from documentary film, an art with revolutionary power —
emotional, educational and social. . . . Documentary film art
captures history in the act and reveals social change to the public
eye.

> — *David Castro and Jerry Stoll,*
> American Documentary Films

Photo by R. Raderman
Courtesy: Stan Vanderbeek

**STAN VANDERBEEK IN
HIS "MOVIE-DROME"**
a simultaneous magic/movie/
space theater

My own work leads me into multiprojection and the
building of the "movie-drome" in
which I plan to
develop a sight and sound research
center, a prototype
theater of the future, exploring
motion pictures,
image transmission and image
storage, video graphics,
electronic sound and music, drama
and experimental
cinema-theater.

— *Stan Vanderbeek*

3 The Film as Communications, Environment, and Politics

Unlike the authors represented in Chapter 2, those in this chapter are not concerned mainly with the aesthetic nature of film. They do not, for the most part, deny that that film is an art form, but they see film as a communications medium, an environment, or an agent for social change. The chapter divisions, however, should not suggest that there are two clear-cut and opposing groups, one seeing film as art, the other as communications. All art strives to communicate, just as most of the communications-oriented films discussed below strive to be art.

Sol Worth, in "Film as a Non-Art," looks at film as a process and a medium of communication. Worth describes some of the major approaches to the study of visual communication as they relate to film and constructs his own model for a filmic encoding-decoding process. He then examines this conceptual framework, more as a scientist than as a humanist or aesthetician, saying that his concern is not film as an art, but rather the process by which the viewer derives meaning from film. If linguistics is the science of language, then Worth can be seen as a scientist of visual language, which he calls "vidistics," attempting to determine its elements and to understand the logic of its structure. "What we are looking for is a logic, a system, a set of rules or definitions by which we can determine units and their sequence in order to know how to infer a meaning from them." Finally, Worth advocates that vidistics be explored further, although he recognizes the problems inherent in this new field of study.

In "The New Languages," Edmund Carpenter's concern is less with the structure and form of film than with the medium's effect upon viewers. He examines film as a language in the context of other media, particularly the written word and television. Like Balazs, Carpenter accuses the printed word of having rendered the faces of men illegible. He says that just as radio helped bring inflection back into speech, so film and television are helping us recover gesture, facial awareness, and the moods, emotions, and thoughts that visual language can convey. Like McLuhan, Carpenter explores differences between media and the effect each medium has upon the ideas expressed and upon persons who come into contact with it. He describes two experiments that examined the effectiveness of print, lectures, radio, film, and television for imparting information and indicates that the results did not show one medium to be superior to the others, but showed differences in kind rather than degree. He concludes: "Can books' monopoly of knowledge survive the challenge of the new languages? The answer is: no. What should be asked is: what can print do better than any other medium and is that worth doing?"

Examining young people's responses to film in "Film as Environment," Anthony Schillaci concludes that they do not respond to film in the traditional ways of which Panofsky, Kauffmann, and others speak. Schillaci asserts that as we come to understand how young people view films, we are forced to revise our notions of what film is. He states that the young think of film as an environment, something in which they can become totally immersed and which demands a mode of attention different from that demanded by the other arts. They hunger for the simultaneity and mind-expanding experiences that film can offer them. To move them, a film must have the pace, novelty, and style of a television commercial. Schillaci contends that the young are the major shaping influence on film and speculates on two developments he says are "revolutionizing" the way the young approach film: student film making and multimedia experimentation. Of the latter, Schillaci says, "Spontaneity, the chance synchronization, overload that leads to breakthrough — these are all part of the excitement that draws people to media rather than film alone." Schillaci is a McLuhanite and his argument can be compared with the counterargument presented by Peter Harcourt in Chapter 4.

Stan Vanderbeek, an experimental film maker who works primarily with computer films and the expanded cinema, continues the discussion of multimedia experimentation. In the poem, "Re: Vision," his main concern is the redefinition of film and the role of the film maker. Vanderbeek's interest in expanding the cinema is similar to that of Schillaci and Gerald O'Grady, whereas his emphasis on using media to change people's attitudes and perceptions is similar to that of Carpenter, Huxley, Balazs, and others in this book.

In my view I see that art and life, man and technology, unite
and seek to renew and re-view. . .
In particular I see that motion pictures will become
"emotion-pictures" and will generate into a new structure,
a new context, becoming a nonverbal international picture
language, in which we can talk to each other. . .

More important, inter-culturally, art and life
must do something about the future; the world is hanging
by a thread of verbs and nouns.

The last three articles deal explicitly with this last point — with
the film as politics, with film as a way of promoting social change.
"Newsreel" is a montage of remarks by members of Newsreel, a
collective of politically active film makers who attempt to use film as
a revolutionary weapon. As San Francisco Newsreel members
Marilyn Buck and Karen Ross state, "In our hands film is not an
anesthetic, a sterile, smooth-talking apparatus of control. It is a
weapon to counter, to talk back to and to crack the facade of the
lying media of capitalism." Newsreel wants its films shown outdoors,
in traveling trailers, in schools — anyplace where they can be shown
to people who would otherwise only come into contact with the mass
media. They try to confront, to stop people in the street, to show
them their films, and to discuss the films with them.

In "On Two Fronts," critic Leo Braudy examines a number of
Newsreel films from the viewpoints of both their aesthetics and their
politics. He points out that earlier Newsreels, although engaging and
provocative, were usually simplistic and expository and did not
confront the audience, but that some later non-sync, less linear, less
chronological films do confront and do not suggest easy solutions.
Braudy's praise for these more experimental Newsreel films is based
on his assertion that they try to integrate commitment with film
technique to achieve more open-minded political results not only
through their content, but also through their aesthetic radicalization
of the viewer.

"Profile of Art in Revolution," by David Castro and Jerry Stoll, is
another statement on the use of film as an instrument of social
change. The authors give a historical, economic, and aesthetic
rationale for the establishment of American Documentary Films.
Perhaps less "radical" than Newsreel, ADF is also a reaction against
the mass media's control over information available to most people.
ADF film makers see themselves as artists responsible to the future
as well as to the past.

Film as a Non-Art:
An Approach to the Study of Film

SOL WORTH

My title is not meant to be a statement of belief, a challenge to the artist, or a manifesto calling for a new "new wave" of non-art or anti-art films. It *is* intended to imply a particular direction of inquiry into the nature of film and the film process — to explore a group of questions that emerge from that inquiry.

This implied direction will lead us to look at film as a process and as a medium of communication, rather than as an art or an art form — and will, therefore, depart from standard aesthetic theory and attempt instead to apply some of the current concepts in communication theory and psychology to the study of this specific form of visual communication.

I would like first to examine briefly the concept of communication and visual communication as it relates to film; then, to outline some previous attempts by philosophers, aestheticians and psychologists to deal with pictures, images and films; and finally, to suggest that film may be examined as if it were a "language," and to explore some of the problems in communication and linguistics that develop from this attempt.

My purpose in examining film and the film process in this way rests on the assumption that the frameworks of communication and linguistic theory may throw new and exciting light on the question, "What does a film communicate, and how does this process work?" The very form of the question — the use of the word "communicate" — helps to clarify the specific nature of the inquiry: to examine film as communication — as a mediating object, and process, through which humans interact in certain ways.

Communication is one of those words that seem to be cropping up everywhere, referring to an ever increasing list of phenomena and behavior; yet it is a word that has only recently come into scholarly and popular use. The 1895 Encyclopedia Britannica, for example, does not even include the word in its index. By now, of course, so much has been written about communication — its processes and problems — that we may rightfully ask whether studying film as communication will help us to understand what happens when we see a film. Although many formulations and definitions of communication have been developed, and many of the current theoretical discussions, definitions and theories of communication would be relevant to this inquiry, so comprehensive a task is beyond the scope and the needs of this discussion.

As I will use the term here, communication can be broadly thought of as *human interaction through messages*.

Just as I have, for the purposes of this inquiry, limited the concept of communication to exclude animal and machine communication, so would I like to limit the concept of visual communication before I define it. A further distinction that must be made is one between the so-called mental or internal image, introduced by Edward Titchener and the introspectionist psychologists, and the commonly observable external image or picture. These psychologists used the word "image" to refer both to what one saw with the eyes, and to what one saw in the "mind's eye." In writing about verbal communication Lev Vygotsky and others have suggested that we distinguish between these two by calling the internal image thought, and its external expression language. Margaret Mead has also suggested the term "pictograph" to distinguish this commonly observable external image from its internal or mental counterpart. I shall use the word image throughout as consistent with Mead's "commonly observable *external* image," and with Vygotsky's concept of external expression.

Such diverse activities as reading, watching facial expressions of people as they talk or respond to talk, the "kinesics" of Birdwhistell, which he calls the language of gesture, the nonverbal communication studied by Reusch and Bateson, painting, architecture, graphic design, the look of a newsstand, television and movies have all at one time or another been treated as visual communications. Obviously they belong together by virtue of being related to seeing, even though we do not yet know enough about the processes of visual communication to describe them all adequately as similar phenomena.

I shall define visual communication as: the *transmission of a signal* received primarily through visual receptors, which *we treat as a message by inferring meaning from it*. (For the purposes of this paper, the range of signals under discussion will be limited to those commonly called film or motion pictures.) This definition offers us several clues that help us to clarify our original question: What and how does a film communicate?

If film is a specific set of signals, that we decide in some as yet unexplained way to treat as a message, we can ask, what is there in any signal, or in us, that tells us to treat it as a message; and, what is it in us or in a film signal that tells us which part is message and which isn't — or even further, which part is more message — has more information — than other parts. We can also ask, what in the signal that we have decided to treat as a message allows us to infer meaning from it? The definition I have just given implies that there is no meaning in the film itself, and from this we can infer a definition of the word "meaning" that we might apply to the study of film. We can say that the meaning of a film is a relationship between the implication of the maker and the inference of the audience. Although the meaning of a film is inferred in large part from the images and sounds in sequence in the film, meaning is clearly that which we *infer* from the film — from its elements, units and parts.

It may be postulated, therefore, that film communication is the transfer of an inferable meaning through the range of materials that a film offers or does not offer as signals, and through the elements and combinations of elements it allows or does not allow. These materials and elements impose their own constraints upon the signals we receive and choose to treat as messages. It is these filmic materials, elements and constraints, and their relation to the meaning we infer from them that we must study in order to know what happens when a film is seen, and when we say it has meaning.

Our question can be reformulated in this light to read, "What does a film mean, and how is someone able to infer this meaning?"

The question of meaning in pictures is hardly a new one. While film communication is a recent development, communication through pictures goes back almost as far as man himself, and questions concerning the meaning of his pictures have been discussed in a great variety of ways. It might be helpful for us to look for a moment at some of the past attempts to analyze pictures, and specifically, at those attempts that have dealt with the question, "What do pictures mean?"

Many of the attempts to analyze pictures, dating back some twenty-three hundred years, were undertaken by philosophers and pursued the normative question of evaluation — is the picture good or bad, beautiful or ugly — rather than the substantive question of meaning. Although the past hundred years have seen the beginnings of a systematic interest by aestheticians and philosophers in the substantive questions related to pictures, and although this interest has wandered freely over the map of human interests and understandings, emphasizing at various times the religious, expressive, sensualistic, perceptive, cognitive, illusionistic, symbolic, nonverbal, semiotic and psychological approaches toward the understanding and analysis of pictures, it has for the most part maintained one basic implicit assumption: All events that undergo aesthetic scrutiny can and should be judged either as good or bad, beautiful or ugly, or as art or not art. The arguments of the various dissenting schools of aesthetics revolved not around the assumption that the normative question of good or bad was at issue but rather on the specific methods and theories of normative determination.

Some workers in aesthetics, communication theory and psychology have in the past fifty to seventy-five years begun to question this value system which forces theorists to make choices between good-bad and art-non-art, or forces analysis of both extremes of some scale but excludes the middle. This does not mean that the concepts, "art" or "beauty," which have in large part governed the analysis of pictures for so long, are no longer applicable to the study of visual communication. What I am suggesting is that current thought, by conceiving of pictures as part of a communication process leads one to see the difference between evaluation and meaning. My concern is not whether film is art or not, but whether the process by which we get meaning from film can be understood and clarified. My objections to the older assumptions of art-non-art are based mainly on their exclusiveness and noncontinuity. While all art might be said to be communicative, all communication is most certainly not art. Assumptions that fail to provide criteria for the analysis of messages falling between the extremes of good and bad, beautiful and ugly and art and not-art must prove singularly unfit as basic assumptions for the analysis of films that so clearly fall between these extremes.

I would like to suggest that we consider the realm of communication as a continuum. All human interaction through messages falls somewhere on that continuum. The determination of the meaning of a message is a necessary if not always sufficient condition for its subsequent judgment. The labeling of poles of judgment values on a continuum — whether good or bad, moral or immoral, beautiful or ugly — depends upon many factors extrinsic to the meaning of the message. Let us leave the questions of evaluation, fascinating though they are, to the value analysts, aestheticians and philosophers. I do not mean that when we look at a film we should ignore judgment, but rather that we should distinguish conceptually between the process of inferring meaning from messages and the process of evaluating those messages.

It would be useful then to digress for a moment and try to trace some of the major concepts and approaches to the study of meaning in visual phenomena. Let us examine some of the more recent arguments about meaning in art, and some of the approaches to the

understanding of visual phenomena that psychologists and psychi-
atrists have taken in the past seventy-five years.

The basic argument in modern times over the place of meaning in
art might be said to start with Kant, who defined aesthetics in his
third Critique as a "judgment of the beautiful in art and nature."
Hegel continued this argument some years later and urged that we
drop the concern with nature and that aestheticians concern
themselves only with art as the aesthetic stimulus.

Although these early nineteenth-century philosophers wrote
about the judgment of beauty in art, they did not specifically exclude
meaning from art. The attribution of meaninglessness to art comes as
a more recent phenomenon, represented by such critics as Sir Herbert Read, who says that "a work of art exists not by virtue of any
meaning, but by virtue of aspects of art that have no meaning." Such
statements seem to be a result of the dogmas laid down by the logical
positivists in the early part of this century.

The logical positivist position on art can be understood through
the works of the logician, Rudolf Carnap, who writes about art that
"only verifiable statements of specific empirical sciences can be
legitimately conceived as knowledge of the states of nature or of
matters of fact . . . no object in any mode of art can be of any value in
acquiring new knowledge. Whatever therefore we take from a work
of art may offer emotional or formal pleasure but cannot offer
intellectual meaning."

The force of this positivist theory and its wide influence on
Western thought in the first half of this century have prompted many
aestheticians to try their hands at countering it.

Clearly opposed to both the positivists and the Readian
no-meaning group is the aesthetician Henry David Aiken, who sums
up the opposing view by saying that "the predominant power of
pictures to arouse, sustain, and project emotion is a function not of
their quality as shapes, but of their meaning and, in the case of art, of
their cognitive meaning."

Lionel Trilling and Jacques Maritain take positions somewhere in
between. Trilling, while denying the validity of the positivist position,
seems to feel the power of their argument so strongly that he is
forced to theorize that the meaning of a work of art is not rational at
all. Trilling's resolution is that works of art offer the appearance of
thought, allowing one the pleasure of feeling that he understands. He
refers to this as cogency, seemingly to differentiate it from the more
scientific concept of "cognition." He adds, "it [the aesthetic response]
is the appearance of thought."

For Maritain, on the other hand, meaning is neither the

appearance of thought, nor a verifiable statement of knowledge. He answers the positivists from the tradition of Thomistic Catholicism. A work of art is "an object of experience." Maritain, like Trilling, does not argue for meaning derived in terms of rational cognition but rather that, "Here is meaning that is different enough from what we commonly call knowledge, meaning which is not expressible in ideas and judgments, but which is rather experience . . . for it wants to be expressed, and is expressible only in a work of art." He equates knowledge and meaning in art as an experience through which we can know God and concludes that "it is a sin for the poet to eat at the tree of knowledge."

Jacques Barzun goes even further and expresses what many of us must sometimes feel when we read the convolutions of thought about what seem to us to be meaningful acts of communication. He throws out entirely the question of what a work of art *is* and how one knows its meaning, and concentrates on an examination of what it *does* for the beholder who enjoys it. "The appreciation of art does not co-incide with intelligence," he writes, "what it correlates with no one knows." Not only is there no determinable meaning, but for Barzun it is an antiegalitarian concept for anyone to think that he knows what "The Meaning" or "The Good" in a work of art is. Criticism, he concludes, "is not the field of Armageddon, where one battles for the Lord, but Dover Beach where ignorant armies clash by night."

Not all people who are concerned with "art," however, feel themselves to be members of ignorant armies clashing by night, nor members of a group thinking about the unthinkable and the unknowable. Some, such as the art historian Meyer Shapiro, or the anthropologist Franz Boas, supported by behavioral scientists in many fields, have been concerned with the meaning of works of art as discoverable in the various styles of art. These theorists feel that the meaning of a work of art can best be determined by "searching in a style for the qualities and structures that can be matched with some aspect of thinking or a world view [of a particular culture]."

The meaning of art and of communication for this group lies not so much in individual works but in the broad sweeps and aggregate changes of style across cultures that are explained by varying forms of social life within the context of cultures, empires, dynasties, cities, classes and institutions.

Henry David Aiken's work can serve as a bridge between the formal aesthetician and the behavioral scientist. He takes the position that "the best model for conceiving the aesthetic response is . . . that of the psychological concept of the consummatory response pattern. So conceived, the whole series of contrasts between the aesthetic and the cognitive . . . become gratuitous. They stand in the way of our theoretical grasp of the variability and complexity of which the aesthetic experience is capable. It is now possible to consider the alleged incompatibility between so-called cognitive meaning, and aesthetic meaning." The impetus for Aiken's argument is empirical — he is acquainted with much of the thinking that has been done by behavioral scientists — but his proof avoids (perhaps out of consideration for the sensitivities of his audience) the examination of the empirical evidence and the theories based on research in perception, cognition and the psychology of art and communication.

What we might call experimental or psychological aesthetics seemed to go through two stages. In the latter part of the nineteenth century, following the work of the psychologist Gustave Fechner, three ideas emerged. First the concept of aesthetic empathy, then the concept of aesthetic "play" and finally the idea of aesthetic, or psychic, distance. These ideas served their purpose; they started a train of thought about aesthetics based on experiments in psychology but the ideas themselves seemed to have been laid aside by the later twentieth-century aestheticians.

Three other approaches that might be called the psychoanalytic, the gestalt, and the early behaviorist seem best to characterize the work done in what may be termed behavioral aesthetics, from the early 1900's to just after World War I. These approaches are more strictly psychological than aesthetic, and were motivated more by a desire to explain human behavior in general than by a desire to explain paintings or art.

Stemming from the work of Freud, the psychoanalytic approach to pictures and films germinates from the fundamental notion that the aesthetic effect, and most of man's behavior, can be explained in terms of the working out of a complex of conscious and unconscious personality needs and drives, at least some of which are erotic, and all of which strive toward and often find symbolic expression in behavior or in dreams and in the arts.

The attempt of the psychoanalytic critics and theorists has been to correlate the inferred meaning of the work with whatever biographical data were available about the maker. Whatever formal elements were found in the work were considered as choices of communication alternatives dictated by the personality needs of the maker, and whatever elements were found to be important in the response of the viewer were considered as inferences dictated by the unconscious needs of the viewer, or as conscious recognition and response by the viewer to the personality of the maker.

The second of these twentieth-century approaches — the concept of the gestalt — is concerned not with the personality of the sender or of the receiver, but rather with the perceptual organizing factors of the "units" or "wholes" that are involved in conditioning the meaning we infer from a communication.

The third approach, the early behaviorist, covers a wide range of conceptions and methods which I would like to distinguish from the other approaches. The experimentalists are those who distrust as unscientific any investigations that make meaning inferences on any basis other than precise measurement of observable behavior, and that make predictions from conclusions not drawn from objective measurement. The early art and music appreciation tests by Meier and Seashore exemplify such attempts to quantify and predict reactions to nonverbal stimuli. If aesthetic stimuli have meaning for the viewer or the listener, they reasoned, we ought to find out what that meaning is, or at the very least we ought to be able to measure and compare one person's reaction to that of a group or to that of another person. Dreher, for example, observed in 1948 that college students trained in music sweat more when they listen to certain pieces than college students untrained in music.

Many of these early workers devoted themselves to measuring preferences as a way of arriving at different reactions. Olsen concluded that people prefer full frequency sounds to limited frequency sounds, that ranges of full frequency sounds were found to be more "good" than those of low frequency. In relation specifically to images it was found, for example, that little boys prefer seascapes to landscapes, and little girls prefer people to either; that children of both sexes prefer bright to dull colored pictures. It has been shown that girls below the age of fifteen give to cartoons a meaning different from that given by girls from fifteen to eighteen. They also evaluate them differently in terms of their funniness.

F. Sander, a gestalt experimentalist, advanced the notion that experiences organized around the unit of the face were more clearly differentiated by a viewer than were experiences organized against a neutral ground. He attempted to prove this conception of physiognomic organization by showing that the distance between two dots is much harder to estimate in its variations when the dots are presented against a ground of blank white paper than when they are made to represent eyes in a schematic face. One could go on at great length describing isolated bits of information that have been found to correlate with other bits.

I have attempted this very brief and incomplete sketch of attitudes, approaches and theories toward the concept of meaning in visual communication to suggest its historical longevity, its complexity and variability. I do not feel that these approaches have taken us very far, or that these theorists are asking the questions we should be most interested in answering, but I do think that such an outline offers us some clues that may help us to develop a more fruitful approach toward stating and solving the problems of film viewing and film analysis that face us today.

Although we are still concerned with the normative questions, they are now seen as social issues. Is violence in films good? Why are Hollywood films bad? In the analysis of films themselves and of pictures, the question of goodness or badness has for the large part been dropped. Similarly few of us today are willing to accept pictures and films as meaningless, or to analyze them as if they merely gave the appearance of meaning, or were an experience of God. The problems of interest today seem to be the substantive ones: to develop theories of meaning about visual communication; and to search for understanding of those processes of cognitive interaction that will help us to formulate the processes occurring when we see a film and when we infer meaning from it.

In the light of this discussion let us turn again to an examination of the process of film. Film communication can perhaps be clarified by the use of a conceptual framework that treats film as a process, and that separates the steps through which that communication takes place. This model should first of all allow us to describe the entire system in which film communication takes place — the maker of the film, the film itself, and the one who sees the film. It should contain the possibility of verification. The description should be clear enough to enable us to know how and where to test it. It should also have face validity, that is, it should correspond to what most people who make or look at films intuitively think happens during this process.

The process of film communication can be thought of as beginning with what I have called a Feeling-Concern. A person has a "feeling," the recognition of which under certain circumstances arouses enough "concern" so that he is motivated to communicate that feeling to others. I have purposely chosen words like feeling and concern that are vague and rather imprecise. After consideration of the entire model, it might prove valuable to try to fit the concepts that these words identify into tighter conceptual frameworks, but for the moment let us use the word "feeling" in the loose sense, by which we mean, "I feel that. . . ."

I use the word concern in the sense that the philosopher Paul Tillich uses it — "each man has his own concern, the ultimate concern is left for man to determine."

This Feeling-Concern then, this concern to communicate

something, which many psychologists feel is almost a basic human drive, is most often imprecise, amorphous and internalized. It cannot be transmitted to another or even to ourselves in this vague, internalized, "feeling" state. With the decision to communicate, a sender must develop a Story-Organism — an organic unit whose basic function is to provide a vehicle that will carry or embody the Feeling-Concern.

The Story-Organism does not need to be a story in the usual sense of the word, but it may be. It is a collection, a set or a cluster, of "things" developed from the Feeling-Concern. I chose the word organism rather than such a word as element, structure, style or system because I want, first, to suggest the living quality and nature of the process that Story-Organism names and to suggest the quality of growth and development as it occurs in a human personality in the act of communication. Second, the use of the word organism suggests the biological concept of function by which most organisms are understood and by which we can examine the story organism, and third, it is meant to call to mind the concept of organization. All of these qualities, developmental, functional and structural, are meant to be implied at the Story-Organism stage of the process.

The Story-Organism mediates between the Feeling-Concern and the next stage of the process of film communication, the Image-Event. Before describing the Image-Event, it might be helpful to look at the Feeling-Concern and the Story-Organism in another light. Suppose we think of the Feeling-Concern as a belief that we want to communicate. We can think of a belief in terms developed by Rokeach as "a proposition we hold to be true which influences what we say or do. Any expectancy or implicit set is also a belief; therefore we can say that a belief is a predisposition to action." In this sense a Feeling-Concern is a belief about which we are predisposed to act. The Story-Organism can be thought of as the next step in that chain of actions. We do not always know, continues Rokeach, "what a person believes by any single statement or action. We have to *infer* what a person really believes from *all* the things he says and does. The organization of all verbal and non-verbal, explicit and implicit beliefs, sets, or tendencies would be the total belief-disbelief system." In this sense what I call the Story-Organism can be thought of as similar to the belief-disbelief system developed by Rokeach.

The Feeling-Concern then is a feeling — a vague, amorphous, internalized belief — that a given person at a given time is concerned or predisposed to act upon, in our case, to act upon specifically by communicating it. The Story-Organism is the organization into a system of those beliefs and feelings that a person accepts as true and related to his Feeling-Concern. It is the structuring of the many constituent units through which, and within which, his Feeling-Concern is clarified, organized and brought to life so that it can be externalized and communicated.

It is at this point only, after awareness of the Feeling-Concern and development of the Story-Organism (either consciously or unconsciously), that a given person, a film-maker, can begin to collect the specific external Image-Events that, when stored on film and sequenced, will become the film communication.

For the moment let's just define an Image-Event as a unit of film. We shall come back to it after we have finished describing the entire process. So far we have talked about the first half only. The sending process has been started. A film has been made.

I would like to suggest that the receiving process occurs in reverse order, as a kind of mirror image of the sending process. The viewer first sees the Image-Event — the sequence of signals that we call a film. Most often he knows nothing of what went on before. He doesn't know the film-maker and his personality, and he usually doesn't know what the film is about, or is meant to communicate. Should our viewer choose to treat these signals as a message, he will first infer the Story-Organism from the sequenced Image-Events. He will become aware of the belief system of the film-maker from the images he sees on the screen. From this awareness of the message he will, if the communication "works," be able to infer — to evoke in himself — the Feeling-Concern.

As you can see from this suggested view of the total process, the meaning of the film for the viewer is closely related to the Feeling-Concern of the film-maker. The single Image-Events of the film are the signals, these specifically sequenced Image-Events are what we treat as messages, and our inference about the Feeling-Concern of the maker is what we call the meaning of the film.

Ernst Kris, in his *Psychoanalytic Explorations in Art*, takes a somewhat similar view of the process. He conceives of art "as a process of communication and re-creation." Communication, he continues, "lies not so much in the prior intent of the artist as in the consequent re-creation by the audience of his work of art. What is required for communication therefore is similarity between the audience process and that of the artist." He deals at great length with the psychic processes that occur when the process of creation is *reversed* within the viewer. Kris suggests that this process proceeds from perception of the work on a conscious level to the understanding of the work on an unconscious level — reversing the sequence that takes place within the artist.

Figure 1

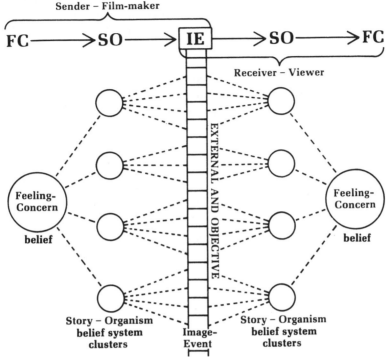

This model that I have suggested [Figure 1] describes the process of film communication. It doesn't, however, explain it. In this concluding section I would like to examine this conceptual framework and explore some of the relationships contained in it to see if we can find some approaches to help us explain why, and how, what has been described happens.

The first notion that emerges quite clearly is the difference between the Image-Event and both the Feeling-Concern and Story-Organism.

The three terms on the left of the drawing can be thought to belong to the realm of the film-maker. The three on the right belong to the realm of the viewer. The Image-Event is the nodal point of the process. It is common to both film-maker and viewer — to both sender and receiver, creator and re-creator. The Image-Event is different from the other two terms, both as a part of the process for the film-maker and as a part of the process for the viewer. It is the only unit of this process that is directly observable.

The parts of the process that lead to the Image-Event and the parts of the process that lead away from it to the inference of meaning on the part of the viewer are internal processes which take place within the human being. The strip running down the page (like a strip of film) is our external objective Image-Event. The series of concepts across the top of the model describing a process represent our internal world.

In our original definition of communication we implied that the inference of meaning from a film was a function — a relationship — of something in the message and something in us. We can look at this model and see that it suggests two separate fields of study — two kinds of questions. The first revolves about the explanation of the human beings involved in the process, and the second about the explanation of the objective Image-Event that is the focus — the mediating agent — of the process. In order to explain the process of film communication we want to know what there is in the Image-Event that allows an individual to infer meaning from it — to re-create what was created. We shall, however, probably never be able completely to separate and distinguish between what is within ourselves and what is within the film that enables us to infer meaning from it. This particular area of study — the interaction between persons and groups, and the stimuli they relate to — has been undertaken by the social and behavioral scientists. Although relevant to our interests, the specific study of the relationships between people and events cannot be the professional concern of those interested in visual communication.

The study of the Image-Event, however — its properties, units, elements and systems of organization and structure that enable us to infer meaning from a film — should be the subject of our inquiry, and of our professional concern.

Most of us who have thought about film and written about film have at one time or another used such phrases as the "language of film," "film grammar," "the syntax of film" and so on. We speak of the "language of dreams," the "language of vision," "the nonverbal languages." Most of us seem to share this desire to call film a language.

Although I am not sure that film is a "language," in the sense in which we define verbal language, my previous work in film and film research has led me to believe that an investigation of film *as if* it were a language offers interesting opportunities for its analysis and understanding. What follows, then, is not an attempt to prove that film is a "language" but rather a direction of inquiry into film as if it were a language — to see where it leads, and to see what paths this search will help to uncover.

The field of language studies, while historically starting with the examination of specific spoken and written languages and their changes over time, has now moved to the examination of *language behavior* encompassing many diverse interests and fields of study. As distinct from psychology, which takes as part of its area of study a concern with verbal behavior in the context of events occurring within the organism, and as distinct from the other social sciences that are to some extent concerned with the analysis of the contents of verbal behavior as it is relevant to shared cultural beliefs and actions, linguistic science has as its traditional subject matter the signal system as such, "the language as she is spoke."

In terms of our description of the process of film communication, the line going from the Image-Event down the page, representing the external Image-Event or film, would be considered the traditional field of interest for linguistic science. Although traditional linguistics has been divided into two main branches, the historical and the descriptive, they complement and are necessary to each other. The major effort, however, of linguistics in recent years has been to develop a system of units, elements and structure of a language that would enable one to describe that language.

The model that I have proposed and the earlier discussion revolving about the definition of visual communication imply an interest not only in the description of the signal system as such but also an interest in the relationship of the film-maker to the film, and the viewer to the film. In a sense the film is a mediating agent between two human beings engaged in an act of communication.

In the last twenty years a new science, or an offshoot of the older science of linguistics, has been developed, concerning itself not only with the descriptive and structural elements of language but with the internal human dynamics of language behavior similar to the problems I have set forth in the line on my model running horizontally across the page — the line represented as internal process. This new science, Psycholinguistics, "is concerned in the broadest sense with relations between messages and the characteristics of human individuals who select and interpret them. In a narrower sense psycholinguistics studies those processes whereby the intentions of the speaker are transformed into signals ... and whereby these signals are transformed into the interpretations of hearers."

It is within this linguistic and psycholinguistic framework that the hypothesis is advanced that film can be studied as if it were the "language" of visual communication, and as if it were possible to determine its elements and to understand the logic of its structure.

Being forced to coin another word — one that sounds like linguistics but is different — I have called this area of study *vidistics* for two reasons: to make a distinction between the process of verbal and that of visual communication, and to preserve some of the connotations of similarity that do exist between these two modes.

Vidistics in this early stage is concerned, first, with the determination and description of those visual elements relevant to the process of communication. Second, it is concerned with the determination of the rules, laws and logic of visual relationship that help a viewer to infer meaning from an Image-Event, and the interaction of Image-Events in sequence. Film as if it were language, as studied vidistically, is thus thought of as the study of specified elements, elements in sequence, operations on these elements, and cognitive representations of them that act as a mediating agent in a communication process between human beings — between a film-maker and a viewer — between a creator and a re-creator.

The first problem then, in studying film in this way, is to formulate the units and elements that, when manipulated in certain ways by the film-maker and the viewer, comprise the system we will study as a language. This is no easy matter.

In a previous paper I have presented the attempts of many film theorists in the past to develop a system of units or elements by which film can be described, and I concluded that, although some of these theorists used phrases such as the "grammar of film," none of them developed a theory of film language embodying filmic elements or units capable of precise syntactic structure. No cohesive body of elements or units and operations has been formulated from which rules of structure, function and syntax can be observed and constructed. Rather than go into the specific elements and hypotheses about these elements in sequence that I have reported elsewhere, I would prefer to discuss some of the theoretical problems involved in looking at film as if it were a language, and to open up for examination some of the possible areas in which further research must be done before we can hope to have even the beginnings of a science of vidistics.

How can a film be analyzed as a language? If we must break it up into units or elements, how do we do this? In what specific ways is film language similar or not similar to spoken language? Are there different film languages as there are different spoken languages? Is there something about the grammar of film that is the same as spoken grammar? Does the notion of grammar or syntax occur in a similar fashion through a variety of film languages? Does the Whorfian hypothesis — that differences in spoken languages make for differences in our experiencing of the world — hold true for differences in language modes between the verbal and the visual? These and a host of similar questions become apparent when we look at film as language through the framework I have presented here.

The very notion of breaking a large thing into its constituent pieces is a complex one. The "pieces" into which a language can be divided are as numerous as the ingenuity and number of the investigators. For example, if we use as our illustration spoken language, we can break up a conversation between two people in some of the following ways. We can start by dividing the utterances into those uttered by each person. We can divide each person's utterances into what we know to be paragraphs, sentences, words, syllables and single sounds. We can divide the utterances into verbs, nouns, adverbs and so on. We can divide them into declarative, interrogative or exclamatory sentences. We can divide the utterances into large words or small words, into words beginning with vowels or consonants, or even into words that begin with specified letters of the alphabet.

What all these divisions have in common, however, is a known group of concepts and categories for organizing utterances. We already know how to define and distinguish among a noun, a verb, a word, a sentence and a syllable and even the utterance of one man from that of another.

Grammarians and linguists are not only involved in constant classification of units, but are constantly concerned with which method of classification and categorization is most efficient and effective. Recent studies in the "new grammar" have shown concern over the relevance of even these forms (noun, verb, et cetera) of grammatical categorization and organization.

In the study of visual communication and of film, no such comprehensive set of categories exists. We share the concern of the investigators of verbal language but lack the backlog of comprehensive work that has been done on oral and written language.

I have up to this point used the words "unit" and "element" almost interchangeably referring to the pieces we divide things into for study. Actually, "unit" and "element" refer to different ways of dividing a thing. According to Vygotsky, the method of breaking complex psychological wholes into elements is comparable to the chemical analysis of water which breaks it into hydrogen and oxygen. He finds this method inadequate for the study of language processes. "Neither of these (hydrogen and oxygen) possesses the properties of the whole and each possesses properties not present in the whole. The student applying this method in looking for an explanation of some property of water — why it extinguishes fire, for example — will find to his surprise that hydrogen burns and oxygen sustains fire."

Vygotsky suggests instead an analytic *unit* for the study of language phenomena. By unit, he means a product of analysis that retains all the basic properties of the whole and that cannot be further divided without losing them. "Not the chemical composition of water but its molecules and their behavior are the key to the understanding of the properties of water. The unit of biological analysis is the living cell possessing the basic properties of the living organism." He feels that the unit of analysis for language is, therefore, the word and the word meaning. He says, "The nature of meaning as such is not clear. Yet it is in word meaning that thought and speech unite into verbal thought. In meaning, then, the answers to our questions about the relationship between thought and language can be found."

It would seem that the concepts of word and word meaning were obviously the starting places for language units. Yet in verbal language studies, "the word as a unit occupies a paradoxical position." No generally accepted and satisfactory definition exists, and some linguists deny the validity of the word altogether. Although we all seem to know what "word" means, linguists have had a difficult time trying to define it in such a way that when we hear a new and unknown language we can apply a set of rules to determine a "word."

In this sense, film can be thought of as a new and unknown language. What would the "word" of a film be? Some theorists of film, starting with Eisenstein, suggest the shot as the basic unit. But this poses many problems. I have suggested elsewhere that the shot — an unbroken length of film depicting a continuous Image-Event — can be broken down into the *cademe*, or camera shot, and the *edeme*, or editing shot, certainly a distinction that must be made. But which of these is the basic unit: The length of film that is taken in the camera — the *cademe* — or the length of film that is used in the final film? I suggest the *edeme*, the unit of film that is constructed from the camera shot, since this is the unit that, when combined in sequence, seems to produce the larger unit that we call a film, and that we might think of as a sentence, a paragraph or a book.

If, on the other hand, the *cademe*, the camera shot, is thought of as a unit, it would be the "word" from which other words are made. Going back again to our analogy with verbal language, there are a finite number of sounds from which we make up the words of any language. In English the twenty-six letters of our alphabet crudely represent these sounds. If the *cademe* is the unit, then the number of possible units (analogous to sounds, and to an alphabet) becomes almost infinite, since the number of images we can photograph is almost infinite. If, on the other hand, the *edeme* — the editing unit made from the camera shot — becomes our unit, the number of *edemes* that can be constructed from one *cademe* is quite small.

The fact that a verbal language has a comparatively small number of sounds from which a large number of word units can be constructed — a sort of building block system — is one of the defining characteristics. The fact that visual language, and film language in particular, has an almost infinitely acceptable number of images creates either a challenge to the concept of building blocks as a requisite of language or the possibility that images as they exist in film can constitute a language. The problem of defining a unit with which to describe film therefore becomes of paramount concern, because upon the unit will fall the responsibility of organized structure in coding a message for the sender and in decoding for the receiver.

The second concept of extreme importance in language is the notion of grammar or syntax. Again let us look at the concepts developed around the study of verbal language. Noam Chomsky of the Massachusetts Institute of Technology, one of the leading linguistic theorists working today, considers a language to be "a set of sentences, each finite in length and constructed out of a finite set of elements. All natural languages are languages in this sense, since each natural language has a finite number of phonemes (or letters in its alphabet) and each sentence is representable as a finite sequence of these phonemes (or letters), though there are infinitely many sentences." This concept of grammar, Chomsky asserts, can be tested scientifically for, "the grammar of language L will be a device that generates all of the grammatical sequences and none of the ungrammatical ones."

The way to test the notion is first "to determine whether or not the sequences that it generates are actually grammatical; *that is*, acceptable to a native speaker." This can be tested by taking sentences that a native speaker holds to be grammatical and seeing if the grammar we have developed can explain and decide what is indeed grammatical. The same should hold true for a sentence that the native speaker holds to be ungrammatical. Futhermore, Chomsky has shown that this notion of grammar or syntax should apply regardless of the semantic meaning of the individual words.

He gives the following two sentences, composed of the same words, as examples to illustrate the notion that judgments of grammaticalness occur regardless of the semantic meaning of the units in sequence. The sentences are equally nonsensical, but any English-speaking person will recognize one as grammatical.

1. Colorless green ideas sleep furiously.
2. Furiously sleep ideas green colorless.

Let us take these definitions and try to translate them into film language. A sentence is constructed out of a finite set of elements. What we are looking for is a logic, a system, a set of rules or defini-tions by which we can determine units and their sequence in order to know how we infer a meaning from them. "Dog bites man" and "man bites dog" mean different things. We know this because we know the units (words) and we know that the difference in their position (sequence) implies a different meaning for the larger unit (the sen-tence). We know about the system of meaning inference, so that we can say that the first word denotes something (an action described by the second word) that is acting on the object described by the third word.

If we consider the *cademe* as a unit, which is finite, what could constitute the filmic sentence into which the *edemes* made from that *cademe* will go? If we consider a sentence as a group of *edemes* made from a *cademe* (which is finite) we have the problem of defining a sentence. How many *edemes* made from one *cademe* are a larger unit (a sentence)? Even if we could arbitrarily determine this, we are still faced with the system — the grammar. How do we define a unit, large or small, whose rules we can describe in such a way that we can distinguish between what is a grammatical sequence and what is an ungrammatical sequence?

I find it almost impossible at this point to construct a sequence of shots that an audience will say is ungrammatical. Nor can I find a sequence of shots that I or a particular audience can say is grammati-cal. If no one can distinguish between grammatical and nongrammati-cal, we have to give up either the concept of grammar in film, or the concept of grammar as we know it — which is a grammatical-ungram-matical polar entity. In the entire literature on film, I cannot find anyone who can make such distinctions. Yet I am not satisfied to say that the concept must be discarded. The answer, it seems to me, lies in a deeper understanding of the concept of syntax as it applies to visual Image-Events in a vidistic structure. The answer must lie some-where in a fuller understanding of the units and combinations of units that humans are able to relate and to infer meaning from — or to re-create. I suspect that the notion of a semantic space having dimen-sions of meaning such as that developed by Charles Osgood can be extended to the notion of grammar in visual language.

We would then have to develop a grammar of probability, a system of possible, of more or less meaningful, sequences based on a concept of dimensions of syntax. Just as we now accept the idea that there is not a single meaning in a poem, a dream or a concept, we would have to accept the idea that there is no absolutely grammatical sequence or ungrammatical sequence. Syntax seen in such a way would be governed not by laws of Aristotelian logic but perhaps by a form of psycho-logic determined by cognitive processes that all human beings share, or by a psycho-logic that is culture-bound and determines whether we speak one visual "language" or another.

The tie between the semantic meaning of images in sequence and the syntactic meaning of the sequence itself will have to be much more fully understood. When a little girl says, "me go up," we know it is ungrammatical, but we also are able to infer meaning from it. When she says, "me go brown" it is just as ungrammatical, but I can infer less meaning from this statement than the other. The problems involved in analyzing film sequences are of this nature rather than like the problem posed by Dr. Chomsky in his "colorless green ideas sleep furiously."

This problem of a syntax, structure or organization of visual language must be solved before we can even attempt to handle the problems of "word" meaning that Vygotsky attempts to solve in his work. All of us are anxious to get to the point where we can relate the structure of film "language" to the semantic, imagistic, metaphoric meaning of an individual unit of film, and of a complete film. The film is akin to a complex poem, but composed of units that are even harder to define than words. Until we know more about the visual "word," until we can at least deal with the image as we can with a combination of sounds in any verbal language, and handle such statements as "That is not a word in this language," we cannot truthfully say that we can understand and analyze the film process.

At this point the area of interest that I have presented amounts to a prolegomenon for a new field of study — vidistics. I have presented more questions than answers, more problems than solutions. But perhaps this is just as well. These are the problems that it seems worthwhile to explore.

The New Languages

EDMUND CARPENTER

> Brain of the New World,
> What a task is thine,
> To formulate the modern
> ... to recast poems, churches, art
> — Whitman

English is a mass medium. All languages are mass media. The new mass media — film, radio, TV — are new languages, their grammars as yet unknown. Each codifies reality differently; each conceals a unique metaphysics. Linguists tell us it's possible to say anything in any language if you use enough words or images, but there's rarely time; the natural course is for a culture to exploit its media biases.

Writing, for example, didn't record oral language; it was a new language, which the spoken word came to imitate. Writing encouraged an analytical mode of thinking with emphasis upon lineality. Oral languages tend to be polysynthetic, composed of great, tight conglomerates, like twisted knots, within which images were juxtaposed, inseparably fused; written communications consisted of little words chronologically ordered. Subject became distinct from verb, adjective from noun, thus separating actor from action, essence from form. Where preliterate man imposed form diffidently, temporarily — for such transitory forms lived but temporarily on the tip of his tongue, in the living situation — the printed word was inflexible, permanent, in touch with eternity: it embalmed truth for posterity.

This embalming process froze language, eliminated the art of ambiguity, made puns "the lowest form of wit," destroyed word linkages. The word became a static symbol, applicable to and separate from that which it symbolized. It now belonged to the objective world; it could be seen. Now came the distinction between being and meaning, the dispute as to whether the Eucharist *was* or only *signified* the body of the Sacrifice. The word became a neutral symbol, no longer an inextricable part of a creative process.

Gutenberg completed the process. The manuscript page with pictures, colors, correlation between symbol and space, gave way to uniform type, the black-and-white page, read silently, alone. The format of the book favored lineal expression, for the· argument ran like a thread from cover to cover: subject to verb to object, sentence to sentence, paragraph to paragraph, chapter to chapter, carefully structured from beginning to end, with value embedded in the climax. This was not true of great poetry and drama, which retained multi-perspective, but it was true of most books, particularly texts, histories, autobiographies, novels. Events were arranged chronologically and hence, it was assumed, causally; relationship, not being, was valued. The author became an *authority*; his data were serious, that is, *serially* organized. Such data, if sequentially ordered and printed, conveyed value and truth; arranged any other way, they were suspect.

The newspaper format brought an end to book culture. It offers short, discrete articles that give important facts first and then taper off to incidental details, which may be, and often are, eliminated by the make-up man. The fact that reporters cannot control the length of their articles means that, in writing them, emphasis can't be placed on structure, at least in the traditional linear sense, with climax or conclusion at the end. Everything has to be captured in the headline; from there it goes down the pyramid to incidentals. In fact there is often more in the headline than in the article; occasionally, no article at all accompanies the banner headline.

The position and size of articles on the front page are determined by interest and importance, not content. Unrelated reports from Moscow, Sarawak, London, and Ittipik are juxtaposed; time and space, as separate concepts, are destroyed and the *here* and *now* presented as a single Gestalt. Subway readers consume everything on the front page, then turn to page 2 to read, in incidental order, continuations. A Toronto banner headline ran: TOWNSEND TO MARRY PRINCESS; directly beneath this was a second headline: *Fabian Says This May Not Be Sex Crime*. This went unnoticed by eyes and minds conditioned to consider each newspaper item in isolation.

Such a format lends itself to simultaneity, not chronology or lineality. Items abstracted from a total situation aren't arranged in casual sequence, but presented holistically, as raw experience. The front page is a cosmic *Finnegans Wake*.

The disorder of the newspaper throws the reader into a producer role. The reader has to process the news himself; he has to co-create, to cooperate in the creation of the work. The newspaper format calls for the direct participation of the consumer.

In magazines, where a writer more frequently controls the length of his article, he can, if he wishes, organize it in traditional style, but the majority don't. An increasingly popular presentation is the printed symposium, which is little more than collected opinions, pro and con. The magazine format as a whole opposes lineality; its pictures lack tenses. In *Life*, extremes are juxtaposed: space ships and prehistoric monsters, Flemish monasteries and dope addicts. It creates a sense of urgency and uncertainty: the next page is unpredictable. One encounters rapidly a riot in Teheran, a Hollywood marriage, the wonders of the Eisenhower administration, a two-headed calf, a party on Jones beach, all sandwiched between ads. The eye takes in the page as a whole (readers may pretend this isn't so, but the success of advertising suggests it is), and the page — indeed, the whole magazine — becomes a single Gestalt where association, though not causal, is often lifelike.

The same is true of the other new languages. Both radio and TV offer short, unrelated programs, interrupted between and within by commercials. I say "interrupted," being myself an anachronism of book culture, but my children don't regard them as interruptions, as breaking continuity. Rather, they regard them as part of a whole, and their reaction is neither one of annoyance nor one of indifference. The ideal news broadcast has half a dozen speakers from as many parts of the world on as many subjects. The London correspondent doesn't comment on what the Washington correspondent has just said; he hasn't even heard him.

The child is right in not regarding commercials as interruptions. For the only time anyone smiles on TV is in commercials. The rest of life, in news broadcasts and soap operas, is presented as so horrible that the only way to get through life is to buy this product: then you'll smile. Aesop never wrote a clearer fable. It's heaven and hell brought up to date: Hell in the headline, Heaven in the ad. Without the other, neither has meaning.

There's pattern in these new media — not line, but knot; not lineality or causality or chronology, nothing that leads to a desired climax; but a Gordian knot without antecedents or results, containing within itself carefully selected elements, juxtaposed, inseparably fused; a knot that can't be untied to give the long, thin cord of lineality.

This is especially true of ads that never present an ordered, sequential, rational argument but simply present the product associated with desirable things or attitudes. Thus Coca-Cola is shown held by a beautiful blonde, who sits in a Cadillac, surrounded by bronze, muscular admirers, with the sun shining overhead. By repetition these elements become associated, in our minds, into a pattern of sufficient cohesion so that one element can magically evoke the others. If we think of ads as designed solely to sell products, we miss their main effect: to increase pleasure in the consumption of the product. Coca-Cola is far more than a cooling drink; the consumer participates, vicariously, in a much larger experience. In Africa, in Melanesia, to drink a Coke is to participate in the American way of life.

Of the new languages, TV comes closest to drama and ritual. It combines music and art, language and gesture, rhetoric and color. It favors simultaneity of visual and auditory images. Cameras focus not on speakers but on persons spoken to or about; the audience *hears* the accuser but *watches* the accused. In a single impression it hears the prosecutor, watches the trembling hands of the big-town crook, and sees the look of moral indignation on Senator Tobey's face. This is real drama, in process, with the outcome uncertain. Print can't do this; it has a different bias.

Books and movies only pretend uncertainty, but live TV retains this vital aspect of life. Seen on TV, the fire in the 1952 Democratic Convention threatened briefly to become a conflagration; seen on newsreel, it was history, without potentiality.

The absence of uncertainty is no handicap to other media, if they are properly used, for their biases are different. Thus it's clear from the beginning that Hamlet is a doomed man, but, far from detracting in interest, this heightens the sense of tragedy.

Now, one of the results of the time-space duality that developed in Western culture, principally from the Renaissance on, was a separation within the arts. Music, which created symbols in time, and graphic art, which created symbols in space, became separate pursuits, and men gifted in one rarely pursued the other. Dance and ritual, which inherently combined them, fell in popularity. Only in drama did they remain united.

It is significant that of the four new media, the three most recent are dramatic media, particularly TV, which combines language, music, art, dance. They don't, however, exercise the same freedom with time that the stage dares practice. An intricate plot, employing flash backs, multiple time perspectives and overlays, intelligible on the stage, would mystify on the screen. The audience has no time to think back, to establish relations between early hints and subsequent discoveries. The picture passes before the eyes too quickly; there are no intervals in which to take stock of what has happened and make conjectures of what is going to happen. The observer is in a more passive state, less interested in subtleties. Both TV and film are nearer to narrative and depend much more upon the episodic. An intricate time construction can be done in film, but in fact rarely is. The soliloquies of *Richard III* belong on the stage; the film audience was unprepared for them. On stage Ophelia's death was described by three separate groups: one hears the announcement and watches the reactions simultaneously. On film the camera flatly shows her drowned where "a willow lies aslant a brook."

Media differences such as these mean that it's not simply a question of communicating a single idea in different ways but that a given idea or insight belongs primarily, though not exclusively, to one medium, and can be gained or communicated best through that medium.

Thus the book was ideally suited for discussing evolution and progress. Both belonged, almost exclusively, to book culture. Like a book, the idea of progress was an abstracting, organizing principle for the interpretation and comprehension of the incredibly complicated record of human experience. The sequence of events was believed to have a direction, to follow a given course along an axis of time; it was held that civilization, like the reader's eye (in J. B. Bury's words), "has moved, is moving, and will move in a desirable direction. Knowledge will advance, and with that advance, reason and decency must increasingly prevail among men." Here we see the three main elements of book lineality: the line, the point moving along that line, and its movement toward a desirable goal.

The Western conception of a definite moment in the present, of the present as a definite moment or definite point, so important in book-dominated languages, is absent, to my knowledge, in oral languages. Absent as well, in oral societies, are such animating and controlling ideas as Western individualism and three-dimensional perspective, both related to this conception of the definite moment, and both nourished, probably bred, by book culture.

Each medium selects its ideas. TV is a tiny box into which people are crowded and must live; film gives us the wide world. With its huge screen, film is perfectly suited for social drama, Civil War panoramas, the sea, land erosion, Cecil B. DeMille spectaculars. In contrast, the TV screen has room for two, at the most three, faces, comfortably. TV is closer to stage, yet different. Paddy Chayefsky writes:

> The theatre audience is far away from the actual action of the drama. They cannot see the silent reactions of the players. They must be told in a loud voice what is going on. The plot movement from one scene to another must be marked, rather than gently shaded as is required in television. In television, however, you can dig into the most humble, ordinary relationships; the relationship of bourgeois children to their mother, of middle-class husband to his wife, of white-collar father to his secretary — in short, the relationships of the people. We relate to each other in an incredibly complicated manner. There is far more exciting drama in the reasons why a man gets married than in why he murders someone. The man who is unhappy in his job, the wife who thinks of a lover, the girl who wants to get into television, your father, your mother, sister, brothers, cousins, friends — all these are better subjects for drama than Iago. What makes a man ambitious? Why does a girl always try to steal her kid sister's boy friends? Why

does your uncle attend his annual class reunion faithfully every year? Why do you always find it depressing to visit your father? These are the substances of good television drama; and the deeper you probe into and examine the twisted, semi-formed complexes of emotional entanglements, the more exciting your writing becomes.[1]

This is the primary reason, I believe, why Greek drama is more readily adapted to TV than to film. The boxed-in quality of live TV lends itself to static literary tragedy with greater ease than does the elastic, energetic, expandable movie. Guthrie's recent movie of *Oedipus* favored the panoramic shot rather than the selective eye. It consisted of a succession of tableaux, a series of elaborate, unnatural poses. The effect was of congested groups of people moving in tight formation as though they had trained for it by living for days together in a self-service elevator. With the lines, "I grieve for the City, and for myself and you ... and walk through endless ways of thought," the inexorable tragedy moved to its horrible "come to realize" climax as though everyone were stepping on everyone else's feet.

The tight, necessary conventions of live TV were more sympathetic to Sophocles in the Aluminium Hour's *Antigone*. Restrictions of space are imposed on TV as on the Greek stage by the size and inflexibility of the studio. Squeezed by physical limitations, the producer was forced to expand the viewer's imagination with ingenious devices.

When T. S. Eliot adapted *Murder in the Cathedral* for film, he noted a difference in realism between cinema and stage:

> Cinema, even where fantasy is introduced, is much more realistic than the stage. Especially in an historical picture, the setting, the costume, and the way of life represented have to be accurate. Even a minor anachronism is intolerable. On the stage much more can be overlooked or forgiven; and indeed, an excessive care for accuracy of historical detail can become burdensome and distracting. In watching a stage performance, the member of the audience is in direct contact with the actor playing a part. In looking at a film, we are much more passive; as audience, we contribute less. We are seized with the illusion that we are observing an actual event, or at least a series of photographs of the actual event; and nothing must be allowed to break this illusion. Hence the precise attention to detail.[2]

If two men are on a stage in a theatre, the dramatist is obliged to motivate their presence; he has to account for their existing on the

[1] *Television Plays,* New York, Simon and Schuster, 1955, pp. 176–78.
[2] George Hoellering and T. S. Eliot, *Film of Murder in the Cathedral,* New York, Harcourt, Brace & Co., 1952, p. vi; London, Faber & Faber, 1952.

stage at all. Whereas if a camera is following a figure down a street or is turned to any object whatever, there is no need for a reason to be provided. Its grammar contains that power of statement of motivation, no matter what it looks at.

In the theatre, the spectator sees the enacted scene as a whole in space, always seeing the whole of the space. The stage may present only one corner of a large hall, but that corner is always totally visible all through the scene. And the spectator always sees that scene from a fixed, unchanging distance and from an angle of vision that doesn't change. Perspective may change from scene to scene, but within one scene it remains constant. Distance never varies.

But in film and TV, distance and angle constantly shift. The same scene is shown in multiple perspective and focus. The viewer sees it from here, there, then over here; finally he is drawn inexorably into it, becomes part of it. He ceases to be a spectator. Balázs writes:

> Although we sit in our seats, we do not see Romeo and Juliet from there. We look up into Juliet's balcony with Romeo's eyes and look down on Romeo with Juliet's. Our eye and with it our consciousness is identified with the characters in the film, we look at the world out of their eyes and have no angle of vision of our own. We walk amid crowds, ride, fly or fall with the hero and if one character looks into the other's eyes, he looks into our eyes from the screen, for, our eyes are in the camera and become identical with the gaze of the characters. They see with our eyes. Herein lies the psychological act of identification. Nothing like this "identification" has ever occurred as the effect of any other system of art and it is here that the film manifests its absolute artistic novelty.
>
> ... Not only can we see, in the isolated "shots" of a scene, the very atoms of life and their innermost secrets revealed at close quarters, but we can do so without any of the intimate secrecy being lost, as always happens in the exposure of a stage performance or of a painting. The new theme which the new means of expression of film art revealed was not a hurricane at sea or the eruption of a volcano: it was perhaps a solitary tear slowly welling up in the corner of a human eye.
>
> ... Not to speak does not mean that one has nothing to say. Those who do not speak may be brimming over with emotions which can be expressed only in forms and pictures, in gesture and play of feature. The man of visual culture uses these not as substitutes for words, as a deaf-mute uses his fingers.[3]

The gestures of visual man are not intended to convey concepts that can be expressed in words, but inner experiences, nonrational emotions, which would still remain unexpressed when everything

[3] Béla Balázs, *Theory of Film*, New York, Roy Publishers, 1953, pp. 48, 31, 40; London, Denis Dobson, 1952.

that can be told has been told. Such emotions lie in the deepest levels. They cannot be approached by words that are mere reflections of concepts, any more than musical experiences can be expressed in rational concepts. Facial expression is a human experience rendered immediately visible without the intermediary of word. It is Turgenev's "living truth of the human face."

Printing rendered illegible the faces of men. So much could be read from paper that the method of conveying meaning by facial expression fell into desuetude. The press grew to be the main bridge over which the more remote interhuman spiritual exchanges took place; the immediate, the personal, the inner, died. There was no longer need for the subtler means of expression provided by the body. The face became immobile; the inner life, still. Wells that dry up are wells from which no water is dipped.

Just as radio helped bring back inflection in speech, so film and TV are aiding us in the recovery of gesture and facial awareness — a rich, colorful language, conveying moods and emotions, happenings and characters, even thoughts, none of which could be properly packaged in words. If film had remained silent for another decade, how much faster this change might have been!

Feeding the product of one medium through another medium creates a new product. When Hollywood buys a novel, it buys a title and the publicity associated with it: nothing more. Nor should it.

Each of the four versions of the *Caine Mutiny* — book, play, movie, TV — had a different hero: Willie Keith, the lawyer Greenwald, the United States Navy, and Captain Queeg, respectively. Media and audience biases were clear. Thus the book told, in lengthy detail, of the growth and making of Ensign William Keith, American man, while the movie camera with its colorful shots of ships and sea, unconsciously favored the Navy as hero, a bias supported by the fact the Navy cooperated with the movie makers. Because of stage limitations, the play was confined, except for the last scene, to the courtroom, and favored the defense counsel as hero. The TV show, aimed at a mass audience, emphasized patriotism, authority, allegiance. More important, the cast was reduced to the principals and the plot to its principles; the real moral problem — the refusal of subordinates to assist an incompetent, unpopular superior — was clear, whereas in the book it was lost under detail, in the film under scenery. Finally, the New York play, with its audience slanted toward Expense Account patronage — Mr. Sampson, Western Sales Manager for the Cavity Drill Company — became a morality play with Willie Keith, innocent American youth, torn between two influences: Keefer, clever author but moral cripple, and Greenwald, equally brilliant but reliable, a businessman's intellectual. Greenwald saves Willie's soul.

The film *Moby Dick* was in many ways an improvement on the book, primarily because of its explicitness. For *Moby Dick* is one of those admittedly great classics, like *Robinson Crusoe* or Kafka's *Trial*, whose plot and situation, as distilled apart from the book by time and familiarity, are actually much more imposing than the written book itself. It's the drama of Ahab's defiance rather than Melville's uncharted leviathan meanderings that is the greatness of *Moby Dick*. On film, instead of laborious tacks through leagues of discursive interruptions, the most vivid descriptions of whales and whaling become part of the action. On film, the viewer was constantly aboard ship: each scene an instantaneous shot of whaling life, an effect achieved in the book only by illusion, by constant, detailed reference. From start to finish, all the action of the film served to develop what was most central to the theme — a man's magnificent and blasphemous pride in attempting to destroy the brutal, unreasoning force that maims him and turns man-made order into chaos. Unlike the book, the film gave a spare, hard, compelling dramatization, free of self-conscious symbolism.

Current confusion over the respective roles of the new media comes largely from a misconception of their function. They are artforms, not substitutes for human contact. Insofar as they attempt to usurp speech and personal, living relations, they harm. This, of course, has long been one of the problems of book culture, at least during the time of its monopoly of Western middle-class thought. But this was never a legitimate function of books, nor of any other medium. Whenever a medium goes claim jumping, trying to work areas where it is ill-suited, conflicts occur with other media, or, more accurately, between the vested interests controlling each. But, when media simply exploit their own formats, they become complementary and cross-fertile.

Some people who have no one around talk to cats, and you can hear their voices in the next room, and they sound silly, because the cat won't answer, but that suffices to maintain the illusion that their world is made up of living people, while it is not. Mechanized mass media reverse this: now mechanical cats talk to humans. There's no genuine feedback.

This charge is often leveled by academicians at the new media, but it holds equally for print. The open-mouthed, glaze-eyed TV spectator is merely the successor of the passive, silent, lonely reader whose head moved back and forth like a shuttlecock.

When we read, another person thinks for us: we merely repeat his mental process. The greater part of the work of thought is done for us. This is why it relieves us to take up a book after being occupied by our own thoughts. In reading, the mind is only the playground for another's ideas. People who spend most of their lives in reading often lose the capacity for thinking, just as those who always ride forget how to walk. Some people read themselves stupid. Chaplin did a wonderful take-off of this in *City Lights*, when he stood up on a chair to eat the endless confetti that he mistook for spaghetti.

Eliot remarks: "It is often those writers whom we are lucky enough to know whose books we can ignore; and the better we know them personally, the less need we may feel to read what they write."

Frank O'Connor highlights a basic distinction between oral and written traditions: " 'By the hokies, there was a man in this place one time by name of Ned Sullivan, and he had a queer thing happen to him late one night and he coming up the Valley Road from Durlas.' This is how a folk story begins, or should begin. . . . Yet that is how no printed short story should begin, because such a story seems tame when you remove it from its warm nest by the cottage fire, from the sense of an audience with its interjections, and the feeling of terror at what may lurk in the darkness outside."

Face-to-face discourse is not as selective, abstract, nor explicit as any mechanical medium; it probably comes closer to communicating an unabridged situation than any of them, and, insofar as it exploits the give-take of dynamic relationship, it's clearly the most indispensably human one.

Of course, there can be personal involvement in the other media. When Richardson's *Pamela* was serialized in 1741, it aroused such interest that in one English town, upon receipt of the last installment, the church bell anounced that virtue had been rewarded. Radio stations have reported receiving quantities of baby clothes and bassinets when, in a soap opera, a heroine had a baby. One of the commonest phrases used by devoted listeners to daytime serials is that they "visited with" Aunt Jenny or Big Sister. BBC and *News Chronicle* report cases of women viewers who kneel before TV sets to kiss male announcers good night.

Each medium, if its bias is properly exploited, reveals and communicates a unique aspect of reality, of truth. Each offers a different perspective, a way of seeing an otherwise hidden dimension of reality. It's not a question of one reality being true, the others distortions. One allows us to see from here, another from there, a third from still another perspective; taken together they give us a more complete whole, a greater truth. New essentials are brought to the fore, including those made invisible by the "blinders" of old languages.

This is why the preservation of book culture is as important as the development of TV. This is why new languages, instead of destroying old ones, serve as a stimulant to them. Only monopoly is destroyed. When actor-collector Edward G. Robinson was battling actor-collector Vincent Price on art on TV's *$64,000 Challenge*, he was asked how the quiz had affected his life; he answered petulantly, "Instead of looking at the pictures in my art books, I now have to read them." Print, along with all old languages, including speech, has profited enormously from the development of the new media. "The more the arts develop," writes E. M. Forster, "the more they depend on each other for definition. We will borrow from painting first and call it pattern. Later we will borrow from music and call it rhythm."

The appearance of a new medium often frees older media for creative effort. They no longer have to serve the interests of power and profit. Elia Kazan, discussing the American theatre, says:

> Take 1900–1920. The theatre flourished all over the country. It had no competition. The box office boomed. The top original fare it had to offer was *The Girl of the Golden West*. Its bow to culture was fusty productions of Shakespeare. . . . Came the moving pictures. The theatre had to be better or go under. It got better. It got so spectacularly better so fast that in 1920–1930 you wouldn't have recognized it. Perhaps it was an accident that Eugene O'Neill appeared at that moment — but it was no accident that in that moment of strange competition, the theatre had room for him. Because it was disrupted and hard pressed, it made room for his experiments, his unheard-of subjects, his passion, his power. There was room for him to grow to his full stature. And there was freedom for the talents that came after his.[4]

Yet a new language is rarely welcomed by the old. The oral tradition distrusted writing, manuscript culture was contemptuous of printing, book culture hated the press, that "slag-heap of hellish passions," as one 19th century scholar called it. A father, protesting to a Boston newspaper about crime and scandal, said he would rather see his children "in their graves while pure in innocence, than dwelling with pleasure upon these reports, which have grown so bold."

What really disturbed book-oriented people wasn't the sensationalism of the newspaper, but its nonlineal format, its nonlineal codifications of experience. The motto of conservative academicians became: *Hold that line!*

A new language lets us see with the fresh, sharp eyes of the child; it offers the pure joy of discovery. I was recently told a story about a Polish couple who, though long resident in Toronto, retained many of the customs of their homeland. Their son despaired of ever

---

4 "Writers and Motion Pictures," *The Atlantic Monthly*, 199, 1957, p. 69.

getting his father to buy a suit cut in style or getting his mother to take an interest in Canadian life. Then he bought them a TV set, and in a matter of months a major change took place. One evening the mother remarked that "Edith Piaf is the latest thing on Broadway," and the father appeared in "the kind of suit executives wear on TV." For years the father had passed this same suit in store windows and seen it both in advertisements and on living men, but not until he saw it on TV did it become meaningful. This same statement goes for all media: each offers a unique presentation of reality, which when new has a freshness and clarity that is extraordinarily powerful.

This is especially true of TV. We say, "We have a radio" but "We have television" — as if something had happened to us. It's no longer "The skin you love to touch" but "The Nylon that loves to touch you." We don't watch TV; it watches us: it guides us. Magazines and newspapers no longer convey "information" but offer ways of seeing things. They have abandoned realism as too easy: they substitute themselves for realism. *Life* is totally advertisements: its articles package and sell emotions and ideas just as its paid ads sell commodities.

Several years ago, a group of us at the University of Toronto undertook the following experiment: 136 students were divided, on the basis of their over-all academic standing of the previous year, into four equal groups who either (1) heard and saw a lecture delivered in a TV studio, (2) heard and saw this same lecture on a TV screen, (3) heard it over the radio, or (4) read it in manuscript. Thus there were, in the CBC studios, four controlled groups who simultaneously received a single lecture and then immediately wrote an identical examination to test both understanding and retention of content. Later the experiment was repeated, using three similar groups; this time the same lecture was (1) delivered in a classroom, (2) presented as a film (using the kinescope) in a small theatre, and (3) again read in print. The actual mechanics of the experiment were relatively simple, but the problem of writing the script for the lecture led to a consideration of the resources and limitations of the dramatic forms involved.

It immediately became apparent that no matter how the script was written and the show produced, it would be slanted in various ways for and against each of the media involved; no show could be produced that did not contain these biases, and the only real common denominator was the simultaneity of presentation. For each communication channel codifies reality differently and thus influences, to a surprising degree, the content of the message communicated. A medium is not simply an envelope that carries any letter; it is itself a major part of that message. We therefore decided not to exploit the full resources of any one medium, but to try to chart a middle-of-the-road course between all of them.

The lecture that was finally produced dealt with linguistic codifications of reality and metaphysical concepts underlying grammatical systems. It was chosen because it concerned a field in which few students could be expected to have prior knowledge; moreover, it offered opportunities for the use of gesture. The cameras moved throughout the lecture, and took close-ups where relevant. No other visual aids were used, nor were shots taken of the audience while the lecture was in progress. Instead, the cameras simply focused on the speaker for 27 minutes.

The first difference we found between a classroom and a TV lecture was the brevity of the latter. The classroom lecture, if not ideally, at least in practice, sets a slower pace. It's verbose, repetitive. It allows for greater elaboration and permits the lecturer to take up several *related* points. TV, however, is stripped right down; there's less time for qualifications or alternative interpretations and only time enough for *one* point. (Into 27 minutes we put the meat of a two-hour classroom lecture.) The ideal TV speaker states his point and then brings out different facets of it by a variety of illustrations. But the classroom lecturer is less subtle and, to the agony of the better students, repeats and repeats his identical points in the hope, perhaps, that ultimately no student will miss them, or perhaps simply because he is dull. Teachers have had captive audiences for so long that few are equipped to compete for attention via the new media.

The next major difference noted was the abstracting role of each medium, beginning with print. Edmund M. Morgan, Harvard Law Professor, writes:

> One who forms his opinion from the reading of any record alone is prone to err, because the printed page fails to produce the impression or convey the idea which the spoken word produced or conveyed. The writer has read charges to the jury which he had previously heard delivered, and has been amazed to see an oral deliverance which indicated a strong bias appear on the printed page as an ideally impartial exposition. He has seen an appellate court solemnly declare the testimony of a witness to be especially clear and convincing which the trial judge had orally characterized as the most abject perjury.[5]

Selectivity of print and radio are perhaps obvious enough, but we are less conscious of it in TV, partly because we have already been conditioned to it by the shorthand of film. Balázs writes:

[5] G. Louis Joughin and Edmund M. Morgan, *The Legacy of Sacco and Vanzetti*, New York, Harcourt, Brace & Co., 1948, p. 34.

A man hurries to a railway station to take leave of his beloved. We see him on the platform. We cannot see the train, but the questing eyes of the man show us that his beloved is already seated in the train. We see only a close-up of the man's face, we see it twitch as if startled and then strips of light and shadow, light and shadow flit across it in quickening rhythm. Then tears gather in the eyes and that ends the scene. We are expected to know what happened and today we do know, but when I first saw this film in Berlin, I did not at once understand the end of this scene. Soon, however, everyone knew what had happened: the train had started and it was the lamps in its compartment which had thrown their light on the man's face as they glided past ever faster and faster.[6]

As in a movie theatre, only the screen is illuminated, and, on it, only points of immediate relevance are portrayed; everything else is eliminated. This explicitness makes TV not only personal but forceful. That's why stage hands in a TV studio watch the show over floor monitors, rather than watch the actual performance before their eyes.

The script of the lecture, timed for radio, proved too long for TV. Visual aids and gestures on TV not only allow the elimination of certain words, but require a unique script. The ideal radio delivery stresses pitch and intonation to make up for the absence of the visual. That flat, broken speech in "sidewalk interviews" is the speech of a person untrained in radio delivery.

The results of the examination showed that TV had won, followed by lecture, film, radio, and finally print. Eight months later the test was readministered to the bulk of the students who had taken it the first time. Again it was found that there were significant differences between the groups exposed to different media, and these differences were the same as those on the first test, save for the studio group, an uncertain group because of the chaos of the lecture conditions, which had moved from last to second place. Finally, two years later, the experiment was repeated, with major modifications, using students at Ryerson Institute. Marshall McLuhan reports:

In this repeat performance, pains were taken to allow each medium full play of its possibilities with reference to the subject, just as in the earlier experiment each medium was neutralized as much as possible. Only the mimeograph form remained the same in each experiment. Here we added a printed form in which an imaginative typographical layout was followed. The lecturer used the blackboard and permitted discussion. Radio and TV employed dramatization, sound effects and graphics. In the examination, radio easily topped TV. Yet, as in the first experiment, both radio

6 Béla Balázs, *op. cit.*, pp. 35–36.

and TV manifested a decisive advantage over the lecture and written forms. As a conveyor both of ideas and information, TV was, in this second experiment, apparently enfeebled by the deployment of its dramatic resources, whereas radio benefited from such lavishness. "Technology is explicitness," writes Lyman Bryson. Are both radio and TV more explicit than writing or lecture? Would a greater explicitness, if inherent in these media, account for the ease with which they top other modes of performance?[7]

Announcement of the results of the first experiment evoked considerable interest. Advertising agencies circulated the results with the comment that here, at last, was scientific proof of the superiority of TV. This was unfortunate and missed the main point, for the results didn't indicate the superiority of one medium over others. They merely directed attention toward differences between them, differences so great as to be of kind rather than degree. Some CBC officials were furious, not because TV won, but because print lost.

The problem has been falsely seen as democracy *vs.* the mass media. But the mass media *are* democracy. The book itself was the first mechanical mass medium. What is really being asked, of course, is: can books' monopoly of knowledge survive the challenge of the new languages? The answer is: no. What should be asked is: what can print do better than any other medium and is that worth doing?

Film as Environment

ANTHONY SCHILLACI

The better we understand how young people view film, the more we have to revise our notion of what film is. Seen through young eyes, film is destroying conventions almost as quickly as they can be formulated. Whether the favored director is "young" like Richard Lester, Roman Polanski, and Arthur Penn, or "old" like Kubrick, Fel-

[7] From a personal communication to the author.

lini, and Buñuel, he must be a practicing cinematic anarchist to catch the eye of the young. If we're looking for the young audience between sixteen and twenty-four, which accounts for 48 per cent of the box office today, we will find they're on a trip, whether in a Yellow Submarine or on a Space Odyssey. A brief prayer muttered for Rosemary's Baby and they're careening down a dirt road with Bonnie and Clyde, the exhaust spitting banjo sounds, or sitting next to The Graduate as he races across the Bay Bridge after his love. The company they keep is fast; Belle de Jour, Petulia, and Joanna are not exactly a sedentary crowd. Hyped up on large doses of *Rowan and Martin's Laugh-In*, and *Mission: Impossible*, they are ready for anything that an evolving film idiom can throw on the screen. And what moves them must have the pace, novelty, style, and spontaneity of a television commercial.

All of this sounds as if the script is by McLuhan. Nevertheless, it is borne out by the experience of teaching contemporary film to university juniors and seniors, staging film festivals for late teens and early adults, and talking to literally hundreds of people about movies. The phenomenon may be interesting, and even verifiable, but what makes it important is its significance for the future of film art. The young have discovered that film is an environment which you put on, demanding a different kind of structure, a different mode of attention than any other art. Their hunger is for mind-expanding experience and simultaneity, and their art is film.

Occasionally a young director gives us a glimpse of the new world of film as environmental art. The optical exercise known as *Flicker* came on like a karate chop to the eyes at Lincoln Center's Film Seminar three years ago. One half-hour of white light flashing at varied frequency, accompanied by a deafening sound track designed to infuriate, describes the screen, but not what happened to the audience. As strangers turned to ask if it was a put-on, if they had forgotten to put film in the projector, they noticed that the flickering light fragmented their motions, stylizing them like the actions of a silent movie. In minutes, the entire audience was on its feet, acting out spontaneous pantomimes for one another, no one looking at the flashing screen. The happening precipitated by *Flicker* could be called the film of the future, but it was actually an anti-environment that gives us an insight into the past. By abstracting totally from content, the director demonstrated that the film is in the audience which acts out personal and public dramas as the screen turns it on. The delight of this experience opened up the notion of film as an environmental art.

Critics have noted the trend which leaves story line and character development strewn along the highways of film history like the corpses in Godard's *Weekend*. The same critics have not, in general, recognized that the growing option for nonlinear, unstructured experiences that leave out sequence, motivation, and "argument" is a vote for film as environment. Young people turn to film for a time-space environment in which beautiful things happen to them. The screen has, in a sense, less and less to do with what explodes in the audience. This new scene could mean either that film is plunging toward irrelevant stimulation, or that there is a new and unprecedented level of participation and involvement in young audiences. I prefer to think the latter is the case. Young people want to talk about Ben's hang-up, why Rosemary stayed with the baby, or what it feels like to be in the electronic hands of a computer like Hal. They do not forget the film the minute they walk out of the theater.

The attention given the new style of film goes beyond stimulation to real involvement. A generation with eyes fixed on the rear-view mirror tended to give film the same attention required for reading — that is, turning off all the senses except the eyes. Film became almost as private as reading, and little reaction to the total audience was experienced. As the Hollywood dream factory cranked out self-contained worlds of fantasy, audiences entered them with confidence that nothing even vaguely related to real life would trouble their reveries. As long as one came and left in the middle of the film, it was relatively noninvolving as environment. When television brought the image into the living room, people gave it "movie attention," hushing everyone who entered the sacred presence of the tube as they would a film patron who talked during a movie. One was not allowed to speak, even during commercials. It took post-literate man to teach us how to use television as environment, as a moving image on the wall to which one may give total or peripheral attention as he wishes. The child who had TV as a baby-sitter does not turn off all his senses, but walks about the room carrying on a multiplicity of actions and relationships, his attention a special reward for the cleverness of the pitchman, or the skill of the artist. He is king, and not captive. As McLuhan would put it, he is not an audience, he *gives* an audience to the screen.

The new multisensory involvement with film as total environment has been primary in destroying literary values in film. Their decline is not merely farewell to an understandable but unwelcome dependency; it means the emergence of a new identity for film. The diminished role of dialogue is a case in point. The difference between *Star Trek* and *Mission: Impossible* marks the trend toward self-explanatory images that need no dialogue. Take an audio tape of these two popular TV shows, as we did in a recent study, and it will reveal that while *Mission: Impossible* is completely unintelligible without images, *Star Trek* is simply an illustrated radio serial, complete on the level of sound. It has all the characteristics of radio's golden age: actions explained, immediate identification of character by voice alone, and even organ music to squeeze the proper emotion or end the episode. Like *Star Trek*, the old film was frequently a talking picture (emphasis on the adjective), thereby confirming McLuhan's contention that technologically "radio married the movies." The marriage of dependence, however, has gone on the rocks, and not by a return to silent films but a new turning to foreign ones. It was the films of Fellini and Bergman, with their subtitles, that convinced us there had been too many words. Approximately one-third of the dialogue is omitted in subtitled versions of these films, with no discernible damage — and some improvement — of the original.

More than dialogue, however, has been jettisoned. Other literary values, such as sequential narrative, dramatic choice, and plot are in a state of advanced atrophy, rapidly becoming vestigial organs on the body of film art as young people have their say. *Petulia* has no "story," unless one laboriously pieces together the interaction between the delightful arch-kook and the newly divorced surgeon, in which case it is nothing more than an encounter. The story line wouldn't make a ripple if it were not scrambled and fragmented into an experience that explodes from a free-floating present into both past and future simultaneously. *Petulia* is like some views of the universe which represent the ancient past of events whose light is just now reaching us simultaneously with the future of our galaxy, returning from the curve of outer space. Many films succeed by virtue of what they leave out. *2001: A Space Odyssey* is such a film, its muted understatement creating gaps in the action that invite our inquiry. Only a square viewer wants to know where the black monolith came from and where it is going. For most of the young viewers to whom I have spoken, it is just there. *Last Year at Marienbad* made the clock as limply shapeless as one of Salvador Dali's watches, while *8¹/₂* came to life on the strength of free associations eagerly grasped by young audiences. The effect of such films is a series of open-ended impressions, freely evoked and enjoyed, strongly inviting inquiry and involvement. In short, film is freed to work as environment, something which does not simply contain, but shapes people, tilting the balance of their faculties, radically altering their perceptions, and ultimately their views of self and all reality. Perhaps one sense of the symptomatic word "grooving," which applies to both sight and sound environments, is that a new mode of attention — multisensory, total, and simultaneous — has arrived. When you "groove," you do not analyze, follow an argument, or separate sensations; rather, you are massaged into a feeling of heightened life and consciousness.

If young people look at film this way, it is in spite of the school, a fact which says once more with emphasis that education is taking place outside the classroom walls. The "discovery" that television commercials are the most exciting and creative part of today's programing is old news to the young. Commercials are a crash course in speed-viewing, their intensified sensations challenging the viewer to synthesize impressions at an ever increasing rate. The result is short films like one produced at UCLA, presenting 3,000 years of art in three minutes. *God Is Dog Spelled Backwards* takes you from the cave paintings of Lascaux to the latest abstractions, with some images remaining on the screen a mere twenty-fourth of a second! The young experience the film, however, not as confusing, but as exuberantly and audaciously alive. They feel joy of recognition, exhilaration at the intense concentration necessary (one blink encompasses a century of art), and awe at the 180-second review of every aspect of the human condition. Intended as a put-on, the film becomes a three-minute commercial for man. This hunger for overload is fed by the television commercial, with its nervous jump cuts demolishing continuity, and its lazy dissolves blurring time-space boundaries. Whether the young are viewing film "through" television, or simply through their increased capacity for information and sensation (a skill which makes most schooling a bore), the result is the same — film becomes the primary environment in which the hunger to know through experience is satisfied.

Hidden within this unarticulated preference of the young is a quiet tribute to film as the art that humanizes change. In its beginnings, the cinema was celebrated as the art that mirrored reality in its functional dynamism. And although the early vision predictably gave way to misuse of the medium, today the significance of the filmic experience of change stubbornly emerges again. Instead of prematurely stabilizing change, film celebrates it. The cinema can inject life into historical events by the photo-scan, in which camera movement and editing liberate the vitality of images from the past. *City of Gold*, a short documentary by the National Film Board of Canada, takes us by zoom and cut into the very life of the Klondike gold rush, enabling us to savor the past as an experience.

Education increasingly means developing the ability to live humanly in the technological culture by changing with it. Film is forever spinning out intensifications of the environment which make it

visible and livable. The ability to control motion through its coordi-
nates of time and space makes film a creative agent in change. Not
only does film reflect the time-space continuum of contemporary
physics, but it can manipulate artistically those dimensions of motion
which we find most problematic. The actuality of the medium, its
here-and-now impact, reflects how completely the present tense has
swallowed up both past and future. Freudian psychology dissolves
history by making the past something we live; accelerated change
warps the future by bringing it so close that we can't conceive it as
"ahead" of us. An art which creates its own space, and can move
time forward and back, can humanize change by conditioning us to
live comfortably immersed in its fluctuations.

On the level of form, then, perhaps the young are tuned in to film
for "telling it like it is" in a sense deeper than that of fidelity to the
event. It is film's accurate reflection of a society and of human life
totally in flux that makes it the liberating art of the time. We live our
lives more like Guido in $8^1/2$ — spinners of fantasies, victims of events,
the products of mysterious associations — than we do like Maria in
The Sound of Music, with a strange destiny guiding our every step.
Instead of resisting change and bottling it, film intensifies the experience of change, humanizing it in the process. What makes the ending
of The Graduate "true" to young people is not that Ben has rescued
his girl from the Establishment, but that he did it without a complete
plan for the future. The film may fail under analysis, but it is extraordinarily coherent as experience, as I learned in conversations about it
with the young. The same accurate reflection of the day may be said
of the deep space relativity of 2001, the frantic pace of Petulia, or the
melodramatic plotting of Rosemary's Baby. Whether this limitless
capacity for change within the creative limits of art has sober implications for the future raises the next (and larger) questions of what
young people look for and get out of film.

When the question of film content is raised, the example of
Flicker and other films cited may seem to indicate that young people
favor as little substance as possible in their film experiences. A casual
glance at popular drive-in fare would confirm this opinion quickly.
Nevertheless, their attitude toward "what films are about" evidences
a young, developing sensitivity to challenging comments on what it
means to be human. The young are digging the strong humanism of
the current film renaissance and allowing its currents to carry them to
a level deeper than that reached by previous generations. One might
almost say that young people are going to the film-maker's work for
values that they have looked for in vain from the social, political, or

religious establishments. This reaction, which has made film modern man's morality play, has not been carefully analyzed, but the present state of evidence invites our inquiry.

As far as the "point" of films is concerned, young people will resist a packaged view, but will welcome a problematic one. The cry, "Please, I'd rather do it myself!" should be taken to heart by the film-maker. It is better to use understatement in order to score a personal discovery by the viewer. Such a discovery of an idea is a major part of our delight in the experience of film art. A frequent answer to a recent survey question indicated that a young man takes his girl to the movies so that they will have something important to talk about. It is not a matter of pitting film discussion against "making out," but of recognizing that a rare and precious revelation of self to the other is often occasioned by a good film. The young feel this experience as growth, expanded vitality, more integral possession of one's self with the consequent freedom to go out to others more easily and more effectively.

Very little of the business of being human happens by instinct, and so we need every form of education that enlightens or accelerates that process. While young people do not go to films for an instant humanization course, a strong part of the pleasure they take in excellent films does just this. Whether through a connaturality of the medium described earlier, or because of a freer viewpoint, young audiences frequently get more out of films than their mentors. It is not so much a matter of seeing more films, but of seeing more in a film. The film-as-escape attitude belongs to an age when the young were not yet born; and the film-as-threat syndrome has little meaning for the sixteen to twenty-four group, simply because they are free from their elders' hang-ups. A typical irrelevance that causes youthful wonder is the elderly matron's complaint that Bonnie and Clyde would teach bad driving habits to the young.

The performance of youthful audiences in discussions of contemporary film indicates their freedom from the judgmental screen which blurs so many films for other generations. In speaking of Bonnie and Clyde, late high school kids and young adults do not dwell upon the career of crime or the irregularity of the sexual relationship, but upon other things. The development of their love fascinates young people, because Clyde shows he knows Bonnie better than she knows herself. Although he resists her aggressive sexual advances, he knows and appreciates her as a person. It is the sincerity of their growing love that overcomes his impotence, and the relationship between this achievement and their diminished interest in crime is not lost on the young audience. The reversal of the "sleep together now, get acquainted later" approach is significant here. These are only a few of the nuances that sensitive ears and eyes pick up beneath the gunfire and banjo-plucking. Similarly, out of the chaotic impressions of *Petulia*, patterns are perceived. Young people note the contrasts between Petulia's kooky, chaotic life, and the over-controlled precision of the surgeon's existence. The drama is that they both come away a little different for their encounter. Instead of a stale moral judgment on their actions, one finds open-ended receptivity to the personal development of the characters.

Youth in search of identity is often presented as a ridiculous spectacle, a generation of Kierkegaards plaintively asking each other: "Who am I?" Nevertheless, the quest is real and is couched in terms of a hunger for experience. SDS or LSD, McCarthy buttons or yippie fashions, it is all experimentation in identity, trying on experiences to see if they fit. The plea is to stop the world, not so that they can get off, but so they can get a handle on it. To grasp each experience, to suck it dry of substance, and to grow in that process is behind the desire to be "turned on." But of all the lurid and bizarre routes taken by young people, the one that draws least comment is that of the film experience. More people have had their minds expanded by films than by LSD. Just as all art nudges man into the sublime and vicarious experience of the whole range of the human condition, film does so with a uniquely characteristic totality and involvement.

Ben, *The Graduate*, is suffocating under his parents' aspirations, a form of drowning which every young person has felt in some way. But the film mirrors their alienation in filmic terms, by changes in focus, by the metaphors of conveyor belt sidewalk and swimming pool, better than any moralist could say it. The satirical portraits of the parents may be broad and unsubtle, but the predicament is real and compelling. This is why the young demand no assurances that Ben and the girl will live happily ever after; it is enough that he jarred himself loose from the sick apathy and languid sexual experimentation with Mrs. Robinson to go after one thing, one person that he wanted for himself, and not for others. Incidentally, those who are not busy judging the morality of the hotel scenes will note that sex doesn't communicate without love. Some may even note that Ben is using sex to strike at his parents — not a bad thing for the young (or their parents) to know.

Emotional maturity is never painless and seldom permanent, but it can become a bonus from viewing good films because it occurs there not as taught but experienced. Values communicated by film are

interiorized and become a part of oneself, not simply an extension of
the womb that parents and educators use to shield the young from
the world. Colin Smith, in *The Loneliness of the Long Distance
Runner*, IS youth, not because he did it to the Establishment, but
because he is trying to be his own man and not sweat his guts out for
another. The profound point of learning who you are in the experience of freedom, as Colin did in running, is not lost on the young who
think about this film a little. Some speak of Col's tragedy as a failure
to realize he could have won the race for himself, and not for the
governor of the Borstal. Self-destruction through spite, the pitfalls of
a self-justifying freedom, and the sterility of bland protest are real
problems that emerge from the film. The values that appeal most are
the invisible ones that move a person to act because "it's me" (part of
one's identity), and not because of "them." Because they have
become an object of discovery and not of imposition, such values
tend to make morality indistinguishable from self-awareness.

It should be made clear, however, that it is not merely the content, but the mode of involvement in the film experience that makes
its humanism effective. In terms of "message," much of contemporary
film reflects the social and human concerns that Bob Dylan, the Beatles, Simon and Garfunkel, and Joan Baez communicate. But the
words of their songs often conceal the radical nature of the music in
which they appear. The direct emotional appeal of the sound of
"Eleanor Rigby," "Give a Damn," "I Am a Rock," or "Mr. Businessman" communicates before we have the words deciphered. Films
with honest human concern, similarly, change audiences as much by
their style as their message. *Elvira Madigan*'s overpowering portrait
of a hopeless love, *A Thousand Clowns*' image of nonconformity,
Zorba's vitality, and *Morgan*'s tragedy are not so much the content of
the images as the outcome of their cinematic logic. If these films
change us, it is because we have done it to ourselves by opening ourselves to their experience.

Expo 67 audiences were charmed by the Czech Kinoautomat in
which their vote determined the course of comic events in a film.
Once again, we find here not a peek into the future, but an insight
into all film experience. In one way or another, we vote on each film's
progress. The passive way is to patronize dishonest or cynical films,
for our box-office ballot determines the selection of properties for
years to come. We have been voting this way for superficial emotions, sterile plots, and happy endings for a generation. But we vote
more actively and subtly by willing the very direction of a film
through identification with the character, or absorption into the

action. The viewer makes a private or social commitment in film experience. He invests a portion of himself in the action, and if he is changed, it is because he has activated his own dreams. What happens on the screen, as in the case of *Flicker*, is the catalyst for the value systems, emotional responses, and the indirect actions which are the by-products of a good film. Film invites young people to be part of the action by making the relationships which take the work beyond a mere succession of images. The reason why young people grow through their art is that they supply the associations that merely begin on the screen but do not end there. When parents and educators become aware of this, their own efforts at fostering maturity may be less frantic, and more effective.

It is not only the films that please and delight which appeal to the young, but also those which trouble and accuse by bringing our fears into the open. The new audience for documentary films highlights a new way of looking at film as an escape *into* reality. From *The War Game* to *Warrendale*, from *The Titicut Follies* to *Battle of Algiers*, young audiences are relishing the film's ability to document the present in terms of strong social relevance. *Portrait of Jason* is more than a voyeuristic peek into the psyche of a male whore; it is a metaphor for the black man's history in America, and this is what young people see in that film. Even the most strident dissenters will appreciate the ambiguities of *The Anderson Platoon*, which leaves us without anyone to hate, because it is not about Marines and Vietcong, but about men like ourselves. In these as in other films, the social content is intimately wed to the film experience, and together they form a new outlook. Ultimately, we may have to change our views on what film art is about.

The foregoing analysis of how young people look at film will appear to some to constitute a simplistic eulogy to youth. For this reason, we may temper our optimism by a hard look at real problems with this generation. There is a desperate need for education. Although they cannot all be structured, none of the better youthful attitudes or responses described came about by chance. Mere screening of films, for example, whether they be classics or trash, does little good. Colleges can become places where the young are taught hypocrisy, being told they "should" like Fellini, Bergman, Antonioni, or Godard. They can accept these film-makers just as uncritically as their parents adulated movie stars. Unless there is encouragement to reflect on film experience, its impact can be minimal and fleeting. Most of the responses I have mentioned came from students who were well into the habit of discussing film. These discussions are best when they flow from the natural desire we have to communicate our feelings about a film. Nonverbalization, the reluctance to betray by treacherous abstractions the ineffable experience of the film, arises at this point. Real as it is, there must be found some middle ground between a suffocatingly detailed dissection of a film, and the noncommunicative exclamation, "like WOW!" Reflecting on one's experience is an integral part of making that experience part of one's self. Furthermore, one can see an almost immediate carry-over to other film experiences from each film discussed.

A problem more crucial than lack of reflection is the poverty of critical perspective. The young can plunge into their personal version of the *auteur* theory and make a fad or fetish out of certain films and directors. Roman Polanski has made some bad films, that is, films which do not reflect his own experience and feelings honestly as did *Knife in the Water*. Fascinating as *Rosemary's Baby* is, it suffers from an uncertain relationship of the director to his work. Some directors are adulated for peripheral or irrelevant reasons. Joseph Losey is a good film-maker, not because of a cynical preoccupation with evil, but because, like Hitchcock and Pinter, he makes us less certain of our virtue. And Buñuel, far from being a cheerful anarchist attacking church and society with abandon, is a careful surgeon, excising with camera the growths of degenerate myth on the cancerous culture.

In their own work, young people can celebrate bad film-making as "honest" and voyeuristic films as "mature." Criticism of poor films is not "putting down" the director for doing his own thing, especially if his thing is trite, dishonest, or so personal that it has no meaning accessible to others. Criticism means taking a stand on the basis of who you are. The current preference of spoof over satire is not just another instance of cool over hot, but is symptomatic of a noncritical stance. *Dr. Strangelove* makes comic absurdity out of the cold war from a certain conviction about what mature political action should be. The *Laugh-In* has no convictions but a lot of opinions. If it is accused of favoring an idea or cause, it will refute the charge by ridiculing what it holds. The cynical, sophisticated noninvolvement of the "won't vote" movement in the recent election has its counterpart in film viewing.

A question that should perhaps have been asked earlier is: Why should we be concerned with asking how young people look at film? Tired reasons, citing *Time*'s Man of the Year, the under-twenty-five generation, or the youth-quake menace of *Wild in the Streets* (they'll be taking over!) are not appropriate here. Anyone who is interested in the direction taken by cinema, and its continued vitality in the current renaissance of the art, will have to take the young into account as the major shaping force on the medium. If the age group from sixteen to twenty-four accounts for 48 per cent of the box office, it means that this eight-year period determines the success or failure of most films. Fortunately, there has not yet appeared a formula for capturing this audience. *Variety* described the youth market as a booby trap for the industry, citing the surprise success of sleepers such as *Bonnie and Clyde* and *The Graduate*, as well as the supposed youth-appeal failures (*Half a Sixpence, Poor Cow, Here We Go Round the Mulberry Bush*). The list may suggest a higher level of young taste than producers are willing to admit. In any case, if the young have influenced the medium this far, we cannot ignore the fact. It is for this reason that we are encouraged to speculate on the future in the form of two developments revolutionizing the young approach to film: student film-making and multi-media experiences.

More and more, the answer to how young people look at film is "through the lens of a camera." In coming years, it will be youth as film-maker, and not simply as audience, that will spur the evolution of the cinema. Students want a piece of the action, whether in running a university, the country, or the world; in terms of our question, this means making films. There is a strong resonance between film-making and the increasingly sophisticated film experience. Young people delighted by a television commercial are tempted to say: "I could do that!" Considering the cost and artistry of some commercials, this is a pretty naïve statement, but it doesn't stop the young from taking out their father's Super-8 or buying an old Bolex to tell their story on film. Today, anyone can make a film. Although Robert Flaherty's longed-for parousia, when film is as cheap as paper, has not yet arrived, the art has come into the reach of almost everyone. The Young Film-Makers Conference held by Fordham University last February drew 1,200 people, 740 of them student film-makers below college age. On a few weeks' notice, some 120 films were submitted for screening. Kids flew in from Richmond, California, and bussed in from Louisville, Kentucky, with twenty-seven states and Canada represented. Numbers, however, do not tell the story. One of the notable directors and actors present sized up the scene by saying: "My God, I'm standing here in the middle of a revolution!" It was the quality of the films that caused Eli Wallach to remark, only half in jest, that some day he'd be working for one of these film-makers. The young look at film as potential or actual film-makers, and this fact raises participation to an unprecedented critical level. The phenomenon also removes the last residue of passive audience participation from the Golden Forties box-office bonanza.

Foolhardy though it may be, one can predict that the new interest in film will take the direction of multi-media experimentation. Expo 67, it seems, is *now*. Our new and growing capacity to absorb images and synthesize sounds demands a simultaneity that cannot be met by traditional forms of film-making. The response so far has been the halfhearted multiple screens of *The Thomas Crown Affair*, not part of the conception of the film, but inserted as fancy dressing. The object of multiple images is not so much to condense actions as to create an environment such as the Ontario pavilion film, *A Place to Stand*. My own students have begun to relegate location shots such as street scenes or mood sequences to peripheral attention on side screens and walls, while the action takes place on the main screen.

It is symptomatic that the staged novelty of the Electric Circus is giving way to a new and interesting experiment in Greenwich Village, Cerebrum — where for a modest fee parties can set up their own media platforms equipped with projectors, tape recorders, and lights to stage their own happening. The idea being developed here is central to multi-media art, that is, the orchestration of contemporary media instruments. Young people are not afraid to carry a running projector around, spraying the images on walls and ceilings for distortions which communicate. An older generation is inclined to think of the media hardware as "machines" to be screwed to the floor or locked in a booth while they "produce" images and sounds. The young, in contrast, recognize this hardware as part of the information environment of electronic technology, and they use it accordingly. Spontaneity, the chance synchronization, overload that leads to breakthrough — these are all part of the excitement that draws people to media rather than film alone.

The young look at film is a revolutionary one, motivated more by love of the medium than hatred of the Establishment. In a sense, the new taste is liberating film for a free exploration of its potential, especially in the area of humanizing change. The hunger for a relativity of time and space will extend to morality, producing films that explore problems rather than package solutions. Nevertheless, the very intensity of young involvement gives promise of profound changes in the youth audience as people open themselves to the reality of the medium. Whether as young film-maker or multi-media entrepreneur, the young will have their say. If we take the time to cultivate their perspective, we may learn an interesting view of the future of media, and a fascinating way to stay alive.

Re: Vision

STAN VANDERBEEK

Vision undergoes re-vision; intention, symbol, reality
are the factors that undergo constant change
in the appearance of any art form.

Motion pictures —
pictures in motion —
seem most suited to the metaphysics of change,
to life in motion,
and as such cinema is becoming the most significant of art forms.

> "One thing that is new is the prevalence of
> newness, the changing scale and scope of change
> itself, so that the world alters as we
> walk in it. . ."
>   (Robert Oppenheimer, from "The Open Mind")

I like to think that life is a dissolve. . .

. . . and that seeing is the real illusion, that a sense of reality
is a sense of the senses. . .
that a sense of reality is a sense of non-sense. . .
that movies should delight the eye and rearrange the senses. . .
that movies are changing the art of seeing. . .
that movies are an art of seeing. . .
that movies are an illusion. . .
that seeing is believing.

The irony of art and life reminds us that "motion pictures"
are really a series of "still" pictures, which are being replaced
in the projector at less than 1/24th of a second . . . reaching
our eye at 186,000 m.p. second.
That we see the illusion of motion is based on the retention
of image, or the eye's inertia.

Motion pictures are apparent motion. . .
The film worker deals with "visual velocity" and "visual inertia,"
laws of sight that seem similar to laws in physics —

or at least to definitions of sight that contemporary
artists are exploring.
If movies and "vision" can assume the same meaning
then visions take the path of least resistance, that is,
intuitive logic, intuitive geometry, image-symbol making, art-
city planning of the mind, a form of research
that is just beginning in motion images. . .

(Retinal art such as strobiscope stimulation that produces
colors from black and white images . . . the possibility of
mental movies. . . .)

> "If confusion is the sign of the time, I see
> at the root of this confusion a rupture
> between things and words, between things and
> the ideas and signs that are their represen-
> tation. . ."
>
> (Artaud)

The apparent image and the approximate image interrelate in
our national sense of photo-reality. It is not inappropriate
that we have a magazine called "Life" — that we take for granted
that movies are reality. . .

That we take for granted much of our American life as it is reflected in
photo-reality is evidenced by a lack of self-criticism
and satire. . . .

> Paul Klee said:
> "Satire is not an excess of ill humor, but
> ill humor resulting from a vision of some-
> thing higher . . . ridiculous man, divine God.
> Hatred for anything stagnant out of respect
> for pure humanity. . ."

Malraux pointed out that life has no real walls . . . and no
real museums. . .
The World's Fair is an example:
It was not very interesting to people, and was a commercial
failure, perhaps because it was designed as an object in
the museum tradition. . . .

But if it had been designed as objects, books, textures,
smells, sounds, motion pictures, that were sent in boxes

to each person in America to own and keep in his possession. . .
to give each of us continuous research pleasure and the stimulation
of international ideas. . .
a direct 20th-century stimulus made possible
by mass production, that would serve as reference material
until the next Fair. . .

In other words a kit of communication tools sent to 150,000,000
Americans — projectors, tape recorders, books,
slides, films, display cases, et cetera — designed by the artist
designers of the world, mass-produced so that the budget for
this kit would cost no more than a pavilion's installation.

Since one had to pay to get into the Fair, the citizen could
have sent this money in return for the kit. For a suitable time
period the Fair would have sent him continuously changing displays
and materials from all over the world . . . some to keep and some
to exchange, like books from a world library.

The World's Fair was at best merely fair. It reproduced the
ideas of 1939, not 1964 . . . It could be
anticipated that audio-visual conditioning will produce new results. . . .

I like the process of making films, because it is a way for me
to have dialogues with myself.
I work in a small studio-dome, which I built myself from a silo
top.

I work in the painter's tradition and do everything by
myself as much as possible, which includes home development
of my negatives, camera work, editing, et cetera. . .

I often make my films without too much conceptual preparation,
using the film process of animation itself as a means
of note-taking.
Thus in the making of one film, a process or idea for another film
often comes about.

I also like to work on a variety of films at the same time
(often as many as six) and don't expect to see a finished
film for several years. . .

Editing a film, often inter-editing from one separate film
into another, continues the conversations with the self. . .

Cinema, like significant painting, must be made on
the basis of self-expression and necessity. . .
There are no geniuses in film-making, only desperate
men. In my opinion the audience cannot be considered as the final
target for their film work, but it may be implicated. . .

The major failure of commercial films made by the film "industry"
is that they represent the range of public-accepted vision that
cannot be made private . . . whereas the film poet is confronted
with the dilemma that his private vision can in no way be made
public. . .

Motion pictures are just now beginning to come out of the literary
perspective of the novel and staged drama they were born in. . .

It is interesting that after nearly 400 years of art that was
preoccupied with realism — growing mostly out of the theory of
perspective and its effect on the senses — this preoccupation
has at last reached its ultimate form in photography, particularly
motion-picture photography.

It is part of the interesting nature of art that at this same
juncture in the crossroads of art, with the perfection
of a means to capture exactly perspective and "realism,"
the artist's vision is turning more to his interior, and in a sense to an
infinite exterior (photos of Mars), abandoning the logic of
aesthetics and springing full-blown into a juxtaposed and
simultaneous world that ignores the one-point-perspective mind
and the one-point-perspective lens.

Another factor of particular interest is that movies represent
a kind of international decompression chamber, being the only
international art form that is portable, reproducible and
universal in popularity. . .

I am fascinated by one of the current theories about dreams
which holds that dreams are a way for the body to get rid of
body poisons (which get burned up in the dream-act).

If this holds true, it seems likely that motion pictures
might be a way for us to burn up international and national
"toxic" attitudes. Perhaps this is an aspect of the
moviegoing ritual, and of the value of the Hollywood "dream
factory". . . .

Clearly, movies help us to re-experience our experiences, which
seems to be a basic human need.

Motion, metamotion, kinetic identity, body-motor response,
homeostasis, continuity. . .
the movement of the spheres. . .
are to be pinned like a moth stuck in the axis of the mind,
to relieve the tensions of change (doubt) — of the movement of
life itself — by studying it. . .
by changing it into a symbolic form that is as real and meaningful as life itself.

I have emphasized that motion pictures are the unique art form
of the 20th century,
that they have produced a revolution in worldwide aesthetics,
(namely, that motion pictures have produced the new aesthetics of
anticipation, as compared to the older idea of painting and art
history as "meditation"). . .
that cinema is just beginning to come into its own. . .

The future holds unknown combinations of some of the present
loosely knit ideas. . .
integration of cinema, theater, dance, drama, electronic sound and
sights, movie-dromes, video tape, libraries of film, kinetic and
"expanded" cinema, "movie-murals," "movie-mosaics" . . .

Some of the ideas that are of particular interest to the
current film-maker are:
simultaneous images and compression,
abstractions, superimpositions,
discontinuous information,
social surrealism,
episodic structure,
loop film (continuous projection),
film as a reflection of private dreams, hallucinations. . .

Some of the vastly expanded techniques available now include:
8mm (some $6^{1}/_{2}$ million 8mm cameras in America)
super 8mm
16, 35, 70, 120mm (over one billion dollars for photo-services
annually),
video tape for home use,
computer-generated graphics,
stereo and laser pictures. . .

television (4¹/₂ hours viewing-time per average family per average
day).

The contemporary artist, facing many opportunities in America,
must find ways to cut across definitions and precensorship of
techniques and medias.

The artist must make use of the force of art, with its influence
on human psychology, to communicate and to announce. He must find
ways to come out of his isolation from his community. He must
find ways to unite technology and the human condition. . .
He must find ways to investigate, to document, to decorate,
to criticize, to love . . . and so add meaning to the life we are all
shaping.

My own work leads me into multiprojection and the
building of the "movie-drome" in which I plan to
develop a sight and sound research center, a prototype
theater of the future, exploring motion pictures,
image transmission and image storage, video graphics,
electronic sound and music, drama and experimental
cinema-theater.

I foresee motion pictures as the tool for a new form of
world communication (via satellite) about to open
the future of "ethos-cinema."

We are on the verge of a new world — a new sense of art,
life and technology — when artists shall deal with the
world as a work of art, and art and life shall again become
the same process. When man's senses shall expand,
reach out, and in so doing shall touch all men in the world.

In my view I see that art and life, man and technology, unite
and seek to renew and re-view. . .
In particular I see that motion pictures will become
"emotion-pictures" and will generate into a new structure,
a new context, becoming a nonverbal international picture
language, in which we can talk to each other. . .

More important, inter-culturally, art and life
must do something about the future; the world is hanging
by a thread of verbs and nouns.

I see that certain films, made in a certain way and presented
in a certain way, will help us and will be used as a technique
to understand and balance the senses.

The development of a nonverbal international picture
language that makes use of cinema and other image-
transmission systems is of utmost importance in the
consistent crises of world peace.

But to realize the possibilities of this new art form
(cinema is only approximately sixty years old) many more
artists and poets must become aware of this media and
attempt to work with it.
I hope that artists from all over the world will do so
and quickly, so that we can realize and enjoy our differences
in a "Culture-Intercom."

Sights and sounds, the changing illusion of the world in which
we live, and the world that lives
only in the mind, are the basic materials of film creation.
The full flow of color, sound, synthesized form, plastic form, light and
picture poetry have in no way begun to be explored in man's
range of experience.

Newsreel

NEWSREEL

NORM FRUCHTER, NY NEWSREEL

Newsreel, for me, is the constant challenge of facing choices which are at once, and indissolubly film-making choices, political choices, activist choices, aesthetic choices. None of us are satisfied with the blend that emerges . . . how to make what we want? Films as weapons? (Historical phrase — badly weathered.) Bullets kill, and some films get into people's heads, to shock, stun, arrest, horrify, depress, sadden, probe, demand. We want that kind of engagement — films people can't walk away from, with "Oh yes, I saw a filmshow last night, sort of political."

Who doubts, any more, that this country is so monstrously damaging, to both its domestic and foreign captive populations, that revolution is essential? The problem is how: what forces we're building, what this multifaceted thing we call the Movement will grow into, what real organizations we're making out of all the disaffection this country breeds. Not that armageddon is coming, or apocalypse — but in small ways the streets explode, and the fabric of consent which sociologists once celebrated shreds visibly on the TV. Who knows what's happening to this country? So our films have to attack, they come out of as close as we can get to the activity we value. Getting deeper, harsher, more corrosive, more inflammatory — those are our problems.

We should hate a lot more. Let it out. Let it dissolve the insufferable smugness which protects everybody. The media. None of us are old enough to have any illusions about infiltrating the major media to reach mass consciousness and change it — we grew up on TV and fifties Hollywood. . . .

MARILYN BUCK AND KAREN ROSS,
SAN FRANCISCO NEWSREEL

This society is one of spectators, who live and perceive through the news media, particularly the visual media. People's lives revolve around the assumptions which are made by which channel they watch or what movie they choose to see. And all the TV channels and American films speak from the same mouth of control and power. We looked around ... and Newsreel was conceived and born. A way for film-makers and radical organizer-agitators to break into the consciousness of people. A chance to say something different ... to say that people don't have to be spectator-puppets.

In our hands film is not an anesthetic, a sterile, smooth-talking apparatus of control. It is a weapon to counter, to talk back to and to crack the facade of the lying media of capitalism.

The radicals who have become involved in San Francisco Newsreel had previously participated in the development of the left political movement. Yet some of these experiences resulted in alienation. A disappointment and frustration with the forms of the left. Creative action was lacking. Newsreel has offered a definite medium in which to work; a weapon to destroy the established forms of control and power over people. We have had to overcome our lack of technical knowledge of film-making. Moreover, we must realize our political responsibility within our chosen form.

Many others who came to Newsreel as film-makers and artists had isolated themselves in their own work and private political fantasies. Newsreel has become an outlet for real political expression in a medium familiar to them. Their political fantasies were exposed. They had to begin relating to more active participation in the movement. They were political but it was necessary to combine the political content with form.

FRUCHTER

Easier to define than make the films we want. We're tied to events, and we shouldn't be: Pentagon, Columbia, Chicago, the Haight. Where should we begin? Most instincts are particular: narrow it down — this group, this action. Follow the officers of the Hanna Company in their jaunts through Brazil? Follow a Peace Corps volunteer? But why document the obvious — none of the people we make films for need that bad joke exposed, they've lived with (and often worked within) the reality. The varieties of domestic and external pacification deserve burlesque, no more. New forms? But how much will time, limited energies, finance, and the wearing pressure of events, the race to stay responsible, limit us?

BUCK AND ROSS

Newsreel is a collective rather than a cooperative; we are not together merely to help each other out as film-makers but we are working together for a common purpose: to make films which shatter the image and reality of fragmentation and exploitation in this society. Yet there are problems in developing and maintaining this collective form. These lie in the question of assimilation. Assimilation of the film-maker and the radical, assimilation of the individual into the collective. In making films together which reflect a collective, a movement of ideas and actions rather than the individuality of the artist, we must develop new values, forms, new criteria for individual interaction. Differences in techniques and analysis of content must be worked out collectively. The body must endorse the resulting film or it cannot be distributed through Newsreel.

FRUCHTER

Responsibility. There's no revolutionary party yet, only fledgling forms of various undergrounds. No coherent strategy, no discipline to stay hewed to, so we make our politics (our films) on the hoof; our discussions often threaten to become interminable. How transcend this transition stage? What's our response, for instance, if we think that sabotage is only marginally effective and yet guys are going to jail for it? What's our response to the police ambush in Cleveland, who among us has doubts about why black men are moved to shoot police? Newsreel is a jumping-off point. Or are we kidding ourselves? In '42, '43, '44 in Italy, what did Zavattini and Rossellini and the rest say to themselves? Were the partisan units a real alternative? What were the terms on which they said, "But we must fight as film-makers"? What historical stage are we in, what categories can we use to decide what we must do?

ROBERT KRAMER, NEW YORK NEWSREEL

We began by trying to bridge the gap between the states of mind and ways of working that we were accustomed to as film-makers, and the engagement/daily involvement/commitments of our political analysis and political activity. This had immediate implications — not only for our film-making, but for interpretations of what, as film-makers, as people engaged in a struggle against established forms of power and control, against established media of all forces, we had to do *with* or *without* cameras.

In regard to our films. I think we argue a different hierarchy of values. Not traditional canons of "what is professional," what is "comprehensive and intelligent reportage," what is "acceptable quality and range of material." No. Nor do we accept a more sophisticated argument about propaganda in general: that if the product isn't sold

well, if the *surface* of the film (grainy, troublesome sound, soft-focus,
a wide range of maladies that come up when you are filming under
stress) alienates, then the subject population never even gets to your
"message" about the product — they just say, "Fuck that, I'm not
watching that shit."

The subject population in this society, bombarded by and totally
immersed in complex, ostensibly "free" media, has learned to absorb
all facts/information relatively easily. Within the formats now popu-
larized by the television documentary, you can lodge almost any
material, no matter how implicitly explosive, with the confidence that
it will neither haunt the subject population, nor push them to
move — in the streets, in their communities, in their heads. You see
Cleaver or Seale on a panel show, and they don't scare you or
impress you or make you think as they would if you met them on the
street. Why? Because they can't get their hands on you? Partly, sure.
(Fear and committed thought exist in terms of the threat that power
will be used against you — in terms of the absolute necessity of figur-
ing out what has to be done — not in terms of some vague decision to
"think it through" in isolation.) But also, because their words are
absorbed by the format of the "panel show," rational (note well:
ostensibly rational) discussion about issues that we all agree are
important and pressing, and that we (all good liberal viewers) are
committed to analyzing. Well: bullshit. The illusion of the commitment to analyze. The illusion of real dissent. The illusion of even
understanding the issues. Rather, the commitment to pretend that
we're engaging reality.

OK. At the point when you have considered this argument then
you start to make films with different priorities, with shapes justified
in a different way. You want to make films that unnerve, that shake
assumptions, that threaten, that do not soft-sell, but hopefully (an
impossible ideal) explode like grenades in peoples' faces, or open
minds up like a good can opener. We say: "The things you see in
these films are happening at this moment, they are our 'news,' they
are important to us and do not represent the droppings of a few
freaks, but the activity of a growing wave of people, your children
who were fighting the pigs at Columbia, your brothers who walked
out of this high school, your sons who deserted the army, your former
slaves who will not now accept your insufficient reparations, etc., etc.
You know this reality. You know enough to know that this is real —
now deal with it, because soon it's going to come to deal with you, in
one way or another." The effect of our films is more like seeing 250
Black Panthers around the Oakland Court House, or Columbia students carrying on the business of revolt at Kirk's desk, or Free Men

occupying the streets of Berkeley, than listening to what some reporter tells us about what these people might have said, and how we can understand "rebellion" psychologically. We strive for confrontation, we prefer disgust/violent disagreement/painful recognition/jolts — all these to slow liberal head-nodding and general wonderment at the complexity of these times and their being out of joint.

We want a form of propaganda that polarizes, angers, excites, for the purpose of discussion — a way of getting at people, not by making concessions to where they are, but by showing them where you are and then forcing them to deal with that, bringing out all their assumptions, their prejudices, their imperfect perceptions.

BUCK AND ROSS

Some viewers make the whole choice to see Newsreels. They are aware of what they are going to see, and the films thus reinforce their conceptions — or they may shake these viewers back into radical action and analysis. Most importantly, Newsreels must be weapons: they must confront people who are not motivated to go see them. Newsreel must make half the decisions for them. Street projection is the first answer we've come up with so far. We take the films into the street, we stop people on the street, and confront them with our films. Involve them as participants. They're not home glued to their TVs, where if subjected to action they merely sit and absorb it in some unconscious place in their heads. The truck, mobile, produces live action on the street. Motion within motion. It has come to them during a walk down the street, they've stumbled upon it. Newsreel has forced itself into their consciousness. They have been confronted. The decision to watch, to register disgust or interest is now theirs. We have the opportunity to talk with them about their reactions, between films. To those inquisitive, we explain more. To those objecting, we can try to break their arguments. We have our confrontation as people, Newsreel has its confrontation through film.

Newsreel can evaluate the effectiveness of its films by looking at its audiences and their responses to the films. Many of our showings have been very discouraging: not many people or no reaction to the films at all. Others have been elating: lots of people who react vigorously to the films, asking questions or arguing about the validity of the films. And the difference in the showings may be only the audience. Middle-class neighborhood groups may feel that the straight documentary sync-sound film on draft resistance is very good to see: informative, encouraging, and perhaps even motivating. But when the same film is shown to young chicanos, it's absolutely useless. The guys walk out, hiss, and ask "When are you going to show us some action?" And so, we run the Haight riot film, a five-minute street film with a lot of action set to contemporary rock music. And they dig it. We show *Garbage*, a cultural exchange between the Motherfuckers of New York and Lincoln Center, a fast-moving film also, thinking this might also turn the guys on, and they are bored by it and finally walk out. But college and excollege radicals say, "Far out, those guys are doing some good things — I like their style." And the older, middleclass people in the audience may not dislike it, but don't quite see the point . . . or register confusion or a polite distaste for the obscene language and people of the film.

KRAMER

We shoot as best we can — but we shoot what's important to us, what meets our perceptions of our lived reality; we cut according to our priorities, our ideologies, not "to make it plain and simple to them." Not to present a "line." Not to present the lived reality as less complex than it really is. Not to enter into that sterile game: modulating our emotions and intensities and intelligences in some vain hope that by speaking your language your way we can persuade you. No, we know the effective outcome of that: only the acceptance of another of the subtle forms of domination and control. Now we move according to our own priorities, and we are justified in this by objective conditions. Five years ago, for example, such a decision would have been suicidal. Our movement was only emerging — few people knew anything about it — few people were involved. But now, all our audiences (and our audiences represent the full spectrum of the society) know the essence of what we're talking about. They read it every day in every paper digested and shaped to their preconceptions. So now we present it to them in its nakedness, in *our* true understanding of it, not vitiated by analyses and "in-depth studies" that we do not accept, but just exactly what counts from our point of view. The established media have done the job of popularizing: now we must specify and make immediate; convert our audiences or neutralize them; threaten.

BUCK AND ROSS

The Columbia film, about the seizure of Columbia and the politics of that seizure, is an important film to college students. It was shown to students at the University of California, Santa Cruz, on the eve of a scheduled protest against the board of regents which was meeting on campus the next day. The film helped to bolster enthusiasm for the students' action and create a mood in which the protest could take place and be successful. The film on the Black Panther Party turns people's heads around, aweing them with the strength and the nature of the Panthers of which they may not have previously conceived. We think the film is politically and visually exciting — it demands that people react to it, and not pass it off. It is a film that evokes response with the most diverse kinds of audiences — liberals on their way to the film festival, students at the universities, the black community in the streets.

KRAMER

Our films remind some people of battle footage: grainy, camera weaving around trying to get the material and still not get beaten/trapped. Well, we, and many others, are at war. We not only document that war, but try to find ways to bring that war to places which have managed so far to buy themselves isolation from it.

So, to return to the issue of propaganda. Our propaganda is one of confrontation. Using film — using our voices with and after films — using our bodies with and without cameras — to provoke confrontation. Changing minds, altering consciousness, seems to us to come through confrontations, not out of sweet/reasonable conversations that are one of the society's modes of absorbing and disarming dissent and movement, of giving that illusion that indeed we are dealing with "the issues." Therefore we keep moving. We keep hacking out films, as quickly as we can, in whatever way we can.

To all film-makers who accept the limited, socially determined rules of clarity, of exposition, who think that films must use the accepted vocabulary to "convince," we say essentially: you only work, whatever your reasons, whatever your presumed "content," to support and bolster this society; you are a part of the mechanisms which maintain stability through re-integration; your films are helping to hold it all together, and finally, whatever your descriptions, you have already chosen sides. Dig: your sense of form and order is already a political choice — don't talk to me about "content" — but if you do, I will tell you that you cannot encompass our "content" with those legislated and approved senses, that you do not understand it if you treat it that way. There is no such thing as revolutionary content, revolutionary spirit, laid out for inspection and sale on the bargain basement counter.

On Two Fronts

LEO BRAUDY

> ... What we demand is the unity of politics and art, the unity of
> content and form, the unity of revolutionary political content and
> the highest possible perfection of artistic form. Works of art which
> lack artistic quality have no force, however progressive they are
> politically. ... We must carry on a struggle on two fronts.
>
> — Mao Tse-Tung, quoted at various moments
> by Kirilov and Véronique in *La Chinoise*

In the approximately nine months of its existence, New York Newsreel has completed fifteen films, with several more almost ready for
release. The films are frequently very good and always interesting,
although sometimes much good will is necessary to disentangle the
web of aesthetics and politics at a particular film's center. But Newsreel shows in general a vital and aggressive willingness to experiment
with traditional documentary methods in a concerted effort to work
"on two fronts" and integrate its political commitment with the
movie-making techniques.

The earlier Newsreels are closer to usual documentary form.
They do imply that the viewer has some knowledge, for example, of
the antiwar, antidraft movement. But they generally take the expository approach dictated by the documentary assumption "I was there
and you weren't." This method is best exemplified by *Boston Draft
Resistance Group*, done mostly in synchronized sound with some narration that describes and explains the group's activities. It is clean
and straightforward in a kind of BBC manner that perfectly suits the
incessant reasonableness of the Boston Draft Resistance Group's
arguments and their decision to look freshfaced and shorn. This fa-
miliarly professional documentary form (even down to the detailed
credits, the only such in the Newsreels I have seen) with its radical
content is one way of attacking the problem.

Two less successful films about draft resistance are *Chomsky*
and *Resist and the New England Resistance*. The frame of the first is
an interview with Noam Chomsky that is then interspliced with antiwar and antidraft activities. It was made just after the Coffin-Spock
indictment, but still has a sense of immediacy in its combination of
shots from the first Call to Resist meeting several months before, an
interview with Coffin, and the actions of several individual resisters.
Resist and the New England Resistance uses the same Call to Resist

footage, but relates it more directly to individual decisions to turn in draft cards and the political implications of such acts.

Except for some close-ups, the camera in *Boston Draft Resistance Group* only records. It is a witness, not a participant or a commentator. Such an approach appears more purely in a film called *Four Americans* released by Newsreel, but edited and synchronized from Japanese footage. Before a dark backdrop the four deserters from the *Intrepid* make joint and later individual statements about their decision. The setting is very stagy and frontal; the camera never moves. But gradually the men emerge in contrast to their rigid aesthetic format.

Later Newsreels do not completely drop this more "objective" and traditional approach because the group preserves a sensitivity to the special kind of treatment each subject demands. A comparatively recent film like *Meat Cooperative* again has a fairly straightforward chronological form, while it describes in a *Consumer Reports* manner the growth of a Lower East Side community meat cooperative that successfully does away with the bad meat and high prices of the local supermarkets until OEO funds are cut off and it must close. The second section, in which the leaders of the cooperative try to get help from the local congressman to have the funds renewed, is inconclusive and abrupt, like the action itself. But the promise of the cooperative, and its potential as an example, carries the weight of the film. Although *Meat Cooperative* like *Boston Draft Resistance Group* is aesthetically traditional, it is politically part of a propaganda of possibilities that stands opposed to what one Newsreel member called "the aesthetically and politically mindless propaganda of the thirties."

The self-help didacticism of *Meat Cooperative* restates the "witness" method of the other Newsreels I have mentioned. But the more pervasive trend in Newsreel has been films that demand much more from the audience in both aesthetics and political response. *Meat Cooperative* can be called open-ended because it suggests the possibility of other cooperatives on its model. But films like *No Game*, *Garbage*, *Riot Weapons*, *I.S. 201*, and *Chicago* abandon the familiar documentary explicitness and chronological linearity to demand more of the audience's attention and engagement. The assumption of these films seems to be that a TV-conditioned desire for pleasant sound and sync dialogue is related to a desire for easy and unabrasive answers to distant problems. Their soundtracks and frequently their spray of images are irritating and confusing. The nonsync film becomes more radical than the sync because sync suggests easy solutions, the effortless marriage of word and image. But these films imply that neither

the problems nor the solutions are easy. Earlier propaganda frequently had little aesthetic appeal, while its political content was simplistic, schematic, and therefore easily ignored. These more experimental Newsreel films attempt to achieve a more open-ended political
result by aesthetically radicalizing the audience as well. The understanding needed to bring together sound and image mirrors the
understanding necessary to translate accurate analysis into appropriate political action.

No Game, Newsreel's Pentagon film, stands uneasily between the
"witness" films and the more experimental ones. The camera moves
about the Lincoln Memorial, recording parts of speeches, incidents,
and faces, and then follows the marchers to the Pentagon. The soundtrack is a frequently hard to understand mix of statements by the
speechmakers, hubbub, and marching noise that synchronizes
momentarily in a Peter, Paul, and Mary song. Finally, when the
camera sweeps down a line of troops before the Pentagon, a studio
voice authoritatively addresses the soldiers about the War, and the
image shifts to Vietnam footage. Although some audiences have complained about this voice and the way it disrupts the more documentary tone of No Game, I found it much less annoying than the many
pointless wide-angle shots. The shift in images is, however, very
effective. The confused charges around the Pentagon give way to the
overexposed blacks and whites of the war scenes; the familiar bushes
and trees change into the landscape of a lunar world; and the helicopter that hovered over Arlington Bridge is transformed into an image
of malevolent destruction.

Despite these striking images of the dreamworld of evil marchers
are trying to fight, the studio voice in No Game does detract from its
final effect; it is too authoritarian and its final optimism about the
value of the march is too easy. The explaining and interpreting overvoice is feasible for films like this primarily because it's cheap. Politically, its effect can be dogmatic and abstract, without a feeling for the
nuances of the concrete situation. Films without the direction of an
overvoice, on the other hand, risk fuzziness or the imposition of even
more simplistic devices. The Jeanette Rankin Brigade, which details a
trip to Washington by a group of militant women, falls too easily into
a series of heavy ironies that juxtapose the resolute women with a
supercilious world of men — cops and otherwise. The effect of the
march is politically inconclusive, and could lead to more understanding of the proper use of this kind of protest. But without an appropriate or compelling artistic form, inconclusiveness appears only as confusion.

In Riot Weapons the last image makes a direct appeal to the

audience to engage the film and the problems it depicts: two black New Jersey National Guardsmen point out of a billboard in Newark, while the camera closes on the pointing hands. But the direction of the film that precedes this image is unclear. Gun advertisements in police magazines, publicity shots of police tanks, and scenes of riot training alternate with footage and stills of riots and their aftermath. The contrast is heightened by the soundtrack: behind the ads is the clatter of guns and the shriek of sirens; behind the riot scenes, only silence. But the riot sequences generally lack any bite or point, in addition to being repetitious. What are the demands that the final image is making on the audience? If the contrast between the two kinds of sequence is the main point, what choice has been made about the length of the film? Does *Riot Weapons* merely document trends in police militarism or does it also imply that black and white radicals should arm themselves too? Is there, for example, a progression from ads for police weapons to ads for ordinary weapons? (I could not tell when I saw the film.) *I.S. 201*, which deals with a memorial parade in honor of Malcolm X and other commemorative activities in a New York public school, similarly tries to find some form other than the chronological narrative of the observing documentary camera. The titles for the separate sequences have a screechy soundtrack behind them (and follow rather than precede the events they describe). The film does capture some sense of the rush of these activities and the energy liberated by Malcolm's influence. But once again there is a lack of effective rhythm in the film itself, an inability to set up its own terms securely enough. For a film that deals with potential action and movement, *I.S. 201* has a curious lethargy, especially in the shots of the destroyed areas of Newark, while an I.S. 201 panel discussion occupies the soundtrack.

Talk, as it is embodied in the discussions that swirl around political action, forms an increasingly important part of Newsreel's films. The films now in progress concentrate even more on developing a kind of "follow" documentary, a film about the dynamics of different groups as they get into, learn about, and try to deal with the society they live in, to bridge the gap between talk and action. *Garbage* and *Chicago* are the two most interesting and most successful attempts I have seen so far to document this process of thought and action and produce a film that has aesthetic form without political finality. *Garbage* follows a Lower East Side group called "Up-Against-The-Wall-Motherfuckers" on a trip to throw garbage into the central fountain of Lincoln Center as a statement about the cultural garbage Lincoln Center purveys and the mounds of real garbage people are living in because of the New York garbage strike. The soundtrack is full of talk — jokes, arguments about the project in earlier discussions, commentary during the trip itself, "America the Beautiful" in falsetto, and discussions afterwards, and more talk about later action to relate the existence of Lincoln Center to the problems of the Lower East Side as a community. *Garbage* was shot by many Newsreel cameramen and therefore embodies many points of view, in its images as well as in its soundtrack, about the appropriateness of the garbage dump as a reaction to the fact of Lincoln Center. One especially ambiguous shot of a black janitor with a broom watching the exuberant Motherfuckers go by introduces the idea that those in power will never be touched by something as whimsical as this; the only effect will be extra work for the people who have to clean up.

Chicago deals with the late March conferences at Long Villa outside Chicago to plan for radical action during the Democratic convention. Most Newsreels start with a "teaser" before the logo and title. In *Chicago* it is a seemingly pointless ride down a long Chicago street, faster and faster, with jumpier and jumpier cuts, until the street dead-ends in the International Amphitheater, site of the convention. This trip appears several more times in the film, together with approaches from other streets, and rides around Chicago by car and elevated. The camera is restless — not content, as in, for example, *Boston Draft Resistance Group*, to follow along and listen to explanations, but dodging in and out, breaking away from the conference discussions with their endless cups of coffee, speakers, and uncomfortable chairs, looking out into Chicago for the relevance of all the talk, for where it connects. The two longest sections devoted to speakers underline this problem. A white committee leader reports on the arguments, the irresolution about what exactly should be done at the convention. Then, towards the end of the film, a black speaker lists in numerical order the demands the convention has decided on and phrased with a rigid certainty, while the camera keeps cutting back to the elevated train ride. Is this the way to Chicago? Is this what should be done?

Films like *Garbage*, *Chicago*, *Boston Draft Resistance Group*, and *Meat Cooperative* have a richness and vitality that repays seeing them several times. Even the less successful Newsreel films are provocative in their deficiencies. Ideally, Newsreel is a community of politically committed film-makers who can progress in artistic ability and political understanding at equal pace. But practically, people come into the group at different levels of sophistication in both film-making and politics, make films, and then change to varying degrees. Making films that strive for some immediacy, with a large group and possibly interminable discussions, forces the need for a series of compromises, with many bad choices being made about both subject matter and treatment. Newsreel members admit that many of their films contain "cheapies" — bald ironies, badly conceived footage, muffed effects. But more important is that many Newsreel films work fruitfully in the terms they have set for themselves.

The Newsreel logo is the words "The Newsreel" flickering violently to the sound of a machine gun — the cinematic equivalent of Leroi Jones's line "I want poems that can shoot bullets," or perhaps an allusion to Yvonne's machine-gun camera in *La Chinoise*. Instead of falling in with apocalypse, Newsreel makes new continuities in both its films and its organization. They have become a group that can work on two fronts, combining their film-making with their activism and obliterating the outmoded barriers between political engagement and artistic detachment.

Profile of Art in Revolution

DAVID CASTRO AND JERRY STOLL

A NEW CONCEPT

Social progress in the U.S. today will only come as the result of irresistible pressure for change from millions of citizens. It will require a drive for public education on a scale unprecedented in history. Unfortunately most people acquire their information about the crucial issues of our time through the mass media, and that media is controlled by those with a large stake in the status quo.

Under these conditions an independent media is vitally needed that can challenge their power to control public information. But reliance upon the old "soap-box media" guarantees failure in the electronic era of instant and massive communication. Instead the challenge must convey reality, directly and immediately, to the millions who feel that old views and old solutions to old problems are no longer relevant to modern life. A broad public understanding of the current crises demands the intense examination of reality through the use of film. But Hollywood has failed to attempt this examination, and television has been brutalized and robbed of its educational potential. The challenge to "controlled" public information, then, must come from documentary film, an art with revolutionary power — emotional, educational and social.

This is why we founded American Documentary Films. It is our instrument of opposition to the cash-register ethic that reduces mass culture to inane irrelevance and makes us indifferent to brutality. Irrelevance and brutal indifference are expressions of the undertakers' art that prepare the body politic for the grave. The threat of war, outbreaks of violence at home and abroad, mass starvation, student and labor unrest are just a few symptoms of a period of social change and widening divisions between social groups. Every day more and more individuals are swallowed up, and the disruption to normal life is increasingly widespread. Survival demands the recognition of reality. Documentary film art captures history in the act and reveals social change to the public eye.

ART AND CHANGE — THE HUMAN VIEW

Art is the precursor of social change and plays a leading role. The novel as an art form was created during the Industrial Revolution to help men and women understand their relation to property and to discover their individuality. In the 20th Century world made smaller and more complex by instant communication and increasingly interdependent organization, film is created to help man understand his relation to his fellow man and society. The development of this kind of communication requires the freest exercise of that creativity which is possible only by the independent artist and his fellow craftsmen.

This too is why we founded American Documentary Films. It is the first time in the history of either documentary or feature film production that the non-profit corporate approach has been used to guarantee independence and solve the problems of both production and distribution which hitherto have made it virtually impossible for socially significant films to exist.

WHY NON PROFIT?

Because the entire history of commercial film making demonstrates that truth and art are poor risks when investment rules the box office.

A CORPORATION

American Documentary Films has been legally chartered by the State of California as a non-profit corporation. The Corporate structure imposes certain rigidities upon its officers but at the same time is the most favorable form of organization, under the present system, for purposes of growth and autonomy. The power of the law, the prestige of public education and the thrust of the economy all combine to preserve the viability of corporate organization. The non-profit character of ADF underscores our emphasis on mass education through the creation of socially significant films. Moreover, the corporation's non-profit status provides for a favorable tax position from which to secure the necessary funds to support independent film production.

PRODUCING AND DISTRIBUTING

The prohibitive expense of film production demands the earliest return of this capital outlay to the film maker in order for new production to continue. But commercial distribution is designed to absorb film income. To avoid the commercial distribution trap, the key to our program is the creation and strict control of an independent distribution apparatus with the simple aims of getting our films to the public and receiving in return enough income to continue production.

FOUNDED BY FILM ARTISTS

We are artists who are responsible to the future as well as the past. We wish to exercise our art freely, to document the profound social changes and political movements that haunt modern life, without sacrificing art and honesty to the demands of the quick sale and volume turnover. Recognizing that our struggle for artistic independence is a struggle for financial independence we have created American Documentary Films to support the film maker by providing organization — the defensive framework that makes creativity possible in a competitive economy by no means dedicated to the progress of enlightenment.

HISTORY

Independent film production had virtually disappeared over the last 40 years. Film art was gradually taken out of the hands of the artists who created it and transformed by giant private corporations into one of the largest business combines the world has ever seen. The film maker as an artist was reduced to a necessary but small cog in a machine organized expressly to do business; the artist existed for the organization and not vice versa. As a result the potential of film medium as a mass art for social understanding degenerated into a mass narcotic manipulated for private gain, and any individual with fewer millions than Howard Hughes no longer even thought of making films.

In addition to the huge capitalization requirements created by the giant studio corporations, independent film production was checkmated by the monopolization of the entire distribution apparatus. Even if a film were independently financed and produced, there was no way for it to be seen by the vast audience necessary to repay the costs of production, because the "majors" owned the theater chains in the cities and controlled the private theaters elsewhere through "block booking."

The key to the old Hollywood monopoly power was the corporate structure which is accorded preference over all other forms of organization under the law, combined with massive financial leverage and strict control over the processes of both production and distribution. This power has since been weakened by the impact of television, by significant anti-trust suits against block booking and other practices, and by court decisions on censorship and free speech. Still far from losing its dominance over the U.S. film "market," the majors have thus been forced to witness the emergence of foreign and independent production and distribution of features, documentary and art films.

DOCUMENTARY FILM

In periods of social stability there is a common tendency to pursue personal or family fortune without questioning the terms by which they are defined. But times of deep social change act as incubators of new ideas and new social groupings as their effects touch the lives of more and more individuals. In such periods reality becomes fashionable once more while people seek out the direction and implications of the great changes taking place around them. Change fosters an attitude of inquiry. Today this attitude finds form in the documentary film, an art always subject to attack because of its social power.

Documentary film art is young in the U.S. In the 1930's, under the impact of the Depression, people were forced by painful reality into a fresh awareness of society and history. This opened the way for a new kind of pictorial journalism, The March of Time.

From this simple beginning in 1934, documentary film developed — through The Plow That Broke the Plains and The River — into that blend of factual observation and dramatic construction which became its characteristic form. It attracted nationwide attention but could not find sponsorship or distribution in the face of hostility from the Hollywood majors. It was thus forced to obtain finance from government, business or educational institutions — and *accept the limitations of purpose which such sponsorship imposes.*

The Roosevelt Administration started the U.S. Film Service where documentary found a brief life of development, until an anti-New Deal Congress decided government production was un-American (especially if it advocated public ownership of utilities). It abolished the U.S. Film Service and put the documentarians back into the streets. There Business closed its doors to them — tinged as they were with New Deal radicalism — and Education, fearful that reality in art threatened the budget, refused then as they do now to finance full-scale film production. And so documentary films in the U.S. floundered into the war years because the little group of enthusiasts who constituted the "movement" lacked the salesmanship and organizational ability required for survival in a competitive economy dominated by giant corporations.

But the pressure for national unity and military-industrial expertise demanded by World War II demonstrated that print is no match for film in the dissemination of ideas and emotions. The result was renewed and widespread government sponsorship of documentaries for training and propaganda.

Here the art flourished, culminating in *Army Navy Screen Magazine*, a servicemen's newsreel which achieved poetic and dramatic as well as ideological power. According to Richard Griffith, " . . . it represented one of the furthest points to which the drive to 'emotionalize facts and rationalize emotions' has been developed — a development which has abruptly ceased."

With victory the great need for unity of purpose dissolved, and in the post-war period documentary art was no longer useful to the cold war and the military ethic. What little film production remained under government sponsorship necessarily demanded a fealty at cross-purposes to its independent growth. Yet the lack of independent film art greatly exacerbates the post-war period of deepening crisis.

Despite the proliferation of electronic mass media, thoughtful citizens agree there is mortal crisis in social communication. There is much talk of gaps: the generation gap, the income gap, the culture gap, the racial gap, the credibility gap. Clearly a means of communication must be found to bridge these divisions in society. We must reach the millions of people alienated by them, and only film can do it. But Hollywood has succeeded in selling only fantasy. Television is also busily selling products and wouldn't care to offend its sponsors. Even educational television is financially dependent on political sponsorship and as a result its offerings are uncontroversial, irrelevant and uneducational. This is another reason why we founded American Documentary Films.

WHO GETS THE MONEY?

Unlike the poet who needs only a pencil and a fairly clean surface to practice his art, the film artist requires precision instruments at each step in the process. The initial capital outlay is enormous for cameras, lenses, lights, sound recording equipment, microphones, synchronizers, electronic control panels, thousands of feet of film and film processing equipment. The question of who benefits from the income returned on this outlay underscores the vital role of distribution in the film making process.

Under the prevailing practice of commercial distribution, the small independent producer owns only the title and the debt incurred in the film production. The income from the film's earnings goes to an alien corporation in control of distribution, with a percentage of net *after* expenses going to the producer.

It may be only coincidence, but the record clearly indicates that distribution expense substantially equals earnings over the years.

This has meant, first of all, that the small film maker was never paid for what he had created; he was forced to the wall only to be replaced by another small film maker who shared the same fate. Secondly, this alienated form of distribution resulted essentially in only two forms of theatrical film making in the U.S. One is the multimillion dollar studio production aimed at the least common denominator in an undifferentiated mass audience, and the other is the low-budget "avant garde" film in 8mm or 16mm keyed to a miniscule audience from the art colony. Between these two extremes waits the rest of the American audience for films evoking insight into the drama of their own lives, with whom neither of the two extremes communicate. Thus present commercial distribution has created a dilemma between making films for millions or making films for nothing.

To avoid being impaled upon these alternatives, the first step is to guarantee that the film maker retains control of his work. In the last two years several film makers have taken this step, evolving an "independent film makers' price policy" with the following essentials:

1. the film maker controls distribution;
2. a relatively high minimum is charged for rental; and
3. a percentage of the gate receipts from attendance returns directly to the producer.

It is true, of course, that these three tenets of independent distribution run directly counter to prevailing distribution procedures. But if we are serious about the need for an independent challenge to controlled mass information, we must be serious about the survival of the independent filmmaker and the growth of documentary film art. We must face the fact that there is no other way to assure both artistic and financial independence.

CREATING A DISTRIBUTION NETWORK

The financial restraints of production expense combined with commercial distribution monopoly explain why feature length films are always behind the times in terms of the culture they reflect. They are always "safe" and are always built around an imaginary theme that hopes to perform two impossible tasks — to offend no one, and at the same time attract everyone.

The widespread myth in the film industry that a motion picture can be made which everyone will want to see has corrupted the entire approach to production and distribution. The result has been an absurd and pitiful reliance by commercial film makers upon fantasy, sex, violence and the grotesque. But a non-profit documentary group can "afford" to treat human reality, to reflect social change, to be quickly flexible without being concerned to make films that please everyone. It can be alive to the changing times and the social pulse of the nation. It operates on the principle that every film it produces must have something to say to an audience within reach of its message.

Feature films thus become possible concerning the sharpest conflicts in the society. The most "controversial" subjects arise from conditions affecting the vital interests of the people as a whole, even though they may become visible only in one or another sub-stratum of society. Placed in a human context, controversy becomes drama. The deeper the effort to explore reality for the roots of controversy, the more personal the drama becomes as the camera reveals people struggling in the web of historic conflict. Here is the broadest basis for audience identification, the universally human.

Contrary to popular mythology, very few independently produced films have been able to recoup the investment for the original producers. This condition, existing for 30 years, has undergone a dramatic and revolutionary change in the past 5 years. It is now highly probable that any competent and sensitively made film will return its cost and earn some net profit for the producers, *if* the distribution is aimed at the new special market which has recently developed.

THE NEW AUDIENCE

This market is initially based around the university, college and academic communities. A market numbering well over ten million film goers, it includes not only the students, but their families and the communities adjacent to academic centers. It is primarily a 16mm market, augmented by churches, social and political organizations, as well as the many hundreds of film societies. All campuses and most of the other organizations have excellent projection facilities for 16mm film. The uses of 16mm film are increasingly widespread and versatile, encouraged by technological developments in camera, projection and sound recording equipment. Another contributing factor of course has been the development of the specialized art house to show foreign films in the U.S.

Another wide audience is the mass of the dispossessed. Recently a guerrilla theater has sprung up among farm workers, company communities and Black ghettos. A modern *commedia dell'arte* travels to migrant camps and "poverty areas," projecting films on the sides of barns and houses, or uses rear-screen projection in a *Guerrilla Cinema*[1] truck parked in the fields at the end of a row, ready to vanish when authorities are summoned to suppress disruptive unprogrammed education.

We live in a new time. People are organizing themselves and are in motion. Not even the massive questioning and social upheaval of the 1930's compares to the demand for a new life now sweeping across these United States. This demand represents a growing audience for new films, films that speak of reality and social change, presented directly to people within the context of their primary local organizations.

[1] Copyright 1967, American Documentary Films, San Francisco.

CONCLUSION

There has been a revolution in 16mm film making, and the implications for the producer are clear: for the first time in U.S. history a film can be made with the assurance of at least recovering the original investment. For those films with particularly contemporary significance the earnings may become extraordinary.

The key is specialized distribution and the refutation of the assumption that conventional distributors know their business. They do not; but they have a practically unbroken record of making a great deal of money from the films they distribute while rarely returning anything significant to the producers. American Documentary Films challenges commercial distribution as it challenges other methods of controlling public access to information; the first challenge ensures the financial independence and basis for the second.

The foundation of a non-profit corporation as the instrument of artistic, financial and political independence is a response to social and technological changes that now allow film artists and film lovers to organize in a way that gives them control of the means of film production and distribution.

This is only a small beginning. We are confident that those millions who crave understanding, dignity and purpose in their lives will support this amplification of their voice, and help forge it into the incontestable expression of their will.

4 Curriculum Design and Evaluation in Film Study

The following articles deal with film curricula and evaluation. The authors are either film teachers or researchers involved in the elaboration of rationales for film study. The approaches they describe are aimed primarily at secondary schools, universities, and teacher-training institutions, but many of the concepts generated are applicable to film study in the elementary school or to informal film study outside of schools.

The first three and the last articles deal with specific modes of film study. They describe various approaches, many of which were discussed more generally in earlier chapters. The other two papers, by Andres Steinmetz and Alan Purves, deal with problems frequently faced by those teaching and studying film in schools — the evaluation of students and programs.

Peter Harcourt's "In Defense of Film History," like most of the articles in Chapter 2, approaches film as an art form. Harcourt believes that film study requires literacy through a sense of film history. He insists that his approach is to film, not to media, saying that although the disciples of McLuhan "think of film as environment," they do so only because they do not fully attend to films per se. Harcourt says his concern with film history is not, as some might suggest, an attempt to make the study of the medium respectable within the academic community. Rather, it is a concern with conveying to students, particularly college students, the wealth of experiences that film can present, the various ways in which it can do so, and the technical flexibility it offers. At the end of his article Harcourt uses his approach to film in an analysis of *Bonnie and Clyde*.

Within the context of curriculum theory for aesthetic education, Ralph Smith, in "Teaching Film as Significant Art," delineates three domains for the study of film: (1) the aesthetic, (2) the social and historical, and (3) the interdisciplinary social problem-solving. Smith deals primarily with the first of these domains, the study of film as significant art. He proposes that aesthetic education is a form of value education and that its goal is "the introjection of desirable standards of preference and justification." He discusses the affective and cognitive components of value education and considers the uniqueness of film as an art form and its ability to enlighten and entertain. Smith, like Kauffmann in Chapter 1, says that if film study does enable a person to gain an understanding of his aesthetic preferences and judgments, it may serve generally to influence and to improve mass media.

My "Interaction and Film Study" examines a particular approach to the study of film in education. I define instruction and schooling and contrast them with the more broadening, generalizing, humanizing process of education. My contention is that interaction is crucial to education and that film study is valuable because, in a variety of ways, it allows for and encourages certain interactive experiences. I conclude with a discussion of how exploitative films affect interaction, drawing examples from three films on student unrest.

The next two articles examine the problem of assessing the successes and failures of film study. In "Educational Innovation and Evaluation," Andres Steinmetz outlines problems of evaluating innovative projects and argues that the traditional method of evaluation should be transcended when dealing with such projects. He examines three issues in the field of educational evaluation: (1) the search for respectability, (2) the need for acceptable evidence, and (3) the matter of objectives. Steinmetz's approach is of particular interest to curriculum-development projects in film and media studies in elementary and secondary schools, but the issues he raises are also relevant to college film teaching and teacher training. The concepts of evaluation and innovation presented here are part of the modus operandi presented in Chapter 1 by the Communications Experience, of which Steinmetz is a member.

Alan Purves, in "A Model for Curriculum Evaluation in Film," continues the discussion of educational research and evaluation. He believes, as does Steinmetz, that accepted evaluative procedures are frequently dysfunctional with film curricula. He uses a grid model for viewing students' cognitive, perceptual, and affective behaviors concerning (1) art objects, (2) the context from which art arises, (3) the experiences with which the art deals, and (4) the responses of the audience to the art. Purves examines the implications of concentrating on any one of the four content areas or on any one of the student behaviors he specifies. He recommends a descriptive, rather than prescriptive, evaluation of the humanities. Such an approach, he says, is more appropriate for film and might assist in convincing students that the arts are open, not closed, systems.

In "The Preparation of Teachers of Media," Gerald O'Grady discusses current confusion and disagreement over the teaching of film at the university level and expresses his preference for placing film in the general context of proposed multidepartmental programs for media studies. He examines how the subject matter of these new programs should be defined and what kinds of curriculum and training they should offer their students. He describes media studies as "the exploration of the creation, the aesthetics, and the psychological, social, and environmental impact of the art forms of photography, cinematography, videography, radio, recordings, and tapes within the broad framework of general education in the humanities." He calls media studies the "new humanities," saying that they borrow from and should interact with the old humanities of literature, drama, and the fine arts. Like Arrowsmith in Chapter 1, O'Grady attempts to integrate the study of film with the older art forms in order to shed light on both. He describes a model program for graduate teacher training and three models for undergraduate programs in media studies. Finally, O'Grady touches on the developing links between media studies and sensitivity training, the work of Lévi-Strauss, and ecology and the future.

In Defense of Film History

PETER HARCOURT

> As long as it is taught with affection and respect, almost any
> approach can increase understanding and appreciation.
> — Jack C. Ellis[1]

> ... "communication" ... that deadly collective.
> — George C. Stoney[2]

Like so many teachers now involved with film, I began as a teacher of
English. Like so many others, I began to use films in the English classroom to stimulate discussion. But this was in England, in schools that
the English euphemistically describe as "further education." In most
cases it is remedial education — education for that large number of
English kids who somewhere along the line have missed the educational bus. They have been left behind; and they feel, more often than
not, that it is the conductor's fault (as it usually is). At the age of
fifteen-plus they have become fed up with the idea of education, with
its emphasis on literacy. So anyone inheriting these kids who still
believes that even in this electronic age a modicum of articulateness
can be an advantage in life, has to find a new way to approach this
perennially central problem. For me, the new way was film.

But I was never concerned with film simply as a visual aid, as a
shortcut to English. At the same time as I was teaching English I was
discovering the cinema. Of course, throughout my Canadian youth, I
had gone to the movies. But about ten years ago in London, I discovered the cinema. I discovered that films, when viewed in a selective
way in some sort of order, conveyed a continuity of development that
I had not thought possible in this popular, industrialized art. With the
manifold film-viewing facilities that London provides, most notably
at the National Film Theatre (a tiny cinema stuck away under one of
the southern arches of Waterloo Bridge), one could see a whole series
of Westerns or the complete works of artists as diverse as Buster
Keaton or Ingmar Bergman. Films from different countries and different times took on a meaning for me that they couldn't have done had
I viewed them piecemeal, in a sporadic way. I remember sitting

---

[1] Jack C. Ellis, "Modes of Film Communication," in *Film Study in Higher Education,* ed. by David C. Stewart (Washington: American Council on Education,
1966), p. 20.
[2] Stoney, George C., "Breaking the Word Barrier," *ibid.,* p. 95.

through a week of Czechoslovakian films several years before the
world started talking about them. I was entranced with the cumula-
tive spectacle of a foreign land and foreign customs. Films seem so
fully to embody the culture they spring from. More than any other
art, they can present directly the social and political values of the
culture that sponsors them. The Czech films I saw then were probably not *great* films if considered individually. (Though they were not
bad, it seemed to me at the time, and they were obviously part of that
growing expertise and artistry that has made possible the current
productions of men like Forman and Passner.) Great or not, however,
when considered together they gave me insights into a world I didn't
know — both the actual world of contemporary Czechoslovakia and
the artistic world of the film industry implicit in the different styles
that the various films conveyed.

Largely thanks to these facilities in London, I was not only an
English teacher aware of the educational potentiality of film in the
classroom but also a budding film fan, a "cinephile" who was fascinated with the medium for its own sake, for the experiences it contains and the emotions and ideas it can convey in its myriad different
forms. Fascinated with the *medium*. *Je souligne*. Not media, medium.
Indeed, scarcely even medium or at that stage even cinema (for I was
not yet terribly interested in making films and was therefore only
subconsciously aware of the abstract technical excitement that a
stunningly executed film can create almost *in spite of* what it pur-
ports to be about). I was interested in films in all the uniqueness and
peculiarity of their plurality: Bergman films, Fellini films — especially
foreign films as they offered me in addition an exposure to foreign
cultures, something that is still one of the great excitements that film
has for me personally. I was developing an interest in discovering
either the individual mind of a particular film maker or the collective
habits of an unfamiliar culture through the medium of cinema, an
interest that was fed by the ordered variety of films available to me in
London.

I begin on this directly autobiographical note because I think
these experiences have gone a long way toward determining my own
educational approach to film. It is of course a truism that the teaching
of *any* subject must begin with the teacher's own enthusiasm, with
his personal interest in the subject *for its own sake*, as of value to
him individually. Yet with the cinema, I have always had to insist
upon this, somewhat to my own amazement. For a time when I served
as Teachers' Advisor within the Education Department of the British
Film Institute I would repeatedly be confronted by teachers, generally English teachers, who had been made aware of the contemporary

importance of "media studies" or who had become interested in "screen education." They always wanted to know what they should do — more specifically, what films they should show. We all know by now the lists that I could have made available and that, indeed, for a while I *did* make available. But always with a shudder; for I always insisted that a teacher must show something that he himself felt offered a tremendous experience, that he himself loved passionately, as I would sometimes overstate my case.

In *Talking About the Cinema* Jim Kitses relates how he screened for his fifteen-year-olds Henri Colpi's *Une Aussi Longue Absence*, a film apparently too esoteric for even the adults of North America as it has scarcely been shown here outside Quebec. But Kitses himself admired it; and his great patience as a teacher, his understanding of how his kids must be seeing the film, made it possible for him to obtain in his class a worthwhile discussion.[3] Through talking about the human content of the film, in terms that some screen educators might now dismiss as "literary," Kitses extracted from his students a sense of the film's uniqueness. And no matter how accepting and sensitive the teacher, a discussion in a classroom is only part of the experience, possibly just the surface of the iceberg. While they were talking about the characters in the film, the most aware of the students would have gained some sense of how different such a film is from those they see week-by-week at their local Odeon, of how *personal* a film experience can be. If *Une Aussi Longue Absence* would not normally be on any list of films for classroom use, Jim Kitses made it one by his personal enthusiasm.

As a teacher, one must begin with what is for oneself a valuable experience. Any other way is educational death, both for the students and for the teacher. But what if the resources necessary for a detailed understanding of one's subject are not readily available? What if, when I began my tentative use of film in English, I had been working in Sarnia, Ontario, instead of London, England? I could not have done the things that I did largely because I could not have learned the things I came to know. My enthusiasm would have been short-circuited by the comparative poverty of the range of film experiences available to me. I might have felt that there is more consistent excitement in the television commercial than in the ordinary run of movies projected, often out-of-focus, in the local movie house.

McLuhanites think of film as environment.[4] But films, I counter-

---

[3] Jim Kitses, *Talking About the Cinema* (London: The British Film Institute, 1966), pp. 1–3.
[4] See, for example, Mark Slade, *Screen* (Canada), II, No. 2, 5.

insist, emphasizing the "s," films offer experiences that we receive or reject, sensitively or crudely, depending on our awareness of what is going on. Film creates an environment only when it is not fully attended to, when it is thought of as a collective, when it is seen as just a part of the big light show that certainly is a pervasive feature of this electronic age. But the idea of film as environment does not especially illuminate my life. Nor does it lend me insights into individual films. The detailed consideration of individual films, however, can give me techniques with which I can find my way around this new, visual environment, distinguish details in the landscape, choose a path to follow. The educational center of any course on film, I have always assumed, involves throwing light on the familiar by comparison with the unfamiliar. When we know a little bit about French films, we might see American films differently. Once we are aware of different possibilities, we are aware of the variety of choices that might be made. And we are aware of the relativity of our own cultural assumptions. Exciting though McLuhan may be as a stimulus for reexamining accepted notions, for making us feel the need to revise in the most basic way our social and educational preconceptions, so much of what he says is so educationally dubious as to hinge upon prophesy. Instead of relating the present to some period in the past, to a degree available to us through the disciplines of history, McLuhan increasingly relates the present to some hypothetical future in which we must believe. "What if he is right?" asks Tom Wolfe, in one of the most sensible and wittiest appreciations of this great and troubling man.[5] Okay, what if he is? What if he isn't? Both questions are simultaneously troubling yet irrelevant — irrelevant because they are not amenable to the test of experience. So they are not much help to us *directly* in the classroom, except as an encouragement to liven things up a bit, to be as audacious in our own analogies and insights as McLuhan himself is.

The McLuhanese litany that now infects so much of our thinking about screen education is, I am sure, educationally dangerous. It encourages a nervousness in the teacher lest he be a medium behind, lest his own culture be thought irrelevant to the culture of his tuned-in students. It incites him to prophesy, perhaps to falsify his own experience, literary as it probably is. In spite of all its talk about environmental control, the McLuhan philosophy serves to endorse the direction in which the world is *assumed* to be going. In its prophetic self-confidence, it actually discourages us from thinking in terms of alternatives and differences. It encourages an irrational and unintelli-

[5] Gerald E. Stearn, ed., *McLuhan: Hot and Cool* (New York: New American Library, 1969), pp. 30–48.

gent belief in dogma, in the acceptance of the Word. It is no wonder that McLuhan is a Roman Catholic. One must have faith. Verily, I say unto you, this is so. So he seems to proclaim. Yet the most valuable stimulus provided by McLuhan is toward a reexamination of the myths by which we live. The McLuhanites actually pervert this aspect of the master's teaching when they simply reiterate the myths by which McLuhan apparently lives. We must reexamine these myths along with our own — accept his probes for the stimulus they provide and then attempt to relate them to our actual experience, to the diversity of our own lives. This seems so obvious that I have often asked myself why the dogmatic implications of his philosophy should have gained such a hold. How did this come about?

This brings me back to a question which I raised earlier, one that I didn't intend to appear rhetorical: what if, as "media" teachers, our experience of film and television has been restricted to what has been brought to us by the uninspired commercial channels of distribution among the standard theater chains and the majority of television channels? What if we have grown up in some out-of-the-way town instead of London or New York or even Montreal? By way of answer, let me offer a probe of my own, an insight that I don't claim to be able to prove: when our experience of a medium has been so limited that we are aware of its potential expressive power yet have never been really enriched by any individual experience that is offered us, that is when we tend to talk about "media," to think of film as a collective. We are more aware of the process than the product because the product seems insufficient fully to engage our attention. There is a sense in this continent in which a good television commercial is more exciting than an average evening on, say, "The Way It Is" or some other, culturally serious program. Why shouldn't it be? Far more money has been spent on it, far greater attention paid to production values, to inescapable impact. The advertisement in this way becomes quintessentially television. As we watch our sets in Canada or in the States, the commercial might well appear to be the most imaginative experience of the medium that we will receive. The entire situation is different in England. There on the BBC, there are no commercials. But there are Ken Russell films on Edgar Elgar or Isadora Duncan, the work of Kevin Billington and a host of others, and regular series of television plays, plays actually conceived for the medium as well as adaptations. After a while one gets to know the names of the livelier writers and producers and begins to stay home on Wednesday night — not for the environment that television provides but for the particular experience that one can receive through this medium. One is less aware of the process because one is engaged by the product, as we were when we used to stay home with the radio in the Jack Benny days!

It is no wonder that McLuhan cuts so little ice in Great Britain. Television does not encourage passive acquiescence there. Every artist in every medium wants to do something for the BBC, in spite of all the bureaucratic hang-ups that they must endure. There is a sense of diversity and standards that is evident in the commercial channels as well. One gets the sense of multiple possibilities for change. The medium remains a kind of environment, but the environment is less important than the experiences it conveys, much as suburban houses, in spite of their uniformity, are less important than the quality of life they can contain. The environment is only primary when we are not really interested in what is going on, have no *active* relationship to it. After his Humphrey Bogart piece in *The Mechanical Bride*, there is no evidence in all of McLuhan to suggest that he has ever really seen a movie. No wonder that for him the medium is the message.

But I do not wish to offer a detailed consideration of the problems posed by the followers of McLuhan. I am simply eager to define a situation, to clarify my perceptions. Since I have been back in Canada, lecturing in film at Queen's University, I have observed that the climate here is very different from what I knew in England. There is an increasing excitement about the value of media studies, but there seem to be so few people who really *care* about films. Our culture is so geared to immediate commercial turnover that it scarcely has time to care about the past. A whole generation of young people who have recently been excited about *Blow-Up* have scarcely heard of *L'Avventura* let alone of *Le Amiche*. But how does a knowledge of *L'Avventura* affect our response to *Blow-Up*? This is a question that I have found worthwhile to ask. But before one can ask it, one has to arrange a screening of *L'Avventura* and eventually (when one finds a way of getting a print into the country) of *Le Amiche* as well. A film teacher's job in North America, especially at university level and when away from the big cities and, most distressingly, in Canada, is in this sense remedial: one has to show miles and miles of film before a serious discussion can really begin. Not miles of *dead* film, cinematic equivalents of *Gammer Gurton's Needle*, [6] but miles of marvelous film the experience of which you really want to share with the students because it is a part of your own life.

Of course, one can make do with lively discussions of the latest trend film like *Petulia* or *Easy Rider*. One can talk about them in

[6] Stoney, *op. cit.*, pp. 82–83.

terms of the television commercials on which Richard Lester, certainly, cut his cinematic teeth. But, speaking personally again, I don't think that students need my help here. They seem to be able to understand the immediate present well enough without my professional help. What I find exciting in the classroom is to mix up their sense of the present with my sense of the past. This way, we both might learn something. If I'm good at my job, some of the students might even get the impression that it is worthwhile growing up, that there is something to be learned from foreign cultures and foreign times, from forty-year-old professors who have their own enthusiasms. Some of the students might come to realize that life need not entail the perpetual endorsement of their present interests and attitudes.

As teachers, unless we are challenging the cultural assumptions of the young people we are dealing with, we are scarcely doing our jobs; and unless they are challenging ours, we have probably stopped being open to them. There must be tension or there will be no growth. But our job is not to turn the students on; they can do that themselves. Our job is to convey to them how people unlike themselves have also been turned on, to give them some sense of the potential diversity of life. Then they might better perceive the relativity of their own cultural assumptions, without which there can be no growth beyond the built-in prejudices that every culture implies.

With this aim in mind and with the memory of the awakening that films provided me with in London, since my return to Canada my strategy has been to dip more and more back into the past, to find the moments still alive there, to give the students a sense of film history that is also a sense of cultural history that is finally a sense of how they came to be as they are. I am *not* concerned with respectability within the academic community — I suppose I had better emphasize that. I am concerned with conveying the multiplicity and diversity of the medium of film, the richness of human experience it contains, the technical flexibility that it offers. By saying "film creates an environment," McLuhanites employ the collective, denying the medium its greatest source of interest for us. Yet even the environment created by *Blow-Up* is very different from that created by *Drums Along the Mohawk*. One has to deal with these different experiences in very different ways, which entails dealing with the values of the different societies that produced them.

Describing my work in this way, I know I run the risk of appearing old-fashioned in my approach, of confronting the medium with supposedly outmoded literary assumptions, of trying to hold back the inevitable sweep forward of contemporary taste. This may indeed be a limitation in my own approach to film. History may prove my efforts futile, and art and youthful sensibility may be destined to become more and more mindless, devoid of content in any traditional sense, offering abstract titilations of a tactile kind, like a perpetual trip. This may be so but there is no *proof* that it will be. And I don't feel it our job as teachers to anticipate future trends, to be other-directed in this way. It is not our job because it leads to passivity in the face of discriminations that still can be made.

One of the most foolish aspects of the McLuhan philosophy is the implication that print is becoming obsolete. Human speech remains the supreme gift of man and its development is still dependent on the inculcation of inwardness within the individual, an inwardness that McLuhan rightly sees as encouraged by the act of reading alone. I still feel it part of our job as teachers to keep alive the finest aspects of this ideal, the essential privacy of the individual imagination, even while recognizing that the ideal will be modified by the electronic atmosphere around it. Modified, not replaced. This is my assumption, the faith with which I work.

But I want now to drop this tone of educational harangue, the tone of a teacher writing for teachers. I will conclude in the tone of a film specialist, of a critic trying within a limited space to present something of the essence of an extraordinary film. I have chosen a film that lends itself very much to a literary approach in terms of its plot and characterizations but that conveys its attitudes more through visual and aural means — through small details of performance, through the quality of the photography, through the constant alternation of natural sound with a musical refrain. The film is, of course, *Bonnie and Clyde*. Critics who have missed its essence and have complained about its violence have, I argue, misread its tone. They have responded too much in an unimaginative literary way, in an unobservant way, not fully aware of the delicate implications of the multisensorial medium of film. *Bonnie and Clyde* offers a complex blend of European intellectual sophistication with the indigenous strengths of American genre. If it is very much a film of our age, it draws upon the strengths of the best films that have preceded it. It is *not* a happening. It is the controlled ordering of experience by a group of extraordinary men. The passages in italics are quotations from the director of the film, Arthur Penn.[7]

> You've heard the story of Jesse James;
> Of how he lived and died;
> If you're still in need of something to read,
> Here's the story of Bonnie and Clyde.

[7] From *Take One*, No. 6. This account of the film appeared in a modified form in the *Queen's Journal* when the film played in Kingston, Ontario, in 1969.

The ballad sets the tone of the film, defines its intentions, and justifies its style. If *Bonnie and Clyde* is a most intimate presentation of two particular people in a particular place and time, it is also concerned with the growth of a legend and with the relationship of this legend to American life. In this sense it is also a political film — at least by implication. For the violence that is such a strong ingredient of *Bonnie and Clyde* can only be understood by reference to the society that would seem, as the film presents it to us, to encourage it and that finally confronts it with an even greater violence of its own. The violence that destroys the Barrow gang is a gratuitous violence, far in excess of any civilized concept of justice or a "debt to society." It is the violence of the lynch-mob, the product of vengeance, fear, and hate. And the final slaughter of our two heroes, for us as spectators, is also the slaughter of everything that was most vital, tender, and alive in the world the film has presented to us — which explains the troubled emotion we are left with at the end. Properly understood, it should be a subversive emotion. It should leave us with an enraged sense of moral injustice and a strong need for social change.

> They were outlaws, they were the sports of nature, they were thrown off by the events of their day, and they did something about it.

Bonnie and Clyde is an extremely moral film, in the traditional, Lawrencian sense of that word. In every scene it seems implicitly to be asking: what are the possibilities for life here and now? How can the characters affirm themselves in a vital and spontaneous way? What are the chances of meaningful, constructive behavior? If the answers to these questions are at odds with the received aspirations of American society, then, the film seems to tell us, the trouble lies as much with that society as with the individuals who try to break free.

After the titles which are intermixed with photographs of the actual Barrow gang, the film opens with assertive shots of Bonnie's boredom and desire: her red lips full on screen; her naked body on the bed, the brass posts like bars between her and the outside world; then her eyes looking straight out at us as if to ask, as Clyde puts it later, "When and how am I gonna get away from this?" A moment later, when she joins Clyde in the street below, the town seems dead. As they strut along, making their first demonstrations toward each other, they pass a boarded-up theater and a Negro sitting in the sun. He grins at them, like most of the other Negroes in the film who are generally standing to one side, looking on — as later when C.W. tries to maneuver his car out of its tiny parking space. The Negroes are part of the atmosphere of the film, part of its sense of passive defeat that Clyde is rebelling against when he sticks up his first grocery store just to prove to Bonnie that he has the "gumption" to use the gun that he is carrying. The Negroes and the farmers are the "little people" neglected by American economic ideals.

The world of *Bonnie and Clyde* is the world of the New Deal, a world most sensitively recreated for us on the screen. Posters of FDR litter the peeling walls that form the majority of locations throughout this film, generally with an ironic sense of irrelevance and perhaps even of deceit. But Bonnie and Clyde are quickly established as folk heroes, instinctively accepted and admired by their own kind — the impoverished, the defeated, the dispossessed. Arthur Penn has described them as "retaliators for the people," and they are received as such wherever they go. "Me and him put in the years here," explains a migrant farmer as he introduces his Negro assistant, now both dispossessed by the Midlothian Citizens' Bank. "They did right by me," explains another, telling the press how the Barrow gang had let him keep his own money when they held up a bank; "I'm gonna bring me a mess of flowers to their funeral." In fact, Clyde's anger toward Captain Frank Haymer of the fabulous Texas Rangers is first provoked by his realization that Haymer is bounty hunting in Missouri for the Barrow gang instead of back home "protectin' the ranchin' poor folks." Finally, when the forlorn "Okies" that look like wan stragglers from *The Grapes of Wrath* immediately accept the wounded legendary figures and provide them, unasked for, with food and a blanket, we are aware of the extent to which these bandit-heroes have come to be valued by their fellow-rejects from the American dream. As C.W. drives his companions away, we might have noticed that even the land is without growth of any kind. The branches on the stunted trees are bare.

> We have a violent society. It's not Greece, it's not Athens, it's not the Renaissance — it is the American society, and I would have to personify it by saying that it is a violent one.

All this is the background to the film, part of what I have called its political implications, part of its surface authenticity and its power to persuade us of the validity of its own point-of-view. Yet the film isn't offering a direct statement about American society: it is telling a story of a more personal kind. In essence, it is a love story — a love story with difficulties. As we are immediately made aware, Bonnie is a woman with strong sexual needs, and Clyde is unable to make love to her. This inability, while not fully explored in the film, lends a compelling barb of psychological complexity to the story and makes for a tenderness between the two of them that intensifies their gentle awareness of one another. Clyde's problem, however, is obviously related to his social insufficiency as a man. He needs to feel he is someone before he can fully act out his masculine role. The robberies and violence stem from this complexity, if you will, on the psychological level; just as Clyde's "cure" is effected by Bonnie's published poem about their lives, thus assuring him that his name will live on. "You've made me somebody they're gonna remember," he shouts excitedly at her just before they begin making love, while the wind — symbolically — blows the paper across the fields, broadcasting their legend.

> The so-called serious play has the air of being stately and literary, but it does not really assault any of the fundamental values of its audience. Movies do — they move in on a highly personal level in the way that a book or a poem does.

In *Bonnie and Clyde,* with the distinguished help of his writers David Newman and Robert Benton, Arthur Penn has succeeded in creating a political, personal, and most artistic film. This political interest and concern with social violence has always been strong in Penn's work, most noticeably in *The Chase* and in *Alice's Restaurant,* as have his formal preoccupations — his attempts to achieve within a conventional Hollywood movie the intensity we would associate with Greek tragedy (*The Chase* again) or a Kafka novel (*Mickey One*). In his first film, *The Left-Handed Gun,* he presented us with a balletically stylized version of the legend of Billy the Kid where Billy is played as an impulsive young idealist seeking vengeance for the death of a close friend. If *Bonnie and Clyde* is remarkably more successful than Arthur Penn's former films, as it certainly is with the general public, it is largely because he has discovered a form for it that enables him to hold all the elements together, that gives us the distance necessary to respond to the film self-consciously as a work of art and yet brings us close enough to the characters to respond to them instinctively as people, as people whose vitality and tenderness we can value immensely.

The form of the film is essentially balladic, the fiddles and banjoes of Flatt and Scruggs providing the refrain, while the story is rich in innumerable details, not only the background details that lend historical authenticity and that imply the political issues, but also the personal details that convey deep feeling and psychological truth. "Pray you undo this button" is a line often singled out by critics of *King Lear,* a small domestic comment introduced into the tragic framework at just the right moment to personalize the story and to move us in a more direct and intimate way than can the awesome, symbolic heath. *Bonnie and Clyde* is full of such effects, too many to enumerate.

Bonnie's return home is a most compelling sequence, all shot through haze as if from a great distance and even the sound seeming faint and disconnected, as if about to be blown away. More than any-where else in the film, this sequence is full of little gestures of ten-derness: Bonnie plays with one of the boys as he falls down a sand dune in gentle slow-motion; Clyde tucks a napkin into C.W.'s shirt-front when he brings him his supper; Clyde assures Mama Parker (as he eats an eskimo pie!) that in a little while now, they'll settle down close to her. But Mama Parker remains unmoved, knowing it is a dream: "You bes' keep runnin', Clyde Barrow, an' you know it!"

Elsewhere in the film there are similar details, the most striking of which (certainly the most *Lear*-like) is Buck's delirium before his death. While the now-blinded Blanche prays and screams hysterical-ly, Buck groans in his brother's arms, trying to hold together his shat-tered head. "I think I lost my shoes, Clyde. I think the dog's got 'em." While C.W., his face always incredulous, looks on.

Throughout its magnificent length, *Bonnie and Clyde* combines the formal authority, the moral implications, and the personal intima-cy of great art. It is a vital, funny, desperate, violent, tender, tragic film that in its movement and execution has the simplicity and power of the ballad that inspired it and that determined its form.

> Someday they'll go down together,
> They'll bury them side by side;
> To a few it'll be grief, to the laws, a relief,
> But it's death to Bonnie and Clyde.

Teaching Film
as Significant Art

RALPH A. SMITH

> In the end we design the tool for the material — in the end, but
> never in the beginning. In the beginning we have still to find out
> the first things about the ways in which the material is and is not
> workable; and we explore it by trying out implements with which
> we have already learned to work other materials. There is no other
> way to start.
>
> — Gilbert Ryle, *Dilemmas*

TOWARD FIRST THINGS

Ryle's comments sum up the situation in film education. It is increasingly acknowledged that the schools should use films in their instructional programs, but just how this new medium should be employed
constitutes the "dilemma." Should film be used primarily as a pedagogical aid in the teaching of conventional subjects? Or does film
help to define a separate field of study? How we answer these questions depends not only on our special interest in film but also on our
interpretation of the aims and purposes of education.

I believe that film — used here to imply dramatic narrative films
shown in theater houses and over television — can be studied in at
least three separate domains of general education in the secondary
grades: (1) the appreciative domain, or what may be called the
domain of aesthetic education proper, in which film would be studied
as an instance of significant art; (2) the social and historical studies
domain, in which the advent of film would be studied as a phenomenon in the evolution of cultural institutions; and (3) an interdisciplinary social problem-solving domain, in which film would be studied
as an element in a mass communications complex whose functions go
beyond the aesthetic and the historical.[1] This essay centers on the
first, i.e., on the study of film as significant art in the appreciative
domain of aesthetic education.

---

[1] These domains of the curriculum are discussed in Harry S. Broudy, B.
Othanel Smith, and Joe R. Burnett, *Democracy and Excellence in American
Secondary Education* (Chicago: Rand McNally & Co., 1964).

THE AESTHETIC APPRECIATION OF FILM

In this section the claim of film to the status of significant art will be examined. What is significant art? And what is it to experience a work of art aesthetically?

The problem of defining art has recently been the topic of several technical writings, the central question turning on whether it is possible, given the great varieties of art, to make any important generalizations about the essence of art.[2] Without denying the complexities of the problem, I don't think it is too difficult to gain acceptance for the following two notions: (1) significant art is always vivid and interesting to perception, indeed so much so that it may be attended to primarily for the intrinsic enjoyment afforded by its sensuous, formal, technical, and expressive properties; and (2) significant art always says something important, in its special way, about human existence or the world.

Now obviously many films satisfy these criteria. Consider briefly Ingmar Bergman's impressive film *The Seventh Seal*. It establishes its intense existential tone with unmatched cinematic virtuosity, and its formal patterning of images, sequences, and rhythms implicates viewers in metaphysical problems of ultimate meaning that are neither solved nor explained but simply left to aesthetic apprehension. That is, *The Seventh Seal* shows what it feels like to engage in the quest for knowledge in a world in which knowledge of certainty is denied; and this grasping of the import of the quest via artistically-shaped images is a central feature of aesthetic experience. *The Seventh Seal* is significant art because it is interesting to perception and says something important in a unique way. The same sort of thing can be said about *Citizen Kane*, *Red Desert*, *Rashomon*, and many other films.

That our interest in films can be primarily aesthetic does not of course preclude them from performing other instrumental or extra-aesthetic functions.[3] "*All* films," writes Martin S. Dworkin, "are 'message' films; *all* films take sides somehow on the issue of whether the audience is to be treated as a mass, whose constituent units are assumed to have no individuality, and are to be seduced to move in predetermined directions, or whether it is to be treated as a group of individual persons, to be persuaded to choose freely."[4] It is important

---

[2] See the section on defining art in R. A. Smith (ed.), *Aesthetics and Criticism in Art Education* (Chicago: Rand McNally & Co., 1966).

[3] A good discussion of the aesthetic and extra-aesthetic functions of art may be found in D. W. Gotshalk, *Art and the Social Order* (New York: Dover Publications, 1962).

[4] Martin S. Dworkin, "Seeing for Ourselves," *Journal of Aesthetic Education*, Vol. 3, No. 3 (July 1969), 50. This article was first printed in *Film Journal* (Melbourne), 1957, and since then has been widely reprinted.

then, Dworkin adds, to understand the manner in which the issue of means and ends is raised in a film.

Film Study as Aesthetic Value Education

The foregoing helps to support the case for including film as an item of study in the program of aesthetic education. Still, the special grounds for including film in the appreciative domain need to be elaborated. The basic proposition stressed here is that aesthetic education is fundamentally a form of value education. What this means will be explained by first juxtaposing aesthetic value education with the notion of education for creative self-expression. A second consideration revolves around an explanation of the components of value education, and a third seeks to show the special pertinence of value education vis-à-vis the enterprise of the popular mass media.

Creative Self-Expression and Aesthetic Valuing

Elsewhere[5] I have indicated that American art education has structured its thinking mainly on the metaphor of the child as a creative artist and on the language and insights of psychology. Accordingly, a popular image in the field portrays the child achieving personal integration and self-identity through the manipulation of expressive materials.

The image of a pupil-artist creatively expressing himself is of course appealing and its charm has not been lost on a generation of art teachers. It is to be appreciated, moreover, as part of the reaction by progressive schoolmen against the restrictive and uninspired formalism of an earlier day. The introduction into the classroom of practices that permitted pupils to work with concrete materials was mostly a sound corrective to the verbalism and meaningless exercises often urged on pupils in older conceptions of teaching. And by emphasizing the readiness and interests of pupils as motivating factors, advocates of art instruction in the schools reasserted proven pedagogical principles — principles which hold that effective teaching adapts its materials and goals to the pupil's rate of maturation and level of ability. In this respect the exponents of public-school art instruction have generally served education well. Through their efforts art offerings have become standard items in elementary-school curricula, and from the elementary level art instruction is moving into the secondary grades where it is certain to become more pervasive.

But if a contribution has been made, it is now time to assess the achievement. And when this is done it can be concluded that the

5 *Aesthetics and Criticism in Art Education, op. cit.,* pp. vii–xiv.

image of the child as a creative artist and an excessive devotion to the cultivation of his inner life foster a subjectivism that downgrades other important aspects of learning in the arts. By stressing the centrality of the teacher's psychological insight into individual needs, theorizing in art education tends to ignore both the nature of the subject matter the pupil manipulates in the course of his learning and the linguistic operations he performs in a variety of verbal activities.

Some current analysis and speculation are meant not so much to reject previous achievements and practices as to build upon them. In contradistinction to earlier ways of talking, a new language stresses moving toward an effective integration of child-centered and discipline-centered conceptions of the curriculum. Instead of emphasizing the child over content, as the "We teach children, not subjects" slogan does, the intent is to teach important topics and ideas in ways that are consistent with a child's learning capacities. To repeat, this way of viewing art instruction is not a return to the older formalism; it is an attempt to build a theory of instruction that respects both the psychological demands of pupils and the logical demands of content.

This renewed emphasis on content in recent curriculum theory derives in part from new challenges facing modern society. Not only does the wise use of abundance and leisure demand a renewal of the ideals of excellence and self-cultivation, but heightened powers of discrimination and judgment are also necessary to cope with the relentless streams of visual impressions flowing from the mass media. The development of critical dispositions is further required to counteract those who in various ways would impose limits on artistic freedom and thereby undermine fundamental tenets of a free society. Finally, the study of the arts as a source of personal knowledge and value orientation in a depersonalized technological society also requires higher levels of reflective discipline than one generally observes today. The components of aesthetic value education will be discussed next before attention centers on the distinctive potential of film for such education.

The Components of Aesthetic Value Education

The goal of aesthetic value education may be stated as the introjection of desirable standards of preference and justification in the domain of significant art. Preferences involve primarily the attitudinal component of value education, whereas justification, since it depends on value judgments and critical argument, features mainly the theoretical component, although in the aesthetic experience of a work of art the difference between attitudinal and theoretical moments is not as apparent as the foregoing might imply. Still, liking and judging are different sorts of things, and it is helpful not to confuse them.

   The Attitudinal Component. It is harmless enough to say that students ought to like good things, including good films, and that the schools therefore should instruct them in proper habits of liking. Yet the cultivation of preferences, since it involves changing value commitments developed over a long period of time, is much more difficult than effecting change in a pupil's store of knowledge. We do not in the first place have sufficient research to proceed confidently in this realm.[6] About the only firm conclusion researchers agree on is that in matters pertaining to a person's values, sole reliance on lecture and exposition is generally insufficient.[7] Rather, the students' opinions must be openly discussed and inconsistencies rendered visible. Second, any kind of effective value education is likely to require seemingly inordinate amounts of time. Above all there is the nagging realization that the schools today may be relatively powerless to change values, given the value crisis in the larger society and the competition the schools receive from youth culture and the mass media. Indeed, some would argue that the schools have no right whatsoever teaching students *what* to think or like; rather they should teach students to decide things for themselves. This argument, when sophisticated, is not without point; yet I find it odd that a teacher should either say or imply that he doesn't really care if his students are indifferent to the finest creative and spiritual achievements of man. I suspect that many teachers do want their students to admire excellence and that, intentionally or not, they attempt to persuade them to do so.

   The Theoretical Component. In its cognitive aspects value education aims at instructing students in the making of well-grounded aesthetic judgments. Reflective critical judgment presupposes the possession of relevant maps of appraisal that have been constructed from a great deal of appropriate practical experience and theoretical understanding. Although stating an aesthetic preference is an act of personal, subjective taste that in no way obligates a person to defend his taste, it is different with an aesthetic judgment that imputes value or disvalue to an object. If called upon to do so, a person is obligated to defend his judgment, which is done by appealing to relevant rea-

   [6] David R. Krathwohl, Benjamin S. Bloom, and Bertram B. Masia, *Taxonomy of Educational Objectives II: Affective Domain* (New York: David McKay Co., 1964), p. 78.
   [7] *Ibid.,* p. 81.

sons and criteria.[8] In other words, there need be no disputing personal preferences, but of a given judgment we may always ask whether it is a good or poor judgment, appropriate or inappropriate, insightful or superficial, and so forth.

The Unique Qualifications of Film
for Aesthetic Value Education

The distinctive character of film has been explained by the late Erwin Panofsky in his influential essay "Style and Medium in the Motion Pictures."[9] According to Panofsky, the development of film reveals the phenomenon of a new medium becoming increasingly conscious of its potentialities and limitations. Contrary to precedent, he points out, moving pictures were not the product of an artistic urge but rather the by-product of a technical invention, and, owing to their origin in a sphere untouched by traditional art forms, early movies became a type of folk art providing vehicles for the primordial categories of success and retribution, sentiment and sensation, pornography and crude humor. After unsuccessful attempts to imitate stage plays, movie-makers realized that the future of the film lay not only in the further development of its folk art character, but also in the development of its unique and specific capability for a dynamic organization of space and time. This potential for a novel space-time organization had two implications: one for the viewer and another for the relations between sound and spoken word and the screen image.

In contrast to the situation of the theatergoer, for example, film viewers occupy their seats only physically. Otherwise they are in perpetual motion as they imaginatively identify with the always active lens of the camera. This kind of identification resulted in new expressive possibilities. Through the use of characteristic cinematic devices it was discovered that states of mind could be projected directly on the screen, thus making practically limitless the ideas and emotions the audience could experience.

The film differs even further from the stage play in the relation between sound and action. Even with the advent of the soundtrack, Panofsky notes, the main emphasis in films remained visual, and the dialogue or script had to conform to the principle of coexpressibility.

[8] See Monroe C. Beardsley, "The Classification of Critical Reasons," *Journal of Aesthetic Education*, Vol. 2, No. 3 (July 1968), 55–63, and R. A. Smith, "Aesthetic Criticism: The Method of Aesthetic Education," *Studies in Art Education*, Vol. 9, No. 3 (Spring 1968), 13–32.

[9] Reprinted in Smith, *Aesthetics and Criticism in Art Education*, op. cit., pp. 412–26, and in this volume, pp. 57–73.

That is to say, the quality of a script derives from the capacity of its lines to be integrated with the events on the screen and not simply from its value as literature. Further, just as a screenplay has no existence independent of its performance, so its characters have no existence outside the actors: a film is written for a specific producer, director, and cast. Those involved in the production of a film, moreover, work in a fashion comparable to that of a painter — piecemeal, discontinuously, and according to the most effective use of materials rather than according to the order of events in the finished product. Because a movie is brought into being by a cooperative effort in which each contribution has the same degree of permanence, Panofsky suggests that the making of a film is the nearest modern equivalent to the building of a medieval cathedral.

Finally, movies are commercial art and hence must acknowledge the requirements of communicability, which for better or worse makes them potentially more vital than noncommercial art forms. Since the primary materials of films consist of physical objects and persons and not a neutral medium, Panofsky suggests that only the film does justice to the materialistic interpretation of the universe that pervades our civilization. Commercial and materialistic characteristics notwithstanding, however, movies do satisfy the canons of art. They manipulate unstylized reality in such a way that the result has style, and this is a proposition no less legitimate and no less difficult than any proposition in the older arts.

So it seemed to Panofsky and so it still is with most of the films made today. Yet we are gaining perspective on this classic essay. A certain kind of empirical researcher, for example, would question the ubiquitous effects attributed to film by Panofsky's statement that "the movies . . . mold, more than any other single force, the opinions, the taste, the language, the dress, the behavior, and even the physical appearance of a public comprising more than 60 percent of the population of the earth." Numerous film makers, moreover, including many working out of university film departments and the "underground," belie the need for Hollywood "cathedral building," nor does the "folk" aspect of films necessarily figure in their filmic intentions. And the idea of "the printed screen"[10] counterbalances excessive claims regarding film's essentially visual nature. In brief, film is still discovering its unique potentialities and limitations.

Film is distinctive in the senses just discussed and in some others, too. Any list of such characteristics must certainly include the

[10] Martin S. Dworkin, "The Printed Screen," *The Educational Forum*, Vol. 32, No. 1 (November 1968), 109–12.

already mentioned space-time organization of filmic elements, the use of physical reality as primary materials, the strong empathic and implicative power, and, in addition, the uniform quality of reproduction and universal appeal. But film is also continuous with other art forms and for some time it will doubtless exhibit those conventional properties commonly referred to as an object's sensuous, formal, expressive, technical, symbolic, and thematic aspects. The sensuous aspects are responsible for the simple look, feel, and sound of films, e.g., the timbre of voices, screeching vehicles, shattering glass, and musical sound tracks. Formal aspects imply the compositional webs of films, the result of juxtaposing elements to achieve the right intensity of expression or meaning. When films have a conventional order, e.g., a beginning, a middle, and an end — and many still do — the common devices of formal patterning are deployed: theme and variations, balance, hierarchy, evolution, etc. Sensuous aspects tend to be noticed casually and in relative isolation from each other, whereas the perception of formal aspects requires synthetic or synoptic vision.

Technical qualities, or evidence of cinematic skill and virtuosity, also figure in our responses to film, as do themes and story lines with their attendant symbolism and import. Themes of course are what films are about: man against the elements, good versus evil, political ambition, love, alienation, hate, youthful rebellion. Then there is overall mood, tone, or dramatic atmosphere: the nervous tension and violence of gangster movies and Westerns, the anxiety and desperation of psychological dramas, the euphoria of musicals. Again, the point is that film, although unique in some respects, is also continuous with other art forms.

The foregoing involved references primarily to the properties of films themselves, but the "industry" that produces and distributes films is also of interest. It is common knowledge that the production and distribution of films are controlled by pragmatic and pecuniary interests that are often, though not always, anathema to the intrinsic and reflective values of significant art.[11] Yet good films as well as mediocre ones need to be distributed and one cannot flatly dismiss the function performed by the public relations aspect of film promotion.[12] Moreover, the film industry is not unresponsive to public pressure. Film companies would doubtless make and promote

[11] In case of doubt see Thomas Guback, *The International Film Industry* (Bloomington: Indiana University Press, 1969).

[12] See Harold Rand's discussion of the effort required to promote *The Pawnbroker* in "Public Relations: Its Place and Function in Society," *Journal of Aesthetic Education,* Vol. 3, No. 3 (July 1968), 72.

more good films if the public demanded them. Yet this happy state of affairs is not likely to materialize so long as the public is relatively untutored in matters of aesthetic quality and excellence. The role of the schools in aesthetic value education, then, is partly defined by the fact that consumers can assert influence over the quality of film production. The issue is not one of entertainment value versus artistic message, for there are too many instances of good film art that has also been a box office success. The task is to educate consumers to demand for their money films in which art and entertainment, pleasure and spiritual uplift, passion and intellect are fused into unified occasions that are the quintessence of aesthetic consummatory experiences. Since there is no other place save the schools in which systematic instruction in film can be undertaken, what form might such instruction take? I cannot go into detail here but the presentation of film exemplars, that is, films that are not only interesting to perception but also say something important, would be consistent with the analysis presented here.[13]

In conclusion, the development of an appreciative and evaluative perspective is the school's contribution to an enlightened, reflective citizenry that, further informed and challenged by responsible professional criticism outside the schools, has the potential power to assert influence over the patterns of good and evil emanating from film and television screens. As a mass technological society tends to encourage the mechanical adoption of life styles, it becomes increasingly important that persons learn to question pseudo-art and aesthetic stereotypes, for film and television have become for the majority of people today what Homer and the poets were for the Greeks of an earlier era. And as educators we have every reason to be as concerned about the mere "opinion" of pseudo-communications as Plato was about the purported pseudo-epistemology of poetry, or at least of certain kinds of it. We now think that Plato's attacks on poetry were ill-conceived, but substitute the art and the popular culture heroes of the mass media today, and his criticism has point.[14]

SOCIAL AND HISTORICAL STUDIES

Since in this essay film study is given over to the development of enlightened preference and justification in the domain of aesthetic

[13] Smith, "Aesthetic Criticism," op.cit.
[14] For a good discussion of Plato's argument see Eric Havelock, Preface to Plato (Cambridge: Harvard University Press, 1963), pp. 3–12, 20–31, reprinted in Alexander Sesonske (ed.), Plato's Republic: Interpretation and Criticism (Belmont, Calif.: Wadsworth Publishing Co., 1966).

education, film as an event in the evolution of cultural institutions and its relations to other societal developments would be emphasized in the social and historical studies domain of the curriculum. Such study would be primarily cognitive in character and would not attempt to cultivate aesthetic modes of response, although obviously some historical information would be used even in the appreciative domain. The reason for the division of labor is that historical and social studies have different aims, and it is a good pedagogical rule of thumb not to attempt to achieve different sorts of outcomes all at once or in the same place.

SOCIAL PROBLEM-SOLVING

Film could also be studied as a significant element in a mass communications network whose functions involve more than providing occasions for aesthetic experience or the development of historical and social understanding. It has been suggested that sometime during the latter years of schooling, perhaps in the junior or senior years, students should be given opportunities to test their mastery of different domains of the curriculum by being required to come to grips with a difficult interdisciplinary social problem, such as ecology and conservation, race relations, or urban planning. The role of the mass communications media in a democratic society might also be studied. On such a problem a student could bring to bear diverse skills, knowledge, and sensitivities developed elsewhere in the curriculum. As a result of his aesthetic studies he would be able to appreciate the aesthetic dimension of the media. As a result of his social and historical studies he would be able to comprehend the intricate web of events that affected the rise of the media as well as the social system in which they are currently entwined. Again, knowing how to use learnings when dealing with a complex social problem is not the same kind of enterprise as experiencing things aesthetically or understanding them historically.

SUMMARY

There are, then, at least three important curriculum domains in which film can be studied, and my brief treatment of the last two in no way implies that I think them insignificant. The rationale for the study of film as significant art in the program of aesthetic education ultimately rests on the importance attached to a person's gaining reflective control over his aesthetic preferences and judgments. Achieving such control is not inconsistent with heightened enjoyment and pleasure.

Indeed, it has been the intent of this essay to emphasize the constant interplay between cognitive and affective moments in the experience of film art.

Interaction and Film Study

JOHN STUART KATZ

INTRODUCTION

As a "discipline" incorporated into the elementary school, high school, or university curriculum, film can be treated like other courses in the arts and humanities and approached primarily as a "subject" to be taught and learned, like English, history, and philosophy. It can also be looked upon as an interdisciplinary study transcending traditional curricular categories, but even this approach frequently fails to utilize qualities film can offer the educational process. Specifically, film study[1] seems valuable for humanizing education because it allows for and, in fact, lends itself to a variety of interactive experiences.

"Interaction" is used here in a relatively specific way. It refers not only to interaction between individuals, but also to interaction between individuals and objects and between the ideas or thoughts of a given individual. However, not all social intercourse or person-object experiences are considered interactions. Experiences that do not result in new learning, either because the experience is not novel or because the individual is not attending to the novelty, are not

---

[1] I am confining these remarks to narrative and documentary film, but much of what I say here applies as well to animated and experimental film. Educational and instructional films are outside the domain of this paper since they seem to serve a different function.

interactive.[2] Not all experiences, then, are interactive, but all interactive experiences are to some extent educational.

Two types of knowing, figurative and operative, result from interaction.[3] The figurative focuses on the external, memorizable aspects of an event or object — its color, name, shape — its present static, sensory qualities. In contrast, the operative aspect of knowing requires the active transforming or structuring of experience into practical or theoretical knowledge. Because it requires conceptual integration, all such knowing becomes meaningful to the life, the humanity, of the knower. Film's potential for the expansion of operative knowing makes it particularly valuable to education when contrasted with the emphasis on figurative knowing in many current curricula.

This paper begins by considering the educational process, by differentiating between instruction, schooling, and education. Second, it posits that operative interaction should be an integral part of education and is important both to film as an art form and to film study. It then explores the idea that such interactions are affected when films themselves are dishonest, exploitative, or pandering.

INSTRUCTION, SCHOOLING, AND EDUCATION

Education, to be understood, must be seen in its relation to instruction and schooling, both of which are frequently confused with the larger process of which they may be parts. Instruction, perhaps the least complex of the three, can be accomplished by using computers, manuals, educational films, or teachers in traditional roles of authorities embodying and purveying knowledge. Instruction implies at least some specific skill, task, or knowledge to be learned — what in Piaget's framework can be called "figurative knowing."[4]

Schooling is what typically takes place in buildings made of red brick, with long corridors and classrooms leading off them. Sometimes the schools are round, made of glass and steel, but they are still only places of instruction if the task that goes on there takes precedence over the development, welfare, and happiness of the students.

[2] This conception of interaction has roots in what is often referred to as the "symbolic interactionist" and "action theoretical" work of Max Weber, George Herbert Mead, Talcott Parsons, and others. For a general discussion of these schools of thought see Don Martindale, The Nature and Types of Sociological Theory (Boston: Houghton-Mifflin, 1960).

[3] Jean Piaget and Barbel Inhelder, The Psychology of the Child (New York: Basic Books, 1969). See also Hans G. Furth, Piaget and Knowledge (Englewood Cliffs, N. J.: Prentice-Hall, 1969).

[4] Piaget and Inhelder, op. cit.

Schooling frequently becomes institutionalized instruction because
the need for efficiency and expediency promotes authoritarian-sub-
servient relationships, neglects peer group involvements, and molds
the persons involved into functionaries who are prisoners of the
schooling imposed upon them.

Education may *involve* schooling and instruction, but it is much
more. Education is not a narrowing, specializing, training procedure;
it is a broadening, a generalizing, a leading-forth process. It is a constant interaction between the individual and those things and persons
with whom he comes into contact that cause and help him to think,
question, feel, and understand — what Piaget calls "operative knowing."[5] It can take place in a school, but it can also take place in
the community, in travel, in a library, while thinking alone, or
through relationships with other people.

Film study offers an excellent basis for operative interaction if
we realize that film is meant to be created, seen, enjoyed, discussed,
and analyzed, not just dissected and cataloged for the sake of puri-
fication and specialization. However, if film study reaches the point
of ossification and irrelevance that the teaching of literature has
reached, particularly in colleges and universities, it will have failed in
its interactive function.

Louis Kampf, professor of literature at the Massachusetts Institute of Technology, assesses the problem as it applies to literature
study, but his ideas apply to film study as well.

> In school we study literature not for the effect it might have
> on our sense of who we are, or on our capacity to relate to others.
> We study literature in order to be certified, and when it performs
> this function, literature is an instrument of social elitism. Rather
> than providing people with a culture, it removes them from the
> possibility of building on their own cultural foundations. Who can
> feel anything but shame when informed by the teacher that one's
> feelings about a literary work are not valid? Curricula originate
> neither from the needs of students nor from the moral imperatives
> of their teachers. Rather, they are shaped to conform to currently
> accepted literary theory or pedagogical methodology. . . .
> . . . Critical methodology has erected a wall between the stu-
> dent and the literary work. The wall is impenetrable and effec-
> tively prevents students from bringing the experience of literature
> to bear upon their daily lives. *Does the study of literature really
> help my students to discover who or what they are? Or how their*

[5] *Ibid.*

joys and pains relate to the world and the culture which have been forced upon them?[6]

The study of film, then, must resist the constraints of overinstitutionalized instruction.[7] Equally, however, film study must resist becoming just a vacuous and thoughtless "grooving" on the flickering images and sounds. Films can be more than mere escape, more than just a diversion from the workaday world. If film does not illuminate that world, it remains a shadow in Plato's cave and its viewers become passive recipients, victims of a kind of cinema-solipsism.

If education, therefore, is seen as an interactive process, the study of film within education is relevant because of film's interactive nature. Film need not be approached primarily as an audio-visual aid for instruction in skills or knowledge nor relegated to a position of respite and reward for students who have completed more "important" classroom tasks. Instead, film study can become an integral part of the total process of education, different from but akin to seminars, discussions, other forms of self expression, and community involvement.

FILM AND INTERACTION

Because interaction is vital to making, viewing, and discussing films, it is a necessary component of film study. But this does not mean using film merely as therapy or as a stimulus for psychodrama or other forms of counseling, sensitivity training, or group work. It means, rather, using an approach that considers how the work of art relates to the context in which it was produced, how the medium affects and is affected by the message or ideas in the film, and how the viewer of the film relates both to what he has seen and to the responses of other viewers.

Interaction occurs at its fullest, perhaps, in film making. In graduate and undergraduate film departments, this usually means training students to work in the field of film production as, for example, technicians, writers, directors, or independent film makers. But film making can also be valuable to students who have no intention of

[6] Louis Kampf, "The Trouble with Literature...," *Change,* 2, No. 3 (May–June 1970), 29. (Kampf's Italics.) Kampf's original title, "Cultural Revolution and the Study of Literature," was changed by *Change.*
[7] See Pauline Kael's famous comment, "If you don't think movies can be killed, you underestimate the power of education," in "It's Only a Movie," *Film Study in Higher Education,* ed. by David C. Stewart (Washington, D.C.: American Council on Education, 1966), p. 137.

working professionally in the field of film. It is important to both
types of students not only because they learn technique, but also
because they interact with others and with their environment. They
find themselves in a position where, if they are working on anything
larger than a single personal film, they must cooperate and coordinate
their activities with those of others, and their activities force them
into contact with the community, institutions, and ideas outside the
school. Students see how the medium works — how it is able to
manipulate issues, controversies, and concepts — through narrative
components, montage, camera angles and movement, lighting, music,
and the juxtapositions of sight and sound. They see how film transforms reality, and they are able to use the medium to order the chaos
of their experience, to structure their own reality.

Similarly, in viewing films, there is always an interaction
between the images on the screen with their accompanying sounds
and the viewer who is seeing and hearing them. It doesn't matter
whether the viewer likes or understands the film; he is still relating to
it as long as he remains awake in front of it. If he has seen any film
before, he comes to this film with certain expectations and an understanding of certain conventions. On one level he can think about the
technique of the film, seeing how a flashback or flashforward works,
thinking a cut or montage particularly effective or inappropriate,
praising or faulting the acting, editing, or sound.

If the viewer's total experience ended with his direct response to
the film he was watching, interaction would not be an important
aspect of film study. But this is seldom, if ever, the case. The viewer
responds not only to the sensory experience as it happens, but also to
the ideas and concepts the film portrays and to others' responses to
the film.

Interaction with a film continues after watching and might begin
with the recognition of the relation between its form and content. Of
course, form and content are not separate and distinct, but an awareness of how the film's ideas and techniques affect each other allows
the viewer to move continually from the art object — the film — to the
ideas and context (historical, cultural, social, economic, etc.) that surround it, and back again to the art object.

In schools, individuals come into contact with the responses of
others who have viewed the film and, perhaps, with the responses of
reviewers and critics. This interactive process facilitates operative
learning when film study is not prescriptive, when compulsions of
high art and respectability are suspended, and when the teacher,
instead of testing students on their knowledge of the accepted clas-

sics, shares in the students' experiences in a collaborative rather than a coercive way.

INTERACTION AFFECTED BY EXPLOITATION

Particular films, however, can either foster or hinder the types of viewer involvement which have been described. The "integrity" of the film seems to have a significant effect upon the type of interaction that follows viewing, and, specifically, exploitative films seem to hamper interaction with the film per se. It is, of course, difficult and perhaps impossible to isolate, objectify, or prove filmic integrity. We infer it from the finished product, much the way we infer the motives of individuals from their behavior.

Nevertheless, judgments of integrity are constantly being made in both the interpersonal and cinematic realms. The film *Bob and Carol and Ted and Alice* illustrates the importance of such judgments on two levels, both within the film, where personal integrity is a focus of interest, and as a filmic entity, where the integrity of the whole is questioned by the audience. Within the film the point is quickly made: if Ted and Alice are to listen to and be influenced by Bob and Carol, they must first determine if their friends are well intentioned and sincere, whether there is integrity behind their behavior.

For the audience the integrity problem is similar, but more complex. We must deal not only with the integrity of Bob and Carol, but also with whether they and others are presented with integrity. When I first saw the film at the Seventh New York Film Festival, uneven and sporadic laughter suggested that the audience was not sure what was included to be funny, touching, thoughtful, snide, or simply lucrative. The film's early action and later development hinge on an Esalen-like sensitivity training, with people self-consciously touching, crying, groping, and psychically exposing themselves in order to find freedom. Was this material included for its relevance, its sexploitative appeal, or as a subject of ridicule and abuse? Was it humorously satirized, taken seriously, or just there to pander? The same questions, or close variations, can be raised throughout the film.

At the press conference, queries to writer-producer Larry Tucker and writer-director Paul Mazursky substantiated the fact that some of the audience found the film exploitative rather than sincerely probing. The responses of Tucker and Mazursky, which at least some of the original skeptics took as sincere, suggested that they intended to offer a serious consideration of the issues involved, but that perhaps poor editing, inept acting, and sensational promoting camouflaged their sincerity. Although many in the audience were convinced by their statements, the integrity of the film will, in the vast majority of its screenings, be assumed from the filmic experience, not from apologies.[8]

The question here is not whether a film actually *has* integrity. Rather, it is the *judgment* of integrity by members of an audience that determines whether the particular filmic experience offers a good basis for interaction. If a film is judged to be exploitative, its substance will be given little consideration and that basis for operative interaction will be diminished.

Consider how the issues of students, schools, and education, when treated exploitatively in films, affect such interaction. Recently a number of films have dealt or have attempted to deal, directly or indirectly, with students and schools. These include *To Sir With Love, Up the Down Staircase, If, The Prime of Miss Jean Brodie, Halls of Anger, Zabriskie Point, The Magic Garden of Stanley Sweetheart, High School*,[9] *The Strawberry Statement, Getting Straight,* and *R.P.M.* The last three films will serve as examples of how the seeming prostitution of controversy, ideas, and events inhibits interaction.[10]

The 1967 novel *Getting Straight* by Ken Kolb has little, if anything, to do with campus unrest, violence, and the role of the university

[8] Filmic integrity can be inferred not only from the film itself, but also from circumstances surrounding the production of the film and from the assumed and stated intentions of craftsmen, artists, and others who have worked on it. The problem of dealing with the intentions of any artist, however, is a difficult and unresolved one. See, for example: William K. Wimsatt and Monroe C. Beardsley, "The Intentional Fallacy," in Wimsatt's *The Verbal Icon* (Lexington, Ky.: University of Kentucky Press, 1954), pp. 3–18; Henry David Aiken, "The Aesthetic Relevance of Artists' Intentions," The *Journal of Philosophy*, 52, No. 24 (November 24, 1955), 742–753; and Peter F. Neumeyer, "Intention in Literature: Its Pedagogic Implications," in *Aesthetic Concepts and Education,* ed. by Ralph A. Smith (Urbana: University of Illinois Press, 1970), pp. 328–365.

[9] Film cannot, by the nature of the medium, be objective and value-free. When dealing with an issue, even documentary reflects a point of view, is selective in what it shows, is not continuous reality but is edited, and can be seen as honest or exploitative. See my "Review of *High School*," in *The Student and the System,* ed. by Bruce Rusk, Tim Hardy, and Bill Tooley (Toronto: Ontario Institute for Studies in Education Publications, 1970), pp. 19–23; reprinted in *Interchange*, 1, No. 2 (July 1970), 105–107.

[10] It is of course possible to interact with any film, exploitative or not. Discussions of technique or plot do not require filmic integrity. In contrast, considerations of a character's social or psychological being or of the film's social or psychological meaning hinge on integrity. Seeing an exploitative film with someone who found it honest might lead to such meaningful dialogue. In these cases interaction will arise from the discussion with that person, with the film playing an incidental role vis-à-vis the learning experience. Similarly, film reviewers writing about exploitatve films sometimes interact with unseen readers more than with the films. But such discussions, whether in person or on paper, frequently rely on an idealized version of what the film should have been or a hypothetical viewer-discussant who found the film meaningful.

in the "military-industrial-educational complex." The closest it comes to dealing with any of these problems is in its crudely painted satire of "mickey mouse" education courses and educationalists and in its farcical rendition of the truly farcical academic rite de passage an MA candidate in literature could be put through in an oral examination. The 1970 film, however, written by Robert Kaufman and directed by Richard Rush, is put into the context of and continually relates back to "student revolution." But rather than raise and examine the issue, Rush glosses over it, using it, it seems, for its box office timeliness. The film is not entirely a cliché. The cops aren't all "just doing their jobs," nor are the students all irrationally acting up; it doesn't distort that much. We see cops beating up on kids and professors who are irrelevant and inhumane. But it still has that Hollywood finality to it, that smugness that does not stimulate one to think about the problems of universities and students. Fluff as fluff is fine, but when a film has pretensions of being substantive, it should have some depth and honesty.

A similarly flagrant example of exploitative handling of the campus issue is The Strawberry Statement based on the book by James Simon Kunen, screenplay by Israel Horovitz, directed by Stuart Hagmann. Kunen's book relates, with Holden Caulfield humor, his involvement in the Columbia University student strikes. In the film, his whimsical joining with student forces in the university president's office loses its adolescent naiveté and becomes more a combination of bandwagon-hopping and boredom. As in Getting Straight, at the end the cops beat up the students; but again, the reality, the verisimilitude is lost, this time in the brightness of the color, in the gimmicky editing from the students to the cops to the people outside, and in the heavy-handed symbolism of ever-widening circles of chanting students. The contrived techniques in The Strawberry Statement can only be seen as pandering to a filmically unthinking and unaware audience.

A third film designed to capitalize on the student revolution is Stanley Kramer's R.P.M., written by Erich Segal and starring Anthony Quinn and Ann-Margret. The focus in the film is on Quinn as Professor Franklin Perez, the new Acting President of the university, and on Ann-Margret, his graduate student and roommate. Quinn's Zorba-like acting, affectations, and clichéd rhetoric fail to convey any sense of a concerned university sociologist just as Ann-Margret's babydoll appearance and inane comments fail to give her credibility. Following in the tradition of the other two Hollywood renditions of student protest, R.P.M. ends with the predictable scenario of an encounter between cops and students. When students occupying a university building threaten to destroy a computer, Quinn calls in the police to evacuate the building. Again, a lyrical ending is attempted. The destruction of a few computer tapes is followed by Kramer's romanticizing of the ensuing struggle — complete with rock music, freeze frames, slow motion, abstract shots of lights and colors, and distorted vaseline-on-the-lens shots, all intercut with close-ups of Quinn's eyes.

These three films do to the issues they deal with what Jacqueline Susann and other pulp writers do to sex. They use their material as best they can to suit their own purposes, but they never really try to understand it or cause the viewer to interact with it on anything but the most superficial level.

It is obviously possible to produce professional slickly scripted films which seem blatantly "false" — *The Strawberry Statement*, *Getting Straight*, and *R.P.M.* are fair examples — as well as rather rough but, to this viewer, honest attempts at "truth" — as Paul Bogart's *Halls of Anger* or Robert Kramer's *Ice*. A naive film such as *Halls of Anger* should not be considered exploitative because it does not satisfactorily grapple with issues any more than a genuinely innocent person should be considered phony. But the apparent lack of honesty in the three films discussed above implies an intent to deceive, not just a failure to communicate. It suggests the decision to exploit by distortion, to present knowingly an economically or socially acceptable cultural myth, a false image of reality that is offensive because it prohibits the kind of growth toward which inter-action can lead.

Although there are not at present films dealing adequately with student unrest, Robert Kramer's *Ice*, which is concerned with young revolutionaries, can serve as an example of a film that would tend to promote interaction. *Ice* does not exploit; it does not gloss over or simplify issues or characters. It is a chronicle of the activities of urban guerrillas who are attempting to overthrow a "future" United States government that is waging war in Mexico and is totally repres-sive at home. Technically, *Ice* lacks polish and filmic flashiness and would be minimally acceptable for many viewers. But the black and white graininess, the result of both budgetary and aesthetic consider-ations, does add to its documentary qualities and its verisimilitude.

Ice seems to have integrity as well as aesthetic value. If Kramer has distorted for box office appeal, it is not obvious. Although the film is sympathetic to them, it portrays the revolutionaries as serious, intent, joyless, sometimes cruel people. Surely conservatives and po-litical moderates would disagree with and dislike most of the people portrayed, whereas politically left and radical viewers who sympa-thize with the characters might find the portrayal too harsh. But the people in the film do seem real, and because we accept the integrity

of the filmic presentation, the questions it raises — about the cost of
personal sacrifice, means-ends relations, the justification of violence,
the nature of human dignity, and man's need for such dignity — become real questions with which we can interact.

The *Strawberry Statement*, *Getting Straight*, and *R.P.M.* are
much more likely than *Ice* to be popular with audiences. As Andrew
Sarris says:

> Popular movies are usually popular because they tell people what
> they want to believe about themselves, and there is no limit to the
> public's capacity for self-deception. . . . It takes guts . . . to make an
> audience face its own cowardice, mediocrity and simple-minded
> sentimentality. It's so much easier and more profitable to make an
> audience rejoice in its own superiority over the characters and
> situations it sees on the screen.[11]

SUMMARY

Involvement with film in education should not be a matter of passive
receptivity to the story or pictures presented, but an active interaction with the content and ideas embodied in the work. Film has the
power both to dull the mind and feelings and to enhance them. What
the viewer sees in a film either is entirely new to him or is consonant
or dissonant with what he knows, believes, and feels. The various
interactions of the viewer with film, with its contexts, and with other
viewers may take the form of fantasy, agreement, disagreement, disbelief, shock, horror, outrage, relief, tension, or combinations of
these. The process of education — the intellectual and aesthetic development of the individual — relies on these interactions not only to
enhance the edification and enjoyment derived from film, but also to
contribute to the humanization of the educational process.

[11] Andrew Sarris, "Films in Focus," *Village Voice*, 15, No. 29 (July 16, 1970), 49.

Educational Innovation
and Evaluation

ANDRES STEINMETZ

The purpose of this paper will be to outline some of the general evaluation problems faced by so-called innovative educational projects, such as film and media education, both of which exemplify the need for departure from the usual outlook on evaluation. As many projects probably face methodological difficulties similar to those examined here, I hope that these remarks will be of use in planning a course of action for them. I will examine three overlapping issues in the field of educational evaluation.

THE SEARCH FOR RESPECTABILITY

When values are challenged, new curricula are proposed, or new conceptions of schooling are offered, there is a reluctance to abandon established and familiar administrative, research, and teaching practices. School districts demand proof that changes are worth trying before they are tried. That may in itself already be contradictory, but it is nevertheless an issue that must be faced, given the realities faced by large school districts. With little hope for radical change, they need a way of deciding which "innovative" project to consider for implementation. This requires a procedure for assessing local problems and cannot be accomplished without some educational and instructional theories that indicate what is of interest and what is not.

    If that suggestion makes sense, then knowledge of how funds are now granted to projects in education is often disillusioning because present methods do not exhibit a clear sense of directed intention. The analysis of needs and procedures for project implementation are usually weak; the conceptual framework out of which a project intends to operate is often extremely vague. A useful and meaningful evaluation of such a project is therefore very difficult to carry out. Although it is of little immediate help to say that such projects should be better planned, it is easy to suggest that in the future project evaluation could begin before the project itself begins. Given that the goal is to make the project as successful as possible, project evaluation seems to require that the role of the evaluator become one of helping the project articulate itself and realize itself, without compromising, in the long run, the goals of evaluation. For the evaluator to assume such a role would also ease the related problem of making educational research relevant to educational practice.

Thinking of the evaluator as something of a change agent, whose responsibility is to provide continuous feedback and to assist project development and implementation, is a logical and even "scientific" approach to take, and it also appears to be responsive to real-life situations. But a serious hindrance to pursuing these avenues of evaluation seems to lie in the singularly stilted approach to science adopted by the educational research profession. Any activity that can call itself scientific seems to enjoy a special prestige, and educational research is very eager to show how scientific it is. In order to project an image of respectability an evaluation report is expected to concern itself with "hard" data, for this is what research has built its promise on. The exclusive emphasis is on data that can be subjected to tests, covariance methodology, and so forth, and it is a foregone conclusion that a report is weak to the degree that it neglects these techniques.

The use of classical or quasi-experimental design and associated statistical techniques is both desirable and inevitable. But to conclude *a priori* that an educational project that doesn't yield such data or that hasn't been subjected to such analyses is bad education, is simply bad logic. It is paradoxical that with the great emphasis on being "scientific," the profession doesn't go about becoming so in a "scientific" way. It tends to close off many avenues by neglecting to explore sufficiently the potential in, for example, careful observation and description, anthropological methods of research, or thorough theoretical appraisal, to name some possibilities, and it is not as conscious as it should be of the limits imposed on the final interpretation of results due simply to the mathematical assumptions inherent in the commonly used statistical techniques.

If the evaluator is implicitly expected to produce a clean and simple summative approach, he starts off at a disadvantage. It seems of little immediate use to point out that this conception of evaluation is probably grounded in a philosophically indefensible view of science. Perhaps it is better to note that such a narrowly construed role of evaluation could place the evaluator in a position that would make him a hindrance to the educational process. For example, in such a framework it would be in his interest if the project did not obtain feedback on itself, did not act upon it, and did not try to improve itself. Such behavior would change the treatment, thus making pretest data questionable, posttesting probably irrelevant, and comparisons between treatments weak. Moreover, in the traditional framework, the evaluator would try to make specific statements about individual projects and so would favor exposing students to only one project at a time because an evaluation design could otherwise get extraordinarily complicated. He would also like to use an evaluation design that would control for as many interacting factors as possible in order to further refine his outcome data. However, from the point of view of ongoing education, a project that changes treatment on the basis of feedback could reflect a very healthy and desirable proce- dure — it could in itself mark a milestone in curriculum implementa- tion. Further, to sort out the specific effects of individual projects in a city where a large number of them are widely distributed among many schools easily becomes an academic exercise when every effort should be made to include students in as many different projects as seems appropriate. Ongoing project evaluation would concentrate on instantaneous feedback because it sees a major source of difficulty located in the purely instructional procedures that surround project implementation, no matter how behavioral the objectives. Summative results become an extra dividend for an approach that does not assume continuity between intentions and final behavior.

ACCEPTABLE EVIDENCE

One finds a depressing lack of concern for broad and systematic theory in educational research. Very few attempts are made to relate individual investigations to larger wholes that are useful in practice, or to plan investigations in order to clarify broad theoretical orienta- tions. The results of an investigation can be interpreted differently depending upon what is valued. It is not enough to approach data gathering with a view of evaluation that is interested only in compil- ing test scores and deciding upon levels of statistical significance.

Laying out alternatives and giving a clear rationale for following one alternative instead of another is a way of infusing order and objectivity into the process of education. It is certainly of greater use than a study that is tightly constructed but lacks a clear enough con- text to allow for the extraction of far-reaching educational meanings. In fact, I would rather argue that the sad state of affairs in which educational research finds itself is not due nearly as much to lack of sophistication in statistical and experimental design as it is to lack of committed and fairly well understood ways of thinking comprehen- sively about education.

In other words, conflict for the evaluator of an educational proj- ect can be identified as arising, basically, out of the relation to edu- cational research of what are philosophical questions. Educational research seems especially removed from the philosophy of education, and it is reasonable to suggest that some clarification in what might be called "philosophy of educational research" could put some basic order into the fragmented efforts at solving problems in education.

To work explicitly from a theory of education is of greatest importance because only in that way is it ultimately possible to decide between what is relevant and what is irrelevant, what is interesting and what is uninteresting. Education must find a way of defining what science means for it, of inventing a mode of inquiry and verification that allows it to reflect upon itself and be objective by being as aware as possible of the context that produced its data.

THE MATTER OF OBJECTIVES

Evaluations in education usually assume that projects are well defined. That assumption sees evaluation as an activity that only begins once behavioral objectives have been specified. The result is that if no behavioral objectives are available then (1) the project is easily dismissed as being confused in its intent (this amounts to an evaluation that the project cannot be evaluated because it does not meet a certain necessary criterion), or (2) a few behavioral objectives are squeezed out of the project staff under the threat of a poor evaluation (the evaluator is then under the illusion that the objectives he is concerned with encompass project activities), or (3) the project is intimidated so that its tone and style change in order to accommodate a standard evaluation design (in which case something that is delicate, tentative, probing, may be extinguished). The point is that very often it is nonsensical to decide that evaluation activities should begin after objectives are specified behaviorally, if in fact a great difficulty is specifying the objectives in a form that allows you to track down what happens with them. Most projects just are not so well defined that they lend themselves to straightforward summative evaluation, and it is often true that if they are and if that is *all* they are, then they are not really alive in any important sense. Besides, there are grounds to suspect that behavioral objectives become, in practice, too closely tied to conceptions of education that are a bit too mechanical and manipulative or unquestioning of existing norms and that have little to offer to education that tries to become serious about personal freedom, self-actualization, social self-realization, and other related concepts in which personal process more than product or superficial appearance becomes central. This is not to say that specific behaviors are not of interest here but only that in a very real sense behavior is often intended to be unpredictable.

Of course, in practice the innovative projects again suffer most of all from the behavioral objectives slogan because they are not easily given the privilege of learning from their mistakes. The results from these and more traditional efforts are used to form different classes of judgments. For example, if it becomes part of a project's aim to teach arithmetic, at no time will that as a general aim be questioned, no matter how many failures various projects undergo. In contrast, suppose there is a notion about "media competence" that one would like to work out. The idea can initially be stated clearly enough so that it contributes to the overall rationale of the project, which is granted some funds. But, as is typical for school district projects, no research help is made available nor much lead time given so that thoughts and staff may be properly gathered while the proposals are being written. After money is granted the evaluator appears asking for behavioral objectives. More likely than not, the innovative project is then forced into too many compromises with respect to its leading idea. The resulting equivocal evaluation helps to curtail funds and the idea of "media competence" disappears while that of arithmetic does not — not because arithmetic is part of some theory of education but because it is sanctioned by tradition.

In sum, whereas behavioral objectives stamp out "vague generalities" they easily, in the real world, encourage meaningless specifics and intimidate the imagination, especially in projects that are exploring avenues of change and new approaches to problems. In their zeal to measure what is more easily quantified, their proponents are also prone to minimize the integration of qualitative processes into a theoretical structure, something that is of immeasurable value to a science of education. In fact, by not considering the relation of objectives to educational theory at large to be worthwhile territory for evaluation, one in effect devalues the objectives themselves, whatever their type, because the importance of the sets of assumptions that make it possible to formulate and value any objective in the first place are minimized.

A Model for Curriculum Evaluation in Film

ALAN C. PURVES

> ... You gotta lot a damn gall to ask me if I've rehabilitated myself.
> I mean ... I mean ... I mean I'm sittin here ... I'm sittin here on the
> Group W bench 'cause you want to know if I'm moral enough to
> join the army, burn women, kids, houses, and villages after bein' a
> litterbug.
>
>   — Arlo Guthrie, *Alice's Restaurant*

One of the educational truisms too often forgotten states that evaluation determines the curriculum. For example, in England the O-level examinations in literature deal primarily with a set list of books about which students are asked questions of recall. A great many classes are devoted to memorizing the books. In the United States, the verbal aptitude test holds sway and vocabulary building is a large part of the senior English course. Even when tests do not affect the teacher's choice of content, they do affect what the students concentrate on, whether it be grammar, dates, or some other weapon by which they think they can beat the system.

Since this truism operates, people in the burgeoning interdisciplinary fields such as film study should pay careful attention to the types of evaluation that are developed. If they do not, evaluation will remain in the hands of the professional tester, who, left to his own devices, will aim for the familiar and the easily measurable and avoid the chancy. The kind of evaluation that may result will make film study as dull and as irrelevant as grammar drill and literary history.

One might attack the very idea of evaluation and say that the humanities are their own reward and that the experience of messing about in books, plays, paints, statues, films, and string quartets suffices as an educational objective. True as I think this is, I recognize a political necessity to prove the pragmatic value of the humanities to those who must decide the place of the humanities in the "marketplace" of the school calendar. Those people, the administration, want to be shown that these experiences have some material value. Even those of us who believe in these experiences because we are "intellectuals" tend to value an intellectualizing reconstruction of the experience. Educational reform leaders, the most interesting force that the university confronts, are challenging that assumption, but even they seem reluctant to abandon it. Further, and perhaps most important, since we are co-opting the film and other forms of creative expression, rather than letting them remain blissfully underground, we want to assure ourselves that we have done it well. The teacher's test, a good teacher knows, measures not his students but himself; it tells him whether he has been successful, not whether they have.

This being so, the teacher must decide what constitutes success. Since we are dealing with film as a humanistic study, I should like to quote a few statements about success in the institutionalized films, statements that might be made about any one of the arts:

> . . . if such a course can nudge the student to turn off the TV set more often or to avoid some of the trash, . . . the imaginative enactment of verbal and visual fiction can help a student find that inner logic of experience.[1]

> We believe a carefully structured program will help these students develop criteria to evaluate film.[2]

> They are capable, however, of sensitively responding to people and of developing some understanding of life.[3]

> The educational task is not only to provide basic tools of perception, but to develop judgment and discrimination with ordinary social experience.[4]

These various statements have been summed up by William Kuhns and Robert Stanley in *Teaching Program: Exploring the Film*. Film is seen as art, and the modes of analysis and criticism of that art are a goal. Film is seen as environment, in McLuhan's sense, and it is studied for its effects on us (film as rhetoric). Film is seen as experience and it is studied to stimulate self-analysis (film as therapy). Film is seen as language and it is studied so for insight into the ways by which the language system can be manipulated. Film is seen as vocation or avocation, as an instrument for creative expression, and it is studied for the acquisition of another expressive tool.[5]

---

[1] The Rev. J. Paul Carrico, "Matter and Meaning of Motion Pictures," *English Journal*, LVI (January, 1967), 24. See also Ralph A. Smith, "Film Appreciation as Aesthetic Education," *The Educational Forum* (May, 1966), 488 (a partial revision of which appears in this volume, pp. 272–280).

[2] G. Howard Poteet, "Film as Language: Its Introduction into a High School Curriculum," *English Journal*, LVII (November, 1968), 1186.

[3] Gay E. Menges, "Movies for Teens," *English Journal*, LVI (October, 1967), 1025.

[4] Marshall McLuhan, "Classroom Without Walls," quoted in John M. Culkin, "Film Study in the High Schools," *Holt's Dialog* (Spring, 1966), 5. (McLuhan's article appears in this volume, pp. 22–24.)

[5] William Kuhns and Robert Stanley, *Teaching Program: Exploring the Film* (Dayton, Ohio: George A. Pflaum, 1968), pp. 3–5.

One of the best ways to make order of these goals is to make use of a behavioral grid, which does not necessarily imply that the curriculum is to be seen behaviorally, but that the student can be so viewed (Figure 1). One must make a clear distinction between models for curriculum and models for curriculum evaluation. The content of this grid is the simplest part of the process in that it consists of films and non-films. Such a division is true of all the arts, for the content of instruction is art objects and non-art objects (artists, history, medium, technique, content, and the art viewer). To be more precise, besides (1) *art objects* the objects of the student's behavior include: (2) *the context from which art arises,* (3) *the experiences with which art deals,* and (4) *the responses of the audience to the art.* Now, the second is an obvious academic object of attention, comprising as it does information about, say, the production of the film, various technical details and terminology, the reception that the film had, and

Figure 1

Content \ Behavior	To know	To apply knowledge to	To discriminate	To express a response to	To express a particular response to	To express a preference	To re-create	To create	To be willing to respond to	To take satisfaction in responding to	To value
1. Art object											
2. Context of art object											
3. Separable content of art											
4. Individual response to art object											

especially the means by which critics connect one film to another. There might well be controversy, however, about whether the third and fourth should be in the curriculum at all. The legitimacy of the third — the experiences with which art deals — arises from, among others, Shelley's claim in "A Defence of Poetry" that poetry is "the creation of actions according to the unchangeable form of human nature" and therefore that to apprehend poetry is to apprehend the essence of human nature. Art is mimetic, and therefore one can learn about what is imitated through the imitation. Critics have argued the contrary, that art is simply form, that it has no content save itself, or that, as Susan Sontag says, "the function of criticism should be to show how it is what it is. ...."[6] Without arguing the merits of the case, let us admit that some people establish the separable content of works of art as objects of study.

From quite a different aesthetic, the rhetorical, comes the idea that the perceiver's response can be an object of study. He can describe the work's effect on himself and what in him and in the work caused that effect. I have argued this position myself,[7] and I realize the force of the counterargument that such a position is anti-aesthetic subjectivism, that it leads to the affective fallacy, that criticism must seek to describe the work "as in itself it really is." Again, we must leave that argument aside, particularly because we must deal with the evaluation of potential curricula and because an evaluative model must deal with the realm of possibilities.

Let us turn, then, to the range of behaviors that seem most powerful in the humanities. In so doing, I shall take the model builder's prerogative of being eclectic, of building upon the twin taxonomies of educational objectives, of adding some terms of my own, and of blending cognitive, perceptual, and affective behaviors. In the humanities, the major behaviors must include: *to know, to apply knowledge, to discriminate, to express a response, to express a particular response, to express a preference, to re-create, to create, to be willing to respond, to take satisfaction in responding,* and *to value.* I am not including *to respond,* because that is an interior behavior, and evaluation can only deal with manifest behavior. Nor am I including some of the lower behaviors in the taxonomy of the affective domain, because they seem to me to be so intimately involved in the expressed response or lack thereof that mentioning them would be redundant.

Several of these behaviors could be subdivided, but for the pur-

[6] Susan Sontag, "Against Interpretation," *Against Interpretation and Other Essays* (New York: Dell Publishing Company, 1964), p. 14.
[7] "You Can't Teach Hamlet, He's Dead," *English Journal,* LVII (September, 1968), 832–836.

poses of model building, some of the subdivisions are of minor importance. *To know* is one of these divisible behaviors, involving knowledge of wholes and of parts, recognition, and recall. *To apply knowledge* is also divisible in that one can apply knowledge of any content
area or any part of any content area to any other. One might divide
the *expressed response* into the main categories of expression of
engagement, of analysis, of classification, of interpretation, and of
evaluation. These in turn can be further subdivided as I have shown
elsewhere.[8] *To re-create* can be divided according to medium and
according to literalness of the re-creation.

Some of these behaviors need further explanation. *To discriminate* refers to the behavior of noting differences between objects,
whether or not the individual analyzes or otherwise deals with those
differences. One might say that it is the behavior of sorting, and it is a
perceptual as well as a cognitive behavior. Discrimination enables
one to observe that a piece of music is not a painting, that a sonata is
not a serenade, and that the mood evoked by a work of art is not the
same as the mood expressed in the work of art. *To express a particular response* includes what I have found to be its contrary: treating
every work of art in a distinct manner. The two goals are contradictory and both appear in humanities curricula — one may read that students should always start with their emotional reaction or that students should not come to the work of art with any prejudice about
how to approach that work — but both may be measured by the same
instrument. The third opaque behavior is *to value*, by which I mean to
hold an intellectual respect for the right of the art object and, by
extension, the artist to exist. This behavior certifies a person as a
"good guy" to the art world: he is against censorship, he is tolerant of
artists, he might even support his local symphony orchestra. He need
not respond to works of art or want to respond to works of art or get
any pleasure out of responding to works of art.

These eleven behaviors cover most of the important behaviors in
the humanities. They deal with the three areas of human action
toward works of art and the art world: knowledge, ability, and attitude. They are not, as I said, related to the curriculum, for they tell us
nothing about how to teach the humanities and nothing about the
learning process. At the same time, however, the minute one begins
to block in the cells of the grid to determine educational priorities,
one begins to influence both what shall be taught and how it shall be
taught. In the rest of this paper I will spell out the implications of

---

[8] Alan C. Purves, with Victoria Rippere, *The Elements of Writing About a
Work of Literature* (Champaign, Ill.: National Council of Teachers of English,
1968).

concentrating on any one of these content areas, or behaviors, and make some recommendations for a balanced evaluation in the humanities. If one tests a behavior with respect to a work of art and only with reference to the work of art, one runs the risk of inculcating in the student the idea that art is unrelated to anything else or that the approved mode of thought is to consider art as separate from the rest of life, from the creator, from the audience, and from the things with which art deals. The perpetuation of such an idea will lead both to a furthering of the dehumanization of art that Ortega so accurately describes[9] and to the perpetuation of an elitist art. Similarly, an emphasis on the non-art surroundings of art work, particularly on the context from which the work springs and on the separable content of art, will lead to an education about art in which the review in *Media and Methods* is more important than the film reviewed. It will lead to what English teachers refer to as the "bad old days" of literary gossip and moral hunting. Overconcentration on the response of the individual can lead to solipsism and subjectivism. It seems, then, that the attention of evaluation should be distributed among the four content areas with major emphasis on the work of art.

The behaviors are perhaps the more important concern of the evaluator since they present the greatest problem to him, particularly the problem of the basis of measurement, and I would propose a major rethinking of evaluation in the humanities. Measurement can be either descriptive or prescriptive; it can tell us whether or not someone is riding a bicycle or how well he is riding that bicycle. Educational measurement has been concerned primarily with prescriptive measures, with measures that operate on a criterion, and with achievement and aptitude tests that seek to rank the individual with some absolute criterion (100%) or with his fellows in the bell-shaped curve. Benjamin Bloom has pointed out the deleterious effects of the normal-curve mentality,[10] and I will demonstrate its particular shortcomings with respect to measurement in film. Let us see what the implications of criteria are for each of the three areas of behavior — knowledge, ability, and attitude.

Knowledge can be tested; it is in fact the easiest of the three areas to test and the one most frequently tested. One can simply ask a student whether or not he can recognize a film, whether he remembers a character's name or a director's birthday, whether he can identify a technique or a camera device, whether he can spot an allusion

---

[9] José Ortega y Gasset, *The Dehumanization of Art* (New York: Doubleday and Company, 1956), pp. 3–50.

[10] Benjamin S. Bloom, "Learning for Mastery," *Evaluation Comment*, UCLA Center for the Study of Evaluation of Instructional Programs, I (May, 1968).

to another work. Literature, art, and humanities tests have been full of questions like these. The only problem in creating tests of knowledge or the application of knowledge to a new piece of data (spotting the symbols in an unfamiliar scene), is deciding what specific bits of knowledge should be tested. The universe of the humanities is too large for any person to encompass it all, much as the humanist would like to be the Renaissance man. So the humanities tester must determine what knowledge is significant. To make this determination, he must have a criterion of significance. Should one know the name of the main character in *On the Waterfront,* the name of the director of *The Graduate,* the type of camera shot that D. W. Griffith perfected? What is the boundary line between serious information and trivia, such as the name of Hopalong Cassidy's horse? One might say that the line divides information on high art and information on low art, or that the line divides art that has endured and art that has become obscure. But Busby Berkeley seems to have emerged from oblivion to be a producer of high film art, although perhaps his prominence will be brief. One might say that only the information about aspects of an art is important — the definitions of techniques,. styles, genres — for only they transcend the individual creation. But another might counter that the arts survive only in the individual creations not in any generalizations that have been drawn from them. The choice of *what knowledge* is arbitrary, not derived inevitably from principle.

Furthermore, the very importance of this kind of knowledge is to be challenged. Education has spent too much of its energy in creating human storage and retrieval systems, rather than systems users. The epitome of the former was Teddy Nader, the mail carrier who could win $128,000 on a quiz program but could not do anything with his knowledge save sort and deliver mail. Ten years after the zenith of Teddy Nader, we realize that machines are more than adequate to perform the storage and retrieval function. The metaphor of the mind as pitcher is fast disappearing from its central place in humanities education because educators have come to realize that the most fruitful experience with an art work comes out of direct confrontation, not out of the half-life of that confrontation in the respondent's memory. The best talk about a poem comes when everyone has a text in front of him; the best talk about a concerto when everyone can refer to a tape; and the best talk about the film when it is available for reference. The temporal media — music, film, theater, dance — do present some problems and do require the retention of information on the part of the audience-discussants, but recording devices now operate to enable them to make more and sharper references to the art object.

Evaluation of knowledge about who wrote or produced what, what characters said or did what to whom, the sequence of events in a film, or the arrangement of figures in a scene, of phrases in a score, or of shots in a montage, should play a lesser role than it has in the past, if only because the humanities have always placed greater stress on abilities and attitudes. The skills in an art are either the skills of production or the skills of criticism, and in general education some of the arts have emphasized one and some the other. Music, dance, and theater have stressed production; literature has stressed criticism; fine arts have stressed both; and film seems close to literature and fine arts in this respect. The evaluation of production has focused either on technical skill or on expressiveness, on the product or on the process. Music has focused on the product, and it has aimed at producing the well-drilled marching band. Dance and theater have also aimed at the recital or "Broadway" production. Art has shifted from a product to a process emphasis: drawing, perspective, and glazes are less important than messing around in paints. Literature has until recently aimed at the school journal, the NCTE Achievement awards, and the perfectly proofread short story. Now curriculum builders are shifting their attention to the process of writing, talking, miming, or performing. Some take the extreme position of "Get the flow going and the rest will take care of itself," but most attempt some manipulation of the creative process, either by comment on the process or by variation of the topics for writing.[11]

Evaluation of the product is, of course, easier than evaluation of the process. We can listen to the piece of music, score in hand, and tell whether it was correctly played. We can look at the painting and tell that it is not as good as a Rembrandt (but did it aspire to be?). We can view the film and compare it to Wiseman, Renoir, or Penn. But we cannot look into the player, the painter, the poet, the film maker, to see whether or not he is being truly expressive. Some inferences are possible from the work he produces, but they are often misleading. Although some external measure, like a general measure of creativity, is possible, a creative person might not be expressive in a particular art form.

Further, we are still reluctant to fail the student, if fail we must, on the basis of whether or not he makes a good film. We might not

[11] See, among others, John Dixon, *Growth Through English* (Reading, England: National Association for the Teaching of English, 1967); Geoffrey Summerfield, *Creativity in English* (Champaign, Ill.: NCTE, 1968); Robert Zoellner, "A Behavioral Approach to Writing," *College English*, XXX (January, 1969), 267–320; Daniel Fader and Elton B. McNeil, *Hooked on Books: Program and Proof* (New York: G. P. Putnam's Sons, 1968).

want to fail him if he refuses to make a film. Although the arts and the humanities respect, stimulate, and examine many facets of man's creative spirit, the teacher of the arts and humanities should respect the child's right not to be creative. The evaluation of a truly creative curriculum of the arts should not seek to measure the extent or even the existence of a child's creative actions. Evaluation should only be of the number of opportunities to be creative that are made use of. If more opportunities are utilized, the curriculum is a success, but I think that is all evaluation ought to do.

Aside from asserting that there is production or re-creation of art, the evaluator can say little more about the value of the art produced that is not ultimately challengeable by the somewhat intelligent aesthetician. The evaluator may say that a poem is not good because it does not have perfect form; and the aesthetician will ask him why form is necessary to an art that expresses formlessness. The aesthetician can always come up with an example of art that is praised for the very factor for which the evaluator has damned another piece of art. Criteria for art works are nonce criteria — although some are more nearly permanent than others — so that the educational evaluator must have a lot of gall to establish absolute criteria. He can, however, do what Northrop Frye says every critic of an art should do: accept the value of every production and seek to describe that production, to say what kind of composition or film or dance the student has created.

If the evaluator has trouble finding a norm for production perhaps he can establish norms for discrimination and response. One can say that it is a higher ability to distinguish between Antonioni and Bergman or between Antonioni and Broccoli than it is to distinguish between a film and a still or between a film and an essay. One can say that a full Judith Crist review is better than a grunted "I like it." Between these extremes, however, continua seem not to exist. To take the example of discriminating verbal ambiguities, which is the harder pun: Mercutio's "When you find me tomorrow you find a grave man," or Anne Sexton's description of a funeral, "Gone I say and walk from church refusing the stiff procession to the grave"? Is it harder to comprehend the symbol of train wheels over tracks or the symbol of dark figures at a graveside in a snowstorm? Is Fellini a more difficult film maker than Hitchcock? In each case there are aspects that make one more difficult than the other, so that it is virtually impossible to sort works of art or even parts of works of art out on a scale of difficulty.

Nor is it possible to assert that one mode of response is intrinsically more complex than another. A full stylistic analysis is as difficult to achieve as a description of one's emotional response, a psychological interpretation as difficult as a formal evaluation, and an archetypal classification as difficult as any of these. A glance at the work of any practicing critic will demonstrate this, despite the prominence he might give his specialty.

Further, as I have recently found, difficulty is in part a function of culture. Two examples will suffice. In an objective test on a short story, one item read, "Which of the following best describes the change in the doctor? (A) He becomes more violent, (B) He becomes more professional. . . ." There were other distractors, but they are unimportant. In all the countries in which this item was tried out, the item was extremely easy, the key being (A). In one country, however, a large and bright segment of the population chose (B). Investigation showed that this was because in that country a doctor is such an authority figure that any action that he performs is considered professional. The second example deals with the apprehension of popular songs. I find that white middle-class students hear the words and are only minimally concerned with the music of artists such as Simon and Garfunkle or the Beatles; lower middle-class and inner-city students do not hear the words at all, but they can mark subtle differences between a Supremes recording and a Beatles recording of "Eleanor Rigby."

With response in particular, and with discrimination as well, evaluation should first seek to describe the differences between and similarities among people. It should seek to describe a person's characteristic patterns of response and his various strengths and weaknesses in discriminating, but it should not assert a criterion for pattern of response or for level of discrimination. It could also seek to determine whether the response patterns to an art work are carried over when dealing with the separable content of art, whether a person looks at a "real" situation as one does a "fictional" one (see footnote 3).

What about attitudes? Surely there can be a norm of attitude, or at least a norm of taste. Is it better to like *Charly* than *The Beverly Hillbillies*; better to like *If* than *Tom Brown's Schooldays*? Well, I think it is, but I'm not convinced that I should impose my taste on everybody, and I'm particularly sure I wouldn't want to flunk a person who preferred *The Beverly Hillbillies* to anything made by Arthur Penn. I'd cry a lot, but I wouldn't flunk him. Most of the preference tests now in print ask the student to subscribe to the taste of the tester and do not allow him to indicate that his preference might be based on a different set of premises than those of the tester.

I for one would much rather get at the basis of taste than see whether someone's taste accords with mine.

Much the same is true with willingness to respond and with pleasure in responding. Teachers would be glad if all were as willing and as enthusiastic about the arts as the Medici family (although I suspect many prefer to be able to be snobbish about their students). Out of all the activities available to a person, the arts are but one set, and to have everyone want to pursue them to the exclusion of anything else would produce a monochrome society.

About the only behavior with respect to which a norm seems both feasible and desirable is that of value. One goal of education in the humanities since the Renaissance has been to develop a tolerance of the right of the arts to exist. Plato challenged it, as have many others, and it is being challenged today (both *Manchild in the Promised Land* and *Birth of a Nation* are embattled works of art, particularly in the schools). Despite these challenges, the good guys seem to have kept on insisting that everything be allowed to exist. I think we might allow a norm to exist here, but I think we need to describe exactly what kinds of constraints on the freedom of the arts and the audience of the arts different people think should exist.

I began this paper saying that evaluation influences education. I have made a plea for evaluation not to seek to establish criteria but to look at what is there. It might then be thought that I was asking that evaluation not influence education. On the contrary, I think the influence should remain, but it should be quite different from the present influence. A descriptive evaluation, ranging over the major types of behavior with respect to the arts, would help convince students that the arts are open systems, not closed ones. It would help convince students that art, not to mention "good art," is an essentially contested concept.[12] From this, I hope it would convince them that the serious consideration of art is not academic punishment, but an exercise of the whole mind of man.

[12] W. F. Gallie, "Essentially Contested Concepts," and Morris Weitz, "The Nature of Art," in *Readings in Art Education,* ed. by Elliot Eisner and David W. Ecker (Waltham, Mass.: Blaisdell Publishing Company, 1966), pp. 49–57.

The Preparation
of Teachers of Media

GERALD O'GRADY

I

Begin with the nature of man and the nature of his social organization: Kenneth Burke has shown us how "man is a symbol-using animal,"[1] and Hugh Dalziel Duncan has explained how "society rises in and continues to exist through the communication of significant symbols" and how "man creates the significant symbols he uses in communication."[2]

Proceed with the nature of education and of pedagogic instruction: J. L. Aranguren has pointed out that "education is the most fundamental means of socialisation and therefore of communication"[3] and Jerome S. Bruner concluded some recent remarks on "Patterns of Growth" with "What I have said suggests that mental growth is in very considerable measure dependent upon growth from the outside in — a mastering of techniques that are embodied in the culture and that are passed on in a contingent dialogue by agents of the culture. This becomes notably the case when language and the symbolic systems of the culture are involved, for there are a multiple of models available in the culture for shaping symbolic usage — mentors of all shapes and conditions."[4]

We have arrived at the nature of our problem. In "Education for Real," John McHale argues that our traditional, so-called cultural, education is now, at best, inadequate and, at worst, a form of creative disenfranchisement from our emergent planetary culture, and makes a plea that the term "arts" be expanded to include our advanced technological media.

> The problem, now, is that those areas of our formal education
> which deal with the symbolic and value content of our culture do

---

[1] Kenneth Burke, "Definition of Man" in *Language as Symbolic Action: Essays on Life, Literature, and Method* (Berkeley: University of California Press, 1966), p. 3.

[2] Hugh Dalziel Duncan, *Symbols in Society* (New York: Oxford University Press, 1968), pp. 44–47.

[3] J. L. Aranguren, *Human Communication* (New York: McGraw-Hill, 1967), p. 158.

[4] Jerome S. Bruner, *Toward a Theory of Instruction* (Cambridge: Harvard University Press, 1967), p. 21.

so almost entirely in terms of the past. By and large, they avoid immediate relevance to the external cultural environs in which the person finds himself. Outside the school, university or other educational institution these environs are those of the film, TV, radio, the pictorial magazine and massive "advertisement" of an enormously proliferated "mass" culture brought into being by our accelerated technology. It is largely within these media, now on a global scale, that the symbolic and value communication of our cultural situation is carried on.[5]

II

The solution — how these new symbolic forms, the media arts, might be incorporated into various stages of our educational processes — is not so easily revealed, as illustrated by the current confusion and disagreement about the teaching of film. . . .

1. Should film criticism or film appreciation be taught, as they are in most colleges and universities which have recently added such courses, by members of the traditional departments in the humanities, such as English, French, classics?[6] Will they misunderstand the very topics, such as structure, theme, and value, which they are usually most capable of examining, because they have almost no knowledge of the techniques by which and circumstances in which the new media are produced?

2. Should such courses be taught solely by departments of communication or of journalism and speech or of radio/television/film? Have even the younger members of such departments been given sufficient preparation in perceiving their subjects as art forms shaping our cultural environment or do they, as often seems the case, perceive them mainly as channels of information? Do members of these departments overemphasize technique and production to the detriment of the symbolic cultural values that concern McHale?

3. Should art departments expand their offerings to include photography, film, and television? Is it clear thinking or just accident that, on many campuses, photography is taught by the art department but film, with the exception of production courses, by other departments? (Why is it, incidentally, that still photography is part of the cinema curriculum in most European film schools but not in their

[5] John McHale, "Education for Real" in Edwin Schlossberg and Lawrence Susskind (eds.), Good News: A Curricula of Ideas to Be Implemented, p. 5. The essay also appears in the World Academy of Art and Science Newsletter (June 1966) and is anthologized in Richard Kean (ed.), Dialogue on Education (New York: Bobbs-Merrill, 1967), pp. 120–25.

[6] Some would include film study under drama. See Richard M. Gollin, "Film as Dramatic Literature," College English, Vol. 30 (1969), 424–29.

American counterparts?) If photography is "still," aren't a great many paintings and sculptures becoming kinetic?

4. Should the teaching of film be placed in a more general context, which might be called media studies? If new departments or programs of media studies are created, there are two questions: how should their subject matter be defined and what kinds of curricula and training should they offer their students?

In the short run, obviously, one simply chooses the most knowledgeable and skilled person, regardless of his departmental affiliation, to teach film. In the long run, I would opt for new multidepartmental programs of media studies.

III

How, then, should media studies be defined? Until a few years ago, the study of media usually meant the investigation of the transformation of information to mass audiences by means of newspaper, radio, and television; film, in its documentary uses, was sometimes included, as was the Hollywood feature film if studied, usually in quantitative fashion, in terms of audience patterns, class entertainment preferences, etc. The word "public" was usually understood to preface "media" and students pursued their programs within a curriculum which was much concerned with government policy and the advertising market — e.g., censorship and sponsorship. With the war came an emphasis on the measurement of propaganda, which continued during the years of the cold war, followed more recently by an emphasis on the relationship of media to voting behavior.

About twenty years ago, a new concept began to emerge in the work of Marshall McLuhan. His three books, the humanistic leitmotif of which is the "man" of their subtitles, approached media from just as many different perspectives. The first, *The Mechanical Bride: Folklore of Industrial Man* (1951), was *mythological* and concentrated on newspapers, magazines, advertising, pulp fiction, and comic books: what was then called popular culture. The second, *The Gutenberg Galaxy: The Making of Typographic Man* (1962), was *historical* and juxtaposed a mosaic of meditations on the cultural interactions arising from the invention of the printing press; turning our attention away from the content and toward the form of print, he explained the cliche, "the medium is the message,"[7] later associated with his work:

[7] McLuhan himself first used the term as the title of the first chapter of *Understanding Media* and punned on it in the title of his next book, with Quentin Fiore, *The Medium Is the Massage* (New York: Bantam, 1967). In a recent interview in *Playboy* (March 1969), he indicates that puns and hyperboles are strategies for drawing attention to new insights. In general, more time has been spent on

"Technological environments are not merely passive containers of people but are active processes that reshape people and other technologies alike."[8] The third, *Understanding Media: The Extensions of Man* (1964), was *formal* and followed seven groundwork chapters dealing with their psychic and social consequences with twenty-six more (symbolically the new alphabet) on the structures of individual media. It was this idea of media as extensions of our senses, as expanders of our psychic environments, and their aesthetically-oriented treatment as forms, structures, and models shaping our physical environment, conceived of as an art form, which caught the contemporary imagination.

According to McLuhan's *formal* treatment, almost everything can be considered a medium, including all our languages — "language is the first mass medium." Pursued, that ideal could reshape our entire educational structure and all its subjects or fields in new ways. Given the completely remote possibility of that happening, I would like to delimit media studies to mean the exploration of the creation, the aesthetics, and the psychological, social, and environmental impact of the art forms of photography, cinematography, videography, radio, recordings, and tapes within the broad framework of general education in the humanities. I would call media studies the "new humanities" to distinguish them from the "old humanities" — literature, drama, the fine arts, etc. — from which they often borrow and with which they continually interact, mutually influencing each other.

I would make a special plea that, in our curricula, the new never be separated from the old.[9] When the student of Greek reads Plato's *Republic* and faces the question of why the whole Hellenic system of education was changing, I would want him to have to ponder Eric Havelock's answer: "The fundamental answer must be in the changing technology of communication. Refreshment of memory through written signs enabled a reader to dispense with most of that emotional identification by which alone the acoustic record was sure to

---

misunderstanding McLuhan as a popular medium than to understanding his work; recent books, subtitled "Hot and Cool," "Pro and Con," "Sense and Nonsense," produce few insights. More accurate "placements" of his work are found in the reviews by Hugh Dalziel Duncan, "Communication in Society," *Arts in Society* Vol. 3 (1966) and John McHale, "The Man from Mascom," *Progressive Architecture* Vol. 6 (February 1967).

   [8] Marshall McLuhan, *The Gutenberg Galaxy: The Making of Typographic Man* (Toronto: University of Toronto Press, 1962), preface.

   [9] This by no means implies that the newer media should be studied only as a means toward interesting students in the classics like Shakespeare and Dickens, an attitude put forth by David Riesman in his introduction to Reuel Denney's *The Astonished Muse: Popular Culture in America* (New York: Grosset and Dunlap, 1964), p. vi.

recall."[10] The student in my period of specialization, the late medieval, undergoes a valuable heuristic process when he is made to
consider the implications for literary form and style of McLuhan's
many insights concerning the transition from script to print. The student of contemporary fiction will gain nothing but profit by meditat-
ing upon Bertold Brecht's remark: "For the old forms of communication are not unaffected by the development of new ones, nor do they
survive alongside them. The filmgoer develops a different way of reading stories. But the man who writes the stories is a filmgoer too."[11]

The interaction of contemporary art forms almost demands that
we inaugurate a field of cross-media studies. In the past, men of letters (today, the phrase seems biased toward print) wrote in different
genres — poems, plays, novels, essays. Some, like Henry James or
George Bernard Shaw, wrote dramatic criticism and novels, or music
criticism and plays. Still others, like the Polish Bruno Schulz or the
Welshman David Jones, were writer-painters or writer-drawers.
Arthur Miller is one key example of the emergence of a new kind of
writer, the writer for many media, who has confronted and been
deeply influenced by the communications revolution of our century.
While his sole medium is writing, his first efforts were the radio
drama, and the style of his stage plays will be better understood
when the latter are examined. Later, he wrote for and was influenced
by film, and his last play, *The Price*, began as a television piece. He
has also written short stories and novels. He has said: "Movies, the
most wide-spread form of art on earth, have willy-nilly created a
particular way of seeing life, and their swift transitions, their sudden
bringing together of disparate images, their effect of documentation
inevitable in photography, their economy of storytelling, and their
concentration on mute action have infiltrated the novel and play writing — especially the latter — without being confessed to or, at times,
being consciously realized at all."[12] The poet Michael Benedikt
concluded an explanation of Godard's *Alphaville* in terms of Paul
Eluard's novels and the philosophy of the Surrealists:

> What I have to say here is that, in considering the background of a
> major creator like Godard, it seems improper to restrict considera-
> tions to the medium in which such a creator happens to be operat-
> ing. Just as it is no longer possible to take a literary criticism seri-
> ously which cuts itself off from the film, and other media, it is no

[10] Eric A. Havelock, *Preface to Plato* (Cambridge: Harvard University Press,
1963), p. 208.
[11] John Willett, trans., *Brecht on Theatre: The Development of an Aesthetic*
(London: Methuen, 1964), p. 47.
[12] Arthur Miller, *The Misfits* (New York: Viking Press, 1961), pp. ix–x.

longer possible to view a creator like Godard as operating solely, or even *primarily*, out of a background of the visual arts — even the cinematic — developments of the past few years. It seems to me that *Alphaville* is an excellent place from which to launch a useful series of fresh confrontations.[13]

Indeed, other critics have pointed out *Alphaville's* allusions to (and thus dependence for meaning on) *Odeipus Rex*, the stories of Orpheus and Lot and detective fiction as well as *Nosferotu* and other films. Godard's first treatment names the scientist Leonardo da Vinci,[14] which explains why the movie version's Dr. Von Braun's first name is Leonardo, that it is Godard's attempt to mythically encircle the entire machine culture, ending with the father of our bomb and beginning with the first artist included in the Museum of Modern Art's recent exhibition, "The Machine As Seen at the End of the Mechanical Age."[15]

IV

Even if we could agree on my rough definition of media studies, on their necessary relationship to the traditional arts, and on the interest and importance of explorations in cross-media studies, we should not rush to formulate curricula for the preparation of media teachers until we have examined our social structure for changes and trends such as the following, which are only a few entries in what would become a long list.

1. Just as affluence and qualitative democracy were topics of the early 1960's, replaced by the later stress on poverty and participatory democracy, so yesterday's interest in distinguishing high, middlebrow, and mass cultures is shifting to today's concern for a new definition of popular culture.[16] The films of Bergman, Antonioni, Godard, and others are high culture in the old sense and popular culture only in the sense that they are seen by a large number of people.[17]

[13]Michael Benedikt, "Alphaville and Its Subtext" in Toby Mussman (ed.), *Jean-Luc Godard: A Critical Anthology* (New York: E. P. Dutton, 1968), p. 220.

[14]*Alphaville: A Film by Jean-Luc Godard* (New York: Simon and Schuster, 1968), p. 97.

[15] K. G. Pontus Hultén, *The Machine As Seen at the End of the Mechanical Age* (New York: The Museum of Modern Art, 1968), p. 15.

[16]The concerns of the contributors to the Spring, 1960, issue of *Daedalus*, devoted to "Mass Culture and Mass Media," are already somewhat dated.

[17]Last year, the Motion Picture Association of America asked Daniel Yankelovich, Inc., to make a survey of the American audience. The report indicated: "The more educated the public the larger the interest in and attendance at movies. The less educated are less interested." See Motion Picture Association of America, 522 Fifth Avenue, New York: *A Year in Review June 1968*, p. 11.

When, in the 1980's, university teachers look back to evaluate the cultural life of the fifties and sixties for their students, they must admit, I think, that the construction, the choice of theme and philosophical treatment, and the influence on thought of the films of these and a dozen other directors were at least as important as the best poetry, drama, and fiction, and perhaps more so because they were so much more widely discussed.

2. Works of similar quality created by artists working with videotape[18] will not become popular in this new sense until we break the commercial stranglehold on television. Robert M. Hutchins has written:

> So a country that is chiefly interested in turning out consumers and producers is not likely to be much concerned with setting minds free; for the connection between selling, manufacturing, and free minds cannot be established. Such a country will transform new opportunities for education into means of turning out producers and consumers. This has been the fate of television in the United States. It could have been used for educational purposes — but not in a commercial culture. The use of television, as it was employed in the United States in the 1960's, can be put in its proper light by supposing that Gutenberg's great invention had been directed almost entirely to the publication of comic books.[19]

While this is by no means completely true, it makes its point by overstatement. Peter F. Drucker has remarked: "Few messages are as carefully designed and as clearly communicated as the thirty-second television commercial. . . . Few teachers spend in their entire teaching careers as much time or thought on preparing their classes as is invested in the many months of writing, drawing, acting, filming, and editing one thirty-second commercial."[20]

3. Higher education, as Peter Schrag recently pointed out "will not only be democratized but will become, in a society that has solved its major production problems, a way of life," and the means will be "via special institutes, books, tapes, films, travel."[21] When we place this beside McLuhan's observation that today's children have

[18] Stan Vanderbeek and Scott Bartlett have both created new film forms by using videotapes. On April 14, 1969, the American Film Institute established a Television Film-makers' Program.

[19] Robert M. Hutchins, *The Learning Society* (New York: Praeger, 1968), p. 127.

[20] Peter F. Drucker, *The Age of Discontinuity: Guidelines to Our Changing Society* (New York: Harper and Row, 1969), p. 337.

[21] Peter Schrag, "The End of the Great Tradition," *Saturday Review,* Vol. 51, No. 11 (February 15, 1969), 26.

had five years of adult education via television before they ever enter class, we can recognize that media teaching and teachers will be at the center of innovation in planning curricula and, more likely, in completely reshaping our educational institutions. In his recent essay, "The Future of University Education As an Idea," Charles Muscatine predicted that "as more and more 'university' instruction goes on in extramural institutions and in field studies here and abroad, the university will tend to lose its character as a place with clear geographical and intellectual boundaries, a place where one spends a definite amount of time and acquires a certain amount of knowledge. It will become, rather, a point or center from which knowledge and teaching radiate into the surrounding environment, and the possible relations of individuals to it will have many gradations, altering with age and circumstances."[22]

4. Individuals in our society will become increasingly mobile because the knowledge explosion means that the organizational charts of all of our institutions — governments and corporations as well as universities — will be made up of project groups rather than stratified functional groups. Warren G. Bennis reports that "Adaptive, problem-solving, temporary systems of diverse specialists, linked together by co-ordinating and task-evaluating executive specialists in an organic flux — this is the organizational form which will gradually replace bureaucracy as we know it."[23] Future media teachers will be entering into many temporary groups, which will require a high degree of adaptability in personality structure, enabling them to establish relationships quickly and intensely and, shortly later, dissolve them. To have the personnel interchange demanded by this application of new knowledge will mean the maximization of sameness among people, and this in turn, as Philip E. Slater shows, can be summed up in the new educational objective: "Less variety from person to person requires more variety within each person." We have to look forward to a changing nature of man within rapidly "self-renewing" community structures.[24] This has been called "the protean style" and involves the idea of a lifetime of personal change, an adulthood of continuing self-transformation and of adaptability and openness to a world in permanent revolution.

[22] Charles Muscatine, "The Future of University Education As an Idea" in Walter J. Ong (ed.), *Knowledge and the Future of Man* (New York: Holt, Rinehart and Winston, 1968), p. 43.

[23] Warren G. Bennis and Philip E. Slater, *The Temporary Society* (New York: Harper and Row, 1968), p. 74. The quotation from Slater is on p. 82.

[24] See J. H. van den Berg, *The Changing Nature of Man: Introduction to a Historical Psychology* (New York: Dell, 1964), and Jerome F. Scott and R. P. Lynton, *The Community Factor in Modern Technology* (Paris: UNESCO, 1962).

V

What kinds of curricula and training should Media Studies programs offer their students? After describing some general guidelines set forth at the Waltham Conference, I shall briefly describe and comment upon a short-term program for current graduate students in the humanities and then propose three models for undergraduate education in Media Studies — a full four-year program, a core curriculum for the first two years of a residential college, and a two-year sequence of courses for a major.

During the weekend of January 19–21, 1968, a group of twenty-eight leading practitioners and advocates of screen education met together in Waltham, Massachusetts, at a conference sponsored by the American Film Institute and the National Film Study Project. The section on the training of teachers in our published proceedings reads in part:

> Screen educators are becoming aware of the need for comprehensive media education, based on the training of sensibility, response and perceptual awareness of the past and present.
>
> We welcome the trend toward interdisciplinary teaching which we find compatible with elements inherent in media education.
>
> Although the prognosis for the immediate future is that screen educators will come from the traditional areas — English, art and the humanities — the more distant future will see specialists from media departments.
>
> To implement such programs teachers need modes of experience and training which are not adequate in existing institutions.[25]

A. Model for a Summer Program in the Preparation of Teachers

One proposal now before several foundations and granting agencies has the aim of encouraging very talented students who are now pursuing graduate studies in the traditional humanities at major centers of higher education to study the media arts in depth during the coming summer and to teach and administer media studies programs at several different educational and social levels next year. The students would be selected from Princeton, State University of New York at Buffalo, University of California at Santa Cruz, University of Southern Illinois, and University of Texas.

---

[25] Jane Anne Hannigan and David J. Powell (eds.), *The Waltham Conference: Screen Education in the United States 1975, K-12* (printed and distributed by Films Incorporated).

The twelve-week summer program would be mainly concerned with instruction in making photographs, films, and videotapes, which would include a review and criticism of the creative traditions in each of these art forms. Faculty members from English, psychology, sociology, drama, and film history would hold month-long seminars on the relationship of the humanities, the behavioral sciences, and media studies; on the availability of media materials (slides, tapes, etc.), their sources and costs, and the variety of ways in which they can be prepared for teaching-presentations; and on current curricula and programs involving media at all stages of the educational process.

During the following year each of the students would be involved in three projects at his location. One student, for example, would teach a freshman course in media at his university and another media course at a junior high school, and would work with a group of ghetto film-makers. Another would teach a media course at a junior college near his university and a film course to a continuing adult education group, and would organize a community media-mart to which local high school teachers could apply for film selections, bibliographies, and film-discussants and lecturers on all kinds of topics embraced by media.

The purpose of simultaneous exposure to several different environments in the learning process is to acclimate the students to assume roles rather than to pursue specialized tasks, and to stimulate them to think concretely, yet broadly, about new solutions for teaching the media arts. Another objective is to create models of interaction and interchange of personnel, knowledge, equipment, and materials between universities, viewed as seminal centers radiating outward, and programs involving urban and minority groups, groups under psychological treatment, and groups of adults engaged in continuing education, as well as programs in junior colleges, and secondary and primary schools.

B. Model for a Four-Year Undergraduate Curriculum

The usual four-year program leading to a degree includes about 120 hours of accredited instruction. The following program in media studies, which began at a small college in one of our largest cities, envisioned combining the experiences of an art school with those of a traditional education in the liberal arts and a domestic "peace corps"-type operation. About forty hours of instruction were to be given to explorations in the new image-making technologies — photography, cinematography, videography — which would provide the focus and *raison d'être* for the program as a whole.

Students would undertake this creative work while simultaneously being exposed, through film rentals, slide collections, and exhibitions, to the best work of the past and present; and from this continued confrontation of tradition with individual talent would evolve discussions of theory and aesthetics: topics not "taught" as formal units but regarded as perpetual and ultimate concerns. This whole process of viewing, making, comparing, debating was conceived as one undivided four-year stream of creation.

Another forty hours would be given to the humanities — literature, philosophy, music, and the fine arts — the experiencing and formal analysis of the great texts, compositions, and art works from the beginning of civilization to the present. It was thought that image-makers in the new media should be rooted in the ways in which man had imaged forth himself and his concerns in the traditional media which continue to be lively and influential. It is just this emphasis which production-oriented curricula usually lack, and the shallowness and "vast wasteland" aspects of contemporary communication are an obvious result.

Finally, a third forty hours of work would concentrate on the behavioral sciences because it was believed that the creators of media should be knowledgeable about and thus responsible for the psychic and social consequences of their work. Each student would be acquainted with the various models and theories of the formation, growth, and abnormalities of the human mind, and special attention would be given to the ways in which visual and auditory images are related to growth from infancy onwards, an area in which research is just beginning. He would also learn to analyze human groups, the ways in which man has organized his relationships with other men, focusing on the media which each group — family, village, globe — uses to bind itself together and how this is accomplished.

A few aspects of the program might be singled out for special comment. A maximum number of the forty hours in the behavioral sciences were to be worked out through participation in community projects. A quote from a recent article in *The Christian Science Monitor* (November 23, 1968) is relevant here. It is headlined "Education: Off-Campus Service":

> At Harvard, the growing interest of students in community involvement has caused Phillips Brooks House to recommend to the college administration that an undergraduate department of urban studies be launched.
> "If the current trend continues, volunteer work at Phillips Brooks House will become an unofficial major for students," Mr. Profit prophesied. "The university should start its own program to

meet this interest. A student's association with the house could then be his way of doing field work in his major."

"This would be the best way to meet the current situation," he concluded.

One example of the possibility for this type of activity in the media studies program involves the day-school education of psychologically disturbed children in one of the city's hospitals. Its director familiarizes the media students, through readings, discussions, and observation, with the psychological and sociological models he uses in treating the children and with the practical problems that arise. The students use cameras and tapes to document the children's activities, and then, having become acquainted with the children through the media, begin to make short videotapes and films for them, and finally, to teach them to communicate with each other through the new media.

Another aspect of the program which deserves comment is the recruitment of film-making teachers. It was thought best to engage a variety of outstanding artists for semester-long residencies, enabling the students to live with a number of styles and attitudes of commitment. The first visitor, appropriately, was Stan Vanderbeek who had produced animated, collage, videotape-generated, and computer films, was then on a Rockefeller Foundation grant for experimentation in nonverbal communication, and had also moved into mixed-media presentations while theorizing on the future forms and functions of cinema.[26] Vanderbeek's legacy was a twenty-five-page curriculum, partly developed in an earlier experience in Allan Kaprow's continuing education program at the State University of New York at Stony Brook, which centered on a developing series of assignments in image-exploration (producing five films in a six-week summer course) and was related to viewing approximately one hundred experimental shorts which were listed (along with their distributors). These covered the entire history of avant garde film-making and comprised what I referred to above as "the tradition." The second film-maker in residence was James Blue, and our juxtaposition was purposeful. Whereas Vanderbeek's background was art — he had attended Black Mountain College — and improvisation, Blue had graduated from the University of Oregon as a drama major and later from the Institut des Hautes Etudes Cinématographiques in France. His course, during which each of the twenty-five students made seven films, was centered on matching

26 Stan Vanderbeek, "Culture: Intercom and Expanded Cinema," *Tulane Drama Review*, Vol. 11 (Fall, 1966), 38–48.

image to sound and was built on a viewing of the classics, giving attention to the image-building (visual and aural) of dramatic structures and roles. Blue had just finished interviewing, on a Ford Foundation grant, the directors around the world who used nonactors in their films.[27] He composed a list of nearly three hundred features which he thought young film-makers should see during the years of their first explorations, and also wrote a twenty-page paper, "Equipment List for a Beginning Film-making Course," a thorough examination of the various capabilities of cameras and sound equipment currently on the market, including a set of purchasing choices directly related to the ability of the students. I believe that the gathering and distribution of these kinds of "practical papers" from contemporary practitioners like Vanderbeek and Blue are one of the essential needs for film and media education.[28]

Finally, a few sentences should be written about the future social roles of graduates from this four-year model program. The program was not narrowly vocational but conceived of as a liberal education stressing exploration in the variety of ways of structuring and using the new image-making technologies or media in relation to man's history of expressing and communicating through his traditional media and to contemporary man's psychic and social awareness, all pointing toward participation in and service to the community. Some of the students, it is hoped, would become tomorrow's artists; others would move, via graduate studies in a variety of departments, into the kind of media research of which McLuhan has made us aware, with the advantage of a thorough familiarity with the creative act in these technologies, often unknown to our present theorists; others would become, in the most immediate way, the media teachers we now need in our primary and secondary schools.

[27] Some of Blue's interviews have already appeared in *Film Comment,* and he will soon publish the whole collection in a single volume.

[28] These papers are being prepared for publication by the staff of the Media Center at the University of St. Thomas, Houston, Texas. Copies of *Light and Vision: Photographs from the Beginning Classes at the Media Center* — introduction by Geoffrey Winningham (Houston, 1969) are available from the Media Center, 3812 Mt. Vernon, Houston, Texas 77006. *The American Film Institute's Guide to College Film Courses 1969–70,* the first of an annual survey, can be obtained by writing to the Institute at 1815 H Street, N.W., Washington, D.C. 20006. It should be complemented by Professor Richard Byrne's *A Survey of Coursework in Cinematography and Film Production in Selected American Colleges and Universities,* sponsored by The Radio-Television-Film Interest Group of the Speech Association of America and distributed by Wisconsin State University, Stevens Point, Wisconsin. The National Association of Broadcasters publishes an annual report entitled "Radio-Television Degree Programs in American Colleges and Universities." It can be obtained by writing to Dr. Harold Niven, NAB, 1771 N Street, N.W., Washington, D.C. 20036.

C. Model Program for a New Residential College

A relatively new movement in the large state university educational systems of California and New York is the establishment of a number of undergraduate residential colleges on campus. These serve the twin purposes of decentralization and curriculum innovation, aiming to identify the student with a group of manageable size for building his personal and educational orientation during his years at the university, and to provide opportunities for faculty and students, working together, to reassess education in the light of new interdisciplinary concerns. Such colleges have a mandate to develop core curricula for their students' first two years, and based on this experience, to develop new departments and programs in which upper-level undergraduates may specialize.

As far as I know, only one of these new residential colleges has decided to concern itself with media studies, and since it is still on the drawing-board, I can give only a very general description of the contours of a program which its faculty have worked out after the first year's planning sessions. Its provisional title is Ernst Cassirer College, and it grows out of his concern with a synthesis of knowledge based on the proposition that symbolic systems engender the whole mental development that sets men apart from their zoological brethren. It will construct its core curriculum around the semiotics of languages, the codes of media, and the study of utopias. In essence, it would place the beginning undergraduate in a forum centered on symbolic forms. It would be hoped that the concerns of anthropologists with structural linguistics could be related to premises in "vidistics" recently put forward in the work of Sol Worth, Christian Metz, and Peter Wollen,[29] and that these, in turn, would flow naturally into the investigation and planning of the social organizations or cultures within which the symbolic modes and codes arise. A media studies program or department, now nonexistent, would arise experientially from the encounter of teachers and students within this context, and its staff would then offer a junior-senior major, centered at this particular college but open to students from all thirty of the projected colleges.

As my opening remarks indicate, the study of symbolic forms seems a proper place for media studies to be situated, and my plea for

[29] See Sol Worth, "Cognitive Aspects of Sequence in Visual Communication," A-V Communication Review, Vol. 16 (1968), 121–45, and "Film as a Non-Art," The American Scholar, Vol. 35 (1966), 322–34 [reprinted in this volume, pp. 180–99]; Christian Metz, Essais sur la signification au cinéma (Paris: Klincksieck, 1968); Peter Wollen, Signs and Meanings in the Cinema (London: Secker and Warburg, 1969).

a connection with the older humanities could be met, though in a formal way, by the study of languages, and by a study of the utopian community in history. The latter, according to its planning committee, would involve the Hebraic prophetic visions — and thus an awareness of "transcendental" media, the voice heard and the light seen;[30] dystopias such as Nazi Germany — and thus the analysis of, for example, "Hitler's theory of rhetoric as a means toward social identification,"[31] and what Kingsley Amis calls "serious science fiction" — and thus the study of expanded cinema, computer-graphics, and satellite intercom. Cassirer's first students will not be finishing their undergraduate education until the mid 1970's, and, by then, its developing programs should be providing information about the preparation of media teachers.

D. Model for a Two-Year Media Studies Major

Since Program B is visionary and Program C is related to the establishment of a new educational community, itself a somewhat utopian idea, I wish to conclude this section with a preliminary course outline for a media studies major which could be developed immediately in any of our larger universities having (or willing to appoint) interested faculty members within the necessary schools or departments.

Junior Year

First Semester	Second Semester
Explorations in Photography I	Explorations in Photography II
Fine Arts Laboratory	Media Laboratory
Narrative Structures I	Narrative Structures II
Media and Technology	Media and Environment
Elective	Elective

Senior Year

Explorations in Film-making I	Explorations in Film-making II
Explorations in Videography I	Explorations in Videography II
Narrative Structures III	Narrative Structures IV
Media and Behavioral Sciences I	Media and Behavioral Sciences II
Elective	Elective

I am dispensing with prerequisites, such as science, philosophy, and languages, which would be completed during the first two years

---

[30]In this connection, see W. Richard Comstock, "Marshall McLuhan's Theory of Sensory Form: A Theological Reflection," *Soundings*, Vol. 51 (1968), 166–83.

[31] See the chapter with this title in Hugh Dalziel Duncan, *Communication and Social Order* (New York: Oxford University Press, 1968), pp. 225–27.

and, in some cases, serve as bases for continuing study under electives. Let us imagine a university which has a College of Fine Arts which could supply the teachers for photography and the creative arts lab, a College of Architecture with faculty members oriented toward technology and environmental study and willing to concern themselves with media, a College of Communication with a Department of Film and Television including some faculty member interested in the applications of these and other media to classroom teaching, and a College of Arts and Sciences which would provide behavioral scientists with an interest in media and collect a group in the humanities — literature, philosophy, history, art — who were students of narrative structures. The faculty members would not leave their departments, but teach one course in the media studies program. An exciting fallout, of course, would be the generation of cross-college communication based on the shared concern for the university as an environment capable of innovating programs relevant to contemporary society and today's students.

The instruction in the image technologies — photography, cinematography and videography — would be exploratory, as indicated, and would include a familiarity with the creative traditions of these forms in ways like those suggested above. Given the great potential of television and the deplorable state of much of its current offering, it is hoped that special attention (and funds) would be centered on this part of the program. The courses offered by the architects could begin with the work of Buckminster Fuller and the topics suggested by McLuhan, Edward T. Hall (The Hidden Dimension), and others, and include community planning which would treat the various media as information systems.

After the student had some experience in using a medium (in this case, photography) the media lab would focus on the basic principles of light and sound as media of artistic expression and information transfer, in the same way that the preceding fine arts lab had concentrated on line, color, volume, etc., and had encouraged an interest in drawing or sculpture that could be developed by the talented in their electives. The behavioral science courses would involve the concerns described in our four-year program and consider media in cross-cultural terms[32] and perhaps make the students aware of the uses and limitations of various media for documenting social and cultural phenomena.[33] The four-semester course in narrative

[32] See John Adair and Sol Worth, "Navaho Filmmakers," American Anthropologist, Vol. 72 (February, 1970), 9–34.
[33] See, e.g., John Collier, Jr., Visual Anthropology: Photography As a Research Method (New York: Holt, Rinehart and Winston, 1967).

structure would be a historical survey of the ways of telling a story or organizing events or constructing an argument in fiction, history, and philosophy and by depiction in the arts — Greek vases, medieval tapestries and stained-glass windows, comic books, etc. The emphasis would be on the formal analysis of individual texts and art works, and the influence of historical conditions and cultural outlooks on their formation. At the end of the course, photography, film, and television would be placed in a new perspective, that of the "older humanities," and rich materials for cross-media studies would have emerged. I should add that such a course in narrative structures would probably be encouraged by teachers of literature on two grounds: (1) some of the best recent books on traditional authors in their area, Rosemund Tuve's study of George Herbert, D. W. Robertson's of Chaucer, Ronald Paulson's of Hogarth in relation to the eighteenth-century novel, and Angus Fletcher's *Allegory: The Theory of a Symbolic Mode*, all of which include pictorial material convincingly demonstrate that literature and depiction are interdependent disciplines;[34] (2) film and television have already and will continue to adapt the texts that they teach: a study like George Bluestone's *Novels into Film: The Metamorphosis of Fiction into Cinema* (1957) is already well established, and Robert Gessner's *The Moving Image: A Guide to Cinematic Literacy* (1968) has recently broken new ground.

VI

These notes on the preparation of teachers of media would be incomplete if I did not touch upon developing links with (1) sensitivity training and group dynamics, (2) Lévi-Straussian structuralism, and (3) ecological studies and futurism.

1. The relationship of media studies to sensitivity training and group therapy seems to have come about in two ways. First, McLuhan's books, which are popular with the students and the younger academics who show the greatest interest in media, are based on a model of the sensory life, which he calls a "ratio," and which enables him to argue that one sense is stunted as another is extended by the development of a certain media technology. Thus made aware, and given some exploratory hypotheses why it is that much of their sensory life is underdeveloped, students have taken a renewed

[34] My use of the term "depiction" is derived from I.A. Richards, *Design for Escape: World Education Through Modern Media* (New York: Harcourt, Brace and World, 1968), p. 16.

interest in the body: in biology and physiology, as well as in the psychoses resulting from its repressed needs, as revealed by Norman O. Brown,[35] and the "therapeutic" excercises designed to "unbind" the psyche by training the senses, put forward in books like William C. Schutz's *Joy: Expanding Human Awareness* (1957) and elsewhere. Second, these same students and younger academics have become interested in the newly developing art forms of expanding cinema,[36] mixed media shows, and happenings, all of which have become associated in one way or another with "New Drama," such as the Living Theatre and the Performance Group,[37] both of which were interested, through the theories of Artaud and Grotowski, in re-establishing the full sensory life in theatrical performance, and in "unblocking" the various psychological inhibitions which hindered them from unification, living and performing as communal groups.[38] The emphasis on community and the willingness of performers to play the roles of the opposite sex (another indicator of the protean style) seem microcosmic analogies to the philosophy of "comprehensive living" outlined below.

Before leaving these topics, it should be mentioned that the new involvement in mixed media, sensitivity training, group therapy, and living as drama (the work of Erving Goffman is relevant) has resulted in a strong interest in multimedia teaching[39] as well as a strong tendency toward the fusion of group therapy and psychodrama with classroom teaching. One of "Cassirer College's" founding faculty members has written:

> Teaching, as most of us know it and have known it, is rather like proscenium theatre with a clear line drawn between art and life; audience and performance. But, unlike traditional theatre, the classroom situation does not have the saving grace of illusion, the will-

[35] Norman O. Brown, *Life Against Death: The Psychoanalytical Meaning of History* (Wesleyan, Conn.: Wesleyan University Press, 1959). The books of R. D. Laing, *The Divided Self* and *The Politics of Experience,* have also contributed to this interest.

[36] The best explanations of expanded cinema have appeared in Gene Youngblood's columns in the *Los Angeles Free Press*. See his *Expanded Cinema* (New York: E. P. Dutton, 1970).

[37] This movement is chronicled in the issues of the *Tulane Drama Review* (now *The Drama Review*).

[38] These groups are also interested in dreams, myth, ritual, and games, relating them to the anthropological concerns treated next, and to McLuhan's chapter on games in *Understanding Media*. See Peter Brook, *The Empty Space* (New York: Atheneum, 1968), Chapter 2; Jerzy Grotowski, *Towards a Poor Theatre* (Denmark: Odin Teatrets Forlag, 1968); Richard Schechner, *Public Domain: Essays on the Theatre* (New York: Bobbs-Merrill, 1969).

[39] A useful bibliography appears in Calvin W. Taylor and Frank E. Williams (eds.), *Instructional Media and Creativity* (New York: John Wiley and Sons, 1966).

ing suspension of disbelief, the projection or interjection of a self and world freer than the self-in-society that we recreate in drama. We have had audience and performance, but little interaction. We have had, in some sense, a theatre of censorship. The performer teacher as authority-figure, consciously or unconsciously, denied by role the very dynamism, process and conflict inherent in the classroom. In order to oppose these tendencies, this stasis, I have tried a number of strategies and techniques in the service of freedom.[40]

Such tendencies will have to be considered by those planning future curricula for the preparation of media teachers.

2. The work of Lévi-Strauss directs anthropology toward a general theory of relationships, and focuses on what the relationships communicate. In his Postscript to chapters III and IV in *Structural Anthropology*, he points out that the study of one language leads inevitably to general linguistics but also involves us in the study of all forms of communication, a development which Haudricourt and Granai, whose article he is commenting upon, call a Copernican revolution. He continues:

> Without reducing society or culture to language, we can initiate this "Copernican revolution," which will consist of interpreting society as a whole in terms of a theory of communication. This endeavor is possible on three levels; since the rules of kinship and marriage serve to insure the circulation of women between groups, just as economic rules serve to insure the circulation of goods and services, and linguistic rules the circulation of messages.
>
> These three forms of communication are also forms of exchange which are obviously interrelated (because marriage relations are associated with economic presentations, and language comes into play at all levels). It is therefore legitimate to seek homologies between them and define the formal characteristics of each type considered independently and of the transformations which make the transition possible from one to another.[41]

Students of literature are already applying Lévi-Strauss's ideas to myth and we can expect this interest to extend to media structures and their messages, a movement which should be welcomed since it interweaves with rather than isolates the study of media from the study of culture.

---

[40] The quotation is from H. R. Wolf's position paper, "New Techniques in Education." One of the Strategies is described in his essay "Teaching and Group Dynamics: The Paradox of Freedom," forthcoming in *Radical Teacher.*

[41] Claude Lévi-Strauss, *Structural Anthropology* (New York: Doubleday, 1967), p. 82. See also Tim Moore, *Claude Lévi-Strauss and the Cultural Sciences,* Occasional Papers No. 4, Centre for Contemporary Cultural Studies, Birmingham University (1968).

3. Concurrent with the interest in man's inner resources has been a developing understanding of his relationship to the material resources of his environment, especially through studies in ecology and futurism. Ecology teaches that man lives, as one type of animal, in a landscape containing many other animals, plants, hills, rocks, streams, ponds, and mountains. To quote C. H. Waddington:

> This whole complex teeming landscape is not a mere jumbled agglomeration of separate items — so many pine trees, so many birds of this species, so many of that, so many wolves, or sheep or what-have-you. It is a community, depending on an organized network of all kinds of relationships, of eater, or eaten, parasite or host, tillers of the soil like earthworms which prepare the land for plants to grow in, bacteria and molds which decompose dead bodies and a multitude of other necessary actors in the total scene.[42]

Waddington believes the basic unit of ecological studies to be energy and the facilities capable of processing it in the forms in which it appears within a given ecological set-up. He continues:

> The system of living things inhabiting any area on the surface of the world is ultimately sustained only by the energy poured into it by the sun. The whole fabric of interactions, which converts that assemblage of living things into a real community, should be understandable in terms of ways in which this basic "income" is parceled out, handed on from one individual to another (by being eaten, for instance), converted into foreign currencies which the recipient cannot use. . . .

His focus on the continuing transformation of energy within a community relates ecology, understood in this sense, to Buckminster Fuller's World Resources Inventory at Southern Illinois University and John McHale's Center for Integrative Studies within the School of Advanced Technology at the State University of New York at Binghamton.[43] The last of a six-volume set called *World Design Science Decade 1965–1975*, on which Fuller and McHale collaborated, is *The Ecological Context: Energy and Materials*, a detailed exposition of the second phase of the ten-year program which

[42] C. H. Waddington, review of Shepard and McKinley (eds.), *The Subversive Science: Essays Toward an Ecology of Man* in *The New York Times Book Review* (April 20, 1969), 32.

[43] Fuller's latest book is *Operating Manual for Spaceship Earth* (Carbondale: Southern Illinois University Press, 1969) and McHale's is *The Future of the Future* (New York: George Braziller, 1969). Related documents are Jon Dieges's syllabus, "Design of Alternative Futures," published as the seventh issue of the *Journal of Environmental Design*, and *The Whole Earth Catalogue* and *The Difficult But Possible Supplement to the Whole Earth Catalogue* (Menlo Park, California: Portolo Institute, 1968).

treats the topic of world energy and materials usage within the overall context of global ecology. One of the most basic concepts of Fuller's *Comprehensive Thinking* (Volume 3) is that man's intelligence is part of nature and that all activities flowing from it are part of the evolutionary process. His total systems-approach to designing the future relates the human biophysical, psychosocial, and technological systems to the environ's atmospheric, terrestrial (lithospheric), and oceanic (hydrospheric) systems. McHale writes:

> We need to extend the physical and biological concepts of ecology to include the social behaviors of man — as critical factors in the maintenance of his dynamic ecological balance. Nature is not only modified by human action as manifested in science and technology — through physical transformations of the earth to economic purpose — but also by those factors, less amenable to direct perception and measure, which are political-ethical systems, education, needs for social contiguity and communication, art, religion, etc. Such "socio-cultural" factors have played and will continue to play a considerable role in man's forward evolutionary trending and its effects on the overall ecology of earth.[44]

The final context of "communication, art" — media studies — will be within this "overall ecology of earth." McHale's references to economies and religion remind us that the contemporary reorganization of the world's economic resources — the war on poverty, aid to underdeveloped countries —runs parallel to the attempted reunification of man's traditional spiritual resources in the ecumenical movement. Economic and ecumenical share a common Greek root with ecological — OIKOS, a house. All are studies in housekeeping and aim at making of the world a home. If Ezra Pound is right, that "beauty is seeing all the relationships," aesthetic education will be the study of this evolutionary process of total planetary interaction as an art form. The arts and sciences would be joined and man's learning would lead toward his wholeness.

[44] John McHale, *The Ecological Context: Energy and Materials* (Carbondale, Illinois: World Resources Inventory, 1965), p. 23. See also his "Global Ecology: Toward the Planetary Society," *American Behavioral Scientist,* Vol. 11 (1968), 29–33. This entire issue, edited by Robert Strausz-Hupé, was devoted to "Society and Ecology."

Selected Bibliography

Agee, James. *Agee on Film: Five Film Scripts*. Boston: Beacon Press, 1964.
——. *Agee on Film: Reviews and Comments*. Boston: Beacon Press, 1964.
Anderson, Joseph L., and Richie, Donald. *The Japanese Film*. New York: Grove Press, 1960.
Anderson, Lindsay. *Making a Film*. London: George Allen & Unwin, 1952.
Arnheim, Rudolf. *Art and Visual Perception: A Psychology of the Creative Eye*. Los Angeles: University of California Press, 1954.
——. *Film as Art*. Berkeley: University of California Press, 1957.
——. *Toward a Psychology of Art*. Berkeley: University of California Press, 1966.
——. *Visual Thinking*. Berkeley: University of California Press, 1970.
Auerbach, Erich. *Mimesis: The Representation of Reality in Western Literature*. Translated by W. R. Trask. Princeton: Princeton University Press, 1953
Balazs, Bela. *Theory of the Film*. New York: Roy Publishers, 1953.
Barthes, Roland. *Elements of Semiology*. Translated by Annette Lavers and Colin Smith. New York: Hill and Wang, 1968.
Battcock, Gregory, ed. *The New American Cinema*. New York: E. P. Dutton, 1967.
Bazin, André. *What is Cinema?* Essays selected and translated by Hugh Gray. Berkeley: University of California Press, 1967.
Benoit-Lévy, Jean. *The Art of the Motion Picture*. New York: Coward-McCann, 1946.
Bluestone, George. *Novels into Film*. Berkeley: University of California Press, 1961.
Bobker, Lee R. *Elements of Film*. New York: Harcourt, Brace & World, 1969.
Brownlow, Kevin. *The Parade's Gone By*. New York: Alfred A. Knopf, 1969.
Bruner, Jerome S. *The Process of Education*. Cambridge: Harvard University Press, 1960.
Burke, Kenneth. *A Grammar of Motives and A Rhetoric of Motives*. Cleveland: World Publishing Co., 1962.
Carmen, Ira H. *Movies, Censorship and the Law*. Ann Arbor, Mich.: University of Michigan Press, 1966.
Carpenter, Edmund, and McLuhan, Marshall, eds. *Explorations in Communication*. Boston: Beacon Press, 1960.

Ceram, C. W. *Archaeology of the Cinema*. New York: Harcourt, Brace & World, 1965.

Cocteau, Jean. *Cocteau on the Film*. Translated by Vera Traill. New York: Roy Publishers, 1954.

Dewey, John. *Art as Experience*. New York: Minton, Balch, 1934.

Duncan, Hugh Dalziel. *Communication and Social Order*. New York: Oxford University Press, 1962.

Durgnat, Raymond. *Films and Feelings*. Cambridge: The M.I.T. Press, 1967.

Eisenstein, Sergei. *Film Form*. New York: Harcourt, Brace & World, 1949.

———. *The Film Sense*. New York: Harcourt, Brace & World, 1942.

Fulton, A. R. *Motion Pictures: The Development of an Art*. Norman, Okla.: University of Oklahoma Press, 1960.

Furth, Hans G. *Piaget and Knowledge*. Englewood Cliffs, N.J.: Prentice-Hall, 1969.

Fuzellier, Etienne. *Cinéma et littérature*. Paris: Les Editions du Cerf, 1964.

Gattegno, Caleb. *Towards a Visual Culture: Educating through Television*. New York: Outerbridge & Dienstfrey, 1969.

Geduld, Harry M., ed. *Film Makers on Film Making*. Bloomington, Ind.: Indiana University Press, 1967.

Gessner, Robert. *The Moving Image: A Guide to Cinematic Literacy*. New York: E. P. Dutton, 1968.

Gombrich, E. H. *Art and Illusion*. 2nd ed. rev. New York: Bollingen Foundation, 1965.

Grierson, John. *Grierson on Documentary*. Edited by Forsyth Hardy. Rev. ed. Berkeley: University of California Press, 1966.

Hall, Edward T. *The Silent Language*. Garden City, N.Y.: Doubleday, 1969.

Hauser, Arnold. *The Social History of Art*. Vol. IV: *Naturalism, Impressionism, the Film Age*. New York: Random House, 1951.

Hodgkinson, Anthony W. *Screen Education*. New York: UNESCO Publications, 1963.

Houston, Penelope. *The Contemporary Cinema*. Baltimore: Penguin Books, 1963.

Huaco, George. *The Sociology of Film Art*. New York: Basic Books, 1965.

Huss, Roy, and Silverstein, Norman. *The Film Experience*. New York: Harper and Row, 1968.

Innis, Harold. *The Bias of Communication*. Toronto: University of Toronto Press, 1968.

Jacobs, Lewis, ed. *The Movies as Medium*. New York: Farrar, Straus and Giroux, 1970.

———. *The Rise of the American Film: A Critical History*. Enlarged edition. New York: Teachers College Press, Columbia University, 1968.

Kael, Pauline. *Going Steady*. Boston: Little, Brown, 1970.

———. *I Lost It at the Movies*. Boston: Little, Brown, 1965.

———. *Kiss Kiss Bang Bang*. Boston: Little, Brown, 1968.

Kauffmann, Stanley. *A World on Film*. New York: Harper and Row, 1966.

Kepes, Gyorgy. *Language of Vision*. Chicago: Paul Theobald & Co., 1944.

——. *The Nature and Art of Motion*. New York: George Braziller, 1965.

——, ed. *Education of Vision*. New York: George Braziller, 1965.

——, ed. *The Visual Arts Today*. Middletown, Conn.: Wesleyan University Press, 1960.

Knight, Arthur. *The Liveliest Art*. New York: Macmillan, 1957.

Kracauer, Siegfried. *From Caligari to Hitler*. Princeton: Princeton University Press, 1947.

——. *Theory of Film*. New York: Oxford University Press, 1960.

Langer, Susanne. *Feeling and Form*. New York: Charles Scribner's Sons, 1953.

——. *Philosophy in a New Key*. New York: The New American Library, 1956.

——. *Problems of Art*. New York: Scribner Pocket Books, 1957.

Lawson, John Howard. *Film: The Creative Process*. New York: Hill and Wang, 1964.

Leyda, Jay. *Kino: A History of the Russian and Soviet Film*. New York: Macmillan, 1960.

Linden, George W. *Reflections on the Screen*. Belmont, Calif.: Wadsworth Publishing Co., 1970.

Lindgren, Ernest. *The Art of the Film*. 2nd ed. New York: Macmillan, 1963.

Lowndes, Douglas. *Film Making in Schools*. New York: Watson-Guptill Publications, 1968.

MacCann, Richard Dyer, ed. *Film: A Montage of Theories*. New York: E. P. Dutton, 1966.

McGowan, Kenneth. *Behind the Screen: The History and Techniques of the Motion Picture*. New York: Delacorte Press, 1965.

McLuhan, Marshall. *The Gutenberg Galaxy*. Toronto: University of Toronto Press, 1962.

——. *The Mechanical Bride*. Boston: Beacon Press, 1951.

——. *Understanding Media: The Extensions of Man*. New York: McGraw-Hill, 1969.

Manoogian, Haig P. *The Film-Maker's Art*. New York: Basic Books, 1966.

Mascelli, Joseph F. *The Five C's of Cinematography*. Hollywood: Cine/Grafic Publications, 1965.

Mercer, John. *An Introduction to Cinematography*. Champaign, Ill.: Stipes Publishing Co., 1967.

Metz, Christian. *Essais sur la signification au cinéma*. Paris: Editions Klincksieck, 1968.

Mitry, Jean. *Esthétique et psychologie du cinéma*. 2 vols. Paris: Editions universitaires, 1963, 1965.

Moholy-Nagy, Laszlo. *Vision in Motion*. Chicago: Paul Theobald, 1947.

Montagu, Ivor. *Film World: A Guide to Cinema*. Baltimore: Penguin Books, 1965.

Panofsky, Erwin. *Meaning in the Visual Arts*. Garden City, N.Y.: Doubleday, 1955.

Peckham, Morse. *Man's Rage for Chaos*. New York: Chilton Books, 1965.

Peters, J. M. L. *Teaching About the Film — A UNESCO Project.* New York: Columbia University Press, 1961.

Piaget, Jean, and Inhelder, Barbel. *The Psychology of the Child.* New York: Basic Books, 1969.

Pincus, Edward. *Guide to Filmmaking.* New York: New American Library, 1969.

Pudovkin, Vsevolod. *Film Technique and Film Acting.* Translated and edited by Ivor Montagu. New York: Grove Press, 1960.

Randall, Richard S. *Censorship of the Movies.* 3rd ed. New York: Holt, Rinehart and Winston, 1965.

Read, Herbert. *Education Through Art.* 3rd ed. London: Faber & Faber, 1958.

——. *The Meaning of Art.* Baltimore: Penguin Books, 1966.

——. *The Philosophy of Modern Art.* London: Faber & Faber, 1964.

Reisz, Karel, and Millar, Gavin. *The Technique of Film Editing.* 2nd ed. New York: Hastings House, 1968.

Renan, Sheldon. *An Introduction to the American Underground Film.* New York: E. P. Dutton, 1967.

Richardson, Robert. *Literature and Film.* Bloomington, Ind.: Indiana University Press, 1969.

Rossi, P. H., and Biddle, B. J. *The New Media and Education.* New York: Doubleday, 1966.

Rotha, Paul. *Documentary Film.* 3rd ed. New York: Hastings House, 1963.

——. *Rotha on the Film.* Fair Lawn, N.J.: Essential Books, 1958.

Rotha, Paul, and Griffith, Richard. *The Film Till Now.* 3rd ed. New York: Twayne Publishing, 1969.

Sarris, Andrew. *The American Cinema.* New York: E. P. Dutton, 1968.

——. *Confessions of a Cultist: On the Cinema, 1955–1969.* New York: Simon and Schuster, 1970.

——. *Directors and Directions: 1929–1968.* New York: E. P. Dutton, 1968.

——, ed. *Interviews with Film Directors.* Indianapolis: Bobbs-Merrill Company, 1967.

Sebeok, Thomas; Hayes, Alfred S.; and Bateson, Mary C., eds. *Approaches to Semiotics.* The Hague: Mouton, 1964.

Seldes, Gilbert. *Seven Lively Arts.* New York: A. S. Barnes, 1962.

Simon, John. *Private Screenings.* New York: Macmillan, 1967.

Smallman, Kirk. *Creative Film-Making.* New York: Macmillan, 1969.

Smith, Ralph, ed. *Aesthetic Concepts and Education.* Chicago: University of Illinois Press, 1970.

——, ed. *Aesthetics and Criticism in Art Education.* Chicago: Rand McNally, 1966.

Sontag, Susan. *Against Interpretation and Other Essays.* New York: Farrar, Straus & Giroux, 1966.

——. *Styles of Radical Will.* New York: Farrar, Straus & Giroux, 1969.

Sparshott, F. E. *The Structure of Aesthetics.* Toronto: University of Toronto Press, 1963.

Spottiswoode, Raymond. *A Grammar of the Film*. Berkeley: University of California Press, 1959.

Stephenson, Ralph, and Debrix, Jean. *The Cinema as Art*. Baltimore: Penguin Books, 1965.

Stewart, David C., ed. *Film Study in Higher Education*. Washington, D.C.: American Council on Education, 1966.

Talbot, Daniel, ed. *Film: An Anthology*. New York: Simon and Schuster, 1959.

Taylor, John Russell. *Cinema Eye, Cinema Ear: Some Key Film-Makers of the Sixties*. New York: Hill and Wang, 1964.

Tyler, Parker. *Sex, Psyche, Etcetera in the Film*. New York: Horizon Press, 1969.

——. *The Three Faces of the Film*. New York: Thomas Yoseloff, 1960.

——. *Underground Film: A Critical History*. New York: Grove Press, 1969.

Wagenknecht, Edward. *The Movies in the Age of Innocence*. Norman, Okla.: University of Oklahoma Press, 1962.

Warshow, Robert. *The Immediate Experience*. New York: Doubleday Books, 1962.

Whitaker, Rod. *The Language of Film*. Englewood Cliffs, N.J.: Prentice-Hall, 1970.

Wimsatt, W. K., Jr. *The Verbal Icon*. Lexington, Ky.: University of Kentucky Press, 1954.

Wolfenstein, Martha, and Leites, Nathan. *Movies: A Psychological Study*. Glencoe, Ill.: The Free Press, 1950.

Wollen, Peter. *Signs and Meaning in the Cinema*. Cinema One series. Bloomington, Ind.: Indiana University Press, 1969.

Youngblood, Gene. *Expanded Cinema*. New York: E. P. Dutton, 1970.

Contributors

William Arrowsmith is Professor of Classics and Professor of Arts and Letters at the University of Texas.

Bela Balazs, who died in 1949, was a Hungarian writer, librettist, and film critic.

George Bluestone, now writing film scripts in England, is a critic and novelist.

Leo Braudy is Associate Professor of English at Columbia University.

Edmund Carpenter is Professor of Anthropology at Adelphi University.

David Castro with Jerry Stoll founded American Documentary Films in 1967 in San Francisco and New York.

The Communications Experience, composed of Kit Laybourne, Andres Steinmetz, and Jon Dunn, is a group of educators and media specialists working with the Philadelphia public schools.

Peter Harcourt teaches film at Queen's University, Kingston, Ontario.

Aldous Huxley, who died in 1963, was a noted scholar, philosopher, and novelist.

Pauline Kael is movie critic for *The New Yorker* and author of three books of film criticism.

John Stuart Katz is Assistant Professor at the Ontario Institute for Studies in Education, University of Toronto.

Stanley Kauffmann is film and theater critic for *The New Republic* and Visiting Professor of Drama at Yale University.

Jonas Mekas, actor, film director, and author, is Publisher and Editor-in-Chief of *Film Culture* and a film critic for *The Village Voice*.

Marshall McLuhan is Director of the Center for Culture and Technology, University of Toronto.

Newsreel is a collective of politically active film makers.

Gerald O'Grady is a member of the Faculty of Arts and Letters at the State University of New York at Buffalo and Visiting Associate Professor of English at the University of Texas.

Erwin Panofsky was a Professor of History of Art and a member of the Institute for Advanced Study at Princeton University from 1935 until his death in 1968.

Ted Perry is Professor and Chairman of the Department of Cinema Studies at New York University.

Alan C. Purves is Associate Professor of English at the University of Illinois.

Michael Roemer, former film critic for *The Reporter*, codirected with Robert Young the film *Nothing but a Man* (1965).

Andrew Sarris is film critic for *The Village Voice* and author of four books on film.

Anthony Schillaci is a freelance writer and teaches at the New School for Social Research, New York.

Ralph A. Smith is Editor of *The Journal of Aesthetic Education* and Associate Professor at the Bureau of Educational Research at the University of Illinois.

Susan Sontag is a critic, film maker, and author of two novels.

Andres Steinmetz is a member of the Communications Experience.

Stan Vanderbeek is Artist-Fellow at the Center for Advanced Visual Studies, Massachusetts Institute of Technology, and is Artist-in-Residence at television station WGBH in Boston.

Slavko Vorkapich, a film maker and montage expert, is now writing a book based on lectures he delivered at the Museum of Modern Art.

Sol Worth is Associate Professor of Communications and Director of the Media Laboratories at the Annenberg School of Communications, University of Pennsylvania.

Index